Disavowing Constantine

Mission, Church and the Social Order in the Theologies of
John Howard Yoder and Jürgen Moltmann

PATERNOSTER BIBLICAL AND THEOLOGICAL MONOGRAPHS

A full listing of titles in this series appears at the end of this book.

PATERNOSTER BIBLICAL AND THEOLOGICAL MONOGRAPHS

Disavowing Constantine

Mission, Church and the Social Order in the Theologies of John Howard Yoder and Jürgen Moltmann

Nigel Goring Wright

paternoster
publishing

First Published 2000 by Paternoster Press

Paternoster Press is an imprint of Paternoster Publishing,
P.O. Box 300, Carlisle, Cumbria, CA3 0QS, U.K.

03 02 01 00   7 6 5 4 3 2 1

British Library Cataloguing in Publication Data
A catalogue record of this book is available from the British Library

ISBN 0-85364-978-2

Typeset by Robert Parkinson
and printed and bound in Great Britain by
Nottingham Alpha Graphics

Dedicated
in loving gratitude to my wife
Judith Mary Wright
partner in life and ministry

Contents

PREFACE

The book the reader now holds is the published version of a PhD thesis of the same title submitted in 1994 at King's College London. As several years have passed since that time and a number of relevant works have appeared, a more extensive revision of the work than has been attempted would have been warranted. Those same years, however, have witnessed my return from the academic world to the relentless concerns of a demanding pastorate. As a consequence I have had to make a choice between a less than perfect manuscript that does exist and a perfect one that does not. Not surprisingly I have opted for the former in the belief that if the present work is to have a wider circulation it is better now than never. I am grateful to Paternoster Press, and in particular to Jeremy Mudditt, for including this volume in the series *Biblical and Theological Monographs*. I am also exceedingly grateful to my friend Robert Parkinson for preparing the original manuscript for publication in such a thorough and painstaking way.

Sadly, John Howard Yoder died in 1997. Many of his previously published articles were gathered together by Michael Cartwright in *The Royal Priesthood: Essays Ecclesiological and Ecumenical* (Grand Rapids: Eerdmans, 1994), to be followed by a companion volume of previously unpublished material in Yoder's *For the Nations: Essays Public and Evangelical* (Grand Rapids: Eerdmans, 1997). Some of the articles referred to in this book can now be located in these works. In addition Yoder's justly well-known, but never published, critique of Richard Niebuhr's *Christ and Culture* can now be found in *Authentic Transformation: A New Vision of Christ and Culture* (Nashville: Abingdon, 1996) by Yoder, Glen H. Stassen and D. M. Yeager. Interested researchers will be in the debt of Mark Thiessen Nation for the appearance of *A Comprehensive Bibliography of the Writings of John Howard Yoder* (Goshen: Mennonite Historical Society/ Goshen College, 1997). Fitting tribute is paid to Yoder in the Festschrift edited by Stanley Hauerwas et al., *The Wisdom of the Cross: Essays in Honor of John Howard Yoder* (Grand Rapids: Eerdmans, 1999). Happily, Jürgen Moltmann has continued his theological work to date, most notably with the latest volume of his 'contributions to systematic theology', *The Coming of God: Christian Eschatology* (London: SCM Press, 1996).

For the thesis stage of this work, I am grateful to Professor Colin Gunton of King's College London, for his patient and gracious supervision of this project over five years; to Professors Moltmann and Yoder for conversations along the way; to the Academic Board and Council of Spurgeon's College for allowing one period of sabbatical leave and another of leave of absence to advance this research; to colleagues on the staff of Spurgeon's College who bore extra burdens during these periods; to the Scholarship Committee of the Baptist Union of Great Britain for financial assistance; to the library staffs of the London Mennonite Centre, New College, Edinburgh, King's College London, the British Library and, supremely, Mrs Judy Powles, Librarian of Spurgeon's College for painstaking and unfailingly generous assistance; to Dr Gayle Koontz, Dean of the Associated Mennonite Biblical Seminaries, Elkhart, Indiana for making available a large number of Yoder's unpublished writings; to Dr Brian Haymes, now President of Bristol Baptist College for loaning articles by the Niebuhrs otherwise difficult to obtain; to Dr Arne Rasmusson of Lund for copying and sending his doctoral thesis at an early stage of drafting and for conversations; to members of the Anabaptist Network, especially Dr Alan and Mrs Ellie Kreider, Dr Stuart Murray and Dr Nelson Kraybill, for their encouragement; to the President and staff of Örebromissionskola, Sweden and especially Dr Per-Axel Sverker, for their hospitality in October 1992 when some of the material here was delivered in prototypical, and now unrecognisable, form as the centenary Ongmann Lectures; to certain anonymous persons whose financial generosity made possible the previously mentioned leave of absence; and to my wife, Judy, for her constant support in this project and her extensive knowledge of the word processor which assisted its production as a thesis. I here record my heartfelt gratitude.

Nigel G. Wright
Altrincham Baptist Church
31 August 1999

ABBREVIATIONS

ABQ	*American Baptist Quarterly*
AfR	*Archiv für Reformationsgeschichte*
AMBS	Associated Mennonite Biblical Seminaries
ASCE	*Annual for the Society of Christian Ethics*
ATR	*Anglican Theological Review*
BQ	*Baptist Quarterly*
BLT	*Brethren Life and Thought*
CC	*The Christian Century*
CD	*Church Dogmatics*
CGR	*Conrad Grebel Review*
CH	*Church History*
CP	*Concern Pamphlet*
CQ	*Covenant Quarterly*
CT	*Christianity Today*
EcR	*Ecumenical Review*
EQ	*Evangelical Quarterly*
ET	English Translation
EvTh	*Evangelische Theologie*
FP	*Faith and Philosophy: Journal of the Society of Christian Philosophers*
GH	*Gospel Herald*
HTR	*Harvard Theological Review*
HBT	*Horizons in Biblical Theology*
IRM	*International Review of Missions*
JAAR	*Journal of the American Academy of Religion*
JES	*Journal of Ecumenical Studies*
JHI	*Journal of the History of Ideas*
JMS	*Journal of Mennonite Studies*
JR	*Journal of Religion*
JRE	*Journal of Religious Ethics*
JTSA	*Journal of Theology for Southern Africa*
JWT	Just War Theory
KTR	*King's Theological Review*
LMC	London Mennonite Centre
MC	*Modern Churchman*
ME	*Mennonite Encyclopaedia*
MG	*Mennonitische Geschichtsblätter*
MQR	*Mennonite Quarterly Review*

MT	Modern Theology
PCTS	Proceedings of the Catholic Theological Society
RIL	Religion in Life
RQ	Restoration Quarterly
RS	Religious Studies
SCE	Studies in Christian Ethics
SIR	Studies in Religion
SJT	Scottish Journal of Theology
SVTQ	St Vladimir's Theological Quarterly
TB	Tyndale Bulletin
THJ	The Heythrop Journal
TZ	Theologische Zeitschrift
ThT	Theology Today
TLS	Times Literary Supplement
TRJ	The Reformed Journal
TS	Theological Studies
USQR	Union Seminary Quarterly Review
ZEE	Zeitschrift für Evangelische Ethik
ZfK	Zeitschrift für Kirchengeschichte
ZNW	Zeitschrift für die Neutestamentliche Wissenschaft

Works by Moltmann and Yoder

References to Moltmann's and Yoder's major works are usually placed in the text using the following abbreviations:

BP	Body Politics, Yoder, 1992
CAW	Christian Attitudes to War, Peace and Revolution: A Companion to Bainton, Yoder, 1983
CCP	The Christian and Capital Punishment, Yoder, 1961
CG	The Crucified God: The Cross of Christ as the Foundation and Criticism of Christian Theology, Moltmann, 1974
CJF	Creating a Just Future: The Politics of Peace and the Ethics of Creation in a Threatened World, Moltmann, 1989
CPS	The Church in the Power of the Spirit: A Contribution to Messianic Ecclesiology, Moltmann, 1977
CWS	The Christian Witness to the State, Yoder, 1964
EFC	The Ecumenical Movement and the Faithful Church, Yoder, 1958
EG	Experiences of God, Moltmann, 1980
EH	The Experiment Hope, Moltmann, 1975
FC	The Future of Creation, Moltmann, 1979
FJC	Following Jesus Christ in the World Today: Responsibility for the World and Christian Discipleship, Moltmann, 1983

GC   *God in Creation: An Ecological Doctrine of God*, Moltmann, 1985

HPP   *He Came Preaching Peace*, Yoder, 1985

HTG   *History and the Triune God: Contributions to Trinitarian Theology*, Moltmann, 1991

JCT   *Jesus Christ for Today's World*, Moltmann, 1994

KBW   *Karl Barth and the Problem of War*, Yoder, 1970

LMS   *The Legacy of Michael Sattler*, Yoder, 1973

Man   *Man: Christian Anthropology in the Conflicts of the Present*, Moltmann, 1974

NS   *Nevertheless: The Varieties and Shortcomings of Christian Pacifism*, Yoder, 1971

OC   *The Open Church: Invitation to a Messianic Lifestyle*, Moltmann, 1978

OHD   *On Human Dignity: Political Theology and Ethics*, Moltmann, 1985

OR   *The Original Revolution: Essays on Christian Pacifism*, Yoder, 1972

PJ   *The Politics of Jesus: Vicit Agnus Noster*, Yoder, 1972

PK   *The Priestly Kingdom: Social Ethics as Gospel*, Yoder, 1984

PKB   *The Pacifism of Karl Barth*, Yoder, 1968

PT   *Preface to Theology: Christology and Theological Method*, Yoder, 1981

PP   *The Power of the Powerless*, Moltmann, 1983

RRF   *Religion, Revolution and the Future*, Moltmann, 1969

SL   *The Spirit of Life: A Universal Affirmation*, Moltmann, 1992

STL   'The Stone Lectures', Yoder, 1979

TH   *Theology of Hope: On the Ground and the Implication of a Christian Eschatology*, Moltmann, 1967

TKG   *The Trinity and the Kingdom of God: The Doctrine of God*, Moltmann, 1981

TRG   *Täufertum und Reformation in Gespräch*, Yoder, 1962

TRS   *Täufertum und Reformation in der Schweiz*, Yoder, 1968

TT   *Theology Today: Two Contributions Towards Making Theology Present*, Moltmann, 1988

WJC   *The Way of Jesus Christ: Christology in Messianic Dimensions*, Moltmann, 1990

WWD   *What Would You Do?: A Serious Answer to a Standard Question*, Yoder, 1983

WWU   *When War Is Unjust: Being Honest in Just War Thinking*, Yoder, 1984

CHAPTER 1

Introduction

In this work I advocate a 'radical' formulation of the theology of church and state and develop it at four levels.

Most formally, the themes of mission, church and social order are expounded in two contemporary theologians who construct 'messianic', missionary theology and develop its social and political implications. John Howard Yoder (1927–97), a Mennonite, first engaged in theological writing to represent Christian pacifism within European ecumenism (*PK*, 1; *EFC*, esp., 23). He exemplifies a renewal movement among Mennonites persuaded that on a 'surprising number of points' the Anabaptists were right, although not infallible.[1] His theological concerns have remained remarkably consistent. A student in Basel in the 1950s, his doctoral research examined the debates between Anabaptists and Reformers (*TRS*, *TRG*). Subsequent writings have concerned Anabaptist history, ecumenical theological conversations, Mennonite perspectives on social ethics and, most distinctively, non-violence. The author of more than a dozen books, much of Yoder's contribution is nonetheless to be found in discussion papers and 'scattered essays'.[2]

Jürgen Moltmann (b. 1926), also representing the 'radical strain'[3] of Christianity, is among the most discussed of contemporary theologians. Although from the Reformed tradition, traditionally opposed to Anabaptism, he asserts that the church's future lies with the 'left-wing' of the Reformation. This statement first suggested to me the possibility of an enquiry into 'Anabaptist convergence' in these two theologians. Reformed–Anabaptist interaction will be a constant theme in this work. Chapters 4 and 5 and then 6 and 7 expound the selected themes in Yoder's and Moltmann's theologies with the intent of engaging critically with their theological logic. Comparison is inevitable, but the aim is primarily heuristic, treating both theologians as conversation partners in constructing a theology of church and social order. The indebtedness of this theology will become clear in the final chapter.[4]

At a second level, Yoder and Moltmann are set within the context of Anabaptism and of a restatement of an Anabaptist theology of church and society. Every tradition offers its own charism to the whole church.[5]

Anabaptism was an innovative movement representing a combination of religious conviction with religious liberty in a manner distinct from, and in my judgement superior to, the majority Christian institutions of its day. Theologically, it has won a remarkably large part of its case. What was once heresy and then a civil offence has now become normative Christian political theory.[6] Indeed, so successful has the free church vision been that a temptation it now faces is that of offering uncritical religious legitimation to liberal democracy when a more dialectical posture is appropriate.

Anabaptism challenged Christendom to abandon religious coercion through an appeal stemming from its understanding of the nature of Christianity.[7] Its conception of the church as free and voluntary and its witness to religious liberty have been accepted with time. Religious liberty has been called a child more of the Reformation than of the Reformers,[8] but Protestantism, originally intolerant, now gives it full support. The principle of liberty triumphed at Vatican II over the doctrine that 'error has no rights'.[9] Some changing theology of the state is implied in these developments, and yet the element in Anabaptism generally to commend itself least has been its 'negative' (better: critical) attitude to 'worldly power', specifically to the state.[10] Its commitment to non-violence has been considered utopian and irresponsible. I argue that, rightly understood, Anabaptism provides a way forward even in the theology of the state, yet only as its theology is reconstructed in directions suggested by the Reformed tradition.

In Chapter 3 I set discussion of Yoder and Moltmann within the Anabaptist heritage by questing for the 'essence' of Anabaptism, reviewing its original conceptions of the social order and then indicating some relevant contemporary Anabaptist–Mennonite reflections. The 'paradox' of the state which emerges is taken as the angle of investigation for the rest of the work.

At the third level, the discussion of Anabaptism takes place within the context of Free Church[11] theology generally and its left wing in particular, my own Baptist tradition. Dissent and political radicalism have been closely associated.[12] English Dissent sprang from two theological sources and has flowed in two distinct but related currents, the radical and the Calvinist.[13] The Calvinist current has undoubtedly been the stronger, even among Baptists, and has led within Dissent to a more positive attitude to the state than in Anabaptism: some even aspired to a comprehensive national church with a reformed religion enforced by a godly prince.[14] For such, advocacy of toleration was a product of their circumstances not their theology. In power they enforced conformity.[15]

The radical current is elusive and sometimes denied by historians. Although it is plausible to posit Anabaptist influence upon early Separatism, the evidence is elusive.[16] Circumstantial evidence suggests links between Lollardy, Anabaptism and the General Baptists of the seventeenth century.[17] Baptist attitudes to the Anabaptists have fluctuated for reasons of ideology and historical scholarship alike.[18] The argument follows the position of

Michael Watts and Ernest Payne[19] that although not identical with the Baptist movement, Anabaptism was one current of air blowing upon the 'turbulent sea of seventeenth century religion' (Payne) and accounting for its more radical notes. Baptists have always had a pacifist element without as a whole adopting peace church status.[20] Crucially, they inherited their convictions concerning religious liberty from the Anabaptists[21] while rejecting their overall view of the state.

Baptists have been fundamentally positive towards the state in its given tasks,[22] even willing to take up arms to achieve their version of it.[23] Here, we argue, the more radical notes within the Free Church tradition need to gain greater resonance and to form a more critical position. The *discontinuity* of human states and divine action needs to be recognised. Dissenters have seen Christianity as dissent from the wiles of surrounding culture. The Constantinian concordat was a betrayal of the gospel whose starting point was in redemption rather than creation or incarnation. Yet Dissent wished both to be different from the world and to gain the approval of the powerful. In the 1914–18 War this showed itself as the anxiety of an increasingly prosperous class to prove its patriotism. They abandoned their principles for the sake of national unity.[24] Wilkinson's judgement that they were let down by having too simplistic an approach should be noted.[25] This was true both of the moral absolutism of the 'Nonconformist conscience' which inhibited more nuanced compromise and, in my judgement, of the absence of a sufficiently penetrating critique of culture and of state. Adrian Hastings describes how the Free Churches became so closely identified with the Liberal Party (Lloyd-George's manipulative 'holy alliance'), that when the Party destroyed itself they suffered a huge loss of identity owing to the consequent politicisation and secularisation.[26] It is a more incisive critique and consequent detachment that Anabaptist sources might provide.

Yet I do not argue for an unreconstructed Anabaptism (even if there were a single Anabaptism). Watts has observed that the impulse behind Eliza-bethan Dissent was the desire not to convert the world but to separate from it[27] and in so far as this is also the logic of Anabaptism it requires amendment. Mission must be the primary concern. This requires us to find some theologically based conception of the nature and limits of political power. The growth of the modern state since the Enlightenment must be reckoned with positively and negatively. Baptists, having become emancipated from civil disabilities, moved from quietism to the politics of righteousness. Their voluntaryist logic inculcated in them a suspicion of state action but this yielded gradually, and questionably, to an evangelical imperative for state action against 'sin'.[28]

I shall argue that a theology of the state cannot be expressed without ambivalence. Yoder and Moltmann will be found respectively to represent the negative and positive poles of this ambivalence although each incorporates elements of the other's position. It will also be argued that

Moltmann does not altogether avoid a veiled form of Constantinianism. Chapter 8 places the insights gained from their theologies within the wider Reformed–Anabaptist debate which itself reflects the ambivalence of the Augustinian tradition towards the state. The heart of the matter concerns the transposition of Yoder's justified critique of worldly power into a Trinitarian framework, as suggested by Moltmann, which allows greater justice to be done to the themes of creation and covenant as counterbalancing elements.

The fourth level for understanding this work is ecumenical. The church is in a 'post-Constantinian situation'. On the whole it acknowledges this fact without evaluating it.[29] To concede the dissolution of Christendom in the face of pluralism is less than appropriating it theologically.[30] The 'disavowal of Constantine' which Yoder and Moltmann advocate and their messianic categories placing the church in a missionary rather than a legitimating relation to the social order, require an approach at variance with the proprietorial assumptions of Western Christendom. John Milbank has drawn attention to the unwillingness of theology to confront the 'severe problem' of possible Christian aversion to the existing social order.[31] Few suggestions are more unwelcome in established church circles than that the proper existence of the church might be in a 'sectarian' mode. The 'political' has assumed a semi-sacred position in modern society.

In Chapter 2 I place this argument within the context of the church's mission. In Chapter 9 I offer a programmatic theological statement fashioned from its entire field of investigation. This statement, drawing from Yoder and Moltmann, intends to be in critical continuity with Anabaptism, to radicalise the Free Church inheritance and to offer an alternative, theologically required by the church's messianic existence, to the explicit or implicit Constantinian assumptions of much theology.

The decline of the churches in the West should not lead to the conclusion that the 'disavowal of Constantine' is an antiquarian discussion. Forms of Constantinianism shape religious witness and political impasse in, for example, Northern Ireland, and inform the programmes of many religiously conservative political movements. The countries of Eastern Europe experience an upsurge of religious nationalism placing the religious liberties and civil freedoms of minorities under threat. New states in Africa and Asia have to face the question of their relation to religion.[32] The religious factor in international conflicts is easily overlooked by secular analysts, but observation suggests that conflicts occur on the boundaries of civilisations shaped by opposed religious traditions.[33] Tensions between cultures and civilisations variously shaped by religion will increasingly determine the nature of international politics.[34] Religion is an integral part of human social existence. The need for a Christian theology of the social order is as great as ever.

1   'What are our concerns?', *CP* 4 (1957), 20–32.

2   S. Hauerwas, *The Peaceable Kingdom: A Primer in Christian Ethics* (London: SCM Press, 1984), xxiv.

3   J. Macquarrie, 'Today's Word for Today 1: Jürgen Moltmann', *The Expository Times* 92:1 (1980), 4.

4   In the course of this research I became aware of a parallel project at the University of Lund undertaken by Arne Rasmusson. This has now been published as *The Church as Polis: From Political Theology to Theological Politics as Exemplified by Jürgen Moltmann and Stanley Hauerwas* (Lund: University of Lund Press, 1994). Hauerwas draws considerable inspiration from Yoder and Rasmusson justifies his choice of Hauerwas as a subject on pp. 23–4. Rasmusson's project is far more extensive and ambitious than the present one but follows Moltmann and Hauerwas in not developing a theology of the state, which is one of the specific concerns of this work.

5   J. Moltmann, 'Nachwort' to P. F. Momose, *Kreuzestheologie: Eine Auseinandersetzung mit Jürgen Moltmann* (Frieburg: Herder, 1978), 176.

6   J. H. Yoder, 'The Believers' Church: Global Perspectives' in J. K. Zeman (ed.), *The Believers' Church in Canada* (Baptist Federation of Canada and Mennonite Central Committee [Canada], 1979), 4–5.

7   H. S. Bender, 'The Anabaptists and Religious Liberty in the 16th Century', *AfR* 44 (1953), 33–4.

8   R. H. Bainton, 'The Struggle for Religious Liberty', *CH* 10 (1941), 95–6.

9   M. Novak, *The Open Church: Vatican II Act II* (London: Darton, Longman and Todd, 1964), 256–8, 275–82; 'Declaration on Religious Liberty' in A. Flannery (ed.), *Vatican Council II: The Conciliar and Post-Conciliar Documents* (Dublin: Dominican Publications, 1975), 799–812.

10   According to Weber, 'a state is a human community that (successfully) claims *the monopoly of the legitimate use of physical force* within a given territory' (my emphasis): M. Weber, 'Politics as a Vocation' in H. H. Gerth and C. W. Mills (eds.), *From Max Weber: Essays in Sociology* (London and Boston: Routledge and Kegan Paul, 1948), 78.

11   The terms 'Independent', 'Separatist', 'Dissenter' and 'Nonconformist', which connote deviation from the norm, were replaced in the nineteenth century by the term 'Free Church', which suggests a constructive alternative to the national church: M. R. Watts, *The Dissenters: From the Reformation to the French Revolution* (Oxford: Clarendon Press, 1978), 2; D. F. Durnbaugh, 'Free Churches, Baptists and Ecumenism: Origins and Implications', *JES* 17 (1980), 4. Some church bodies entitled 'Free Church' would not be embraced by the more precise use of the term which denotes a voluntary gathering of Christian disciples who believe it wrong to be governed in their discipleship by the state. In the USA all churches are, in the formal sense, Free Churches. The title 'Free Church' is an accident of legal history when, for example, the Episcopal Church in Scotland is so described. Not all English 'Free Churches' are opposed in principle or to the same degree to *some* form of 'establishment'. Yoder prefers to speak of the 'Radical Reformation' (G. H. Williams) to refer to his own tradition: *PK*, 104–5. Throughout this work 'Free

Church' denotes those *institutions* usually so called and 'free church' identifies the more precise *theological tradition of conviction*. The latter use of the term is therefore interchangeable with the term 'believers' church' as defined by F. H. Littell: 'The Concept of the Believers' Church' in J. L. Garrett (ed.), *The Concept of the Believers' Church* (Scottdale: Herald Press, 1969), 15–32.

12 M. Walzer, *The Revolution of the Saints: A Study in the Origins of Radical Politics* (New York: Atheneum, 1968); M. G. Baylor (ed.), *The Radical Reformation* (Cambridge: Cambridge University Press, 1991), xvii–xix.

13 Watts, *Dissenters*, 4; P. T. Forsyth, *Faith, Freedom and the Future* (London: Hodder and Stoughton, 1912), 91–110; D. F. Durnbaugh, 'Theories of Free Church Origins, *MQR* 41:2 (1968), 83–95; I. B. Horst, *The Radical Brethren: Anabaptism and the English Reformation to 1558* (Nieuwkoop: B. De Graaf, 1972), 56, 177–80.

14 Watts, *Dissenters*, 47–50.

15 Ibid., 378.

16 A. P. F. Sell, 'Anabaptist–Congregational Relations and Current Mennonite–Reformed Dialogue', *MQR* 61:3 (1987), 321–2.

17 Watts, *Dissenters*, 7–14 and passim. See also P. Pauls, '"A Pestiferous Sect": The Anabaptists in England from 1530–1660', *JMS* 3 (1985), 60–72.

18 I. Sellers, 'Edwardians, Anabaptists and the Problem of Baptists Origins', *BQ* 29 (1981–1982), 105–7. Most agree that Baptists are a development from English Separatism: K. R. Manley, 'Origins of the Baptists: The Case for Development from Puritanism–Separatism' in W. H. Brackney and R. J. Burke (eds.), *Faith, Life and Witness* (Birmingham, Alabama: Samford University Press, 1990), 56–69.

19 'Who were the Baptists?', *BQ* 16 (1955–6), 340, 342. See also A. J. D. Farrer, 'The Relation between English Baptists and the Anabaptists of the Continent', *BQ* 2 (1924–5), 30–6.

20 P. R. Dekar, 'Baptist Peacemakers in Nineteenth-Century Peace Societies', *BQ* 34:1 (1991), 3; R. S. Trulson, 'Baptist Pacifism: A Heritage of Non-violence', *ABQ* 10:3 (1991), 200.

21 E. A. Payne, 'The Anabaptists of the 16th Century and their Influence in the Modern World', The Dr Williams's Trust Lecture, Carmarthen, 1948, 5–6.

22 W. S. Hudson, 'Who were the Baptists?', *BQ* 16 (1955–56), 312.

23 W. T. Whitley has shown the considerable extent of the Baptist contribution to the New Model Army: *A History of British Baptists* (London: Charles Griffin and Co., 1923), 73–6.

24 A. Wilkinson, *Dissent or Conform? War Peace and the English Churches 1900–1945* (London: SCM Press, 1986), 3–4, 15–17, 19–20, 44, 57.

25 Ibid., 81.

26 *A History of English Christianity: 1920–1985* (London: Collins, 1986), 125–127, 271–2.

27 Watts, *Dissenters*, 439.

28 D. W. Bebbington, 'The Baptist Conscience in the Nineteenth Century', *BQ* 34:1 (1991), 17, 22.

29 J. H. Yoder, 'The Otherness of the Church', *MQR* 35:4 (1961), 286.

30 J. H. Yoder, 'The Disavowal of Constantine: An Alternative Perspective on Interfaith Dialogue', *Tantur Yearbook of the Ecumenical Institute for Advanced Theological Studies* (Jerusalem: Tantur, 1975/76), 67.

31 J. Milbank, *Theology and Social Theory: Beyond Secular Reason* (Oxford: Blackwell, 1990), 209.

32 N. Q. King, *The Emperor Theodosius and the Establishment of Christianity* (London: SCM Press, 1961), 9.

33 P. Marshall, *Thine is the Kingdom: A Biblical Perspective on the Nature of Government and Politics Today* (Basingstoke: Marshalls, 1984), 116–18.

34 S. P. Harrington, 'Im Kampf der Kulturen', *Die Zeit* 33, 13 August 1993, 3.

CHAPTER 2

A Free Church In A Free State

Péguy's dictum 'Tout commence en mystique et finit en politique'[1] lamented the degradation of ideals into self-interest. It also suggests the fertility of religious ideas for the social order. Ecclesiologies in particular seek their image in the political order. This work shows that the reverse can also be the case, with destructive consequences. The free church 'mystique'[2] has frequently found expression in the axiom 'a free church in a free state'.[3] The relation is not incidental: what the church *is* enables what it *accomplishes*. How the church has its being is of missiological significance.

The Mission Paradigm and Ecclesiology

The theological context for Christ's church is the mission in and for which it exists. All true ecclesiology is missionary. The church's form therefore stems from its nature as the first fruits and primary earthly means of reconciliation. This should constitute it, this work claims, as a free church and requires the disavowal of 'Constantinianism', that alliance of church and state which while passing for an extension of the church's mission actually obstructs its fulfilment. Yet God's mission embraces all creation and so disavowal necessitates alternative strategies for church, society and state. The work develops these in conversation with the missionary ecclesiologies of John Howard Yoder and Jürgen Moltmann.

The *Missio Dei*

Since the 1950s the *missio Dei* paradigm of the mission of the triune God[4] has become normative for both Catholic and Protestant theology.[5] Christianity is a missionary faith, its God a sending God. The sending of Son and Spirit reveals God's self-giving love and expresses the centrifugal movement of God's being; indeed, the word 'mission' was once used exclusively of the inter-Trinitarian relations[6] in which mission is rooted.[7] Where pluralistic monotheisms render mission redundant, Trinitarian confession undergirds it both by distinguishing the gospel as unique[8] and by showing its origin in the divine life. Of the successive paradigm shifts mission has undergone, David Bosch describes the latest as this ecumenical paradigm in which the *missio Dei* relates christology, soteriology and Trinity.[9] Mission, the movement of God to the world, first defines God's being and then the church's.[10] Previously, the church sent; in the new paradigm, the church is sent. It is itself the object of mission and finds in the *missio Dei* the *missiones ecclesiae*.[11] God's mission is not confined to the church[12] but the church, in particular the local church, exists as its sacrament, sign and instrument.[13]

The missionary nature of the congregation is complemented by the congregational nature of the mission. Frustration with a bourgeois church has led some to regard the world as the locus of encounter between God and humanity. But, argues Bosch, the New Testament knows of no christology or pneumatology which is not ecclesial. Mission is rooted in the living worship of a pilgrim, ex-centric, temporarily resident church called from the world for the world. The church's failure means it itself requires the *missio Dei*, bringing to it repentance, conversion and continual reformation.[14]

Expressing missionary ecclesiology in *messianic* categories serves to integrate the personal, social and political dimensions of mission. Christ is the prototype of all faithful mission. He set out not to win proselytes[15] but to free people to serve God. He forbade his disciples to impose themselves. The church gives loyalty to a Messiah who frees the world from the idols of power. It is an eschatological community shaped by the power of the *eschaton* and continuing the messianic task.[16] Deformations of mission lose continuity with this Messiah and assume false responsibility, forgetting that mission is God's and proselytising or, since the time of Constantine, coercing in order to gain adherents.[17]

Christ's mission generates and continues through microsocieties interacting with the socio-political order. The prophetic, messianic microsociety is the means whereby God's kingdom, seeking the renewal of all society, advances through alternative structures of solidarity.[18] Alternative patterns of government develop which reject imposition. Power to govern is corporately owned and based on voluntary participation.[19] Distinguished from the macrosociety, the microsociety-church relates to it through missionary witness not withdrawal or revolutionary hostility. Larry Miller argues that the Messiah's mission requires the creation of such microsocieties addressing all human existence; indeed *only* churches of this type ('alternative, voluntary, missionary, pacifist microsocieties') can be messianic instruments.[20] The Messiah brings liberation from the 'powers', from world enslavement to the 'dominion system' and its legitimising myth of redemptive violence.[21] Only in voluntary, non-hierarchical and non-violent communities can the church pose an alternative to the system. The identity of the church is crucial to mission.

Church Identity in the Service of Mission

Karl Barth first articulated mission as an activity of God and developed a missionary ecclesiology.[22] In the *Dogmatics* ecclesiology is integrated with Christ's work of objective reconciliation and the Spirit's subjective application of it. The church is the 'provisional representation (*vorläufige Darstellung*) of the whole world of humanity' justified, sanctified and called in Christ.[23] It addresses others as 'designated Christians', 'Christians in hope' in the light of God's love.[24] It gathers around the Messiah who has come and represents those who will be gathered at the end of history, 'holding in trust for the world the kind of relationship of men with men that will ultimately be universally established'.[25] Traditionally, the 'true church' is a place where something is done, the Word proclaimed and the sacraments administered,[26] but by relating pneumatology and ecclesiology the true church can emerge as that which is awakened, gathered, upbuilt and sent by the Spirit. The church emerges, in Zizioulas' words, from the 'co-incidence and con-vergence of relationships freely established by the Spirit'.[27] So passive, institutional definitions are replaced with relational, dynamic and missionary approaches.

In the visible community, in so far as it is the 'true church' arising from the quickening power of the living Lord by the Spirit,[28] we glimpse God's will for all. The church's law is exemplary, serving as a pattern for the formation of human law generally.[29] Barth expounded the implications of this for the social order in *Gospel and Law, Church and State* (ET 1939) and *The Christian Community and the Civil Community* (ET 1946).[30] He rejected the Lutheran division of church and state founded on the law/gospel distinction. Law is the form of the gospel and its content is grace,[31] so the gospel determines that sphere commonly regarded as under law. The basis of both church and state is christological, the state being appointed by Christ to serve the work of redemption by means of preservation.[32] Christ's kingdom is a final goal for both church and state, yet the spheres are not identical. There is no duplicate of the church in the political sphere, no Christian state or single doctrine of the just state. There is instead a 'direction' taking bearings from the Christian centre and making analogies or parables possible. The church may see the state as an allegory, correspondence or analogue of the kingdom even though the state is not and cannot become the kingdom.[33] So the 'real Church must be the model and prototype of the real State. The Church must be an example so that by its very existence it may be a source of renewal for the State and the power by which the State is preserved.'[34]

The church's primary duty is therefore to be itself, so preserving the true nature of the state and preventing its demonisation. Barth is aware that the 'true church', as the state, fails to realise its true potential, but the vision acts as a powerful eschatological symbol that challenges both church and state.[35] Christian social theory is first and foremost an ecclesiology, a sociology which is a reading of other societies at the same time. It embodies a moral practice in the historical emergence of a unique community.[36] So the way the church has its being must determine the shape of its mission, its visible form confessing or denying what it represents (Moltmann *CPS*, 290–291, 294). Here, free church distinctives which stress voluntary discipleship and free community are given a missiological grounding.

The sacral state in which religion binds tribe or *Volk* together does not need mission. By definition all participate in a common life reinforced by sacramental actions. In Constantinian Christianity the means by which the sacral order was maintained and enforced were passively received, infants being baptised and the elements of the Eucharist received kneeling with the bread placed in the mouth.[37] By contrast the apostolic church proclaimed the *kērygma* to elicit an active but inevitably unequal response which divided society into the responsive and unresponsive.[38] Such proclamation implies, unlike the sacral state, that society is *composite* and does not possess a religious unanimity. It is therefore among those repudiating sacralism and stressing the responsive nature of faith that a sense of mission is found.

Despite recovering the *kērygma* the Reformers were not evangelistically minded.[39] Their provincialism and concept of the *Volk* as the object of mission undercut personal decision. By rejecting monasticism they removed the last vestiges of a 'responsible otherness' of Christian commitment.[40] The Anabaptists were among the first to make the Great Commission binding upon all church members,[41] preceded to a degree by some voluntary monastic orders which bore free church characteristics.[42] Rooted in a missionary consciousness, the Anabaptist mission was inspired by apostolic leaders, but application of the priesthood of all believers meant their actions were complemented by the Anabaptist 'laity', male and female, whose exemplary lives, independent convictions and zeal as members of a persecuted sect surpassed anything comparable in the Reformation churches.[43]

The Reformers were diverted from mission for reasons intrinsic to their ecclesiology,[44] inhibited by the state church principle.[45] The Reformation churches were institutional with an inward focus and an emphasis on control.[46] The state fulfilled the evangelistic imperative by coercion. The free churches broke this link.[47] They opened the way to recover evangelization and in the process came to be seen as seditionists.[48] The Pietists of Halle and Herrnhut (both movements marked by free church ideals) later took up the task[49] but the Anabaptists were 'originally and intensely evangelistic'.[50] Bosch attributes the Anabaptists' 'remarkable programme of missionary outreach' to their theology of church and state.[51] That evangelization re-emerged from the free church tradition suggests that this ecclesiology is conducive to mission.[52]

Evangelization implies more than conversion. It initiates people into God's kingdom that they may share in the quest for justice,[53] so *ekklēsia* is a 'theo-political category'.[54] The church's life is its mission. The believing community embodies provisionally the new humanity and is political in that it follows a corporate way contradicting prevailing patterns. It dissents from dominant cultures in order to offer back to them creative possibilities. Dissent is not therefore merely negative response to establishment religion: it is the conviction that there is a higher form of churchmanship[55] and church discipline is the realistic recognition that its aspirations are only partially realised.

Dissent has led to the development of 'a pluralist society in which men would learn to live in peace with others with whom they disagreed without resort to the scaffold or the firing squad'.[56] Democracy was, according to A. D. Lindsay who credits its inspiration to the Anabaptists, the social application of the priesthood of all believers, the political analogy of the democratic religious congregation.[57] The nexus between the free church and the free society is in the method used for decision-making.[58] Rejection of coercion in religion contributed to its avoidance in other areas. The call for freedom of conscience, from a trajectory found in Luther and Calvin but undeveloped by them,[59] stimulated other liberties, though it required the upheavals of the eighteenth century and the transitional role of such as John Locke to remove the forces which had suppressed them.[60] Christ's new community produced and arguably may continue to produce such 'political' inklings in so far as it lives out its life under Christ's rule.[61]

Barth, having rooted the church in God's mission and Spirit, logically moved towards free church convictions. He distinguished three modes of the church, *Volkskirche*, *Freikirche* and *Bekenntniskirche* of which the first involved solidarity with the state, the second voluntary community independent of the state but not in conflict with it and the third a threat from the state to the essential nature of the church.[62] Barth's movement, continued as we shall see by Moltmann, is paralleled elsewhere by tendencies towards free church ecclesiology under the impetus of missionary concerns.[63]

The Church and the Social Order

Barth insisted on the primacy of revelation in Christ. Knowledge of God is found in the Word, and the Word is believed in the church, so we are to look within the church for insight into God's will for the social and political order. The social order is not an independent norm. Typically, Barth saw the future state (to which Christians belong here and now in anticipation) as the only real state.[64]

The church has as a rule proceeded otherwise to determine its relation to the social order. Appealing to theories of 'natural law' or 'orders of creation', it has accommodated itself. This is clear in 'Constantinianism', the church's rise to legality under the Edict of Milan in AD 313, then to privilege and finally to political and religious dominance.[65] Theocracy triumphed through imperial favour over the fact that faith comes from inner conviction not exterior compulsion.[66]

All primitive societies sought validation of the social order, safeguarding community health through religious observance. Religion made sedition and impiety synonymous: to question the ruler was tantamount to blasphemy.[67] In the Empire an imperial cult undergirded the ruler's authority while offering hospitality to a range of cults that confined themselves to the private sphere or a social ghetto.[68] Early Christianity could not accept these options.[69] Neither could it be public in the way Rome allowed, as a form of observance to which all might gain access lest society be fragmented.[70]

Christian political theology was always bound to be distinctive.[71] Its theological tensions implied restructuring the social order so that political and religious communities did not coincide.[72] Its Trinitarian doctrine, its centre in the cross, its Christ who claimed his kingdom was not 'of this world' and its hope of a kingdom to supersede the kingdoms of this world, implied criticism of the *status quo* and made Christianity a potentially awkward public religion. Conversely, pressing it into the mould of a civil religion corroded its identity; it is arguably easier to see the crucified Christ as the end of all political theology rather than as the source of a new one.[73] In the Old Testament the political order is not holy and beyond question. God *reverses* the existing order. Biblical theology cut political systems down to size, denying their divine pretensions and claims to absolute loyalty.[74]

A political theology must be constructed from the unlikely materials which constitute the centre of Christian belief. The easier option was to look to alternative ideological resources. This is how Christendom emerged.[75] Early political theologies ranged from Tertullian's 'withdrawal' theology to Eusebius' court theology with Augustine's uneasy understanding of church–state relations in between. This constituted a perennial spectrum of positions for later theology.

Tertullian's concentration on the gospel and the true church produced a theology with the potential to revitalise political thought in the longer term.[76] He represented the majority of pre-Constantinian Christianity in which non-participation in state service was the norm, although not necessarily on principle.[77] Augustine's strengths were his realism about the corruption of government, his stress on justice and the only partial fulfilment of God's kingdom in the church, which nonetheless served as a spur to the state.[78] However, Eusebius' theology was the first to triumph.

An Analysis of 'Constantinianism'

As their Lord was crucified by the state and they themselves knew its antagonism, the early Christians were likely to regard the state as an enemy.

However, belief in forgiveness and God's sovereignty combined with the desire for acceptance and power in a world where the powers had come to stay suggested a different possibility. Animosity to the state was therefore bound to change when those who were the state were converted.[79]

Constantine's influence has been enormous.[80] He symbolises the church's rise from obscure sect to world religion. For some he merits the title of 'thirteenth apostle' accorded him by the Council of Nicaea.[81] Constantinianism might be regarded as an appropriate and faithful response for that historical moment.[82] For Newbigin, it was right that the church should at that time provide spiritual cohesion and sustain the political order[83] and equally right that at other times it take the dissenting role.[84] He asserts the public truth of the gospel and finds the determinant of Western culture in the Enlightenment's privatisation of religion. While we are sympathetic to Newbigin's thesis and acknowledge his desire to avoid the 'Constantinian trap',[85] to regard the church's reversal under Constantine as the 'experiment of a Christian political order that had to be made'[86] is surely, in the light of its consequences, too mild a position.

Eusebius translated the emperor cult into Christian terms with the consequence that Christianity mirrored the features and functions of the old paganism.[87] Pre-Christian societies were sacral, held together by a single religiosity, an ultimate loyalty of the soul common to each member of that society.[88] The need for cohesion in a sprawling empire had led to the requirement of Emperor veneration.[89] Rejection of this demand occasioned the persecution of Christians. However, Constantine recognised in Christianity a religiosity needed by the Empire when the old religiosity was crumbling. This was more likely political expediency than Christian conversion.[90] So two inherently incompatible religious traditions were joined issuing in an hybrid and bequeathing future difficulties to the church.[91] It represented the loss of authentic Christianity.[92]

Before Constantine the church was a counterculture in the Empire, imitating Christ's 'detached involvement'.[93] Modifications to its internal life, growing awareness of its universality, pressures to move from its charismatic origins towards hierarchy and institution, liturgical tendencies towards a sacrificial dimension with its own priesthood and ritual, growth through adhesion rather than conversion, and the tension between remaining separate whilst reassuring outsiders, were preparing the way for change. To a remarkable degree the counterculture was sustained, principally because of the polarity maintained by the state's hostility.[94] Once removed, the stage was set for the counter-cultural element, itself of the essence of the church, to be lost.

Despite persecution, the church had maintained a surprisingly positive understanding of the state, avoiding a stark dualism. The increasing participation of the wealthy within the church and the debilitating pressure of persecution meant that when offered the opportunity to move beyond confrontation was seized. The new relationship offered protection not persecution, a framework for expansion and the context for transforming culture. Its downside was the revival of religious monarchy, subservience to secular power, the lowering of ethical standards and the growth of nominalism.[95] The church was obliged to support the emperor's undertakings and legitimate his institutions. This was bound to change it.[96] The church acquired power under Constantine linked with a sense of territoriality. Political annexation carried with it the imposition of a different religiosity upon another people.[97] The gospel thus assumed overtones of conquest.[98]

The state embodies a whole culture[99] and so adjustment in its relationship to the church has widespread ramifications. The pre-Constantinian church was consistently non-violent.[100] But the requirement of defence and increasing army converts led to a sudden change. With the abandonment of non-violence the church was deprived of its most visible and most effective means of re-creating the praxis of Jesus.[101] A key factor in forwarding God's kingdom was in effect repudiated. But this followed logically upon the change of relationship to the state as a consequence of which alien values replaced those of Jesus.[102]

Alistair Kee's spirited analysis interprets Constantine not as the triumph of Christ over Empire but of ideology over Christianity with the norms of Christ being replaced by those of imperial theology. Constantine needed a new ratifying sign to legitimate his imperial claims. The *labarum*, the symbol revealed before the battle of Milvian bridge in AD 312, was no cross but an adaptation of a Roman cavalry standard.[103] In a crucial distinction Kee argues that Constantine's devotion was not to Christ but to the God of the Christians.[104] Analysis of the writings of Eusebius and Constantine's imperial decrees shows that Christ played no part in Constantine's religion, that he did not regard Christ as his mediator, that he remained unbaptised and outside of the church until the end of his life and even then saw baptism not as forgiveness but as conferral of immortality.[105] Constantine's religion replaced Christ by Constantine himself. Eusebius portrays him as one in whom the Logos is expressed in a new divine initiative. He assumes messianic status, but this is pre-Christian messianism, uninformed by Christ. Constantine continued the Jewish messianic expectations that Jesus did not fulfil. He is thus an anti-Christian figure fulfilling a vision Jesus rejected.[106] Consistent with his covenantal vocation, Constantine assumed authority in the church, calling and chairing councils in a precedental fashion; but his motive was to maintain imperial unity without schism rather than the will to truth.[107]

If Kee's analysis is even partially correct[108] its implications are considerable. Ideology triumphs. By projection God, the unknown Sovereign, assumes the form of the earthly sovereign who *is* known and so God legitimates the emperor.[109] Constantine, according to Kee, replaced Christ to the extent that European history is determined by the values of

Constantine as if they were the values of Christ, the son of the carpenter being passed by in favour of one more like the *mimesis*[110] of the Eternal. This is most clearly seen in relation to combat. Constantine was the Warrior-King subduing and chastising the opponents of truth by the law of combat. He gained absolute power and exercised it. He had no equal in battle and his wealth was beyond compare. Next to him Jesus was almost embarrassing. Constantine 'represents in every aspect of his being precisely what Christ rejects, point for point'.[111] In Christ God is revealed in weakness and in suffering. Christ dies rather than seek victory through evil. He washes the feet of the disciples, touches the leprous and harms none, not even his persecutors and not even to save his own life. Constantine defends his honour by killing his enemies. His victorious trophy is covered in blood, but that of other people.[112]

Kee's contrast is stark and clear. In Constantine, whatever the short term benefits to the church, the foundation for mediaeval Caesaro-papism was laid.[113] Seduced from revolutionary faith in its crucified Messiah, the church exchanged the values which had previously inhibited its loyalty to the emperor. The unreasonable *kenosis* revealed in Christ was avoided. The teaching of Jesus on wealth and property was spiritualised.[114] The church, the religious arm of the state, replicated the imperial hierarchy. Clergy became civil servants and adopted the familiar justifications of accommodation to power.[115] Kee relates his analysis to political theology which finds Christianity influenced by alien values. To unmask them he indicates how they first entered. But the tradition has taken over. History has been reinterpreted. The imperial ideology determines the way the Bible is read. Even the recovery of Jesus' teaching makes little difference in changing what has been received.[116]

That Christ is Lord of all demands an account of how his lordship embraces the social order. But Kee has indicated the magnitude of the departure from Christ. Others have shown how christological doctrine came under pressure to undergird imperial authority and the earthly Jesus was lost in the glory of the Pantocrator.[117] The Constantinian compromise is so deeply embedded in the church's thought that it might claim to be the position of historic Christianity. Verduin has shown[118] the degree to which Augustine, Luther, Zwingli and Calvin justified the *corpus Christianum* and the systematic use of coercion, the service of the *sacerdotium* by the *regnum*. They have done so through questionable exegesis against the background of an uncooperative New Testament, employing defective hermeneutical methods and inwardly contradictory ecclesiologies.[119] And Christianity always risks legitimising ruling-class ideology, serving oppression, ceasing to be a resource for revolutionary change.[120] This analysis of Constantine enables us to offer a working definition:

> *Constantinianism is the explicit or implicit attempt by the Christian church acting from a position of power, privilege or patronage to impose*

Christian values by the use of social and political power in what are believed to be the interests of the kingdom of God.[121]

Associated with this is the implicit shift of hope for salvation away from the church to the political sphere. As Hauerwas has observed, 'Constantinianism is a hard habit to break' because of the assumption that by being in power it is possible to do so much good, an assumption shared by left and right alike.[122] But the Constantinian project also represented the attempt to allow Christians to share power without being a problem for the powerful.[123] The real challenge is to witness to God's rule without ruling.[124]

The issue of violence will play a certain hermeneutical role in what follows. Disregard of Christ's example of non-violent love of enemy will indicate that an ideology is at work which is not rooted in Christ however much it appears in the guise of Christianity.[125] This raises inevitable questions concerning the nature and extent of Christ's non-violence and the ways in which it may be interpreted for contemporary problems.

The Vitality of the 'Sectarian'

After Constantine, monasticism emerged as an internal opposition.[126] Troeltsch believed that the New Testament contained conservative and radical impulses and inspired both accommodating and radically anarchic expressions in the later church.[127] A history of protest is discernible throughout church history. Verduin speaks of the presence of 'rival churches'.[128] The established church has often institutionalised the radical element in monastic orders[129] in the belief, according to Troeltsch, that both institutional and radical expressions are of the gospel and only conjointly exhaust its range.[130] This work gives an account from within the radical tradition. Is it possible to describe the church's relationship to the state in missionary terms so as to avoid Constantinianism and yet in a way which takes realistic account of the tasks the state has to do in a fallen world? A dichotomy of politics and Christian truth is after all no improvement on the previous error.[131]

Only the sectarian style of committed membership is likely to keep the church alive in a disestablished future.[132] The word 'sectarian' carries the force of a theological insult,[133] immediately disadvantages this understanding of the church,[134] is synonymous with 'ghetto mentality'[135] and so needs interpretation. The distinction is properly made between 'sect' as an *ecclesiological* and as *a sociological* category.[136] Here the term is used in that sense originated by Troeltsch in distinguishing 'church-type' and 'sect-type' sociological variations.[137] The sect-type also exists as a reforming presence within church-type structures.

The sect-type was the original sociological form of Christianity and continued within the Constantinian church in monasticism. With the late Middle Ages it emerged as specific sects and then proliferated from the time of the Reformation. Where the church-type aspires to *universality* and so compromises, the sect-type practises *intensity* and is arguably in more direct contact with Jesus and the gospel.[138] George Lindbeck has argued that the church's future requires its de-institutionalisation and reconstitution. He distinguishes between the sociological sectarianism which adds to itself a theological justification and that sectarian form which emphasises an internal, diversified unity. In this form, sharply distinguished from society at large and rooted in the unsurpassable finality of Jesus Christ, early Christianity had its existence. Its manifestation today may be described, with Rahner, as a 'diaspora' existence.[139] The stark opposition between world-affirming church and world-denying sect is to be refused. The balance is rather as suggested by Barth: '[The Church] exists... to set up in the world a new sign which is radically dissimilar to [the world's] own manner and which contradicts it in a way which is full of promise'.[140]

The struggle between models of church and social order is a struggle between *historic* and *authentic* Christianity.[141] In the postmodern paradigm of mission to which Bosch refers, faith will possess a voluntary character, rooted in intentional communities critically detached from the prevailing cultural power interests. The church is a pilgrim church not least because it does not call the tune. It is everywhere in a diaspora situation, existing eccentrically as an alien element with temporary residence status.[142] The universal church could come to terms with a pluralist, post-Constantinian era by adopting increasingly the character of a free or confessing church. The state-church nexus hinders rather than furthers the mission because the church's form communicates the wrong message. The church should rather rely upon the inherent authority and creativity of its life and message and so the present situation opens up the crisis-opportunity of truly being the church.[143] The church may then re-emerge as a distinctive community, existing over against the world as a political community of salvation and demonstrating the truth of Christian convictions.[144]

But a postmodern paradigm must also question the sect-type. Churches belonging to the sect-type are facing again the Constantinian challenge. Talk of God implies a claim upon the whole of life. The early church could not apprehend the responsibility of transforming social and political structures, but our situation is not theirs; the contemporary Christian has access to economic, political and social power. It becomes impossible to insist that power be exercised elsewhere. Yet even cultures in which church and state are legally separated pose the Constantinian temptation. Alongside the sacral state there stands sacral culture, the idolising of national and cultural values. Churches may be technically free but bound to loyalties other than Christ or to a Christ no longer recognisable as the crucified. Troeltsch's distinctions here are questionable. There are some 'churches' which resist the dominant ideology while many 'sects' defend it.[145] The political hermeneutic we develop in this situation must be missionary[146] and in creative continuity with the mission of the early church. Relating the way of Christ to the exercise of power means attempting once more what has been badly done throughout history. Barth argued that the free church must face the question posed by its own internal life in which Christ is proclaimed as Saviour alone. The church cannot exist for itself but must be a '*freie Volkskirche*' with a prophetic responsibility towards the state. This restores the question of what stance it is commanded in faith to entertain towards the state.[147]

Troeltsch's and Richard Niebuhr's typologies have shaped modern discussion of Christian social ethics. Troeltsch's typology of church, sect and mysticism was followed by Niebuhr's of church, denomination and sect. Niebuhr then developed a fivefold typology in his seminal work *Christ and Culture*. Yet apart from the fact that the same church may adopt different attitudes to culture at different times[148] the typologies narrowed down the discussion. Both typologies are determined by evaluative criteria and presuppositions. Troeltsch assumed synthesis and compromise to be necessary if Christian ethics were to be culturally effective,[149] so the credibility of the church-type was exaggerated. The very word 'church' is bound to have a normative significance.[150] Niebuhr chose the principle of transformation. Both approaches closed off those positions they did not represent and were implicitly polemical, extrapolating foils to their preferred types.[151] Yoder here finds the options fixed by a Constantinian logic requiring social ethics to accept the responsibility of politics or be doomed to withdrawal (*PJ* 110). This position requires the church to engage the world on the world's own terms and excludes or defines out of existence unorthodox options.[152] Niebuhr set up his argument to undergird the transformationist approach and allow only a world-affirming church or world-denying sect, offering no discriminating modes for the discerning of culture but requiring an all-or-nothing relationship to it.[153] Typologies are valuable as heuristic tools with limitations, as open rather than closed 'boxes'. Yet the dialectic between engagement or withdrawal is a false version of the eschatological tension between church and kingdom. Duality is necessary but is eschatological rather than sociological and historical. It functions as a continual juxtaposition leading to an interaction of confirmation and confrontation.[154]

The current challenge is to develop a post-Christendom political theology based upon the recovery of an authentic ecclesiology. According to Forrester, such a theology would be more akin to Tertullian and Augustine than Eusebius, would treat the political sphere seriously without making it absolute and would be forward-looking and missionary in character. The post-Constantinian age, with the church reduced to a minority status, may prove to be the time for recovering a pre-Constantinian understanding of the church, able to be the church indeed.[155] Close attention to the theology and legitimacy of the state is required here within a christologically determined framework. Political theology has been criticised as superficial, giving inadequate attention to the theological issues which underlie the 'political existence of the Christian'. Socio-political positions are arrived at intuitively or derived from social context rather than from the Word made flesh and attested by Holy Scripture.[156] A theology of church and state is required here to determine a theologically driven approach to the state rather than a politically driven approach to God.[157]

The absence of an adequate theology of church and state was at the root of the churches' failure under the Third Reich[158] and made necessary Barth's christological reformulation. One approach is to derive a 'political option transcending both tyranny and anarchy' and so to 'identify the moment of prophetic resistance to the state, which is theologically related to the affirmation of government as a God-given institution for the common good of society'.[159] Alternatively, not necessarily in contradiction, it may be necessary to relativise the legitimacy of the state by questioning the nature of the 'God-given' status which is ascribed to it. Traditional approaches to the state and the related issue of violence all tend to be 'monist'. They assume a Christian solution to organising society and that the discordant elements in the enterprise can be satisfactorily resolved. Our discussion will reckon with the possibility that the values of Christ and of fallen society may remain unreconciled and that attempts to assimilate 'world' and faith are as wrong as attempts to separate them.[160] But a theological statement remains necessary as a guide for realistic action.

Conclusion

The quest for a non-Constantinian and missionary theology of church and social order, most specifically of the state, is undertaken in the chapters that follow. It begins with an examination of Anabaptist approaches with their emphatic rejection of the sacral state. This provides an angle of approach for the exposition of our selected modern theologians to be found in the subsequent four chapters.

NOTES

1   *Notre Jeunesse* in A. Suarès (ed.), *Oeuvres Complètes de Charles Péguy 873–1914: Oeuvres de Prose*, (Paris: Nouvelle Revue Française, 1916), 59.
2   Free churches rejected the state's right to dominate conscience in favour of the 'crown rights of the Redeemer'. This rejection may be related to the biblical tradition of freedom from idols, any final claim other than that of the true God. So freedom is both personal and political in nature. 'Religious liberty has always been by implication political dissent': Yoder, 'The Believers' Church: Global Perspectives' in J. K. Zeman (ed.), *The Believers' Church in Canada: Addresses*

and Papers from the Study Conference in Winnipeg, May 1978 (1979), 5. Freedom from idols is also correlated with the service of God, which implies a freedom for obedience which comes through acceptance of his authority.

3   E. Y. Mullins, *The Axioms of Religion: A New Interpretation of the Baptist Faith*, (Philadelphia: Judson Press, 1908), 74, 185–200. The 'free church in a free state' formula used by advocates of separation of church and state is attributed to Camillo Cavour (1810–61), Piedmontese statesman and first prime minister of a united Italy. In making Rome Italy's capital, separation of church and state was his answer to the problem of the papacy. He saw the liberty of the church, its spiritual existence and renunciation of temporal power, as the means of renewal of the world and revival of humankind. Pius IX did not respond positively: *Encyclopaedia Britannica: Micropaedia 2* (Fifteenth Edition, Chicago, 1990), 976–8. Moltmann attributes the phrase to Cavour's contemporary and fellow-countryman Guiseppe Mazzini (1805–72): *SL*, 107.

4   G. R. Vicedom, *the Mission of God: An Introduction to a Theology of Mission*, (St Louis: Concordia Publishing House, 1965), 4–11.

5   A. M. Aagaard, 'Missio Dei in katholischer Sicht: Missionstheologische Tendenzen', *EvTh* 34:5 (1974), 422.

6   D. J. Bosch, *Transforming Mission: Paradigm Shifts in Theology of Mission* (Maryknoll: Orbis Books, 1991, 1.

7   Aagaard, 'Missio Dei', 423–4.

8   C. E. Braaten, 'The Triune God: The Source and Model of Christian Unity and Mission', *Missiology: An International Review* 18:4 (1990), 415, 420–1.

9   Bosch, *Transforming Mission*, 9, 182, 389.

10   Cf. Vicedom, *Mission*, 6.

11   Bosch, *Transforming Mission*, 370.

12   Aagaard, 'Missio Dei', 422–33.

13   Bosch, *Transforming Mission*, 374–5, 380.

14   Ibid., 374 384–7.

15   W. R. Shenk (ed.), *The Transfiguration of Mission: Biblical, Theological and Historical Foundations* (Scottdale: Herald Press, 1993), 12.

16   Ibid., 29, 31.

17   Ibid., 9.

18   L. Miller, 'The Church as Messianic Society: Creation and Instrument of Transfigured Mission' in Shenk (ed.), *Transfiguration*, 130, 139.

19   Ibid., 142, 144 cf. Mark 10:42–45.

20   Ibid., 145, 149–50.

21   W. Wink, *Engaging the Powers: Discernment and Resistance in a World of Domination* (Minneapolis: Fortress Press, 1992), 13ff.

22   Bosch, *Transforming Mission*, 389, 373; Aagaard, 'Missio Dei', 421.

23   K. Barth, *CD* IV/1, 643; IV/2, 614, 702–4; IV/3:2, 681.

24   *CD* IV/3:2, 810.

25   G. W. Martin, *The Church: A Baptist View* (London: Baptist Publications, 1976), 21.

26   Bosch, *Transforming Mission*, 249.

27   J. Zizioulas, 'The Doctrine of God the Trinity Today: Suggestions for an Ecumenical Study' in *The Forgotten Trinity 3* (London: BBC, 1991), 28.

28   *CD* IV/2, 617.

29   *CD* IV/2, 719, 722–6.

30   These have been brought together in K. Barth, *Community, State and Church:*

Three Essays edited and with an Introduction by Will Herberg (Gloucester, Mass.: Peter Smith, 1968).

31   Ibid., 80.

32   Ibid., 118.

33   Ibid., 168–9.

34   Ibid., 186.

35   C. Villa-Vicencio, *Between Christ and Caesar: Classic and Contemporary Texts on Church and State* (Grand Rapids: Eerdmans, 1986), 92.

36   Milbank, *Theology and Social Theory*, 380–1.

37   L. Verduin, *The Anatomy of a Hybrid: A Study in Church–State Relationships* (Grand Rapids: Eerdmans, 1976), 113–18, 94, 112, 148.

38   Ibid., 16, 19, 92, 112–14.

39   K. S. Latourette, *A History of the Expansion of Christianity: Volume 3: Three Centuries of Advance 1500–1800* (New York: Harper and Row, 1939), 25; J-M. Chappus, 'Who Are the Reformed Today?' in H. G. Vom Berg et al (eds.), *Mennonites and Reformed in Dialogue* (Geneva: WARC; Lombard, Ill.: Mennonite World Conference, 1986), 36–7.

40   J. H. Yoder, 'Reformation and Missions: A Literature Survey', *Occasional Bulletin of the Missionary Research Library*, June 1971, 4–5.

41   F. H. Littell, *The Origins of Sectarian Protestantism* (New York: Macmillan, 1964), 112 and 'The Anabaptist Theology of Mission' in W. R. Shenk (ed.), *Anabaptism and Mission* (Scottdale: Herald Press, 1984), 13–23.

42   Yoder, 'The Otherness of the Church', *MQR* 35:4 (1961), 215.

43   W. Schäufele, *Das missionarische Bewusstsein und Wirken der Täufer* (Neukirchen-Vluyn: Verlag des Erziehungsvereins, 1966) and 'The Missionary Vision and Activity of the Anabaptist Laity' in Shenk (ed.), *Anabaptism and Mission*, 80, 85–97.

44   Bosch, *Transforming Mission*, 245–6.

45   H. S. Bender, 'Evangelism', *ME 2*, 269.

46   Shenk (ed.), *Transfiguration*, 22–3.

47   'The essential meaning of the Free Church system... is the destruction of the mediaeval and early Protestant idea of a social order welded together by one uniform State Church, and of one infallible authority with a uniform control of the whole of civilisation. From the very outset, therefore, its attitude towards the fundamental social ideas of the previous era was revolutionary': E. Troeltsch, *The Social Teaching of the Christian Churches* 2 (London: George Allen and Unwin, 1931), 656.

48   Yoder, 'Reformation and Missions', 6.

49   D. F. Durnbaugh, *The Believers' Church: The History and Character of Radical Protestantism* (London and New York: Macmillan, 1968), 230; cf. Moltmann *CPS*, 8–9.

50   Bender, 'Evangelism', 269; Yoder, *EFC*, 34.

51   Bosch, *Transforming Mission*, 246–7.

52   Durnbaugh, *Believers' Church*, 238.

53   Bosch, *Transforming Mission*, 420.

54   Bosch, *Transforming Mission*, 377 citing J. C. Hoekendijk, *Kirche und Volk in der deutschen Missionswissenschaft* (Munich: Chr. Kaiser Verlag, 1967), 349.

55   Watts, *Dissenters*, 2.

56   Ibid., 4.

57   A. D. Lindsay, *The Churches and Democracy* (London: Epworth Press, 1934), 14,

24, 26, 31–2.

58   F. H. Littell, 'The Work of the Holy Spirit in Group Decisions', *MQR* 34:2 (1960), 83.

59   E. A. Payne, *The Free Church Tradition in the Life of England* (London: Hodder and Stoughton, 1965), 26–7; Durnbaugh, *Believers' Church*, 3–4; Moltmann, *OC*, 117.

60   Verduin, *Anatomy*, 242–8; W. S. Hudson, 'John Locke: Heir of Puritan Political Theorists' in G. L. Hunt (ed.), *Calvinism and the Political Order* (Philadelphia: Wetminster Press, 1965), 108–29.

61   Cf. Lindsay, 'The ideal of a free Church in a free State is not less necessary or less likely to be fruitful in the world of the present than it has been in the past': *Democracy*, 87.

62   'Volkskirche, Freikirche, Bekenntniskirche', *EvTh* 3 (1936), 411–12, 416–17. I have traced Barth's development in this regard in 'Mission, the Shape of the Church and Ecumenism' in Beasley-Murray (ed.), *Mission to the World* (Didcot: Baptist Historical Society, 1991), 52–6.

63   Yoder, 'Believers' Church', 4; Moltmann, *OC*, 117–18, *CPS*, 329–30; R. R. Ruether, 'The Free Church Movement in Contemporary Catholicism' in M. E. Marty and D. G. Peerman (eds.), *New Theology No 6: On Revolution and Non-Revolution, Violence and Non-Violence, Peace and Power* (London: Collier-Macmillan, 1969), 268, 287 esp. 285–6; K. Rahner, *The Shape of the Church to Come* (London: SPCK, 1985), 23–5, 32, 48, 108–9, 120; M. E. Marty, 'Baptistification Takes Over', *CT*, September 2 1983, 32–6; G. Lohfink, *Jesus and Community: The Social Dimension of Christian Faith*; L. Boff, *Church, Charism and Power: Liberation Theology and the Institutional Church* (London: SCM Press, 1985), *Ecclesiogenesis: The Base Communities Reinvent the Church* (Glasgow: Collins, 1986).

64   K. Barth, *Church and State* (London: SCM Press, 1939), 38.

65   This shift is associated with Constantine but took time to effect. Ramsey MacMullen, in *Christianizing the Roman Empire: AD 100–400* (New Haven and London: Yale University Press, 1984), traces three stages: Up to the Peace of the Church in 313 new members entered the church impressed by the proofs and content of the faith, 109. After this the church grew because there was financial advantage in being a Christian, 115. After 380 there was the systematic application of persuasion and armed force (flattery and battery) to finish the task of Christianisation, 119. By 407 it could be claimed that non-Christians were outlaws and that a state religion had emerged, 101. The turning point however was AD 312/3, p. 102. The original toleration was intended as a pluralism in which Christianity would triumph over paganism by persuasion without coercion: H. Dorries, *Constantine and Religious Liberty* (New Haven: Yale University Press, 1960), 21, 23, 26, 28–9. Coercive measures began against heretics but even here Constantine realised their ineffectiveness, 93, 101. Toleration gave way to repression of paganism as Constantine's position became stronger: N. Baynes, *Constantine the Great and the Christian Church* (London: Oxford University Press, 1934 and 1972), 18–19. Paganism was penalised by Constantine's sons and then comprehensively by Theodosius the Great (379–95) whose policy of enforced conformity became the starting point for subsequent legislation, 49, 51–2. As imperial office supposedly involved sins, the rule was to delay baptism, as with Constantine, but Theodosius received emergency baptism and so ruled as a church member: King, *The Emperor Theodosius*, 30. In theory he and his contemporaries

knew heresy should be overcome by love and patience, but coercion had crept in unobtrusively under Constantine and no alarm had been raised. At first Theodosius was lenient but after 392 the orthodox Christian state was established, 50, 93–6. He confirmed Christianity as a religion of victory in battle. Theodosius saw it as his duty to smite the enemy, but showed moderation. Church leaders came round to advocating force persuaded by arguments first elicited by the need to deal with heresy, 32. Imperial need for a unifying religion and the absolute claims of Christianity resulted in messianic fusion of the kingdoms of Christ and Caesar by the time of Justinian (527–65) into 'Christendom'. Catholic church joined catholic Empire to produce a universalism which in the end turned out to be a form of tribalism: R. R. Ruether, 'Augustine and Christian Political Theology', *Interpretation* 29 (1975) 255–58; A. Hastings, *Church and State: The English Experience* (Exeter: University of Exeter Press, 1991), 17–18.

66   G. H. Williams, 'Christology and Church–State Relations in the Fourth Century', *CH* 20:4 (1951), 21.

67   D. B. Forrester, *Theology and Politics* (Oxford: Basil Blackwell, 1988), 3–4.

68   Ibid., 5.

69   Ibid., 28.

70   Verduin, *Anatomy*, 22–3.

71   Forrester, *Theology and Politics*, 1.

72   Verduin, *Anatomy*, 29, 91.

73   Forrester, *Theology and Politics*, 19, 29, 54.

74   Ibid., 10, 13–14, 17.

75   Ibid., 20, 38.

76   Ibid., 20–6.

77   Villa-Vicencio, *Christ and Caesar*, 6.

78   Forrester, *Theology and Politics*, 25. Augustine in the Donatist conflict advocated coercion after seeing its effectiveness, justifying it through strained exegesis (Verduin, *Anatomy*, 105–11; Dorries, *Constantine*, 58–64). After the sack of Rome in 410 and the pagan charge that it was due to Constantine's defection, Augustine responded in the *City of God*. In this an eschatological critique de-absolutised the state and charted a course between Eusebius' fusion of church and empire and the apocalyptic dualism of Donatism in such a way as to recognise the principle of secularity and the political order as legitimate in its own limited terms: Ruether, 'Augustine and Christian Political Theology', 261. It also removed the historical expectation of the Kingdom from the political realm, reduced hope for messianic redemption within history and abandoned the state to 'love of self'. Augustine, further, diminished hope for the visibility of the true church, seeing it as an imperfect shadow of the spiritual church. P. Brown, *Augustine of Hippo: A Biography* (London: Faber and Faber, 1967), 221–4. His position fails to take the possibilities of either civil order or church with sufficient seriousness.

79   R. J. Neuhaus, *The Naked Public Square: Religion and Democracy in America* (Grand Rapids: Eerdmans, 1986), 171.

80   A. H. M. Jones, *Constantine and the Conversion of Europe* (Harmondsworth: Pelican, 1972), 232–40.

81   Baynes, *Constantine the Great*, 30.

82   Neuhaus, *Naked Public Square*, 172.

83   L. Newbigin, *Foolishness to the Greeks: The Gospel and Western Culture* (Geneva: World Council of Churches, 1986), 100–1.

84   L. Newbigin, *The Gospel in a Pluralist Society* (London: SPCK, 1989), 195–6.

85   L. Newbigin, *The Other Side of 84: Questions for the Churches* (Geneva: World Council of Churches, 1983), 2, 32–7.

86   Ibid., 100; Bosch takes a similar position: *Transforming Mission*, 222.

87   Forrester, *Theology and Politics*, 22.

88   Verduin, *Anatomy*, 11.

89   Villa-Vicencio, *Christ and Caesar*, 4–5.

90   Verduin, *Anatomy*, 102.

91   Ibid., 251–3.

92   Cf. Edwyn Bevan: 'Such a view is worse than a corruption of Christianity; it is a denial of the very essence of the Church, of the character which it had from the beginning as a society in which membership represented a personal individual act of will: it is an assimilation of Christianity to the State religions of paganism': *Christianity in the Light of Modern Knowledge*, 104 cited by Payne, *The Free Church Tradition*, 146.

93   R. S. Giles, 'The Church as a Counter-Culture Before Constantine'. MLitt Dissertation, Newcastle-upon-Tyne, 1988, 2. A counter-culture is 'a social construction set up as an objective reality within society, but which is quite distinct from that society, from which it experiences some degree of alienation', 3.

94   Ibid., 80–1, 273.

95   Ibid., 13–132.

96   Ibid., 141–3.

97   Ibid., 19–20.

98   Shenk (ed.), *Transfiguration*, 33 n. 6. Christendom was later to collapse because of the Enlightenment but also because the modern mission movement patiently and persistently breached the boundaries of historic Christendom: 19–20.

99   Troeltsch, *The Social Teaching* 1, 80–1.

100 There was, however, some diversity at this point and it is ambiguous whether military service was rejected because of the violence or the idolatry involved: F. Young, 'The Early Church: Military Service, War and Peace', *Theology* 92 (1989), 491–503.

101 Giles, 'Counterculture', 210.

102 Ibid., 210–11.

103 A. Kee, *Constantine versus Christ: The Triumph of Ideology* (London: SCM Press, 1982), 2–4, 8, 18.

104 Ibid., 23. Contra Baynes, *Constantine the Great*, 29.

105 Ibid., 28, 88–101; 58; Verduin, *Anatomy*, 95–105.

106 Ibid., 36–8, 44, 50, 121–5.

107 Ibid., 100.

108 D. M. MacKinnon judged that Kee makes a convincing case for a 'monstrous distortion of Christian understanding in the conversion of Constantine and its *sequelae*': Review in *SJT* 36:2 (1983), 261. A. Louth questions his familiarity with the field he is dealing with: Review in *Theology* 68 (1983), 140; W. Klaassen finds him buttressing the Constantine critique but recognises that he is on a crusade and so produces insecure conclusions: Review in *MQR* 57:4 (1983), 400. H. Chadwick faults Kee at many points and finds him 'essentially wrong-headed'. He can agree that the emperor's intense ambition became fused with religious allegiance but concludes: 'The emperor was not striking for his saintly qualities but to treat him as the devil incarnate is a bit much': 'The Emperor as Antichrist', *TLS*, May 28 1982, 574.

109 Kee, *Constantine*, 129, 134.

110 Ibid., 140–1. Eusebius had developed the idea of Constantine as the *mimesis* of the Eternal: Villa-Vicencio, *Christ and Caesar*, 16–19; N. H. Baynes, *Byzantine Studies and Other Essays* (London: Athlone Press, 1955), 168–72. Here Kee, following Feuerbach, stands the argument on its head.

111 Ibid., 125, 146–7.

112 Ibid., 151–2, 155.

113 J-P. Hornus, *It Is Not Lawful For Me To Fight: Early Christian Attitudes Toward War, Violence, and the State* (Scottdale: Herald Press, 1980), 212.

114 Kee, *Constantine*, 156–7, 159, 164.

115 Ibid., 162–4.

116 Ibid., 166–8.

117 Moltmann, *WJC*, 153–4; T. N. Finger, 'The Way to Nicea: Reflections from a Mennonite Perspective', *CGR*, 3:3 (1985), 321–49. D. A. Shank claims that 'christology' evacuates the biblical, messianic language of its historical, social, economic and political content. He advocates the rediscovery of a series of words cognate with 'Messiah': 'messianist', 'messianic', 'messianism', 'messianity' and 'messialogy': 'Jesus the Messiah: Messianic Foundation of Mission' in Shenk (ed.), *Transfiguration*, 39, 42. However, it is not christology as such which is here at fault but the tendency under political pressure to forget how the absoluteness of God is associated with the account of a vulnerable and contingent human career: C. E. Gunton 'The Political Christ: Some Reflections on Mr Cupitt's Thesis', *SJT* 32:6 (1979), 527, 534–40.

118 Verduin, *Anatomy*, 105–11, 163–8, 178–83, 198–212.

119 Ibid., 110, 225.

120 Villa-Vicencio, *Christ and Caesar*, xv–xvi.

121 Cf. P. P. Peachey: 'At the core, Constantinian Christendom represents a synthesis in which religion provides sacred legitimation for the secular order and the polity secures monopoly and protection for the religious institution': 'Constantinian Christendom and the Marx–Engels phenomenon', *MQR* 55:3 (1981), 184.

122 S. Hauerwas, *After Christendom? How the Church is to Behave if Freedom, Justice, and a Christian Nation are Bad Ideas* (Nashville: Abingdon Press, 1991), 18, 39.

123 S. Hauerwas and W. H. Willimon, *Resident Aliens: Life in the Christian Colony* (Nashville: Abingdon Press, 1989), 27.

124 Ibid., 43.

125 B. Goudzwaard, *Idols of our Time* (Downers Grove: InterVarsity Press, 1984), 24–5.

126 Kee, *Constantine*, 162; Moltmann, *OHD*, 137.

127 Troeltsch, *The Social Teaching* 1, 82–5.

128 Verduin, *Anatomy*, 30 n. and passim.

129 Troeltsch, *The Social Teaching* 1, 329–30.

130 Ibid., 340.

131 Neuhaus, *Naked Public Square*, 172.

132 J. H. Yoder, 'Another "Free Church" Perspective on Baptist Ecumenism', *JES* 17:2 (1980), 155.

133 Troeltsch acknowledged this term suggests groups regarded as 'inferior side-issues, one-sided phenomena, exaggerations or abbreviations of ecclesiastical Christianity' by the dominant churches which believe that their type alone has any right to exist: *The Social Teaching* 1, 333–4.

134 Martin, *The Church*, 15.

135 Rahner, *The Shape of the Church*, 29–30.
136 G. A. Lindbeck, 'The Sectarian Future of the Church' in J. P. Whelan S. J. (ed.), *The God Experience: Essays in Hope* (New York: Newman Press, 1971), 227.
137 'The Church is that type of organization which is overwhelmingly conservative, which to a certain extent accepts the secular order, and dominates the masses; in principle, therefore it is universal, i.e. it desires to cover the whole life of humanity. The sects, on the other hand, are comparatively small groups; they aspire after personal inward perfection, and they aim at a direct personal fellowship between the members of each group. From the very beginning, therefore, they are forced to organize themselves in small groups, and to renounce the idea of dominating the world. Their attitude towards the world, the State and Society may be indifferent, tolerant or hostile, since they have no desire to control and incorporate these forms of social life; on the contrary, they tend to avoid them; their aim is usually either to tolerate their presence alongside of their own body, or even to replace these social institutions by their own society. Further, both types are in close connection with the actual situation and with the development of society. The fully developed Church, however, utilizes the State and the ruling classes, and weaves these elements into her own life; she then becomes an integral part of the existing social order; from this stand-point, then, the Church both stabilizes and determines the social order; in so doing, however, she becomes dependent upon the upper classes, and upon their development. The sects, on the other hand, are connected with the lower classes, or at least with those elements in Society which are opposed to the State and to Society; they work upwards from below, and not downwards from above': Troeltsch, *The Social Teaching* 1, 331; see also 335ff. A third type is identified as 'religious individualism which has no external organization', 381. Littell draws attention to the neglect of the third type identified by Troeltsch, the mystics or spiritualisers, and believes that, with the elimination of doctrinal and disciplinary order, it is between this type and the sect that the real tension now exists in Protestantism: 'Church and Sect', *EcRev* 6 (1954), 266–7.
138 Troeltsch, *The Social Teaching* 1: 335–7.
139 Lindbeck, 'The Sectarian Future', 227–8.
140 Barth, *CD* 4/3.2, 779.
141 Verduin, *Anatomy*, 20.
142 Bosch, *Transforming Mission*, 373–4.
143 Ibid., 2–3.
144 Hauerwas, *After Christendom*, 26, 35–7.
145 Villa-Vicencio, *Christ and Caesar*, xviii.
146 D. L. Migliore, 'Biblical Eschatology and Political Hermeneutics', *ThT* 26 (1969–70), 118, 123.
147 'Volkskirche, Freikirche, Bekenntniskirche', 419.
148 L. Newbigin, 'Christ and the Cultures', *SJT* 31:1 (1978), 14.
149 B. K. Jennings, 'A Critical Appraisal of Typologies of Religious Orientation in the Theology and Ethics of Ernst Troeltsch and H. Richard Niebuhr.' MPhil Dissertation, Open University, 1988, 70.
150 Littell, 'Church and Sect', 268; D. K. Friesen, 'Normative Factors in Troeltsch's Typology of Religious Association', *JRE* 3:2 (1975), 271–83.
151 Jennings, 'A Critical Appraisal', 152, 223.
152 Ibid., 30.
153 *Resident Aliens*, 40–1. B. Johnson suggests instead: 'A church is a religious group that accepts the social environment in which it exists. A sect is a religious group that

rejects the social environment in which it exists': *American Sociological Review* 13 (1974), 542 cited by A. Snyder 'The Monastic Origins of Swiss Anabaptist Sectarianism', *MQR* 57:1 (1983), 6. This allows for a spectrum of positions.

154 Jennings, 'A Critical Appraisal', 226–30.

155 Forrester, *Theology and Politics*, 55, 143.

156 A. J. Torrance, 'Introductory Essay' in E. Jüngel, *Christ, Justice and Peace: Towards a Theology of the State in Dialogue with the Barmen Declaration* (Edinburgh: T. and T. Clark, 1992), ix–xiii.

157 Ibid., xx.

158 J. Begbie 'The Confessing Church and the Nazis: A Struggle for Theological Truth', *Anvil* 2:2 (1985), 125–7.

159 Villa-Vicencio, *Christ and Caesar*, xiii, xi.

160 J. Ellul, *Violence: Reflections from a Christian Perspective* (London and Oxford: Mowbrays, 1978), 24–5.

CHAPTER 3

Anabaptism, Power And Paradox

This chapter clarifies Anabaptism's historical origins, its 'essence' and its characteristic concepts of church and society in order to provide a context within which to examine Yoder and Moltmann. It further identifies the distinction between Anabaptism and Baptist movements to illustrate a tension between Anabaptist and Reformed traditions and reviews some recent internal criticism of Anabaptist–Mennonite positions.

Anabaptism in History

The tangled roots of Anabaptism have yet to be successfully unravelled.[1] Long subject to its detractors' interpretations, the renaissance of Anabaptist historiography has offered more positive appraisals.[2] The identification of a type of 'evangelical Anabaptism' in the Swiss Brethren emerging from the circle around Zwingli, and distinguished from him after 1525, came to function as normative for the whole movement,[3] allowing 'a sort of posthumous excommunication' to exclude unacceptable elements.[4]

The diversity of the Reformation's radical wing is clear from Williams' survey and included three main thrusts: Spiritualists, Anabaptists and Evangelical Rationalists.[5] Williams identifies seven Anabaptist regional groupings resolved into three morphological types:[6] (1) The Swiss Brethren, (2) South German and Austrian Anabaptists, (3) The communitarian Hutterites of Moravia, (4) The anti-Chalcedonian Melchiorites of Lower Germany, the Netherlands, England and Prussia in line with Melchior Hofmann's and Menno Simons' pacifism, (5) The revolutionary Münsterites in line with Melchior Hofmann's apocalypticism and the violence of Jan Mathys, (6) The predestinarian and psychopannychist, anti-Nicene North Italian Anabaptists and (7) the anti-Nicene Lithuanian and Polish Brethren. These groups are unevenly distributed into Evangelical Anabaptists, or 'suffering servants' (groups 1–4), Maccabean Anabaptists, or 'militant heralds' (group 5), and Spiritualising Anabaptists, or 'watchful brooders' (from various groups).

The early debate over Anabaptist origins isolated one of two points, Saxony or Switzerland, Zwickau or Zurich, and drew parallel value judgements. By locating its origin in Luther's confrontation with the Wittenberg radicals (1521–1522),[7] Karl Holl associated the movement with the Zwickau Prophets and Müntzer. The Münster *débacle* (1535) was thus Anabaptism's logical extension. This association has been vigorously contested.[8] Yet recent scholarship, reconciling Mennonite and Marxist interpretations,[9] recognises revolutionary concern for reconstructing property ownership in Anabaptism[10] while heightening the non-violent elements in the 'German Peasants' War'.[11] Troeltsch, opposing Holl, found the origins in Zürich and concluded that Anabaptism was mainly pacifist. Münster was an extreme and uncharacteristic consequence of persecution.[12] Anabaptism, it may be agreed, was a refuge for ex-revolutionaries rather than a violent organisation.[13]

In the 1960s a historiographical shift rejected the search for normative Anabaptism as a confessional device for dismissing embarrassing incidents. Anabaptism was polygenetic[14] or at least trigenetic,[15] centred upon the Zwinglian-humanist Swiss Brethren, the mystical-humanist South Germans and the sacramentarian-apocalyptic Dutch.[16] Evangelical Anabaptism was an abstraction of limited utility, the consequence of a 'high ideology'.[17] Anabaptism was a series of interacting groups embodying distinct sectarian traditions and oscillating between the poles of pacifism and revolution provided by Zwickau and Zürich.[18] Similarly, 'the Reformation' is a misnomer. There was a series of reformations of plural origins and theologies, not 'purely religious' but part of the larger social and political revolution.[19] This polygenetic approach is itself not unideological: it legitimates growing Mennonite pluralism and interest in radical politics.

This diversity is further attested by ways of accounting for the movement. Williams' 'Radical Reformation' and Bainton's 'Left Wing of the Reformation'[20] defined Anabaptists as radical Protestants, more courageous than Luther and Zwingli in applying Reformation principles. Differences between Reformers and Radicals were quantitative. Others identified a debt to mediaeval dissenting movements and so a qualitative distinction from Protestants and Catholics.[21] The focus here is on evangelical resistance to totalitarianism. An alternative finds traces of mediaeval asceticism mediated through the monastic orders (several Anabaptist leaders were former monks), the influence of Erasmus and the *Devotia Moderna* or the *Theologia Germanica*.[22] For Marxists the movement resulted from social forces, the search for religious motives being a bourgeois illusion.[23] Still others locate its origins in the ability of the revolutionary strains of the biblical canon, already being suppressed within the canon itself, to reassert themselves throughout history.[24]

ANABAPTIST IDENTITY

Given the varieties of Anabaptism, is it meaningful to use the name at all? The nominalist use of the description corresponds to its literal meaning:

Anabaptists were united by an outward sign, the baptism of believers. It is necessary however to identify a common body of ideas.

The quest for the essence of Anabaptism and its related traditions is almost as extensive as that for the essence of Christianity.[25] Amidst the plurality, Weaver finds the regulative principles in discipleship, community, non-violence and separation from the world.[26] Similarly, McClendon finds among the wider 'heirs of the Radicals':

(1) Biblicism, understood not as one or another theory of inspiration, but as a humble acceptance of the authority of Scripture for both faith and practice. (Related themes are restitution and restoration.)

(2) Mission (or evangelism), understood not as an attempt to control history for the ends we believe to be good, but as responsibility to witness to Christ – and accept the suffering that witness entails.

(3) Liberty, or soul competency, understood not as the overthrow of all oppressive authority, but as the God-given freedom to respond to God without the intervention of the state or other powers. (Related themes are intentional community, voluntarism, separation of church and state.)

(4) Discipleship, understood neither as a vocation for the few nor an esoteric discipline for adepts, but as life transformed into service by the lordship of Jesus Christ. (Signified by believer's baptism; a related theme is the regenerate or believers' church.)

(5) Community, understood not as privileged access to God or to sacred status, but as sharing together in a storied life of obedient service to and with Christ. (Signified by the Lord's Supper.)[27]

Various themes have been applied as organising centres for this total vision and are reviewed by McClendon. For Smucker[28] biblicism has priority; but this is shared with other Christians. Mullins advanced liberty and 'soul-competency',[29] although in a culturally conditioned way. Troeltsch attributed separation of church and state, religious toleration, voluntaryism and development of the liberal society to the Anabaptist legacy[30] but reduced these themes from theology to political theories. 'Discipleship' emerged from Bender's seminal essay 'The Anabaptist Vision', with its christocentric stress on *Nachfolge Christi* as the meaning of baptism and its combination of discipleship, the church as brotherhood and non-resistance.[31] But by itself the theme does not express the vision. Community was stressed by Littell in his working definition: '[T]he Anabaptists proper were those in the radical Reformation who gathered and disciplined a "true church" (*rechte Kirche*) upon the apostolic pattern as they understood it'.[32] He expounded this definition within a primitivist view of church history involving a fall from apostolic purity, variously dated[33] but associated with Constantine, and the subsequent Anabaptist restitution of the true church.[34] This McClendon believes to come closest to the mark because it joins history and community. To a degree, all parties of the Reformation were restitutionists; but the Reformers gloried in a restoration of the gospel while the Anabaptists gloried in that of the church.[35] Unlike the Spiritualists, they looked for a restitution of the visible community.[36]

McClendon's own 'hermeneutical motto' finds the essence of the vision in:

> shared awareness of *the present Christian community as the primitive community and the eschatological community*. In other words, the church now is the primitive church and the church on the day of judgement is the church now; the obedience and liberty of the followers of Jesus of Nazareth is *our* liberty, *our* obedience.[37]

This captures the sense of immediacy before the biblical testimony: the church now is the apostolic church, often fallen and often restored. So McClendon existentialises the themes of fall and restoration while avoiding the detailed interpretations of history and the unself-critical attitudes that have accompanied this motif.

Anabaptists and the 'Sword'

Anabaptist variety is illustrated, and generalisations questioned, by examining how the church's relation to society and government was conceived. Stayer's work on this topic illustrates the degree of disagreement. By 'sword' is meant the ethics of coercion, the use of force by the authorities.[38] In the sixteenth century coercion was the largest part of the state's activities. The Reformers moved from the Two-Sword theory of mediaeval papalism to a One-Sword view confining the legitimate use of the sword to the *Obrigkeit*, the civil authority. Luther intended not to divide between secular and sacred but to illuminate the twofold nature of God's rule.[39] The Anabaptists generally followed this, sharing his presuppositions but few of his conclusions. All *Obrigkeit* is of God and under God but is qualified by the Fall. It was established as a sign of God's mercy and an instrument of his wrath, not always being excluded as a place of service on principle, but in practice conflicting with redemptive love.[40] The primary setting for their discussion was not the war of the nation-state envisaged in the present century but *holy* war in defence of the faith or against fellow Christians in the exercise of church discipline.[41] The only governments the Anabaptists knew, therefore, were those who persecuted them today or might well persecute them tomorrow.[42]

Stayer uncovers the variety of Anabaptist responses to the sword, identifying four points on a compass as positions between which the varying groups oscillated.[43] This typology clarifies the raw stuff of Anabaptist teachings for the modern reader and elaborates Bainton's prior classifications of crusade, just war and pacifist positions.[44]

The *crusading stand-point* embraced coercion as legitimate and effective. At Münster Anabaptists became the civil government and practised a reign of terror. Hofmann's apocalyptic visions were interpreted violently. Rothmann, the Münsterite theoretician, located Münster within the temporal unfolding of Providence by reading the signs of the times.[45] Vengeance was the prelude to Christ's coming and found expression in mass executions and a general Anabaptist uprising. Violence was not isolated: revolutionary Melchioritism died a lingering, festering death.[46] Disillusioned apocalypticism incited Anabaptist terrorism in Germany and the Netherlands.[47] Violence often resulted from desperate social conditions and persecution. But Anabaptism became identifiable with violent revolution even though, as Stayer indicates, the balance of its membership was peaceful.[48] Elton's judgement that it was 'a violent phenomenon born out of irrational and psychologically unbalanced dreams..' is not entirely uninformed.[49]

The *realpolitik stand-point* is associated with Balthasar Hübmaier. Although identified with the Swiss Brethren, Hübmaier was not 'in the middle of the Anabaptist movement'.[50] In Yoder's judgement, he failed to see that the state which claims to reform the church can also claim to halt its progress.[51] He is accurately described both as a Reformed Anabaptist, standing half way between Anabaptism and Zwinglianism,[52] and as a Catholic Anabaptist.[53] A reforming priest in Waldshut when the village was resisting the Habsburgs,[54] he was baptised in 1525 and led the majority of the town to be baptised, constituting the first Anabaptist city. He aimed, like Zwingli, at a general reformation of the church, believed in a Christian society and shared Zwingli's real-political teaching on the sword.[55] By this Stayer means the recognition that values enforced by the sword are tarnished, but this is better than making no attempt to realise those values.[56]

Between his baptism and his martyrdom in 1528, Hübmaier spent time in Zürich, where he briefly recanted, and then migrated to Nikolsburg in Moravia. His temporary recantation affirmed that a Christian may govern: 'Ever and always I have said that a Christian can be in government, and that the more Christian he is the more honourably he would rule'.[57] Nikolsburg became a refuge for Anabaptists of all shades[58] and an experiment in Anabaptist civil government in which Hübmaier was influential as theologian and Reformer. The arrival of Hans Hut in 1527 occasioned a dispute which divided the town's Anabaptists into *Schwertler*, like Hübmaier adopting a positive attitude to civil government, and *Stäbler*, rejecting any identification with the sword. Hut himself taught an apocalyptic doctrine of the vengeance of the elect against the rulers after the second coming: meanwhile Christians were to be non-violent.[59]

The reconstruction of the Nikolsburg dispute and the articles there discussed is complex.[60] Bergsten has clarified the contradictory positions of Hübmaier and Hut at the time.[61] Hübmaier's position is stated in his pamphlet 'On the Sword', produced immediately after the dispute. It expounds the texts cited to deny that the Christian should sit in authority and wield the sword.[62] The sword belongs to the divine order to watch over orphans, protect widows and the righteous and to free those who are threatened. Killing belongs necessarily to this order. Subjects are obligated to help their superiors root out the evil ones; yet they are also to test whether governments act from other motives than love of peace and the common good. If not, migration is the solution.[63] Christians may bear the sword and punish evil-doers provided they are duly appointed to 'wield' the sword and do not 'take' the sword to themselves.[64] What a Christian government does in wielding the sword is not motivated by hatred of enemies but exercised as a mandate of God.[65] Next to the preaching task, the office of temporal ruler is the most dangerous on earth because of the temptations of power. But it can be exercised in servant fashion and this requires 'that we should not quarrel, fight and strive about it, nor conquer land and people with the sword and with force. It is against God'.[66] Ironically, Hübmaier was arrested shortly after this with the acquiescence of his protector von Liechtenstein as a prelude to trial and martyrdom.[67]

Hut's position is less easily determined. In Nikolsburg he maintained Christians should participate neither in violence nor in government. He and Hübmaier thus occupied different positions, Hut being the 'typical' Anabaptist and Hübmaier remaining, in this respect, a Protestant Reformer[68] advocating a 'Reformed Anabaptism'.[69] The most considerable theologian[70] produced by Anabaptism, certainly its only trained theologian and most prolific author, was therefore atypical on the sword. The more Reformed and militant Baptists have embraced him as a forerunner.[71] Stayer makes a strong case that although unique as a real-political theorist, Hübmaier was far from unique as a real-political practitioner, even among the Swiss Brethren.[72]

Stayer identifies as *apolitical moderates* those who agree that force is necessary to the life of society but deny that it can achieve the highest values. Force maintains the order within which the higher values are pursued but remains ethically neutral. Moderates accept the benefits of the maintenance of order by coercion.[73] This position distances itself from the sword without denying it. It might also be described as 'moderate non-resistance' and is found in Denck, Marpeck and Simons.[74]

Hans Denck belonged to the Anabaptism influenced by Müntzer, especially by his mysticism, yet avoided his crusading attitude. He moved from an early position of ambiguity concerning whether a Christian could use the civil sword to non-resistance. But even here was paradox. Openness to dialogue with the world and belief in the ethic of true love as universal demand led him to agree that coercive authority might be exercised in a spirit of love, as might do the head of a household, the foundation and model for social authority. Yet the difficulty of achieving such love in government meant government should be avoided.[75] Killing and ruling might be Christian if performed, as did God, without vengeance and egoism.[76] Although a separatist, Denck held his position with subtlety and denied participation in civil government on pragmatic moral grounds rather than in principle. His characterisation as the 'founder of undogmatic Christianity' is widely accepted.[77]

Pilgram Marpeck ranks with Hübmaier for intellect in the early movement and occupied civil positions out of sheer ability.[78] As town engineer in Strasbourg (1528–31) and Augsburg (1544–56) he was practically in government.[79] He was no separatist[80] nor friendly with Hutterites and Swiss Brethren who were. He renounced self-defence and denied the government any ecclesiastical function. The government should neither dispense with power nor use it in the church.[81] This would blaspheme against the Spirit and reject Christ's rule. Force is not even to be used against false teaching; the Word and the Spirit are enough. The sword belongs in the world but not the church. His primary objection to force was its use under the pretext of faith in Christ.[82] Yet the civil sword was also dangerous: 'It is difficult for a Christian to be a worldly ruler... since no one can serve two masters, that is the king or emperor in the worldly magistracy, and Christ in the spiritual, heavenly kingdom'.[83] 'Christ's wisdom is merciful and will not serve [the magistrate] in his office because he is not merciful in his office but rather an avenger'.[84] Stayer has followed previous arguments in claiming that Marpeck was fitting himself into South German traditions reaching back to Denck. Doubt about serving as a ruler does not absolutely rule it out. Stayer cites Marpeck's close association with Georg Rothenfelder who argued that if a Christian could be the ruler of a household he could also be the ruler of a country. Other South German Anabaptists manifested a less-than-hard-line position in this regard.[85]

Menno Simons is particularly instructive. Menno, a priest, broke with Rome only in 1536 (after Münster) and shepherded the scattered flock of Melchiorites as one untainted by violence. He was closer to Zwingli than to the Swiss Brethren,[86] opposing the sword of war but not forbidding Christians to rule and wield the sword. He distinguished between the sword of war and the sword of justice.[87] Christian rulers protect widows and orphans, punish the immoral and criminal and even, surprisingly, aid true religion against deceivers, although by reasonable means of restraint and not by tyranny or bloodshed.[88] Menno followed this outline all his life with two alterations. He came to reject altogether the application of force in strictly religious matters.[89] This brought him into line with Marpeck. He came to reject capital punishment for more humane forms of punishment.[90] He never developed a political ethic separating Christians from maintaining the natural order of society but wavered between withdrawal from society and its transformation. The Old Testament ideal of the godly ruler is not lacking in his writings. He does not adhere to 'non-resistance' and is not doctrinaire concerning the sword.[91]

The fourth point of the compass, with which Stayer confesses himself to be unsympathetic,[92] is *radical apoliticism*[93] or separatist non-resistance. To exercise force is to become corrupt. This is ethical absolutism with an unambiguous view of reality. It was represented by the Swiss Brethren, became codified in the Schleitheim Brotherly Union drafted by Michael Sattler, and triumphed by virtue of its radicalism wherever Anabaptism survived.[94] Yoder describes Schleitheim as the most important event in the history of Anabaptism. Here emerged the growing conviction that the sword was a pagan arrangement (*TRS*, 99–100, 169). The first Anabaptist sect thus came to define thinking on the sword,[95] but the beginnings of Anabaptism generally need to be distinguished from the founding of the Swiss Brethren sect at Schleitheim.[96] Snyder believes Schleitheim to be decisive for the Swiss and Hutterites but less so for other streams of the movement.[97]

The radical position was outlined in Grebel's letter of 1524 to Müntzer, expressing both admiration and unease over Müntzer's position, of which he was only partially informed. The church is a suffering minority which has forsaken the sword and war.[98] This was developed by Michael Sattler at Schleitheim.[99] Sattler can thus be claimed as the real founder of the Swiss Brethren.[100] The sectarianism of this strand, uncharacteristic of most early Anabaptists, has been convincingly explained as having its intellectual taproots in the Benedictine monasticism to which Sattler previously belonged and in which the theme of christocentric discipleship was dominant. Anabaptism is in part a Protestantisation of monasticism.[101]

Schleitheim advances extreme separation of church and world in Article IV. Its pessimistic anthropology and sociology envisage the sword as the power which holds society together[102] without any neutral ground between God and Satan for God's preservation ordinances. The non-Christian is the anti-Christian. The world is devilish and only Romans 13 prevents radical apoliticism becoming anarchy.[103]

Article VI, on the sword, contrasts the ban used for admonition and exclusion 'within the perfection of Christ', in the church, and the sword prevailing 'outside the perfection of Christ'. The sword is a diabolical weapon (Yoder: *LMS*, 38), yet also an *ordering of God* to punish the wicked and protect the good, to be wielded by secular rulers. Believers can have nothing to do with it, nor serve in civil government as magistrates, nor can they swear oaths (Article VII). Nonconformity is justified by the example of Jesus. The Christian life is adherence to his example. Zwingli interpreted this rejection of the sword as rejection of the state. His logic moved from rulers as servants of God, through the fact that Christians should serve God to the conclusion that therefore Christians should be rulers (Yoder: *TRS*, 107, 116).

Schleitheim was reaffirmed at disputations in Zoffingen (1532) and Bern (1538) but not all Swiss Brethren accepted it. Hans Bruback, a member of the first Anabaptist congregation in Zollikon, argued in 1530 that Christians could be rulers and that the government should imprison thieves and murderers but not execute them.[104] Yet Schleitheim predominated because, Stayer suggests, radical ideas tend to survive. Moderate apolitical conciliation was not suited to the violence and extremism of the times.[105] More sympathetically, Verduin finds the Confession an excellent statement which avoided making the *regnum* the devil's realm while establishing a clear, necessary and progressive distinction between the instruments of preserving and redeeming grace, that is, state and church.[106]

The arguments of the Confession were repeated in the writings of Peter Rideman of the Hutterites, the most doctrinaire of all Anabaptist groups in rejecting the established state.[107] While allowing that government is ordained by God and right and good within its own limits (when it does not presume to 'lay hands upon the conscience and to control the faith of man'),[108] he developed the logical outcome of the separatist position: 'But governmental authority was given in wrath, and so it can neither fit itself into nor belong to Christ. Thus no Christian is a ruler and no ruler is a Christian, for the child of blessing cannot be the servant of wrath'. Governmental authority, itself a rejection of the rule of God's Spirit (Genesis 6:3), is no concern of the children of God. Because vengeance is God's alone it should be neither practised nor exercised by Christians.[109] Likewise, taxes devoted to making war and the manufacture of armaments should be refused.[110]

By the 1560s radical apoliticism characterised all surviving branches of Anabaptism except the Dutch Waterlanders who maintained a more moderate position. According to Stayer, once the forty-year process of separating the Anabaptist congregations from the world and its natural maintenance was complete, the Waterlanders became the first labourers in the four hundred-year process of bringing them back into the world.[111]

SUMMARY AND EVALUATION

Yoder criticises historians, including Stayer, for bringing to the discussion of Anabaptist history a 'definitional dualism' which is a product of Constantinianism. This systematic bias renders the nuances of the history difficult to grasp, imposing a consistency out of the mind of the analyst.[112] Anabaptists accepted the non-resistant teaching of Jesus without concluding dogmatically that his disciples would always reject civil responsibility. Stayer's analysis shows this, yet is still committed to the dualist approach and finds an undogmatic position inconsistent.[113] This distorted reading assumes ideas which were impossible for the Anabaptists, including that of participative government. The governments with which Anabaptists interacted were closed authority structures not responsible even to technical citizens. A contextualised question to ask the Anabaptists would be: 'Is it the calling of the Christian to exercise unaccountable sovereignty, to oppress the poor, to brake the pace of the reformation of the church, and to punish with death those of another religious opinion?' That they said No should not be taken as systematic separatism or an 'ideal type' of social stance.[114] The majority of free church believers in the sixteenth century rejected both radical dualism and theocracy. Schleitheim should be read as time-bound, calling for discernment as the meanings of actions and symbols change with the times.[115] Sattler's Confession was against the backdrop of governments which denied his right to free religious expression and which shortly would take his life. It is unfair to project from this a vision of civil 'absenteeism' in contexts where public involvement without moral disobedience can be contemplated.[116] Despite persecution the Anabaptists consistently affirmed the legitimacy of the civil order. They prefigured a democratising, pluralising, disabsolutising thrust in social thought for which the language of their century was not ready.[117]

While sympathetic with aspects of Yoder's appraisal, Stayer denies that his framework of approach distorts the evidence.[118] Yoder's analysis is itself determined by an ethical norm close to the Quaker principle of speaking truth to power for which radical apoliticism is an embarrassment.[119] He obscures the position of the Schleitheim majority, being reluctant to admit to the predominance of a stance for which, like Stayer, he has distaste.[120] Yoder and Stayer agree upon the ideological nature of radical apoliticism. It emerged out of the concrete experience of a group under intense persecution.[121] Given the circumstances separatist non-resistance was entirely 'realistic' and allowed Anabaptism to survive.[122] Peachey finds here a movement which lost its early intellectuals and, forced to confine itself largely to artisans and farmers, became distanced from mainstream culture and so impoverished.[123]

Granted these cautionary comments, within the Anabaptist thought that predominated is a paradox,[124] a basic structural ambiguity,[125] a theological dilemma without solution.[126] The state is an ordering of God, necessary and legitimate, protecting the good and punishing evildoers. Yet, it is outside the perfection of Christ. Its means are in conflict with the teaching of the Christ whom the disciple follows.[127] The magistrate's office is left to the non-Christian to administer. It will never lack occupants. The few who want to follow Christ should follow him wholeheartedly.[128] This position, despite similarities with general Reformation thought, is unique.[129] The state is both an 'ordering' of God and outside the 'perfection of Christ'. The discussion permits a summary:

All Anabaptist groups acknowledged the necessity of coercion and saw this as the right and duty of civil government.[130] The state is an indication of God's wrath but expresses God's grace in bringing order and peace. Governmental power and authority are good and necessary in their own way.[131] Anabaptists were not anarchists seeing force as the source of all wrongs.[132] They were realistic about human wrongdoing. On the validity of the civil order they have been misrepresented, as if the claim that the sword has no place in the church meant that it has no place in society.[133] This must be attributed to the thought system of the magisterial reformers which so intertwined church and state that the first claim was heard to equal the second.[134]

Anabaptists rejected force in the internal affairs of the church and against false teaching. This was true of all groups but the Münsterites, except that Menno excluded false teaching from the state's concern more slowly. For Yoder the turning point in the Zwinglian Reformation hinged around this rejection of state involvement.[135] Reformation thought allowed individuals private faith and believed that true faith could not be compelled. But when belief was held publicly it could conflict with the authority of the state to regulate external faith in its territory. The Reformers did not question this authority.[136] The Anabaptist claim implies religious pluralism and a de-sacralised state.

Anabaptists were suspicious of the sword because it was at the service of the sacral state. Some differentiated the sword in war and in the administration of justice, declaring the former illegitimate and the latter legitimate. The question of whether a country might engage in defensive armed conflict was not generally addressed.[137] There were different opinions about the participation of the faithful believer in the legitimate functions of the sword. Hillerbrand understands the prevailing answer to be negative, but notes 'the minority within the minority', including Hübmaier, which stood closer to the Reformation position.[138] Yoder has argued for a large proportion of 'undogmatic non-resistants'. Some could conceive of the administration of the coercive functions of the state so as to avoid bloodshed and capital punishment. Some conceptualised the distinction between the state as an oppressive instrument and as the protector of the widow and the orphan.

A basic quandary of political reality, and the point of conflict between Anabaptists and Reformers, concerns the tension between the requirements of the whole of society and those of its parts, between 'holism' and 'elementarism': how to build a comprehensive order without destroying the autonomous integrity of the component units.[139] The Radicals were groping towards an arrangement which did not as yet exist.[140] The Schleitheim statement that 'the sword is an ordering of God outside the perfection of Christ' replaced the concept of dual offices, *sacerdotium* and *regnum*, within a united Christendom by returning to the pre-Constantinian order of two distinct and coexisting conditions. It rejected anarchy and the pretensions of rulers. Yet Schleitheim's dichotomy of good and evil and its rejection of participation in voluntary or civic associations, which are essential if pluralism and liberty are to be safeguarded, saws off the pluralist limb on which the radical claim rested.[141] It remains to be seen how a doctrine forged in a time of religious and political despotism[142] can be translated into present relevance.

Baptist and Anabaptist Attitudes to the State

The paradoxical nature of the Anabaptist understanding of the state is well illustrated in early disagreements between English Baptists. John Smyth and forty-two others signed their names in 1610 to an English translation of a Confession of Faith drawn up in 1580 by Waterlander Mennonites. This Confession affirmed (Article 18) that the redeemed 'do lift up no sword, neither hath nor consent to fleshly battle'. Article 35 asserted: 'Worldly authority or magistracy is a necessary ordinance of God, appointed and established for the preservation of the common estate, and of a good, natural, politic life, for the reward of the good and the punishing of the evil'. This article goes on to deny the role of the magistrate in the church and adds:

> Neither hath he called his disciples and followers to be worldly kings, princes, potentates, or magistrates; neither hath he burdened or charged them to assume such offices, or to govern the world in such a worldly manner... therefore we avoid such offices and administrations.[143]

This is characteristically Mennonite. The paradox was identified by those separating from Smyth's congregation upon its admission to the Mennonite church. This group, which was to return under Thomas Helwys to establish the first Baptist church on English soil, clarified its position in a Confession written by Helwys and published in 1611 under the title 'A Declaration of Faith of English People Remaining at Amsterdam in Holland'. Article 24 records:

> That Magistracie is a Holie ordinance off GOD, that every soule ought to bee subject to it not for feare onelie but for conscience sake. Magistraets are the ministers off GOD for our wealth, they beare not the sword for nought. They are ministers off GOD to take vengance on them that doe evil, Rom 13 Chap... And therefore they may bee members off the Church off CHRIST, reteining their Magistracie, for no Holy Ordinance off GOD debarreth anie from being a member off CHRISTS Church. They beare the sword off GOD, – which sword in all Lawful administracions is to bee defended and supported by the servants off GOD that are under their government with their lyves and al that they have according as in the first Institucion off that Holie Ordinance. *And whosover holds otherwise must hold, (iff they understand themselves) that they are the ministers of the devill, and therefore not to bee praied for nor approved in anie off their administracions,* – seing all things they do (as punishing offenders and defending their countrees, state and persons by the sword) is unlawful.[144]

After his death in 1612 the followers of Smyth responded to the criticism of the Helwys party with 'Propositions and Conclusions concerning True Christian Religion' published between 1612–1614 and in its first draft the work of Smyth himself. It contains the following paragraphs:

83. That the office of the magistrate, is a disposition or *permissive ordinance* of God for the good of mankind: that one man like the brute beasts devour not another (Rom. xiii.), and that justice and civility, may be preserved among men: and that a magistrate may so please God in his calling, in doing that which is righteous and just in the eyes of the Lord, that he may bring an outward blessing upon himself, his posterity and subjects (2 Kings x. 30, 31).

84. That the magistrate is not by virtue of his office to meddle with religion, or matters of conscience, to force or compel men to this or that form of religion, or doctrine: but to leave Christian religion free, to every man's conscience, and to handle only civil transgressions (Rom. xiii), injuries and wrongs of man against man, in murder, adultery, theft, etc., for Christ only is the king, and lawgiver of the church and conscience (James iv. 12).

85. That if the magistrate will follow Christ, and be His disciple, he must deny himself, take up his cross, and follow Christ; he must love his enemies and not kill them, he must pray for them, and not punish them, he must feed them and give them drink, not imprison them, banish them, dismember them, and spoil their goods; he must suffer persecution and affliction with Christ, and be slandered, reviled, blasphemed, scourged, buffeted, spit upon, imprisoned and killed with Christ; and that by the authority of magistrates, *which things he cannot possibly do, and retain the revenge of the sword*.[145]

The exchange illustrates the relationship and the difference between Mennonites and early English Baptists. At the point of church and state Baptists show their dependence upon Anabaptism in the insistence on religious liberty. But in accepting Anabaptist doctrine they revised it in a Reformed direction allowing them to embrace and participate in the state in its secular function while denying its jurisdiction in the spiritual. Anabaptism consigned the coercive function of the state to the 'world' and separated from it. It was a 'permissive ordinance' only. Behind the Baptist position lay the nationalism of English Puritanism and belief in England's destiny as an elect nation. It needed to conceive that England's king could be a Christian. In a way parallel with the Smyth/Helwys rejection of the Calvinist doctrine of election, Helwys argued that God would not destine a ruler to rule and then damn him for it.[146]

Baptists, like Hübmaier, developed a view of the state between Anabaptism and Zwinglianism/Calvinism. Yet by affirming state power positively in matters temporal and civil it became harder to argue that such beneficial powers should not also be used in the religious sphere.[147] Historically, the Baptist position has rendered it vulnerable to nationalism[148]. The Baptist–Mennonite distinction, reflecting that between Reformed and Anabaptists and so of wider relevance, concerns a duality: the civil power as a fallen, rebellious power overruled by divine providence or as a benign power given as a blessing by divine grace.

Church and Society in Present Mennonite Perspective

Evidence that the most direct heirs of the Anabaptists, Mennonites, are emerging from separatism and adapting their heritage is considerable.[149] This shift was advanced by J. Lawrence Burkholder in a thesis submitted in 1958 at Princeton but only published in 1989.[150] The work criticises Mennonite social thought of the 1950s, especially the apolitical non-involvement of G. F. Herschberger's *War, Peace and Non-resistance*[151] which it saw as a metamorphosis of the early Anabaptists' political radicalism.[152]

Mennonites, emerging from the isolated, agrarian existence of a German-speaking minority in an English-speaking society, were encountering the ambiguities of power. The extent of the Christian's responsibility for secular society was problematic. Holding power is dangerous, not doing so is desertion from responsibility.[153] Anabaptist–Mennonites faced their own Constantinian dilemma. Non-resistance, from which Mennonite social thought was inferred, needed re-examination.[154]

Social responsibility required an identification with the world of which attitudes to political office were present tests, as during the Reformation.[155] The tension is to reconcile the God of the cross with the God who makes politics a calling. The Sermon on the Mount placed pure principle above practical possibility and so could prove irresponsible.[156] Mennonites stressed discontinuity between church and world, yet love implies involvement with the neighbour and in a society where life is no longer composed simply of primary relationships, the neighbour was now a corporate neighbour. When Jesus renounced physical and institutional power, where does the disciple find norms when the absolute ethic of love is no longer a simple possibility?[157]

Non-resistance was a particularly acute problem. The Anabaptist position on the sword was paradoxical, ordained by God yet not to be wielded by the Christian. Government exercised a negative function. Even providentially ordered and though its administration be just, the sword is 'devilish'. Schleitheim rejected for Christians the administration of retributive or distributive justice.[158] Mennonites had a theology for separation but not for the political participation opening up to them. Justice lay outside their vocabulary, being seen as an Old Testament concept.[159] Christ's lordship was practically limited to the church, separating the work of God the Creator and Christ the Redeemer and neglecting the implications of Logos christology and the christological passages in Ephesians and Colossians. The broader implications of Christ's rule were excluded.[160]

Burkholder's stance was informed by the Christian realism of Reinhold Niebuhr and John C. Bennett which talked of ambiguity, compromise, balances of power and impossible possibilities.[161] Churches were socially responsible if they sought a Christian culture and political order, and irresponsible if they concentrated on a separate church.[162] Yet, for Burkholder, the 'responsible society' extended the *corpus christianum* under the conditions of secular pluralism and represented the ideal of total society under the domination of the Christian ethos.[163] Too many questions were left theologically imprecise concerning the relation of church to society and consequently the church merely echoes existing 'responsible' opinion. Here the Anabaptist tradition can help supply the deficiencies.[164]

Burkholder's programme for a responsible ethic true to the Anabaptist heritage involves seeking brotherhood, peace and mutuality under the conditions of compromise. Solidarity with the world involves ambiguity and responsibility for corporate evil. The place of power needs to be recognised. Christians cannot live without the exercise of power, including compulsion and force. Small communities with agreed values minimise such power but the growth of institutions brought increased political power whose use may nevertheless be mitigated by the service motif. As a comprehensive norm for all relations non-resistance needed re-examination. As an absolute principle it would remove Christians out of the world altogether. A practical alternative is non-violent resistance, allowing participation in the ambiguous struggles for justice but without violence.

Love must take the form of justice to be effective. This reawakens questions of interpreting Jesus' commands, of how church–society relations in the New Testament are normative for later periods, of the relation of Jesus' ethic to Paul's and of the Old Testament's authority for Christian conduct. These questions need re-examination while reaffirming the values of non-conformity and obedience to Christ fundamental to Anabaptism.[165]

In a more recent taxonomy, which takes account of the immense changes in Mennonite thought, Burkholder has charted opinions among contemporary Mennonites on the subject of 'peace'. He discerns four positions:[166]

(1) *Traditional 'biblical' non-resistance* rejects all force far beyond war alone and neglects the biblical category of justice. It places government outside the perfection of Christ.

(2) *Witnessing non-violence* endorses resistance towards evil through non-violent uses of power, favours peace-making above pacifism and recognises the claims of social justice. This requires a reappraisal of government: *Universal christological non-violence* requires all governments

to be non-violent on the basis of the unity of God's will and so risks anarchy. *Middle-axioms non-violence* calls governments to non-violence as an ideal but accepts that the limitation of violence is the reasonable outcome. Violence used by government even in a just cause remains sin however. *Two-kingdom non-violence* views government as a natural phenomenon and the minimal use of violence as mandated by God in the maintenance of order. The two kingdoms are however destined for an eschatological unity.

(3) *Dialectical pacifist political responsibility* rejects detachment from the political order for direct involvement in politics, translating the Old Testament offices of king and prophet into the political process and accepting compromises.

(4) *Vocational pacifism* resolves the tension between moral fidelity and political realism by understanding pacifism as a calling given to some. Others may have a vocation to participate in a just war.

Burkholder's thesis calls for legitimate *aggiornamento* of the Anabaptist tradition. But does it too easily jettison the Anabaptist criticism of government? Vernard Eller claims that the Bible's socio-political stance amounts not to 'radical discipleship' but to 'Christian anarchy'.[167] Christ's kingdom is not of this world; it does not pursue its aims through impositional means or what Eller calls the 'arkys', structures of power and domination.[168] Believers in the messiah are unimpressed by the claims of all worldly powers.[169] Anabaptism rejected all 'impositional pressure' and 'arky power', not only violence.[170] Christian anarchy rejects both legitimation of the status quo and revolution. Justice is brought into being by God and not the 'powers'.[171] This is 'apolitical' only in rejecting deliberate calculation of effects. It is thoroughly political in being critical of the world's definition of politics. It stands apart from all adversary contest and power play and offers a political theology of liberation intent upon liberating humanity from its enslavement to worldly politics.[172] By rejecting confidence in impositional pressure it exercises considerable political influence but only in the long term.[173]

Neither Anabaptism nor the New Testament church wished to legitimate the status quo, to subvert it by revolutionary power, or to amass power. Neither made large claims about transforming a lost world. Both trusted God to accomplish his purpose.[174] Yet Christian anarchists are close to being revolutionists. Characteristically they have emerged in the wake of failed revolutions, whether the Peasants' War, or (as the Quakers) the Puritan Revolution. The 'political' resemblance between revolutionism and Christian anarchy exists in the commitment to peace, justice, freedom and human welfare. But this obscures their radical theological opposition.[175]

Eller's argument refuses messianic significance to any other than Jesus Christ as the bringer of God's kingdom and justice.[176] This does not preclude seeing relative merits in social movements. Neither does it mean that anything beyond the church is of the devil or that all states are equally wicked. But social progress is not advanced by human power structures pitting power against power or by adopting the adversary's values. This dictates that human values are obscured, truth is disregarded and perspective lost in the adversarial mode such structures require.[177] Worldly politics are to pass away: we need to be liberated from them not enslaved to them, a freedom anticipated in the church.[178]

The theological issue here concerns the doctrine of creation and whether engagement with structures of power leads to Constantinian compromise.[179] A theology of creation affirming the goodness, if imperfection, of God's world and the redemption of fallen creation, must include societal structures.[180] Governments are important for human life and are produced by all communities. They are a given of human existence and Christians are involved in the 'push and pull of interests, rights and obligations of citizenship'. Yet scepticism is required about the presumption that God's purposes can be achieved through governmental action. Governments are still Machiavellian.[181]

It is relevant to this discussion that Conrad Brunk identifies two philosophies of law. *Legal positivism* grounds law in the will of the ruler and the coercive power that supports it. For *natural law*, law is not essentially coercive but the product of shared aims, values and principles of conduct reliant upon a moral consensus.[182] The latter allows law to be a way of promoting, maintaining and even establishing moral norms.

The Anabaptist view of law and state derives from the Lutheran, two-kingdoms, legal positivist context. No concept of social justice is found either in traditional Lutheran or in most Anabaptist thought. It is unsurprising therefore that the Anabaptists had difficulty reconciling the demands of the two kingdoms. All state functions are referred to as 'the sword' and seen as intrinsically coercive.[183] This basic, criminal law paradigm made all governmental activity suspect. Yet even Mennonite communities establish law to regulate and create moral conduct. Here is a weakness of the tradition: failure to see that law arises out of the moral consensus or agreement of a community. Christians do not obey the law because of the command to obey authority but out of respect for their neighbours. By contrast with Brunk's analysis of Anabaptism, the traditionally Reformed approach to government has greater affinities with the natural law approach and a strong commitment to achieving a just civil realm. Both Lutheran and Reformed traditions can be seen to reflect the socio-political contexts from which they emerged, the Lutheran the princely territory or oligarchically-ruled city and the Reformed the corporate ethos of the early modern city.[184]

Law is necessary and communities of love need orderly systems and the sanctions which motivate compliance. Even church discipline is a coercive sanction. Applied to the state this pattern of thought allows a contractual approach in which law can be used to pursue justice and righteousness. Anabaptism inclined because of its suspicion of rulers toward a minimalist view of the state.[185] But as long as law does not outrun public morality it can serve as a moral teacher. It can help heal the sick, feed the hungry and free the captives; and the church helps to build the public morality out of which law grows.[186] In this sense, we shall argue, the search for justice in the public and civil realm is not Constantinian because it seeks for consensus and agreement and not imposition, but it does make its claim upon the state. These distinctions, which expose the theological complexity of social and political reality, provide a useful backdrop for our expositions of Yoder and Moltmann who will in general be found to represent respectively the legal positivist and contractual or covenant, 'natural law' approaches.

Conclusion

The Anabaptist view of the state is paradoxical in asserting simultaneously the legitimacy and illegitimacy of the state, but not only so. Its initial vision for social change was changed into quietism and pessimism about the world which in turn led to irrelevance. This remains in tension with its inherent missionary commitment.[187] The expositions of Yoder and Moltmann will assist us in working through these complexities and in the search for a theology of 'creative dissent'.[188]

NOTES

1   A. Snyder, 'The Influence of the Schleitheim Articles on the Anabaptist Movement: An Historical Evaluation', *MQR* 63:4 (1989), 323.
2   H. S. Bender, 'Historiography: Anabaptist General', *ME* 2, 754.
3   Pre-eminently J. Horsch, 'Is Dr Kuehler's Conception of Early Dutch Anabaptism Historically Sound?', *MQR* 7:1 (1933), 48, 50–2. G. H. Williams identifies evangelical Anabaptism but suggests that the Swiss Brethren's chronological priority and eventual dominance should not be mistaken for normativeness: *The Radical Reformation* (Philadelphia: Westminster Press, 1962), 118ff, 853–4.
4   J. R. Coggins, 'Toward a Definition of Sixteenth Century Anabaptism: Twentieth-Century Historiography of the Radical Reformation', *JMS* 4 (1986), 187.
5   Williams, *Radical Reformation*, 846.
6   Ibid., 853–4.
7   K. Holl, 'Luther und die Schwärmer' in *Gesammelte Aufsätze zur Kirchengeschichte I: Luther* (Tübingen: J.C.B. Mohr, 1932), 420–67. This follows the early lead of Heinrich Bullinger who was concerned to clear the Zwinglian Reformation of guilt by association: Williams, *Radical Reformation*, 851–2.
8   H. S. Bender, 'The Zwickau Prophets, Thomas Müntzer and the Peasants' War' in J. M. Stayer and W. O. Packull (eds.), *The Anabaptists and Thomas Müntzer* (Dubuque and Toronto: Kendall/Hunt Publishing, 1980), 145–51.
9   Coggins, 'Toward a Definition', 196.

10   D. W. Brown, 'The Radical Reformation: Then and Now', *MQR* 45:3 (1971), 251;
      W. Klaassen, 'The Nature of the Anabaptist Protest', *MQR* 45:4 (1971), 300–4.

11   J. M. Stayer, *The German Peasants' War and Anabaptist Community of Goods*
      (Montreal: McGill-Queen's University Press, 1991) e.g., 35, 38, 57, 73, 77, 92, 99.
      This undermines characterisations of the Anabaptists as 'withdrawn'.

12   Troeltsch, *The Social Teaching* 2, 703–5.

13   Coggins, 'Toward a Definition', 197.

14   J. M. Stayer, W. O. Packull and K. Deppermann, 'From Monogenesis to
      Polygenesis: The Historical Discussion of Anabaptist Origins', *MQR* 49:2 (1975),
      83–121.

15   Coggins, 'Toward a Definition', 201.

16   W. Klaassen, 'Sixteenth-Century Anabaptism: A Vision Valid for the Twentieth
      Century?', *CGR* 7:3 (1989), 242.

17   J. M. Stayer, *Anabaptists and the Sword* (Lawrence, Kansas: Coronado Press,
      1972), 14, 17.

18   Ibid., 1, 19–20.

19   J. M. Stayer, 'Reublin and Brötli: The Revolutionary Beginnings of Swiss
      Anabaptism' in *The Origins and Characteristics of Anabaptism* (The Hague:
      Martinus Nijhoff, 1977), 83, 89, 91, 96.

20   'The Left Wing of the Reformation', *JR* 21 (1941), 124–34.

21   L. Verduin *The Reformers and their Stepchildren* (Exeter: Paternoster, 1966), 15.

22   K. R. Davis *Anabaptism and Asceticism: A Study in Intellectual Origins* (Scottdale:
      Herald Press, 1974), 296.

23   G. Tschäbitz, 'The Position of Anabaptism on the Continuum of the Early
      Bourgeois Revolution in Germany' in Stayer and Packull (eds.), *Müntzer*, 29.

24   C. Rowland, *Radical Christianity: A Reading of Recovery* (Oxford: Polity Press,
      1988), 45, 101–2.

25   C. Redekop, 'The Community of Scholars and the Essence of Anabaptism', *MQR*
      47:4 (1993), 429–50.

26   J. D. Weaver, 'Becoming Anabaptist–Mennonite: The Contemporary Relevance of
      Sixteenth Century Anabaptism', *JMS* 4 (1986), 167–8, 178–80. Cf. Troeltsch: 'The
      following were its main characteristics: emphasis on Believers' Baptism, a voluntary
      church, the precepts of the Sermon on the Mount, the rejection of the oath, of war,
      law, and authority, and finally, the most far-reaching mutual material help and the
      equality of all Church members, the election of elders and preachers by the local
      congregations, and, to a large extent, the unpaid character of the pastoral office;
      these principles were in close agreement with the democratic tendencies of the
      masses': *The Social Teaching* 2, 703. As other traditions based infant baptism on
      fides aliena or *fides infusa*, it is arguably more accurate to describe the Anabaptist
      position as 'confessor baptism' rather than 'believers' baptism': J. H. Rainbow,
      '"Confessor Baptism": The Baptismal Doctrine of the Early Anabaptists', *ABQ* 8:4
      (1989), 286–97. The oath was used as a means of ensuring political loyalty.
      Strasbourg, for instance, held an annual *Schwörtag* when citizens pledged allegiance
      in front of the cathedral: A. L. Fitz-Gibbon, 'A Study in Church–State Relations in
      the Writings and Teaching of the Anabaptists of the Sixteenth Century'. MLitt
      Dissertation, University of Newcastle-upon-Tyne, 1992, 144.

27   *Systematic Theology: Ethics* (Nashville: Abingdon Press, 1986), 28.

28   'The Theological Triumph of the Early Anabaptist–Mennonites', *MQR* 19:1 (1945),

5–26.

29   Mullins, *The Axioms of Religion*, 59–69.

30   *Protestantism and Progress: A Historical Study of the Relation of Protestantism to the Modern World* (London: Williams and Norgate, 1912), 123–6.

31   H. S. Bender, 'The Anabaptist Vision' in G. F. Herschberger (ed.), *The Recovery of the Anabaptist Vision* (Scottdale: Herald Press, 1957), 43ff. Non-resistance embraces the rejection of violence, self-defence and coercion.

32   Littell, *Origins*, xvii. The Anabaptists believed in a 'gathered' rather than a 'pure' church. Church discipline aimed to purify the gathered church: J. E. Colwell, 'A Radical Church? A Reappraisal of Anabaptist Ecclesiology', *TB* 38 (1987), 134.

33   The Zwinglian party, and other Protestants, dated the fall in the sixth century and associated it with the papal hierarchy. This explains something of their distance from the Anabaptists: P. P. Peachey, *Die Soziale Herkunft der Schweizer Täufer in der Reformationszeit* (Karlsruhe: Buchdrückerei und Verlag Heinrich Schneider, 1954), 98.

34   Littell, *Origins*, 46–108; F. Wray, 'The Anabaptist Doctrine of the Restitution of the Church', *MQR* 28:3 (1954), 189–96. W. Klaassen's summary of the Anabaptist critique of Christendom is that (i) infant baptism, the motor of Christendom and so the object of Anabaptist criticism, denied the liberty of the children of God; (ii) governments were established to restrain evil in matters relating to physical life whereas religious persecution *created* chaos; (iii) Christendom obliterates the distinction between church and world; (iv) it secularises the church without sanctifying the state, Christian magistrates being obliged to adopt the world's standards not Christ's; (v) it leaves no place for a truly mutual Christian community by placing spiritual leadership in the hands of rulers; (vi) it neglects ethics in favour of doctrine, incorporating the ethics of vengeance and neglecting the suffering or 'bitter' Christ: 'The Anabaptist Critique of Constantinian Christendom', *MQR* 55:3 (1981), 228.

35   H. J. Hillerbrand, 'Anabaptism and History', *MQR* 45:2 (1971), 112–13, 119.

36   J. L. Garrett, 'The Nature of the Church According to the Radical Continental Reformation', *MQR* 32:2 (1958), 115.

37   McClendon, *Ethics*, 31 (his emphasis).

38   Stayer, *Anabaptists and the Sword*, 1. For summaries see also W. Klaassen, '"Of Divine and Human Justice": The Early Swiss Brethren and Government', *CGR* 10:2 (1992), 169–85 and H. J. Loewen, 'Church and State in the Anabaptist–Mennonite Tradition: Christ *Versus* Caesar?' in R. T. Bender and A., F. Sell (eds.), *Baptism. Peace and the State in the Reformed and Mennonite Traditions* (Waterloo: Wilfrid Laurier University Press, 1991), 145–65.

39   Neuhaus, *Naked Public Square*, 174.

40   C. Bauman, 'The Theology of the "Two Kingdoms": A Comparison of Luther and the Anabaptists', *MQR* 38:1 (1964), 44–7.

41   W. Klaassen (ed.), *Anabaptism in Outline: Selected Primary Sources* (Scottdale: Herald Press, 1981), 265.

42   F. H. Littell, 'The New Shape of the Church–State Issue', *MQR* 40:3 (1966), 184. This leaves open the question of an Anabaptist response to a more representative government, 185.

43   Stayer, *Anabaptists and the Sword*, 3.

44   J. M. Stayer, 'Reflections and Retractions on *Anabaptists and the Sword*',

MQR 51:3 (1977), 200. Cf. Bainton, *Christian Attitudes Toward War and Peace* (Nashville: Abingdon Press, 1960 and 1986), 14.

45 J. M. Stayer, 'The Münsterite Rationalization of Bernhard Rothmann', *JHI* 28:2 (1967), 181.

46 Stayer, *Anabaptists and the Sword*, 249, 297.

47 Ibid., 191, 196–7, 285ff.

48 Ibid., 336.

49 G. R. Elton, *Reformation Europe 1517–1559* (London and Glasgow: Collins, 1963), 103.

50 H. W. Pipkin and J. H. Yoder (eds.), *Balthasar Hübmaier: Theologian of Anabaptism* (Scottdale: Herald Press, 1989), 13, 15. In Yoder's judgment, Hübmaier as a trained theologian approached baptism as a single issue in its own right. For the Swiss Brethren it was one expression of a new understanding of faith and the church: 'Balthasar Hübmaier and the Beginnings of Swiss Anabaptism', *MQR* 33:1 (1959), 7, 17; *PT* 54; *TRS*, 59.

51 Yoder, 'Balthasar Hübmaier and the Beginnings of Swiss Anabaptism', 17.

52 R. Friedmann, 'The Nicolsburg Articles: A Problem of Early Anabaptist History', *CH* 36:4 (1967), 404.

53 J. Wm. McClendon Jr, 'Balthasar Hübmaier, Catholic Anabaptist', *MQR* 65:1 (1991), 20–33.

54 Stayer, *Anabaptists and the Sword*, 104.

55 Ibid., 104–5.

56 Ibid., 3.

57 Hübmaier, 'Recantation at Zurich' in Pipkin and Yoder (eds.), *Hübmaier*, 132

58 Stayer, *Anabaptists and the Sword*, 141.

59 Ibid., 151–2.

60 The research is summarised by R. Friedmann, 'The Nicolsburg Articles', 391–409. Attitudes to the state were not the only or primary issue at stake.

61 T. Bergsten, *Balthasar Hübmaier: Seine Stellung zu Reformation und Täufertum 1521–1528* (Kassel: J. G. Oncken Verlag, 1961), 464–7.

62 Hübmaier, 'On the Sword' in Pipkin and Yoder (eds.), *Hübmaier*, 493–4.

63 Ibid., 519–21.

64 Ibid., 503; 'Apologia' in Pipkin and Yoder (eds.), *Hübmaier*, 558–61.

65 Ibid., 511.

66 Ibid., 517; Bergsten, *Hübmaier*, 465. See also 'On the Christian Baptism of Believers' in Pipkin and Yoder (eds.), *Hübmaier*, 98, 'Recantation at Zurich', 152, 'A Brief Apologia', 304.

67 'On the Sword' in Pipkin and Yoder (eds.), *Hübmaier*, 494.

68 Bergsten, *Hübmaier*, 466–7. Bergsten's judgment that Hut was 'typical' is questionable in the light of his quasi-Müntzerite position: Stayer, *Anabaptists and the Sword*, 150–1.

69 Bergsten, *Hübmaier*, 324.

70 Pipkin and Yoder (eds.), *Hübmaier*, 15.

71 J. Loserth, 'Hübmaier, Balthasar', *ME 2*, 826; Friedmann, 'The Nicolsburg Articles', 399.

72 Stayer, *Anabaptists and the Sword*, 109.

73 Ibid., 3.

74 Ibid., 22, 313.

75   Hans Denck, 'Concerning True Love' (1527) in Klaassen (ed.), *Anabaptism in Outline*, 249.

76   Stayer, *Anabaptists and the Sword*, 147–9.

77   W. F. Neff, 'Denk, Hans', *ME 2*, 32.

78   *The Writings of Pilgram Marpeck* Translated and edited by William Klassen and Walter Klaassen (Scottdale: Herald Press, 1978), 15–18.

79   Stayer, *Anabaptists and the Sword*, 178.

80   Klaassen, 'Of Divine and Human Justice', 181.

81   'Pilgram Marpeck's Confession of 1539' in *The Writings of Pilgram Marpeck*, 113, 150–1.

82   Stayer, *Anabaptists and the Sword*, 181.

83   Marpeck, 'Defense' in Klaassen (ed.), *Anabaptism in Outline*, 263.

84   'Explanation of the Testaments' in *The Writings of Pilgram Marpeck*, 556–8.

85   Stayer, *Anabaptists and the Sword*, 185–6.

86   Klaassen, 'Of Divine and Human Justice', 181.

87   Stayer, *Anabaptists and the Sword*, 312–14: See e.g. Menno Simons, 'Brief Confession on the Incarnation' (1544) in J. C. Wenger (ed.), *The Complete Writings of Menno Simons c. 1496–1561* (Scottdale: Herald Press, 1956), 424 and 'Reply to False Accusations' (1552), ibid., 555.

88   Menno Simons, 'Foundation of Christian Doctrine' (1539), *The Complete Writings*, 193; 'Supplication to all Magistrates' (1552), 526; 'Epistle to Micron' (1556), 922.

89   Stayer, *Anabaptists and the Sword*, 315.

90   H. S. Bender, *Menno Simons' Life and Writings* (Moundridge, Kansas: Gospel Publishers, 1983), 93–4.

91   Stayer, *Anabaptists and the Sword*, 318.

92   Ibid., 22.

93   Ibid., 3.

94   Ibid., 22; Yoder, *LMS*, 33.

95   Ibid., 92.

96   Stayer et al, 'From Monogenesis to Polygenesis', 100.

97   Snyder, 'The Influence of the Schleitheim Articles', 323.

98   'Letter to Thomas Müntzer by Conrad Grebel and Friends', G. H. Williams and A. M. Mergal (eds.), *Spiritual and Anabaptist Writers* (Philadelphia: Westminster Press, 1957), 80.

99   Appendix 1.

100   Stayer, 'Reflections and Retractions', 207.

101   Snyder, 'The Monastic Origins of Swiss Anabaptist Sectarianism', 5, 9, 17, 26.

102   Stayer, *Anabaptists and the Sword*, 119.

103   Ibid., 122.

104   Ibid., 129–30.

105   Ibid., 186.

106   Verduin, *Anatomy*, 202.

107   J. M. Stayer, 'Anabaptists and the Sword', *MQR* 44:4 (1970), 373.

108   'Concerning Governmental Authority' in *Confession of Faith* (London: Hodder and Stoughton / Plough Publishing House, 1950), 103.

109   Rideman, 'Whether Rulers Can Also Be Christians', ibid., 107.

110   Ibid., 108, 110–11.

111   Stayer, *Anabaptists and the Sword*, 325–6, 328.

112 Yoder, '"Anabaptists and the Sword" Revisited: Systematic Historiography and Undogmatic Non-resistants', *ZfK* 85 (1974), 274.

113 Ibid., 276; Stayer, *Anabaptists and the Sword*, 22.

114 Ibid., 278; *CAW*, 199.

115 'The Limits of Obedience to Caesar: The Shape of the Problem'. Address delivered to the Study Conference of the Commission on Home Ministries, June, 1978, 8.

116 Yoder, 'The Believers' Church: Global Perspectives:', 14.

117 Yoder, '"Anabaptists and the Sword" Revisited', 283; Fitz-Gibbon, 'A Study', 42, 217.

118 J. M. Stayer, 'Anabaptist Non-resistance and the Rewriting of History: Or, is John Yoder's Conception of Anabaptist Non-resistance Historically Sound?', (Unpublished and undated paper deposited in the library, LMC), 3.

119 Ibid., 2.

120 Ibid., 9.

121 Ibid., 11 and Yoder, '"Anabaptists and the Sword" Revisited:', 283; *CAW*, 265.

122 Stayer, 'Reflections and Retractions', 200.

123 Peachey, *Die Soziale Herkunft*, 93.

124 Smucker, 'The Theological Triumph', 7, 21–2.

125 Fitz-Gibbon, 'A Study', 218.

126 J. W. Miller, 'Schleitheim Pacifism and Modernity: Notes Toward the Construction of a Contemporary Mennonite Pacifist Apologetic', *CGR* 3:2 (1985), 156–7.

127 H. J. Hillerbrand, 'The Anabaptist View of the State', *MQR* 32:2 (1958), 100–1, see also 95.

128 H. J. Hillerbrand, 'An Early Anabaptist Treatise on the Christian and the State', *MQR* 32:1 (1958), 32.

129 Hillerbrand, 'The Anabaptist View of the State', 83.

130 Ibid., 85–8.

131 Ibid., 85–7. The legitimacy of government is repeatedly and strikingly affirmed in subsequent Anabaptist–Mennonite confessions: e.g. H. J. Loewen (ed.), *One Lord, One Church, One Hope: Mennonite Confessions of Faith* (Elkhart: Institute of Mennonite Studies, 1985), 67, 77, 78, 99, 123–4, etc.

132 Stayer, *Anabaptists and the Sword*, 3.

133 J. Calvin, *Treatises Against the Anabaptists And Against the Libertines* edited by B. W. Farley (Grand Rapids: Baker Book House, 1982), 91.

134 Verduin, *Anatomy*, 203, 205, 226.

135 'The Turning Point in the Zwinglian Reformation', *MQR* 32:2 (1958), 137–40.

136 Hillerbrand, 'The Anabaptist View of the State', 90.

137 Ibid., 105.

138 Ibid., 101–3.

139 P. P. Peachey, 'The Radical Reformation, Political Pluralism, and the Corpus Christianum' in *The Origins and Characteristics of Anabaptism*, 10–11, 13.

140 Ibid., 22.

141 Ibid., 19, 24.

142 S. J. Holland, 'God in Public: A Modest Proposal for a Quest for a Contemporary North American Anabaptist Paradigm', *CGR* 4:1 (1986), 44.

143 W. L. Lumpkin, *Baptist Confessions of Faith* (Valley Forge: Judson Press, 1959), 107, 111–112.

144 Ibid., 122–3 (my emphasis).

145 Ibid., 139–40 (my emphasis).

146 J. R. Coggins, *John Smyth's Congregation: English Separatism, Mennonite Influence and the Elect Nation* (Scottdale: Herald Press, 1991), 101, 130–2, 147, 157–8.

147 T. George, 'Between Pacifism and Coercion: The English Baptist Doctrine of Religious Toleration', *MQR* 58:1 (1984), 49.

148 P. P. Peachey, 'New Ethical Possibility: The Task of "Post-Christendom" Ethics', *Interpretation* 19 (1965), 30. Peachey finds major strongholds of neo-Constantinianism in those 'Free Churches' which most demand the separation of church and state: 'The End of Christendom', *CP 9* (1961), 23.

149 J. L. Ruth, 'America's Anabaptists: Who They Are', *CT*, 22 October 1990, 29.

150 J. L. Burkholder, *The Problem of Social Responsibility from the Perspective of the Mennonite Church* (Elkhart: Institute of Mennonite Studies, 1989).

151 R. J. Sawatsky's Review of *The Problem of Social Responsibility from the Perspective of the Mennonite Church* in *CGR* 8:2 (1990), 223.

152 B. S. Hostetler, 'Non-resistance and Social Responsibility: Mennonites and Mainline Peace Emphasis, ca. 1950 to 1985', *MQR* 64:1 (1990), 56, 58.

153 Burkholder, *The Problem of Social Responsibility*, 2.

154 Ibid., 6.

155 Ibid., 17.

156 Ibid., 19.

157 Ibid., 30.

158 Ibid., 70–71.

159 Ibid., 181.

160 Ibid., 215.

161 Ibid., 11.

162 Ibid., 20.

163 Ibid., 213.

164 Ibid., 205.

165 Ibid., 223–224.

166 'Mennonites on the Way to Peace', *GH*, 19 February 1991, 1–4, 8.

167 V. Eller, *Christian Anarchy: Jesus' Primacy Over the Powers* (Grand Rapids: Eerdmans, 1987), 5.

168 Ibid., 9.

169 Ibid., 2.

170 Ibid., 32.

171 Ibid., 33.

172 Ibid., xii–xiii.

173 Ibid., 34–36.

174 Ibid., 42–43.

175 Ibid., 40–41.

176 Ibid., 26.

177 Ibid., 12.

178 Ibid., 184, xiv.

179 Villa-Vicencio, *Christ and Caesar*, 63.

180 Holland, 'God in Public', 54–5.

181 Klaassen, '"Of Divine and Human Justice":', 183.

182 C. G. Brunk, 'Reflections on the Anabaptist View of Law and Morality', *CGR* 1:2

(1983), 6. To clarify Brunk's argument, which will be important for what follows, it should be appreciated that Brunk uses 'natural law' in a carefully defined way here and certainly not as an epistemological category.

183 Ibid., 7–9.

184 W. O. Packull, 'Between Paradigms: Anabaptist Studies at the Crossroads', *CGR* 8:1 (1990), 6.

185 Brunk, 'Reflections', 11–15. In the nineteenth century liberals were helped by T. H. Green to see the positive potential of the state. The law could create freedoms rather than just eliminate them. Baptists were slow to grasp 'the state as friend': J. H. Y. Briggs, *Freedom: A Baptist View* (London: Baptist Publications, 1978), 22–3.

186 Brunk, 'Reflections', 16–17, 19–20.

187 Fitz-Gibbon, 'A Study', 217, 219.

188 The term is coined by Wilkinson to denote that form of dissent which is aware of and sympathetic to the ambiguities and difficulties of the use of power: *Dissent or Conform?*, xiii.

CHAPTER 4

Yoder:
Free Church, State
And Social Responsibility

Chapters 4 and 5 outline critically Yoder's understanding of the church, its relationship to society and to the state. Foreshadowed by his historical-theological research into Anabaptists and Reformers (see *TRG*, 155–206), his exposition illustrates the claim that for the Anabaptist–Mennonite tradition the orders of church and state are incommensurable (*PK*, 174). Zimbelman's description of his theology as 'phenomenological, confessional, partisan and political' is here confirmed.[1]

Anabaptism and 'Christian Realism'

Yoder's theology may be understood as a sustained response to the agenda-setting[2] criticism of pacifism by Reinhold Niebuhr (1892–1971) and the analysis of Christian social thought of H. Richard Niebuhr (1894–1962) (*STL*, 29–42; *NS*, 130).[3] Despite early differences,[4] both advocated 'Christian realism' in the encounter between Christ and culture providing positions from which Yoder's theology has distinguished itself, including the 'faithfulness' and 'effectiveness' polarity (*CAW*, 314).

In an early paper Yoder identified Reinhold Niebuhr's project as 'the principal system of thought with which to come to grips... to consider pacifism as found in America today'.[5] Himself a disillusioned pacifist, Niebuhr agreed that Jesus taught a non-resistant ethic of absolute love, denying that he provided any ground for violent action. Yet Jesus' ethic was 'not immediately applicable to the task of securing justice in a sinful world'.[6] Fallen society required force to maintain justice. Absolute love was relevant as a principle of indiscriminate criticism exposing the sinfulness in all existence, and also as a principle of discriminate criticism between relative forms of justice. The 'impossible ethic' of the Sermon on the Mount hovers over every situation as an impossible ideal, not as a simple alternative for schemes of justice.[7] Society is a balance of egotisms. The Christian is involved in its ambiguities, serving relatively just purposes and yet becoming guilty and so trusting in the forgiving grace of God. This is Christian realism. It discerns the 'right sin to commit' (*STL*, 36).[8] Niebuhr respects the pacifist as true to Christ and as a reminder of absolute love. But to demand that all follow this example is self-righteousness.[9] Adherence to Jesus means withdrawal from 'responsibility' since pursuing the absolute the church neglects the relativities of the world's actuality and embraces irrelevance.

Yoder finds encouragement in Niebuhr's identification of Jesus' 'non-resistance' but denies that following him is impossible or irrelevant.[10] Pacifism for Niebuhr implied that a state can function without violence. Yoder distinguishes this from 'historic Christian pacifism' which differentiates between what is necessary for a fallen state and what is commanded for disciples. Niebuhr does not engage with this distinction and so cannot refute it.[11] He reacts against his former liberal pacifism (*CAW*, 282–3, 339). Conversely the pacifist can affirm Niebuhr's powerful analysis of personal and social sin. Niebuhr's theology is primarily derived from analysis of the human predicament, not revelation (*CAW*, 344). This analysis corresponds with Scripture but undervalues redemption, transferring it to a transcendent realm expressed in myth. It has a cross but no resurrection and neglects altogether the church which is 'the bearer of the meaning of history'.[12] These omissions render Niebuhr's social ethics inadequate. The analysis that societies are less moral than individuals[13] is reversed in the church's supranational society which is more moral than its members (*CAW*, 207).[14] Niebuhr's ethics run into impossible possibilities by constructing Christian ethics for unregenerate society, ignoring the duality of judgements involved. Omission of resurrection, church and regeneration is attributed to neglect of the Spirit who enables 'crucial possibilities' of obedience. Acceptance of the cross in obedience to God's love is not perfectionism but pleases God and is useful to people.[15]

Yoder criticises Niebuhr for 'his unbiblical assumption of responsibility for policing society and for preserving Western civilization'.[16] Because Christian ethics prove unrealistic for immoral society Niebuhr resorts to categories of 'impossibility', 'necessity' and 'responsibility' to fashion something workable. Yoder rejects these axioms. 'Responsibility' amounts to

> an inherent duty to take charge of the social order in the interest of its survival or its amelioration by the use of means dictated not by love, but by the social order itself. This social order being sinful, the methods 'necessary' to administer it will also be sinful... sinful society is accepted as normative for ethics.[17]

So 'responsibility' finds nuclear warfare potentially a bitter necessity.[18] It deprives the church of its visible specificity.[19] New norms cancel out the way of love, the motives of self-preservation being rehabilitated as ethical determinants. Belief that God's will can be known normatively is rejected[20] and alternatives labelled as withdrawn irrelevance (*PK*, 11).

Equally formative for Yoder's polemic is Richard Niebuhr's analysis in *Christ and Culture*.[21] In the 'enduring problem' of 'the double wrestle of the church with its Lord and with the cultural society with which it lives in symbiosis', Niebuhr typified five responses: Christ against Culture, the Christ of Culture, Christ above Culture, Christ and Culture in Paradox and Christ the Transformer of Culture. The Christ against Culture type, rejecting culture's claim to loyalty, is represented by Mennonites who 'renounce all participation in politics'.[22] Niebuhr has in mind the most conservative Mennonite variant, the Old Order Amish.[23] His preference is revealed in that the Christ the Transformer of Culture type alone escapes critical comment.

Yoder's paper indicates that Niebuhr's criticism is directed mainly against the first type which also comes closest to his description of Christ. Niebuhr relativises Jesus, subordinating him to the critic's attachment to culture. Jesus is non-resistant, and yet this is not necessary for all. His demands are avoided by appeal to Trinitarian doctrine, 'a set of concepts with enormous historical prestige' which he employs in partisan fashion.[24] A Trinitarian balance relates the Son's Lordship to the Father as creator of nature and governor of history and to the Spirit as immanent in creation and the Christian community.[25] Christ is relativised by the Father's demands in nature and history and the church's historic conclusions led by the Spirit. The affirmation of culture results. Yet the doctrine of the Trinity, according to Yoder, intended not to balance revelations of Father, Son and Spirit but to affirm one unique, divine revelation in Christ's incarnation (*HPP*, 82).[26] Niebuhr's Jesus is a moralist who points away from culture, not Lord over history and nature through resurrection and exaltation. Yet this Christ is a 'straw man'. Jesus' humanity was cultural and his followers are necessarily within culture.[27]

Yoder is equally critical of Niebuhr's understanding of culture. 'Culture' is used univocally (*STL*, 30), seen as monolithic and autonomous. Those 'against culture' are found inconsistent since while criticising culture they partake of it.[28] But having defined culture as inherent to human existence,[29] it becomes impossible to be 'against culture' unless what is meant is *prevailing* culture. This changes the discussion. Niebuhr attributes an ontological dignity to the 'world' and 'culture' without reckoning with their rebellion.[30] He treats the Anabaptists unhistorically as paradigms illustrating a typology determined by their opponents.[31]

Disciples are within culture but challenge its pretensions. The church discriminately rejects some aspects of culture, accepts others within limits, motivates others anew and creates yet others without treating culture monolithically or 'globally' as though it were autonomous. Niebuhr offers no help in distinguishing these elements. Culture must *all* be rejected, merged with or transformed (*STL*, 38). The minority tradition is therefore seen as disjunctive rather than integrative (*PK*, 11).

The New Testament speaks of the 'world' as self-glorifying, autonomous and rebellious culture,[32] a collective solidarity in selfishness which killed Jesus (*HPP*, 31). The church represents within society 'a real judgement upon the rebelliousness of culture and a real possibility of reconciliation'.[33] Yoder offers an ecclesiology neither identical with nor isolated from the world, in and for and therefore sometimes against the world in dissent.[34] His preferred, triangular typology, drawn from Reformation experience, distinguishes the 'theocratic' vision locating historical meaning in the movement of the whole society, the 'spiritualist' moving the locus of meaning to the inner spirit, and the 'believers' church' which rejects individualism while insisting that Christianity's social form is the covenanted fellowship not the *corpus christianum*.[35] Theocratic and spiritualist types (better: traditions)[36] retain the sociological base of the *corpus christianum*. The believers' church type encourages in ecumenical conversation a theocratic correction which revalues the minority community and the spiritualist search for personal authenticity requiring support from a visible community. When these types refuse these corrections they are reduced to chaplaincy of the established order.[37]

The Church: The Bearer of the Meaning of History

God's ecclesial activity is fundamental to Yoder's theology: the church is the 'bearer of the meaning of history'[38] taking priority over the state and preceding the world epistemologically (*CWS*, 17; *PK* 11)). This theology undergirds those rejecting social action through legislation in favour of developing Christian community, parallel institutions and forms of non-violent action.[39] Political power is not the fundamental force shaping history. What the church is is its mission, testimony and first task. It is the 'motor of history', for good or ill, depending whether it be faithful or apostate.[40] The church is defined as *community* and *mission* not by superstructure, as the Anabaptists understood and as missiology is realising.[41] Community can be realised without lordship and without the coercive givenness of establishment or atomistic individualism (*PK*, 24–5).

This theology has a particular historical identity. The Radical Reformation offers a vision of renewal, a paradigm illuminating the church's pilgrimage (*PK*, 2, 5) with perennial validity for all communions as mission and ecumenism stimulate new interest in ecclesiology. As Constantinian patterns are recognised as dubious (*PK*, 8),[42] majority denominations retrieve elements of the 'sectarian' witness (*PK*, 5–6). Rediscovery of the 'world' as the totality of humanity rejecting God's will accompanies recovery of the believers' church[43]. This determining insight, the antithesis between the essential natures of church and world, is present from Yoder's earliest writing.[44]

The free church embraces voluntary membership and rejects government intervention in its internal affairs. It may discard infant baptism for a baptism of informed confession or baptise infants and make congregational membership dependent upon further commitment (*PK*, 105–6). Because the term 'free church' changes meaning within theocratic or spiritualist frameworks,[45] Yoder prefers the designation 'Radical Reformation'.[46] This 'genuinely distinctive vision of what the church is about in the world' is exemplified in the sixteenth century Swiss Brethren, Quakers and Baptists emerging from seventeenth century Puritanism and in cognate but organically unrelated groups preceding or succeeding them (*PK*, 106).

The radicals extended the Protestant Reformation as 'a fundamentally critical renewal of all Christian thought oriented by a renewed simplicity of understanding of the authority of Scripture' involving 'the perennially unfinished task of critiquing the developed tradition from the perspective of its own roots' (*PK*, 16). The minimal or maximal pursuit of this task constituted the difference between mainstream and radical Reformers and the cause of their alienation (*EFC*, 30).[47] Under pressure the mainstream preferred another authority, the state's, revealing diminished confidence in the preached Word (*PK*, 22).[48]

All Protestantism believed that something had gone wrong in the early church and sought restitution. For mainstream Reformers this primarily concerned things 'necessary for salvation'. For the radicals, it included church order (*PK*, 16). The New Testament represented a paradigm of order and ministry accessible to all Christendom.[49] The term 'Magisterial Reformers' (G. H. Williams) was coined to indicate that the Protestant church was managed by the state (the 'magistracy') and relied upon doctrinal standards set in the universities (the 'magisterium').[50] For the free church/radical Protestant concept, scriptural authority supplied an essential 'primitivism',[51] a thought pattern judging the present in the light of the classical documents. Centrality was given to 'a critical principle of appeal to the sources, which can reach unpredictably farther than those who first called themselves "Protestant" dreamed' (*PK*, 17). This principle supplied the tradition's radicality. Anabaptists found the Bible's unity in the movement from old to new testaments, from promise to fulfilment whereas their opponents saw equal authority in all its parts (*PT*, 281). Unlike the radicals, the Reformers surrendered the visible church as an hermeneutical community and located the focus of infallibility in the inspired text and the qualified expert.[52]

Yoder describes the Anabaptist position as 'biblicism', neither uncritical fundamentalism nor insensitivity to the extent to which the Scriptures are read within particular contexts but acceptance of the canonical witness as a baseline. The object of knowledge is distinct from the way of knowing, just as in examining an organism by a microscope the microscope never becomes the microbe (*PK*, 66). This engenders confidence concerning the 'knowability of the divine will' (*PK*, 3). Appeal to the original tradition can help distinguish between right tradition and treason (*PK*, 67, 69–70).

Yoder's ecclesiology is thus uneasy and arguably implies that the church he aspires to has never existed. Judgement and realignment are its characteristic motifs,[53] expressed in the thought pattern of 'restitution' or 'restoration'. Far from being the claimed 'timeless imitation of first century details', this takes history seriously in its capacity for faithfulness or failure, finding in the faith's origins an historical criterion for judging and renewing the church.[54] Church history has three moments – a normative state, a 'fall' into degeneration irreparable without discontinuity, and a radical renewal.[55] Among those Yoder identifies as 'ecclesial Anabaptists'[56] (originating in Zürich in 1525), the *incarnation* was normative. This norm was applied to church order in a wider-ranging criticism than the Reformers', who referred to figures other than Jesus (Joshua, David, Josiah) to justify adherence to the *corpus christianum* and dependence upon it for reform.[57] Both aspired to a believers' church but the radicals could not accept the church's 'invisibility' to justify contemporary affairs.[58] An alternative to fallen Christendom needed to be identified within Scripture and interpreted with awareness of the relationship between the testaments, not by the establishment but within the congregation.[59] Yoder denies that this is schismatic. Since unity characterised the New Testament church restitutionism cannot in principle be schismatic, although uncontrollable factors might make one church unattainable.[60]

Yoder everywhere asserts the validity of Radical Reformation ecclesiology. The church's roots were in God's dealings with Israel. In Jesus God gathered his people around his word creating the hitherto unseen, a voluntary community of religiously and economically diverse elements forming in a corrupt world a new order where forgiveness, willingness to suffer, service, sharing, mutual submissiveness and love replaced the old patterns (*OR*, 28–9). Its sign was the baptism of believers. It practised discipline and had its own sociology. Rejecting alliances with the political power, it propagated itself through evangelism and persuasion (*OR*, 108–9). Wider expressions of this church are constituted by the covenant of its members, deriving authority not from law but from the congregation.[61] In this community the new aeon supersedes the old (*CWS*, 9–10). By implication, the church alone can be prophetic and redemptive. This magnifies the church's role: the meaning of salvation and therefore of history unfolds through it (*CWS*, 13). The believing community is deterritorialised (*PK*, 189–90). No nation has a calling from God that can claim priority; any such claims are extra-biblical (*KBW*, 79–80).

This ecclesiocentrism conflicts with locating salvation in progressive or liberation movements, a temptation which is a form of natural theology. One biblical motif (exodus) is chosen to the despite of others (exile, captivity, cross, law). 'Liberation' becomes a slogan with flexible content, a general theistic affirmation. It is 'neo-Constantinian' to bless political movements.[62] Not all historical movement is forward: some destructive movements, including fascism, claimed to read a moral lesson from history. Specific political victories should not be read as providential signals, as Eusebius did in heralding Constantine: this is triumphalism.[63] This does not deny that there are good pagans and pagan goods, but it is a circumspect judgement. The biblical Exodus is not a paradigm for all kinds of groups with all kinds of values to attain all kinds of salvation, but is linked with the historical identity of Israel's God. It has prerequisites and postrequisites.[64] Liberation's form is the creation of a confessing community, a distinctive moral minority. This involves liberation from Mars and Mammon and the necessity which their fallen rationality requires.[65]

Church and State: The Constantinian Fall

The concept of restitution implies a fallen institutional church. Littell's analysis suggests the Anabaptists discerned the church's incipient fall at various points, but associated it primarily with Constantine.[66] Even the dominant reading of church history recognises Constantine as a fundamental shift (*CAW*, 41). For Yoder, Constantine represents 'a fundamental flaw of structure and of strategy' changing the church's very nature (*PK*, 107). The alliance between Rome-as-Empire and Church-as-Hierarchy was a tactical error and a structured denial of the gospel.[67]

'Constantine' functions as a cipher for this shift but it was underway before him (*CAW*, 39, 45). A characteristic was the renunciation of the faith's Jewish roots and the substitution of Greek or Roman provincialism for Hebrew universality (*STL*, 13).[68] Mission became inseparable from propagation of a religious culture and cultural religion, the message of the kingdom adapted to religiosity.[69] Christendom's fundamental error was its illegitimate take-over of the world, ascribing Christian confession to those who made no profession (*STL*, 7). Church and ethics became tied to the *civitas* as the norm of ethical reference,[70] replacing the conviction that the church pursues her task while leaving society's functions to pagans, over whom Christ was also Lord.[71] Here is the 'Constantinian postulate' assuming a state church and Christian control of the levers of power: *the Christian ethic for the state and the ethic of Christians under the state is one and the same*. The paradigm case for moral decision became the ruler who manages society (*CAW*, 40).[72] Religious sin, ethical wrongdoing and political crime all now coincided (*CAW*, 594–5). God is with those who triumph, so ethics became the imperative to make history come out right (*CAW*, 50–1). Here lies Zwingli's misunderstanding of the Anabaptists: seeing reformation as the rebuilding of society from the top down he read the Anabaptist programme as an attempt to abolish the state, which it was not.[73]

There is, Yoder argues, a distinction between a state ethic and a Christian ethic because of the difference between belief and unbelief. Christian and state duties might in given cases be identical but require independent examination.[74] The reasoning which asks what would happen if everybody adopted a given stance is meaningless because discipleship is for those few who have counted the cost. The real question is 'will it be redemptive if it is done by a few?'[75] Constantine symbolises the shift in the relation of church and world. From being a persecuted and convinced minority, the church came to embrace all unless they were of strong conviction otherwise. The Empire declared paganism illegal, ruled on the nature of orthodoxy and punished dissent. Understandings of being Christian changed under sociological and political pressure, coming to new theological expression in Augustine's doctrine of the invisibility of the true church. The true church was a minority of elect persons within the outwardly baptised majority (*PK*, 135–6). For the non-elect majority, outward conformity to Christian practice made them more decent than they might otherwise be, but not regenerate disciples (*CAW*, 43).

At a second level a shift in eschatology opposite in kind to that in ecclesiology occurred. The early church was the visible community of Christ's rule. That Christ was Lord also of the powers was taken on faith. As the church in Augustine's theology assumed neo-platonic invisibility, an opposite movement found the emperor embodying God's visible rule in the world. The millennium was pulled from the future into the present (*PK*, 136–7). Social ethics were reshaped from being appropriate for a minority awaiting the kingdom to serving the regime now understood as the means of God's providential rule. Jesus' ethic was redirected inwardly for the religious few not the mass (*PK*, 137). The realities of power demanded a pragmatic ethic. Mission no longer summoned people to discipleship but served Rome's expansion, the system with which the church was identified. This then led to pronouncing Jesus' name over Germanic culture without any radical conversion and to that opposition to the 'infidel' called the Crusades (*PK*, 137–8). These shifts generated a view of history in which civil government became the main bearer of movement. Social ethics became the discussion of what people in power do with their power. The church assumed the role of 'chaplaincy' concerned with the duties of office rather than the ethic of Jesus (*PK*, 138).

At a third level the shift led to utilitarianism in moral deliberation. The identification of history's meaning with a particular regime once made, the good of that regime measured what was right which in turn was measured by whether it worked. This Yoder calls the 'engineering approach' to ethics, 'a long range echo of the Constantinian wedding of piety and power' which assumed that power and the responsibility to make it work were in the church's hands (*PK*, 140).

At a fourth, doctrinal level the shift was a victory for neo-platonic metaphysical dualism. The visible/invisible duality justified the distinction between the conforming visible church and the invisible elect. In ethics appeal was made to the 'orders of creation'. The ethics of love were reserved for the inward life while the ethics of power were for the outward structures of the world. Through interiorisation and individualisation the growing ethical distance from Jesus in favour of other authorities was justified (*PK*, 141).[76]

The mediaeval church, the product of the process Yoder describes, found the clergy allied with the sword, wealth and social hierarchy, corrupted by power. By Luther's time the church needed radical reformation (*PK*, 107). Yet having rejected episcopal authority the magisterial Reformers sought secular support to legitimate reform and guard against social disorder, so failing to reverse the structural decisions of Constantine's age. Locating the state in creation rather than redemption (where it had been for Eusebius) reason not Christ became its norm. Its dignity was thereby decreased but its autonomy increased, laying the foundation for modern secularism.[77] The radical Reformers discovered more profoundly that the 'world' must occupy that place in theology which God's patience allows it in history. It is neither all nature nor all culture but 'structured unbelief, rebellion taking with it a fragment of what should have been the Order of the Kingdom'[78] and lacking ontological dignity because it is estranged from what really is.[79] The official Reformation was a manoeuvre of consolidation by established religion, whereas the Radical Reformation was committed to continuing change.[80] Faithfulness to Jesus was the key Reformation issue and ethical issues, particularly the use of sword and wealth, were consistently evident in Anabaptist debates with their opponents (*PK*, 107–8). The contended issue was the 'fundamental axiom that it is the obligation of the Christian to direct the course of history so that it attains the goals he chooses, in more traditional words, 'to be lord' over other men and over the social process' (*OR*, 132–3).

Yoder suggests that Constantinian assumptions are not dead, the establishment simply assumes new shapes (*PK*, 141–4). The difference between mediaeval Constantinianism, American civil religion or revolution is one of timing.[81] Christianity became identified with Rome and Byzantium. With the nation states imperial Christendom was displaced but the arrangement of church and state remained on a national scale. This Yoder here calls 'neo-Constantinianism'. After the Ages of Enlightenment and Revolution, religious liberty and disestablishment severed some formal church–state links. Yet the United States shows that the alliance of church and state could continue informally through moral identification. Even in Baptist circles the design to put the civil sword behind white Anglo-Saxon Protestant values emerges (*PK*, 187). This Yoder calls 'neo-neo-Constantinianism'.[82] A further step was taken with governments hostile to Christianity, as in the 'People's Democracies' of Eastern Europe. Even here Christians claimed their faith did not produce disloyalty and states supported churches financially in the interim before their final Marxist withering away. This continuing moral identification despite ideological disavowal is 'neo-neo-neo-Constantinianism'. A final possibility, 'neo-neo-neo-neo-Constantinianism', concerns future regimes brought about by revolution where a better model of partnership with the power system is hoped for (*PK*, 143).

Each of these positions rejects the former as wrong while transposing the structural error into a new key. That error is 'the identification of a civil authority as the bearer of God's cause' (*PK*, 143). Thus Yoder sustains his dual thesis that 'the fourth-century shift continues to explain much if not most of the distance between biblical Christianity and ourselves, which is a distance not merely of time and organic development, but of disavowal and apostasy' and that 'many efforts to renew Christian thought regarding power and society remain the captives of the fallen system they mean to reject' (*PK*, 144). Explicit and profound disavowal of Constantinianism which recognises that the church has only pilgrim status in somebody else's world is required (*PK*, 145).

The 'disavowal of Constantine' is also necessary for inter-confessional and interfaith dialogue which are bedevilled by past abuse of power and Christianity's identification with the self-fulfilment of nation, race, culture or class (*HPP*, 53–4).[83] As the word 'mission' has been abused, Yoder advocates the non-coercive word 'herald'. The herald is vulnerable and affirms the dignity of the interlocutor. This overcomes triumphalism which was wrong not because it was tied to Jesus but because its disrespect for the neighbour denied him, not because it propagated Christianity but because what it propagated was not Christian enough (*PK*, 44). The remedy is not to talk less about Jesus and more about religion but the contrary, with new emphasis on his message's content. The scandal of particularity and the uncoercive vulnerability of faith are intrinsic to the gospel and evident in the occasionalistic nature of the primary narratives.[84] Repentance for triumphalism and tribalism is required, not a new pluralist triumphalism still working with the criterion that the true faith can sweep everyone in. Yoder's proposal refuses to leave people in the national-cultural mould in which they were born (itself a capitulation to Constantinianism). No-one should be shut into an inherited faith by accident of birth but should have the genuineness of choice throughout life since no one's faith is final in this life.[85] Disavowing particularism to include Christianity in the wider wisdom is a new form of unbelief, both sectarian and missionary, which avoids the risk of allegiance to the crucified Jesus, continuing rather than correcting the Christendom ethos, so ultimately defending the dominant social and value system (*STL*, 910, 11–13).

Yoder insists upon the finality of Jesus Christ as the goal towards which things point.[86] This is saved from provincialism by the missionary nature of the church (undefined by race in God's purpose of election) and by an ethic which forbids it to impose itself or to withhold itself from any (*STL*, 13). His universalism trusts that the Lordship of Christ reaches beyond those who know him by the right name. This exalted view of Jesus rejects a universalism rooted in a high view of the human and that of the 'anonymous

Christian' (Rahner), an inclusivism which still wants to give meaning to the cultural mainstream.[87]

Does the structural fault of identifying civil government as the bearer of God's cause imply that any vision of the state as the servant of peace and justice may be labelled 'Constantinian'? This discussion must consider the state's status in the pattern of creation, fall and redemption. Critics have found Yoder failing to furnish a theory of justice for the state and ambiguous concerning whether the state is rooted in a pre-fall ordering of creation and is a legitimate tool for resisting the fallen powers.[88] Further discussion will clarify this.

Church and State: Prophetic Dissent

Anabaptism rediscovered the 'world' as a 'structured reality taking concrete form in the demonic dimensions of economic and political life' and did not share the Reformers' confidence in the 'Christian state'.[89] The *church* is 'the bearer of God's cause'. To transfer this to the state recapitulates Constantine's errors. Christians are not insufficiently *in* the world but excessively *of* the world, yielding to Mars and Mammon. Nonconformity is the indispensable dimension of their visibility. Ethics is mission.[90] The call to follow Jesus requires a distinctive political stance imitating his prophetic nonconformity. This missionary posture is incompatible with that of an established church.[91]

The state has a conserving role and defends against a worse reality.[92] The New Testament offers a theology but no doctrine of the state; the state is related to God and so cannot be outside the realm of theology,[93] but there is no doctrine of the state *as such* (*CAW*, 26, 452)[94] since the state is not a platonic abstraction but certain people doing concrete things. Classical doctrines of the state define its essence and evaluate this as good by divine institution (*PJ*, 200). This suggests a distinction between good and bad states. But the New Testament lacks this body of thought.[95] The state is always fallen. It can show degrees of submittedness and be partly Christianised but never ceases to be a domination structure. Therefore it can never become part of the church.[96] When fulfilling welfare functions its nature as dominion remains since welfare can be prostituted. Even democracy (itself an element of 'submittedness') is legitimized by non-factual myths such as 'government by the people'.[97] Although it is possible to speak of social progress (*CAW*, 454) the church continually relates critically to the state, urging it to improve and never expecting perfect justice (*CWS*, 5).[98]

Because of its priority, the church understands that the state exists 'to serve God by encouraging the good and restraining evil, i.e., to serve peace, to preserve the social cohesion in which the leaven of the Gospel can build the church, and also render the old aeon more tolerable' (*CWS*, 5, 16). This is positive and negative: the state preserves social cohesion but the real drama concerns gospel and church. For now it is modestly hoped that the 'old aeon' be rendered 'more tolerable'. 'The good are to be protected, the evildoers are to be restrained, and the fabric of society is to be preserved, both from revolution and from war' (*CWS*, 5). Yoder distinguishes between war and policing to establish the relative validity of the police function (*CAW*, 106; *PJ* 206–7; *WWD*, 24–5). Policing exists under legislative and judicial control whereas war kills without discrimination between innocent and guilty (*KBW*, 102). War abrogates the obligation to maintain peace.

War is therefore to be rejected. The sword (*machaira*) in Romans 13:4 symbolises judicial authority rather than capital punishment or war. Policing is welcomed as legitimate but by way of concession since 'legitimate does not mean right and good; it points rather to the minimal level of wrong' (*CWS*, 59). Police action by a state or under the United Nations cannot be condemned in principle. It might extend to 'the localized readjustment of a tension', but more than this or its prosecution by indiscriminate means is wrong not only for the Christian but also for the state judged on the basis of its assignment. The civil sword is a minimally legitimate means of maintaining peace but not, as some have thought, an especially important instrument of God in the service of human community (*STL*, 33). It is not given to instigate vengeance, since God wants to swallow evil up not repay one evil with another, but to channel in a concessionary way and limit to a level equivalent to the offence that vengeance which is already happening. In this sense it is a way in which God's grace works against sin (CCP, 7). The state is rooted in creation but remains questionable, the difficulty being to distinguish between the good creation and fallen reality.

At this point we approach the nodal issues. If it is ordained by God to restrain chaos believers, one assumes, might legitimately serve God by participating in the state's coercive functions.[99] What is ordained by God cannot be intrinsically wrong. This implies an ethical duality according to the *social* capacity in which the believer functions. But for Yoder the state's coercive functions are inherently fallen or fallen to the point of being unrecognisable from their created form. Participation in them inescapably leads to unfaithfulness. Disciples are prohibited from the avenging functions of state by the rejection of vengeance (*PJ*, 199).[100] Although God's servants, the state's coercive functions are concessions only. From the fallen structures God extracts those which turn the force of human violence against itself in order to restrain it and maintain peace and order. These structures are unwilling servants of God in their fallenness. They are ordered by God even while discipleship prevents participation in their coercive functions. *This* duality is created by the unwillingness of some to submit to God and by his patience in allowing them their way. It is indicated by the Schleitheim's reference to 'inside' and 'outside' the 'perfection of Christ' (*CWS*, 31).[101]

The state is an accommodation to sin rather than a 'pure' ordinance of God. Yoder follows the Anabaptists who here followed the early Zwingli: not only the abuse of the law (or state) but its existence and normal functioning are the fruit of sin.[102] The state is first an instrument of power struggle not a welfare institution.[103] Through it Christ 'channels violence, turning it against itself, so as to preserve as much as possible of the order (*taxis*) which is the pre-condition of human society' (*CWS*, 12–13). The state's force is not a good but an evil subdued by Christ (*OR*, 67). Biblical justification is found for this in that in judging Israel Assyria is used by God as 'the rod of my anger' but once used becomes liable to judgement (Isaiah 10:5–19) (*PJ*, 204).

Romans 13, consistently read as a charter for government as part of God's good creation (*PJ*, 194, 197), indicates God's ordering of the state, fitting it into his providential plan, rather than his 'ordaining' or decreeing it (*PJ*, 193–214; *CAW*, 451). Without creating the sword God orders it providentially (*PJ*, 203; *CAW*, 184). This excludes the use of this text as a conservative legitimation of the social order (*PJ*, 194–8). It provides no basis for distinguishing the 'state-as-such' or the just state from a demonic state so as to legitimate violent revolution (*PJ*, 201–2). Only after Constantine could this passage provide the model for the righteous state within Christendom (*CAW*, 448–9, 451).

The fallen state cannot be the 'bearer of God's cause' or an agent of God's redemption.[104] The 'order of providence' restrains disobedience and is distinct from the 'order of redemption' (*CWS*, 12). There is no expectation that the state will advance the church's purposes. What Yoder designates the 'Puritan option' seeks a single morality for all society leading to its imposition by force upon the unwilling. The Anabaptist tradition has recognised that Christian ethics is for the Christian (*PJ*, 28–30).

The church is not identical with any local, ethnic or national solidarities but exists as a holy nation from among all nations. Its task is evangelism and: 'History is the framework in which the church evangelizes, so that the true meaning of history is the fact that God has chosen to use it for such a '"scaffolding" service' (*CWS*, 10–11). The church is to be distinct in structure and sociology and independent from the world (*OR*, 108). Its pattern is seen not in Constantine but in Abraham who broke with the continuities of human civilisation and of local human loyalties (*OR*, 112). It enters into spiritual potency after the pattern of *kenosis* and sacrificial love which is the manner of Christ's Lordship. Its mission as the church is dependent upon its faithfulness to this task.

To be the 'primary social structure through which the gospel works to change other structures' (*PJ*, 157) the church remains a nonconforming and dissenting community and so contributes to the community's health. The question for the disciple concerns the integrity of involvement both in a fallen state and in redemption's beginnings (*CAW*, 280). Yet Christian social involvement is not a question of scrupulosity but of stewardship, the management of scarce resources (*CAW*, 284). Yoder replaces the casuistic question 'what can I do and still call myself a Christian?' with 'what does the Call ask of me, and can I be called to obey or collaborate with the state in the light of the prior claim of Christ?'. This removes the question of serving as a police officer, for instance, from the legalistic to the vocational framework. For Yoder it would involve an exceptional call which would need to be justified (*CWS*, 57).[105]

The extension of government from a law state to an enabling, democratic, welfare state provides room for discerning involvement where Christian obedience is not threatened (*PJ*, 159). Disciples acknowledge the necessity (albeit critically) of the extreme cases of violence which policing functions may require, but not as part of their own reconciling ministry (*PJ*, 214). The duality involved here is not that degenerate form which rejects war for non-resistants while not disapproving of it for others.[106] The duality of church and world belongs not to God's sphere but to that of human response. The obedience which leads to pacifism cannot be expected, let alone required, of statesmen for whom the presuppositions of the Sermon on the Mount are lacking (*CWS*, 32). Discipleship must be combined with a realism about what is possible 'outside the perfection of Christ'.

The issue here involves a theological judgement on the state's ontology within God's good creation. Yoder acknowledges within the state the existence of authentic, created values of peoplehood ('ethnicity, a sense of place and forms of community') but finds these fused with the claims of rulers and of states to sovereignty.[107] He can argue that sociality as a created good may include pressures and sanctions to teach and motivate wholesome behaviour but not that the state's created 'nature' demands the sword. With no epistemologically reliable access to the original creation, the evidence suggests that the fallen powers are inherently warped (*STL*, 53). Grounding a state metaphysically gives it authority independent of Christ. There is no 'legitimate state' metaphysically distinguishable from actual states which are ambivalent political realities internally composed of competing forces. The concept of 'legitimacy' has value in discriminating these forces but even where the 'citizen is the state' Mammon, Mars, 'public opinion', the press and other powers are the effective rulers.[108] Power is neither neutral nor intrinsically evil. It is in tension, sometimes good, sometimes intrinsically fallen, sometimes capable of reclamation and sometimes unusable (*STL*, 53). Sometimes the believer must determine there is nothing he or she can do to control events. At other times 'responsibility' is to be accepted with modesty and without millennial illusions.[109] But access to power should not be purchased at the cost of changing moral guides. Responsibility does not mean being prepared to do things which are not according to Christ (*STL*, 37). This clarifies that Yoder's aversion to controlling history is not a rejection in principle of the cultural mandate.

Yoder distinguishes between power and coercion, coercion and force, force and violence (*NS*, 40).[110] The Anabaptist understanding of the sword does not settle the question of coercion (*CAW*, 267). Any structure has sanctions and pressures, including the church. Their existence as a way of changing people's minds is not a moral problem. The real question is whether to destroy people or their dignity to keep a society going. Correction does not necessarily require this (*CAW*, 279).

Christ, the Powers and Power

The state's ontology is clarified by Yoder's analysis of the 'powers'. He published his translation of Hendrik Berkhof's, *Christ and the Powers*[111] to assist development of 'an up-to-date, yet Christian world view, capable of understanding the state and the structuredness of culture, yet without overvaluing them' and without robbing them of their creaturely dignity. His summary of this theme (*PJ*, 135–62) is an expansion of Berkhof and challenges the claim that Jesus says nothing to power politics.[112] Jesus speaks to social ethics (*PJ*, 136–7).

Many evils are structural so the most unselfish cannot 'use for good' fundamentally vicious structures.[113] 'Structure' as a concept points to 'the patterns or regularities that transcend or precede or condition the individual phenomena we can immediately perceive' while 'power' points 'in all its modulations to some kind of capacity to make things happen' (*PJ*, 140). The New Testament powers and principalities denote orders created by God, subsisting in the creative Word, which have fallen with humanity and seek through domination to hold people in servitude. Though fallen they are not limitlessly evil but exercise an ordering function under God (*PJ*, 143–4).

These religious, intellectual, moral and political structures are more than the sum total of their parts. They are necessary but have absolutised themselves. Lostness and survival both depend upon them. Here is 'a very refined analysis of the problems of society and of history' (*PJ*, 145–6). Christ came living a free and human existence to be opposed by the powers of religion and politics acting in collusion. He broke their rule at the cost of death by refusing to support them in their self-glorification and opened up the way for restored humanity (*PJ*, 147–8). In this work of Christ the church's work is found. The church, brought together from Jews and Gentiles, is a token to the powers that their dominion is ended (Ephesians 3:11). Its very presence is an aggressive fact, a resistance and an attack on the powers, yet only in so far as it lives freely. The 'otherness' of the church therefore signifies not withdrawal but its existence as a herald of liberation (*PJ*, 150–1). Only from authentic and free community life can the church address the social order, but such communities can renew society from the bottom up (*PJ*, 153–5).[114] A fundamental Constantinian error assumes that renewal is achieved by mastering the powers which determine society. The disciple does not shun power, which is God's good creation, but certain kinds of power are so incorrigible that responsibility involves refusal to collaborate with them or to achieve worthy ends through unworthy means (*PJ*, 156–8).

The church contributes to the creation of structures more worthy of humanity. It needs to discern how God is using the powers, a task assisted by the outlined exousiology (*PJ*, 159). The Lordship of Christ over church and state (apparently a new concept to Mennonites in the 1950s) provides a basis to articulate concern for society while recognising that church and world relate to Christ differently (*CAW*, 568). The state belongs in some sense to the powers created by God and is therefore to be reconciled at the last (Colossians 1:20).

Because the powers are necessary for life, the church cannot escape involvement in them even in their idolatrous form, but this takes the form of a revolutionary or voluntary subordination, an acquiescence in their ordering function while maintaining an inner freedom which refuses them an ultimate value (*PJ*, 185–9). The call to subordination in the early church arose from the temptation to insubordination derived from the new dignity experienced as a fruit of the gospel. This call was 'revolutionary' since it called both subordinate and dominant members of society to reflect the self-abasement-in-freedom of Jesus himself (*PJ*, 178, 181, 184). The subordinate person lives freely without resentment while the superordinate person renounces domineering. This is not conservative accommodation to hierarchy but a principle of revolutionary change in a situation where Christians lacked power. Because the powers were about to pass away Christians had no need to smash them (*PJ*, 190–2). This is part of a process of maximising freedom. Unalterable situations can be accepted freely by those who are free in Christ (*PJ*, 187). This is the church's position faced with an idolatrous state, although the outworking of subordination cannot naively be transposed from the New Testament but is reworked in each situation.[115]

The contrast between Romans 13 and Revelation 13 is not between two different states. It is the enduring ambiguous reality of any state.[116] The church will be the community of prophetic dissent while it is in the world but not of it, not apolitical but hyperpolitical, dealing with the themes and issues that politics deals with but in a more original and intensive way. Caesar's world and Christ's are not separate compartments but intersecting paths through the same terrain.[117]

Romans 13 suggests the radical possibility that the powers have legitimacy in the service of the subject's welfare. This represents a progressive view of the state (*PJ*, 210). Without needing to control the world Christians may both serve God and seek the good of the country in which they are set, not excluding, as with Joseph and Daniel, helping the pagan king 'solve one problem at a time'. But they will avoid idolatry.[118] The recurrent

Joseph/Daniel/Mordecai pattern rather than David's state sovereignty was by Jesus' time the standard for the community liberated for covenant. These stories concerned changes of social structure through nonconformity inspired by a vision of divine liberation beyond the boundaries of present historical existence and the planning of human agency.[119]

Yoder distinguishes in principle between the state's functions of coordinating social co-operation and of policing evils (*CWS*, 59). This leads to paradox because there is an interaction of factors and apparently contradictory elements are held together.[120] The co-ordinating function, the divinely given function of being the means of community and voluntary common effort, belongs to the order of creation. The disciple participates freely in these aspects. There is common ground between the agenda of the kingdom and the welfare function, which is Caesar's least tyrannical vision, the 'dialogical pluralistic quality of governments becoming more liberal'.[121] This is distinguished from the state as 'sword', a coercive power with violence as its ultimate recourse. This dimension is found in the use of force to curb evils and, less blatantly, in the action taken by government to establish institutions and controls for the well-being of society which are backed ultimately by force. Here the disciple is posed with greater difficulty and seeks in the fallen system the minimal level of wrong.[122]

The 'sword' therefore belongs to the fallenness of the powers and has no place in creation's ontology or the final reconciliation of the powers. It is inevitably and always wrong compared to the ultimate revelation of God's will in Christ. It exists by virtue alone of God's accommodation to estranged humanity. It is not the proper sphere for the disciple but belongs to the sphere of the 'incorrigible'. There is paradox in Yoder here in that any role that is necessary for the well-being of society ought to be a possible Christian vocation.[123] For him the police function is legitimate but also wrong, God's servant for the believer's good and yet God's enemy in the coercive function.

Summary: Dissent or Sectarianism?

The redemptive activity of the Spirit is predominantly ecclesial. Yoder depicts the state's fallenness while offering the vision of a believers' church unambiguously manifesting the glory of God's reign.[124] This position, and those which follow it, is routinely labelled as withdrawn, perfectionist or sectarian.[125] Hauerwas rightly protests against shortcutting engagement with his or Yoder's work by this charge.[126] He opposes the 'serious error' that we have to be church-type or sect-type.[127] The true sectarianism is denial of the church's universality in favour of narrow national loyalties and exaltation of the nation-state.[128] Scriven's review of social ethics has argued that the radical vision of the church has most potential to transform culture. Other approaches accommodate prematurely and lose their transformative power.

When the church offers a 'transformative example' it is most potent and this depends upon its solidarity with Christ.[129]

But the key issue in rebutting the charge of sectarianism concerns not social typology but *the adequacy of the doctrine of creation* and its use as a basis for ethics.[130] Yoder's christological ethics, although indicating signs of a created ontology within fallen reality, for the most part subordinate creation to redemption. Even here the charge of sectarianism is scarcely justified since the agent of redemption is also agent of creation and so the key to the future of the universe. His relevance therefore cannot be limited.[131] No aspect of creation is in principle excluded as a place of service nor is there a radical discontinuity between discipleship and 'worldly' endeavour.[132] The christocentric approach appropriates the concerns of creation as illuminated by the revelation of the Word made flesh. But the question is whether this fills out adequately the fullness of God's involvement with his world beyond the communally mediated Word-event.[133] This is clearest in Yoder's scepticism about the ability of politics to do what is needed.[134] He does not spurn a place for political action, indeed establishes it, provided it proceeds out of Christian community.[135] Yet his emphasis on the fallenness of the powers overshadows their createdness and redeemability.[136] Yoder's reaction to Niebuhr's use of the term 'responsibility' and his objection to controlling history means that the very proper responsibility to steward creation comes only reluctantly to the fore in his theology.

Hauerwas considers that Yoder's predispositions hinder a more positive understanding of the nature of political community. For Yoder, violence is of the essence of the state. But human community is sustained not by violence but by the common wills of its members. Mainly the state functions without physical threat, through non-violent power directing the individual to the good of the whole.[137] Yoder hints at this dimension without greatly developing its implications. Conversely his ecclesiology takes little account of the church's actual performance. It is portrayed as either apostate or faithful when most of the time it is somewhere in between. A more 'Augustinian' approach to its sanctification might lead to a more positive appraisal of what can be learnt from its history even in its unfaithfulness. The line between old and new aeons is not as sharp as Yoder makes it, the relationship between them more dynamic.[138]

We miss in Yoder's theology a fuller recognition that the church exists in thorough dependence upon its environment and in solidarity with it. There is a tendency here toward *ecclesiological docetism*.[139] The church exists for the world, in solidarity with it but not in conformity to it.[140] Yet in the concern to express its otherness this element is suppressed. As Yoder finds the issue of violence crucial in distinguishing church and world, this will be a theme in the following chapter.

NOTES

1   J. Zimbelman, 'The Contribution of John Howard Yoder to Recent Discussions in Christian Social Ethics', *SJT* 45:3 (1992), 367, 372–3.
2   Wilkinson, *Dissent or Conform?*, 212.
3   H. J. Loewen, 'Peace in the Mennonite Tradition: Toward a Theological Understanding of a Regulative Concept' in R. T. Bender and A., Sell (eds.), *Baptism, Peace and the State*, 99.
4   See the exchange: H. R. Niebuhr, 'The Grace of Doing Nothing', *CC*, 23 March 1932, 378–80 and R. R. Niebuhr, 'Must We Do Nothing?', *CC*, 30 March 1932, 415–17.
5   'Reinhold Niebuhr and Christian Pacifism', *MQR* 29:2 (1955), 101–17, see 101.
6   *Why the Christian Church is not Pacifist* (London: SCM Press, 1940), 15–16.
7   Ibid., 36; *An Interpretation of Christian Ethics* (London: SCM Press, 1936), 113–45.
8   Niebuhr holds 'a strategy for (discriminately) sinful living in an (indiscriminately) sinful world, rather than a strategy for transformed life in a world become new in Christ Jesus': McClendon, *Ethics*, 320.
9   *Why the Christian Church is not Pacifist*, 45–47; R. Harries, 'Reinhold Niebuhr's Critique of Pacifism and his Pacifist Critics' in Harries (ed.), *Reinhold Niebuhr and the Issues of our Time* (London and Oxford: Mowbray, 1986), 113.
10   'Reinhold Niebuhr and Christian Pacifism', 101, 103.
11   Ibid., 104, 111.
12   Ibid., 102, 115.
13   *Moral Man and Immoral Society: A Study in Ethics and Politics* (London: SCM Press, 1963) e.g., 19–22, 93; 'Must We Do Nothing?', 416–17.
14   'Reinhold Niebuhr and Christian Pacifism', 115.
15   Ibid., 116. See also C. E. Gunton, 'Reinhold Niebuhr: A Treatise of Human Nature', *MT* 4:1 (1987), 80.
16   Ibid., 117.
17   Ibid., 113.
18   'Continental Theology and American Social Action', *RIL* 30:2 (1961), 225.
19   'The Otherness of the Church', 295.
20   'Reinhold Niebuhr and Christian Pacifism', 114, 116.
21   *Christ and Culture* (New York and London: Harper and Row, 1951 and 1975).
22   Ibid., 45, 56.
23   Yoder, '"Christ and Culture": A Critique of H. Richard Niebuhr'. Unpublished paper, drafted in 1964 and revised in 1976, 2.
24   Ibid., 6–8.
25   *Christ and Culture*, 80–81.
26   '"Christ and Culture": A Critique', 10, 15.
27   Ibid., 10–11.
28   Ibid., 8–9.
29   'Culture is the "artificial, secondary environment" which man superimposes on the natural. It comprises language, habits, ideas, beliefs, customs, social organization, inherited artefacts, technical processes, and values': *Christ and Culture*, 32.
30   'The Otherness of the Church', 294.

31   'A Review and Discussion', *MQR* 35:1 (1961), 85.

32   '"Christ and Culture": A Critique', 10–11.

33   Ibid., 13.

34   C. E. Gunton, *The Actuality of Atonement: A Study of Metaphor, Rationality and the Christian Tradition* (Edinburgh: T. and T. Clark, 1988), 180–1.

35   'A People in the World: Theological Interpretation' in J. L. Garrett Jr (ed.), *The Concept of the Believers' Church* (Scottdale: Herald Press, 1969), 256–7. Stassen suggests a 'mission group type' whose norm is redemptive process and which need not withdraw because it hopes for redemption, healing and peacemaking in the world: G. H. Stassen, 'The Politics of Jesus – Moving Towards Social Ethics' (An unpublished address to the Mennonite Peace Theology Colloquium, Kansas City, 8 October 1976), 5–6.

36   'The Third World and Christian Mission'. Address to the Theological Conference of the International Federation of Free Evangelical Churches, North Park Seminary, Chicago, 3 September 1971, 5.

37   'A Clarification of Views of the Church'. Paper presented at a Mennonite Board of Missions Study Meeting, Brussels, Belgium, 1–2 January 1969, 4, 6–7, 10.

38   'Continental Theology and American Social Action', 230.

39   S. C. Mott, 'The Politics of Jesus and Our Responsibilities', *TRJ* 26 (1976), 7.

40   'A Light to the Nations', *CP* 9 (1961), 15–17.

41   'A People in the World', 259, 261–2.

42   'Marginalia', *CP* 8 (1960), 47.

43   'A Review and Discussion of *Kirchenzucht bei Zwingli* by Roger Ley (Zurich: Zwingli Verlag, 1948)', *MQR* 31:1 (1957), 63.

44   'Caesar and the Meidung', *MQR* 23:2 (1949), 77, 89.

45   'Theses on the Definition of the Free Church Vision', Second Draft, 30 May 1968, 2–3.

46   Williams, *Radical Reformation*, xxiv–xxv.

47   'The Turning Point in the Zwinglian Reformation', 38; Article 'Zwingli', *ME 4*, 1053–4.

48   'The Evolution of the Zwinglian Reformation', *MQR*, 43:1 (1969), 96–7; 'Der Kristallisationspunkt des Täufertums', *MG* Neue Folge 24 (1972), 32.

49   'The Fullness of Christ: Perspectives on Ministries in Renewal', *CP* 17 (1969), 82.

50   Ibid., 72.

51   This trait was identified by Roland Bainton of the whole Reformation, carried through most consistently by the Anabaptists. It was systematised as a definition of Anabaptism by Littell, *Origins*, 46–65. Yoder finds it an inadequate description of the functioning of biblical authority ('The Fullness of Christ', 70) but it conveys a characteristic mode of thought.

52   'The Hermeneutics of the Anabaptists'. Paper delivered to Goshen College Biblical Seminary Regional Alumni Meetings: 29 March, 18 April, 2 May 1966, 11.

53   'Anabaptist Vision and Mennonite Reality' in A. J. Klassen (ed.), *Consultation on Anabaptist–Mennonite Theology* (Fresno: Council of Mennonite Seminaries, 1970), 22.

54   'Anabaptism and History: "Restitution" and the Possibility of Renewal' in Hans-Jürgen Goertz (ed.), *Umstrittenes Täufertum, 1525–1975, Neue Forschungen* (Göttingen: Vandenhoeck and Ruprecht, 1975), 245, 253.

55   Ibid., 245–6.

56 Ibid., 247. Yoder prefers this term for the 'evangelical Anabaptists'. It indicates their attempt to create ordered hermeneutical communities: '"Spirit" and the Varieties of Reformation Radicalism', *De Geest in het Gedin: opstellen aangeboden aan J. A. Osterbaan* (Willink: H. D. Tjeenk, 1978), 304; 'The Enthusiasts and the Reformation', H. Küng and J. Moltmann (eds.), *Concilium 128: Conflicts about the Holy Spirit* (New York: Seabury Press, 1979), 43–5.

57 Ibid., 249.

58 'Review and Discussion', *MQR* 37:1 (1963), 136.

59 'Anabaptism and History', 249, 257.

60 Ibid., 248.

61 'Is There Historical Development of Theological Thought' in C. J. Dyck (ed.), *The Witness of the Holy Spirit* (Nappanee: Evangel Press, 1967), 378.

62 'Exodus and Exile: The Two Faces of Liberation', *Crosscurrents*, Fall 1973, 297–309.

63 'To Serve our God and to Rule the World', *ASCE* 1988, 6.

64 'Withdrawal and Diaspora: The Two Faces of Liberation' in D. S. Schipani (ed.), *Freedom and Discipleship: Liberation Theology in Anabaptist Perspective* (Maryknoll: Orbis Books, 1989), 81.

65 'The Anabaptist Shape of Liberation' in H. Loewen (ed.), *Why I am a Mennonite: Essays on Mennonite Identity* (Scottdale: Herald Press, 1988), 339–40. Yoder's analysis provokes social-ethical thought beyond his own tradition, especially through Stanley Hauerwas. Hauerwas provides alternatives to 'quandary ethics', which approaches ethical decision making from hard cases (*The Peaceable Kingdom*, 4), to 'foundationalism' which bases ethical thought on agreed foundations established in dialogue with extra-Christian thought (10), and to catholic 'natural law' approaches, 51. He proposes to focus on the virtues and character out of which we act, nurtured by the contexts and communities to which we belong, in turn shaped by narratives, xvi–xxi. Hauerwas' developing understanding required a church with an integrity of its own functioning as a community of virtue sustained by the story of Jesus. In view of Niebuhr's omissions, the discovery of the priority of the church in Yoder was significant, xxiv; *Christian Existence Today* (Durham, North Carolina: Labyrinth Press, 1988), 7–8. The church's first social and political task is to be the church, xviii.

66 Littell, *Origins*, 62. See also Rowland, *Radical Christianity*, 14.

67 'The Disavowal of Constantine', 49.

68 'Tertium Datur: Refocusing the Jewish–Christian Schism'. Address to the Notre Dame Graduate Union, 23 October 1977, 8, 25, 37. Yoder finds anti- or non-Jewish Christianity always accommodating to pagan gods and so the relation with Judaism continues to be important. Judaism exists as a paradoxical sign that the grace of God in election persists, a fact attested by unbelieving Israel, although the state of Israel is not the best incarnation of Jewish identity. Christian mission takes a special form to the Jews because of the depth of repentance marking it and because the messianic promise is directed in an historically distinct way to them: 'Judaism as a Non-non-Christian Religion'. Lecture in 'The Theology of the Christian World Mission' course, AMBS 1964–73, transcribed 1981, 4, 8–9.

69 'The Finality of Jesus Christ and Other Faiths', Manuscript prepared as background for the course 'Ecclesiology in Missional Perspective', AMBS, Fall 1983, 9.

70 Review of *La Guerre et l'Évangile* by Jean Lasserre, *MQR* 28:1 (1954), 76–7.

71   'The Otherness of the Church', 288.
72   'A People in the World', 264.
73   'The Evolution of the Zwinglian Reformation', 122.
74   'Von göttlicher und menschlicher Gerechtigkeit', *ZEE* 6 (1962), 171–2.
75   'The Way of the Peacemaker' in J. A. Lapp (ed.), *Peacemakers in a Broken World* (Scottdale: Herald Press, 1969), 120.
76   Le Masters points out that Constantinianism is for Yoder a crucial metaphor for the perversion of Christian ethics:, Le Masters, *The Import of Eschatology in John Howard Yoder's Critique of Constantinianism* (San Francisco: Mellen Research University Press, 1992), 1, 91, 128. It is designed to strike at the heart of the language of 'Christian civilisation', 130. He faults Yoder for failing to display historically how the conversion of Constantine altered the church–state relationship. The concept operates as abstract rhetoric too thinly constructed to be an adequate historical metaphor, 117, 136–7, 140–1, 209. It is shorthand for (i) compromising the gospel in order to gain worldly power, (ii) 'baptising' uncritically a dominant cultural order, (iii) seeing the church as another human organisation with no peculiar moral identity: *Discipleship for all Believers: Christian Ethics and the Kingdom of God* (Scottdale: Herald Press, 1992), 153.
77   'The Otherness of the Church', 210–211.
78   Ibid., 213.
79   Ibid., 298.
80   'The Finality of Jesus Christ', 26.
81   'Mennonite Political Conservatism: Paradox or Contradiction' in H. Loewen (ed.), *Mennonite Images* (Winnipeg: Hyparion Press, 1980), 8.
82   The Southern Baptists occupy in some areas a quasi-established position linked with the centres of power and prestige. Yoder notes their Lutheran dualism of church and state in which legal separation has become an internal division of labour and the tendency towards 'infantile baptism' (baptism at a very young age). In the Radical Reformation separation of church and state meant refusal of provincialism and nationalism, both of which characterize Southern Baptists: 'A Non-Baptist View of Southern Baptists', *Review and Expositor* 67 (1970), 219–28. Identification of church and culture is also true of traditional Mennonite communities. Mennonitism has become a *corpusculum christianum* reproducing the mentality of the *corpus christianum*. This can only be guarded against by sustaining a missionary relationship to the outsider and voluntaryism within the church: 'Anabaptist Vision and Mennonite Reality', 4–7.
83   'The Disavowal of Constantine', 51, 53.
84   'The Use of the Bible in Theology' in R. K. Johnston (ed.), *The Use of the Bible in Theology: Evangelical Options* (Atlanta: John Knox Press, 1985), 144.
85   'The Disavowal of Constantine', 56–67.
86   'The Finality of Jesus Christ', 6.
87   'The Basis of Barth's Social Ethics'. Extempore lecture at the Midwestern Section of the Karl Barth Society, Elmhurst, Illinois, 29–30 September, 1978, 11.
88   Zimbelman, 'The Contribution of John Howard Yoder', 293.
89   'The Prophetic Dissent of the Anabaptists' in Herschberger (ed.), *The Recovery of the Anabaptist Vision*, 97, 102.
90   'A People in the World', 264–5.
91   Ibid., 267.

92 'Von göttlicher und menschlicher Gerechtigkeit', 181.

93 'The Theological Basis of the Christian Witness to the State' in D. F. Durnbaugh (ed.), *On Earth Peace* (Elgin, Illinois: Brethren Press, 1978), 140.

94 'Church and State According to a Free Church Tradition' in Durnbaugh (ed.), *On Earth Peace*, 282–3; 'The Spirit of God and the Politics of Man', *JTSA* 29 (1979), 70.

95 Ibid., 283.

96 'The Theological Basis of the Christian Witness to the State', 141.

97 'Church and State According to a Free Church Tradition', 285.

98 'The Theological Basis of the Christian Witness to the State', 143.

99 Cf. R. R. Niebuhr, 'Must We Do Nothing?', 416.

100 Yoder reads the distinction between Romans 12:19 and 13:4 as between vengeance and no vengeance rather than individual and state vengeance: Mott, 'The Politics of Jesus', 9.

101 See also, 'Helpful and Deceptive Dualisms', *HBT* 10 (1988), 74–76.

102 'A Review and Discussion', 84.

103 'Marginalia', *CP* 10 (1961), 39.

104 Yoder's suspects civil religion as captive to the fallen powers: *PK*, 173–95. This raises the question of social beliefs and values with transcendent sources which are held in common and not derived from the state. Wogaman argues that Yoder only gives the negative aspect of the issue and that when common values can judge the state they have validity: *Christian Perspectives on Politics* (London: SCM Press, 1988), 131. There are common values despite differences in ultimate grounding, 135–7. The church is not *exclusively* the bearer of God's redemptive action and Christians do well to be both confident of God's actions in history and humble about discerning the details. Christ is the criterion for this, 137. There is no necessary conflict between loyalty to the community of faith and openness to the civil community, 140. Civil religion is not a violation of integrity so long as no tenets or rituals are imposed, 197.

105 Zimbelman, 'The Contribution of John Howard Yoder', 399.

106 'Was Jesus a Political Person?' Address delivered at Goshen College, 22 October 1973, 2.

107 'A "Peace Church" Perspective on Covenanting', *EcRev* 38 (1986), 320.

108 'Von göttlicher und menschlicher Gerechtigkeit', 180–1.

109 Stassen sees Yoder taking a pluralist view of politics. It includes the effort of the powerful to lord it over others and the merciful ordering of God in the midst of the oppression, falsehood and idolatry: Stassen '*The Politics of Jesus* – Moving Towards Social Ethics', 3–4.

110 Zimbelman, 'The Contribution of John Howard Yoder', 396.

111 *Christ and the Powers* (Scottdale: Herald Press, 1962 and 1977).

112 Ibid., 6, 70.

113 'The Biblical Mandate' in R. J. Sider (ed.), *The Chicago Declaration* (Carol Stream: Creation House, 1974), 95.

114 Ibid., 94–102.

115 'The Limits of Obedience to Caesar: The Shape of the Problem'. Address delivered to the Study Conference of the Commission on Home Ministries, June, 1978, 10–11. Yoder has in mind the withholding of war taxes in an age when respect for

the international community also makes its claim and when government rhetoric concerning serving the people invites debate.

116 'Mennonite Political Conservatism', 11.

117 Ibid., 11–12.

118 'To Serve our God and to Rule the World', 8–9.

119 'Withdrawal and Diaspora', 82–3.

120 'Mennonite Political Conservatism:', 15.

121 Ibid., 13.

122 'Mennonite Political Conservatism', 59. Stassen faults Yoder for not saying enough about the proper purposes of government. Even if Christians participate primarily in the church as a servant community they are involved beyond it and need greater clarity about the uses and abuses of power: Stassen '*The Politics of Jesus* – Moving Towards Social Ethics', 23–5.

123 Wogaman, *Christian Perspectives on Politics*, 259.

124 Le Masters, *The Import of Eschatology*, x, 75–6, 210.

125 E.g. J. M. Gustafson, 'The Sectarian Temptation: Reflections on Theology, the Church and the University', *PCTS* 40 (1985), 83–94; W. D. Miscamble, 'Sectarian Passivism?' *ThT* 44:1 (1987), 69–77; J. Wogaman, *A Christian Method of Moral Judgement* (London: SCM Press, 1976), 32–35. See also S. J. Holland, 'The Problems and Prospects of a "Sectarian Ethic": A Critique of the Hauerwas Reading of the Jesus Story', *CGR* 10:2 (1992), 157–68.

126 *Christian Existence Today*, 8.

127 'Will the Real Sectarian Stand Up?', *ThT* 44:1 (1987), 87.

128 Hauerwas, *Against the Nations: War And Survival in a Liberal Society* (Minneapolis: Winston Press, 1985), 7.

129 *The Transformation of Culture: Christian Social Ethics After H. Richard Niebuhr* (Scottdale: Herald Press, 1988), 26, 147–58, 181.

130 Gustafson, 'The Sectarian Temptation', 88. Scriven's thesis has been criticised for using the non-violence criterion ideologically so obstructing his capacity to hear the other positions he examines. He is said to share the common Anabaptist fault of lacking a doctrine of creation owing to his form of christocentricity: B. J. Walsh, 'The Transformation of Culture: a Review Essay', *CGR* 7:3 (1989), 265.

131 Le Masters, *Discipleship for all Believers*, 31, 46, 80–1, 103–33.

132 Ibid., 128, 140.

133 Holland, 'Problems and Prospects of a "Sectarian Ethic"', 167.

134 R. B. Fowler, *A New Engagement: Evangelical Political Thought 1966–1976* (Grand Rapids: Eerdmans, 1982), 127–8.

135 Ibid., 161.

136 Cf. the criticism that Anabaptism seeks not a *recreatio* but a *nova creatio*: A. A. van Ruler cited by W. Baltke, *Calvin and the Anabaptist Radicals* (Grand Rapids: Eerdmans, 1981), 270.

137 S. Hauerwas, 'The Non-resistant Church: The Theological Ethics of John Howard Yoder' in Hauerwas, *Vision and Virtue: Essays in Christian Ethical Reflection* (Notre Dame: University of Notre Dame Press, 1981), 218–19.

138 Ibid., 220.

139 Barth, *CD* IV/3.2, 723, 734, 762–3.

140 Ibid., 773, 796.

CHAPTER 5

Yoder:
The Messiah, The Messianic Community
And The Way Of Peace

This chapter clarifies the church's relationship to Christ in Yoder's theology particularly with reference to politics and violence. Yoder reasons by means of solidarity: discipleship involves unity with Jesus (*CAW*, 186) and Christ is the model for ethical action (*PJ*, 12). Even politically therefore the church is involved in his pattern of cross and resurrection.[1]

Jesus of Nazareth as Socio-ethical Norm

The Politics of Jesus argues that the life and teaching of Jesus have direct social and political implications.[2] This theme, the organising principle of Yoder's work,[3] was anticipated by Anabaptist disagreements with the Reformers over biblical authority. They denied any distinction between 'prescription' and mere 'description'. New Testament injunctions, arising as responses to questions, and examples, presupposed without being questioned, had equal authority.

The early church encountered religious cosmovisions and hammered them into new shapes with Jesus, the crucified Jewish criminal, at the bottom and the pre-existent Son transcending each new cosmos at the top.[4] Christ is the canon within the canon, supreme over the later church and the earlier revelation in Judaism. The canon allows the church to be judged by its prehistory, sustaining Jesus' memory to stimulate faithfulness to him in every age, discriminating the growing tradition and demonstrating how the early church proved faithful to Jesus in new contexts (*PT*, 117–19). This process, not the past decisions themselves, is the normative factor in the inter-cultural mission of the church.[5] The hermeneutic community applies Jesus' memory through conversation to its changing historical settings, legitimately modifying New Testament examples within principled constraints.[6]

Trinitarian doctrine establishes this christological concentration. There is no independent doctrine of the Father or of the Spirit (*PT*, 76). The Nicaeno-Chalcedonian formulae point to Jesus as the Word of the Father, true God and true Man (*PJ*, 105). Yoder inclines towards a monistic doctrine of God, downplaying the distinction of the persons and regarding pluralist doctrines that magnify the community, communion or multi-personality of God's being as 'interesting speculation' or poetic. This was not the original point of the doctrine (*PT*, 140, 142). A Trinity of three persons is neither biblical nor Nicene. The concept that Father and Son have separate identities and make transactions with each other is without grounds in orthodox doctrine or the New Testament (*PT*, 222). The doctrine of the Trinity intended to establish Jesus' significance as God's revelation.

Christ's total existence is the Word of God to humanity and he was a political figure from the beginning, his ethical involvement being described in his teachings.[7] The Anabaptists rediscovered Jesus' ethical demand on the church in realising that the world, the 'structuredness of evil', existed over against the church.[8] Yoder holds together christological, ecclesial and political themes through his messianic emphasis. Bethlehem can thus speak to both Rome and Masada. Mainstream thought denied Jesus' immediate relevance to such realms: Jesus proposed an 'interim' ethic, or his model of social relations was inappropriate for institutional societies, or his company conceived only of being a faithful minority, or he dealt only with the infinite, with atonement rather than ethics (*PJ*, 15–19). Some 'theology of the natural' was posited in dialectical tension with Jesus' example. Paul was said to stress grace to correct Jesus' ethical radicality into a more conservative stance (*PJ*, 20–1). But the doctrines of revelation and incarnation establish Jesus as normative in his humanness and go beyond general truths accessible to believer and non-believer. Jesus presented a particular social-political-ethical option (*PJ*, 22–3).

The coming of the kingdom in Jesus is a social reality liberating people from bondage (*PJ*, 28) whose first-fruits are found in the social existence of believers (*STL*, 1). Jesus' missionary platform (Lk. 4:18–19) 'states the messianic expectation in the most expressly social terms' (*PJ*, 35) announcing a jubilee, a 'visible socio-political, economic restructuring of relations among the people of God, achieved by his intervention in the person of Jesus as the one Anointed and endued with the Spirit' (*PJ*, 39).[9] The cross was not an instrument of propitiation but a political alternative to both insurrection and quietism (*PJ*, 41–3). In the Jesus movement the power of the coming kingdom enabled a jubilee, messianic lifestyle of forgiveness, remission of debts and imitation of God's boundless love in a manner foreign both to the Jewish leaders and popular expectations. This community was to be willing to endure social hostility, to practise servanthood and be distinct through a nonconformed quality of involvement (*PJ*, 39–40, 45–7). It existed as a foretaste/model/herald of the Kingdom (*STL*, 6), an alternative politics in its approach to power, wealth and decision-making.[10]

Yoder concludes that Jesus was

> in his divinely, mandated (i.e. promised, anointed, messianic) prophethood, priesthood, and kingship, the bearer of a new possibility of human, social and therefore political relationships... who threatens

society by creating a new kind of community leading a radically new kind of life (*PJ*, 62–3).

His political stance presented a contrast between politics in human rebelliousness and politics under the teaching and empowerment of God's Spirit[11] which is not to be avoided by denying his normative status or relegating it to a special vocation (*PJ*, 75). Yet New Testament literature offers no *general* concept of the imitation of Christ. It rather draws attention in every strand to the cross as the pattern for the church's life. This is the

concrete social meaning of the cross in its relation to enmity and power. Servanthood replaces dominion, forgiveness absorbs hostility. Thus – and only thus – are we bound by the New Testament thought to 'be like Jesus' (*PJ*, 134).[12]

This is a political option. Jesus' context offered four potential political stances (*OR*, 18–33). The *Sadducees* opted for realism in an unavoidable situation, accepting and infiltrating the establishment. The *Zealots* waged holy war against their oppressors. Jesus rejected this as mirroring Roman tyrannical violence, changing too little, producing the new order by the sword and reproducing the self-righteousness of the mighty (*OR*, 23–4). By contrast he acted on occasion compassionately towards Romans. Despite similarities such that he could accurately be called a non-violent Zealot (*CAW*, 428, 432), Jesus adopted a lower view of state sovereignty and a higher view of the adversary. The alternative to the Zealot sword was not neutrality but servanthood enabled by a new divine presence.[13] The *Essene* option represented withdrawal in search of purity; yet Jesus forsook his village community for the city. The *Pharisees* represented the option of 'proper religion', living in urban societies and keeping themselves apart yet in the limited and deceptive fashion of avoiding certain elements of culture. Such separation took the establishment's side through non-involvement (*OR*, 25–6).

Jesus' option, the 'original revolution', was to create a community with deviant values. It involves more than individual conversion (which alone can lead to progressive or reactionary social strategies). The new creation is a new community.[14] The gospel's preferred social form is where different kinds of people are reconciled.[15] This fulfils God's purposes beginning with Abraham and is a voluntary, mixed society which forgives offenders and deals with violence by suffering. By drawing upon the gifts of its members, by revaluing human relations in general and the enemy in particular, it builds a new order without smashing the old. Its heart is a new way of dealing with the fundamental temptation of power, the way of servanthood (*OR*, 28–31).

Christ's normative and non-resistant cross makes it imperative for Yoder to delineate an understanding of God's wrath which absolves God from inflicting punishment. He is aware of the challenge posed by ideas of divine judgement and indeed of church discipline (*CAW*, 28–9) and by the language of the Apocalypse. The New Testament portrays God and Jesus as angry (*CAW*, 585). But does not the ultimate destruction of rebels contradict suffering love? (*CAW*, 454). Yoder is sharply critical of substitutionary theory in both Anselmian and penal forms on the grounds that it unbiblically makes God the object not the agent of reconciliation (*PT*, 220).[16] God responds to evil by bearing the suffering we inflict, not by causing humans to suffer what their rebellion deserves.[17] '[N]on-resistance is part of the essential nature of agape, of God's way of dealing with evil' (*PT*, 227).

God's wrath is his decision out of respect for human freedom and dignity to allow humans to damn themselves. History contains the possibility of real decision and therefore of real tragedy. Love means respecting the freedom of the beloved to reject love; so the love and wrath of God are one.[18] The atoning God in Christ absorbs and nullifies human hostility and so restores communion. Wrath is not an attitude of God and has no need of propitiation. It is the process actuated when humans reject God (A. T. Hanson) (*PT*, 236–7). The Anselmian tradition leads to tritheism and fails to integrate the theme of discipleship within the atonement (*PT*, 223–4). The atonement expresses God's non-resistant bearing of sins and is the model for discipleship (*PT*, 229–30).

The Church as a Transforming Community

Yoder embraces a 'minority-missionary' perception of the church distinct from the 'established-pedagogical'.[19] The focus on the autonomous self needing assurance of its destiny is unbiblical. Christian faith is, instead, enrolment in the divine mission.[20]

For Christianity to be society's official ideology jeopardises something definitional about the faith at the cost of Christ's Lordship, as for instance in seeking a quasi-autonomous law within the social setting (orders). The church is a moral minority adopting a counter-establishment stance: this change of consciousness accompanies the disavowal of Constantine. Banding together in social dissonance produces social leverage. The church has a modelling mission, being now what the world is called through its functioning to become.[21] Here, renunciation of the sword is crucial to evangelical and ecumenical integrity (*NS*, 9).

Progress in history is borne by the underdogs (Tolstoy).[22] Christian ethics take as their proper paradigm not the Charlemagnes and Carnegies but believers in lesser roles who give allegiance to the Jesus story and form supportive, corrective and ethical communities standing, as did God, with the victims.[23] The major characteristics of civilisations are contributed by minority groups, both those exercising domination and those which, unengaged in political responsibility, are liberated for exceptional creativity (*EFC*, 22–3). So the church is 'an instrument for serving and saving the wider culture' (*PK*, 11). Creation's goodness and the duties of building culture are not denied but an autonomous world being served on its own terms is.[24] Disciples are in the world, not of it. This affects their manner of exerting social pressure but does not mean withdrawal. It allows freedom for critical independence and even radical opposition.[25] Yet violence (willingly and knowingly violating the dignity and physical or psychic integrity of any person)[26] is exchanged for non-violence (the intentional renunciation of intent to harm).[27] Nor does seizing the levers of power to enforce change cohere with Christ's sacrificial servanthood. How then does the church effect change and exercise power in Christ's name?

As the worship of God is the source of renewal and the preached Word unmasks the enslaving powers, the church has power to recreate from the bottom up (*PJ*, 154–5). Power is God's creation and its exercise cannot of itself be wrong, but it is to be used worthily. The church therefore engages in conscientious participation and conscientious objection (*PJ*, 158, 161).

The church influences the world by prefiguring God's will for human social existence and then generalising its own patterns. It is called to be today what the world is called to be ultimately so that a Christian social witness is derived from the faith community's witness (*BP*, ix, 71–80). Internal activities, such as fraternal admonition (the process of human interchange and of the 'binding and loosing' of ethical discernment),[28] the universality of charisma and the freedom of the Spirit in the meeting, are generalised as the empowerment of the humble and the end of hierarchy. This becomes the ground-floor for democratic ideas.[29] The breaking of bread becomes an economic solidarity ethic of family or 'socialism'. Baptism constitutes a new people in which stratifications are relativised, so creating a path into 'egalitarianism' (although such words are never fail-safe and univocal). The church's God-empowered sociology, enabled and illuminated by its Messiah and so belonging to the order of redemption, functions paradigmatically for other social groups and even for the political and economic order. Being rooted in the order of redemption does not make these sacramental practices less public but rather more realistic about sin and more hopeful about reconciliation. This differs from Brunner and the Niebuhrs who sought roots in creation rather than redemption, in reason rather than revelation and in the Father's rather than the Son's work.[30] The apostolic communities proceeded conversely.[31]

In addressing the ethical issues it faced, the early church applied Jesus' messianic ethic (*PJ*, 192). The first step in its contemporary application recognises the church's diaspora, minority situation. To assume that those who govern are also Christians confuses ethical thinking by fusing elements distinguished in the key servanthood text Luke 22:24–30. They are: (i) 'dominion' as a system of government within the nations, (ii) the moral justification which legitimates it, (iii) the different 'ethical game' played by the church. With minority status the church is free to engage the self-justifying language of rulers which, though not that of Christian discipleship, enables it to address rulers on their own terms and according to political circumstance (*PK*, 156–8). Democratic machinery helps to achieve this end and this is its strength. Democracy is not truly 'the rule of the people', since even democracies are ruled by an élite. But its ideological legitimation permits a critique which has penetrated the rhetoric and understood the prior reality of political systems to be domination. Yoder calls this the 'priority of the facticity of the sword' (*PK*, 159). Democracy is the least oppressive political system, a less overtly violent way of administering human justice, but not a fundamentally new kind of sociology (*KBW*, 110). The coercive use of power even here creates problems for Christians practising servanthood.

The third step in Yoder's analysis notes that the church adopts a distinct servant lifestyle, practising the true politics which the world's palely reflect. This is its primary form of political involvement (*PK*, 163–5). Democracy grew out of the church's radical form. The church processed sacred truths dialogically and respectfully and proved this could be done with other issues. One version of the democratic urge came from Puritanism as expressed in the 'Cromwellian adventure'. It failed because it both developed consensus as a moral mandate for government and enforced rule over one's neighbour, so falling into contradiction. The Massachusetts Puritan experiment denied to others the religious freedom which its founders claimed for themselves. These failures illustrate that the way to apply as a governmental paradigm the 'open conversation of the church under the Word' is to 'assure to any and all churches their own freedom by denying to any and all churches any civil privilege'. A truly Christian society grounds the right of dissent theologically. Democracy, for Yoder, is based upon the dignity of dissent, not majority rule but the privileged status of minorities and their right to be heard (*PK*, 167).[32]

Democracy is the product of a long spiritual history dependent upon the general osmotic effect of evangelical witness. Yet the essential nature even of democratic societies involves dominion and coercion. This is a realistic view of even the most liberal society; but Yoder does not deal extensively with the fact that the church also is shaped by power relationships, perhaps more covertly expressed. Church and society thus confront the same reality. The church falls short of its vocation but, Yoder claims, the radical tradition has internal instruments of correction. It can claim that its members are committed to the right way of working at their own unfaithfulness.[33] The church's validation is in the call to which it responds, not in its achievements (*STL*, 16). Yet the distortions that lead to war, especially the 'crusading' mentality, have their roots in the church, so pacifist polemic must first be directed here (*PJ*, 247). We now examine what Yoder describes as 'the ripple effect from faith community forms' (*PK*, 168).

The Process of Social Change

Minority communities are change agents. They support dissenters pursuing deviant paths and discharge 'modelling missions' for alternative visions of society (*PK*, 191–2; *OR*, 171–4). Christian communities are paradigmatic, providing places to stand from which to say and to test something critically new. The church represents the kind of community that society ought to be and has the enablement to become what society as yet cannot become, a dialogical democracy where justice, dignity, equality, peace and social pluralism are found (*PK*, 92–4).[34] It serves the community by pioneering. It functions as a witness but only under certain conditions: it must speak from the authenticity of its own life, from shared convictions and a base community living consistently with its claims (*CWS*, 22–3). The church affects society by 'moral osmosis', its influence through existence and example (*CWS*, 21). It produces new creative openings or possibilities (*OR*, 157). It recognises the power of weakness and the weakness of power, bringing about change from within itself, when for all their power governments are unable to bring about the changes that really matter. For these reasons, the church's commitment to evangelical nonconformity is its greatest contribution to social responsibility (*OR*, 174–6).

The incarnation is by definition involvement, yet Christ was involved without sin (*CWS*, 57–8). The question of Christian involvement in the political process concerns the points at which the messianic witness is surrendered for the sake of the tired formulae of an unbelieving world. The disciplined community can advocate general disciplines of law in the public forum (*CWS*, 21 n. 5). It can use without compromise selective democratic means of participation. The vote is a witness. The witness can be made even as legislators if it is without excessive concern for re-election or for developing a power-bloc (*CWS*, 27–8).

The argument therefore is not for minimum government but for sobriety, humility, reality, decentralisation and humane tolerance in all that the government undertakes (*CWS*, 58–9). The state's work as society's agent for co-ordinating common effort is a more appropriate point of involvement than its forcible curbing of evils. There is a temptation to expect other forces in society to be more effective than the body of believers, but legislation is only meaningful when it extends the commitment of a Christian community, so demonstrating that commitment's fruitfulness.[35] Some sins cannot properly be dealt with in the courts even were there a majority to declare them worthy of civil punishment, so it is wisdom to accept that some things cannot be stopped.[36]

God is certainly active beyond the church. The criterion of 'what God is doing in the world' must however be 'jesuological', the earthly servant Jesus, since abstract slogans can mislead. Concrete acts of servanthood, rather than statecraft, are what resonate with Jesus. What God does beyond the church is still to be seen in relation to the church, often as a judgement of its faithlessness. God condemns its failures, not its ecclesiocentricity as such, by letting another messiah temporarily fill the gap with the intention of restoring faithfulness.[37]

God has one standard for the whole of society, the *agapē* revealed in Christ. There is no lesser justice for society at large ascertainable through natural theology alongside a higher ethic for vocational groups. Those in the church are committed to *agapē* although their performance falls short of it. Nothing less is laid upon society and the statesman, but without faith *agapē* appears a suicidal demand for self-sacrifice not a meaningful alternative. From the faith community the demands of love rebound into the as yet unbelieving community, being translated in the process into 'pagan' categories such as liberty, equality, fraternity, education, democracy and human rights. These represent the highest standard of appeal in the world of unbelief, although not commensurate with a full Christian vision. Through these 'middle axioms' the Christian appeals to the statesman in his own, secular terms without conceding an alternative set of standards to the *agapē* revealed in Christ.[38] Christian social responsibility calls the statesman to fulfil his own best rhetoric while embodying in the church the life of the loving community which affects the community at large by osmosis, example and creative transformation (*CWS*, 71–3).

Messianic Pacifism

The major distinction between church and world concerns the uses of power. The church's power of loving servanthood reflects the messianic lifestyle. The world maintains itself through dominion, coercion and violence. The messianic community lives non-violently and proclaims a gospel to which non-resistance is integral not peripheral.[39] Yoder sees the rejection of violence as the New Testament proclamation from beginning to end (*PJ*, 250). The world seeks for forms of self-protection with which believers may dispense through their abandonment to God. Yoder entitles his distinctive approach 'the pacifism of the messianic community' (*NS*, 123).

The issue here is not the casuistry of whether violence breaks the rules nor is a pacifist position necessary which can be institutionalised to 'work' (*NS*, 125–7). 'Pacifism' concentrates on political goals rather than the Anabaptist priority of loving concern for people and the refusal to harm intentionally.[40] Yoder's position does not promise to succeed. It deals with a human community experiencing and expressing the kingdom of God in foretaste. The issue is lifted from the realm of the heroic individual into that of the community which reinforces the witness (*NS*, 126). The church is called to be a 'reconciling presence' in the neighbour's life (*WWD*, 40). Christological pacifism depends on confession of Christ as Lord and on repentance initiating a new human existence. The person of Jesus is indispensable, the only ground on which it makes sense. It is right not because it works but because it anticipates the triumph of the Lamb that was slain.[41]

The prudential ethics of the just war theory (JWT) calculate probabilities of success. Messianic pacifism accepts the probability of crucifixion without believing that resurrection can be mechanically predicted (*NS*, 126). The JWT, more accurately 'justifiable' war theory, resembles pacifism in its presumption against war and its intention to restrain state violence (*CAW*, 62, 83),[42] yet operates with a confusing multi-logic which renders it unwieldy as an instrument of decision-taking.[43] It lacks the test case of a war or a particular form of weaponry in which Christians have refused to take part.[44] Its honesty is questionable because of the lack of provision for surrender which the theory requires but which national psychological reality forbids (*WWU*, 64–7).[45] Its power to restrain conflict therefore comes into question.[46] In the middle ages it had its locus in the confessional and so in 'discipline after the fact' rather than in decision-making.[47] It has often cloaked uncritical espousal of the ruler's cause as if it were God's,[48] its demands being set aside by those who proclaim moral absolutes in other areas but whose involvement in the establishment has subordinated loving one's enemy to pragmatic and managerial considerations.[49]

War is the only sin which has been systematically advocated with a good conscience by theologians; there is no doctrine of just adultery,[50] righteous false witness or legitimate polytheism.[51] Proclaimed as necessary because of human depravity, the JWT optimistically trusts the wielders of great destructive force to exercise restraint.[52] The possibilities of non-violent action are left unexplored, rejected because of failure to 'work', when no investment is put into them, while armed conflict is planned and budgeted for. In violent conflict casualties are expected while in non-violent action they are grounds for rejection.[53] The JWT makes no provision for forming people able to make moral judgements independent of and sometimes against the authorities (*WWU*, 19, 22). It cloaks the predominant justification for war which is *raison d'état* or national interest. Yoder calls this the 'blank check' reality of the theory (*CAW*, 13, 82), worsened by the trend to national autonomy of which the Reformation was a part and which freed the state from mediaeval restraints on war (*WWU*, 29, 36, 71; *CAW*, 100–1). The JWT cannot appeal to the Old Testament: holy war was not 'just war' but a miracle of the gracious God who protects and preserves his people. These strange events are not normative but exceptional signs of God's grace, an awareness which would with time form a people who were also concerned for the enemy and the foreigner (*CAW*, 445–7).

Messianic pacifism involves a risk of faith rooted in Christ and therefore in God in the service of reconciliation. Those who risk this faith are later recognised as truly representative of the church. Their deaths have often made the greater contribution to God's cause and the world's welfare (*WWD*, 26). Yoder objects to an approach which determines that martyrdom, which reflects God's way with the world, is the one thing we should not let happen (*WWD*, 40). The church has undergone the re-orientation of repentance which makes possible a different response (*NS*, 126–7). If Reinhold Niebuhr's concern was that in pursuing the absolute we become blind to the relativities of the present, Yoder's concern is that in tackling the relativities of the present we might betray the absolute.

Yoder believes making history 'turn out right' to have been the dominant concern of Christian social ethics since Constantine, leading to consequentialism and the sacrifice of subordinate values to overriding immediate concerns (*PJ*, 233–4, 248). He questions concern with calculated effectiveness because Jesus refused so to direct history. The 'cross and not the sword, suffering and not brute power, determines the meaning of history'. The triumph of the right is assured by the resurrection. The obedience of God's people and God's triumph are related as cross and resurrection (*PJ*, 235–6, 238). The pattern of resurrection, ascension and Pentecost demonstrates that our death and that of our causes is not final. With God weakness is true strength.[54] Non-violence corresponds with the shape of divine action in moving history and thus with the way things ultimately are and will be (*PJ*, 238–9; *HPP*, 46). When legitimate ends are unattainable except by violating the dignity of others they should be renounced. This reflects the 'character of God's struggle with a rebellious world'. Yoder distinguishes here between *crusade* and *cross* (*PJ*, 244–7).

This position is sometimes called 'non-resistance' (Matthew 5:39), a frequent word in Yoder's earlier writings but which he finds inadequate because it suggests not opposing evil (*CAW*, 315–16).[55] An older Mennonite scholar argued that: 'The doctrine of the New Testament is an absolute non-resistance which makes no compromise with the relativities of politics' and resisted turning this rejection of all coercion into non-violent resistance.[56] Yoder's respect for Gandhi and Luther King indicates that he does not share this view.[57] It is indeed difficult to argue that the Jesus who cleansed the temple and engaged in other provocative acts was passively non-resistant.[58] Non-retaliation is not the same as absolute non-resistance[59]. Yet Yoder does not clarify the uses of power, coercion and force in non-violent resistance.[60]

Granted that the norm is non-violent imitation of the Messiah, are there any circumstances in which violence might be countenanced? Yoder approaches this question negatively. His analysis of Barth's attitude to war, revealing him as 'nearer to pacifism than any other major theologian within the European Protestant tradition in modern times' (*KBW*, 103–4),[61] criticises his insistence on the *Grenzfall*, the borderline case where God's command received directly or intuitively means that 'in certain contexts [Barth] is convinced of the necessity of not acting according to the way God seems to have spoken in Christ' (*KBW*, 74). Yoder mistrusts this resort to 'unconditional subjective certainty' in certain situations (*KBW*, 73, 90). For Barth ethics is one with dogmatics, yet we do not find limiting cases elsewhere suggesting that certain doctrines might not apply under certain circumstances (*PKB*, 25–6). Appeals to principle and to God's command rightly reject legalism but maintain so much room for manoeuvre as to evade Jesus' offensive but ultimately liberating demands. What Jesus demanded in his day, or any day, was unreasonable behaviour.[62]

The frustration for critics of Yoder's position is its unwillingness to address situations of inescapable ambiguity where not to use force would allow worse evil. The transferability of Jesus' teaching is problematic because he was not addressing this kind of situation. Why should the demand of non-resistance take precedence over equally fundamental demands of neighbour welfare and of distributive justice?[63]

Scriven's otherwise strongly affirmative analysis of Yoder defends openness to exceptional practice in exceptional circumstances. The New Testament accords human welfare a higher place than the letter of the law. He dissents from Yoder's claim that Christian love 'seeks neither effectiveness nor justice, and is willing to suffer any loss or seeming defeat for the sake of obedience' (*OR*, 56).[64] Jesus ranked justice among the law's weightier matters. Both love and justice are effective action for the weak and the oppressed, so effectiveness cannot be a matter of indifference. Although radical virtue calls for creative and non-violent action it cannot be denied that sometimes recourse to violence might alone effect justice. Circumstances might arise when non-violence loses 'all semblance of constructive witness' and a disciple commits an 'utterly strange act'. This 'nonlegalistic account of the radical tradition' still preserves the distinction between the radical community with its virtues and majority culture.[65]

Yoder's short book on this moral dilemma (*WWD*) agrees there are hard choices but insists on the need to choose not the lesser but the least evil. It is false to posit only two options and ignore non-violent resistance (*KBW*, 85–6). The dilemma so posed makes any answer other than that desired impossible (*WWD*, 15). The non-violent approach a limit situation with an armoury of possibilities which the violent deny themselves, not excluding that of miraculous intervention. Being a 'reconciling presence in the life of my neighbour' might 'justify firm non-violent restraint but never killing' (*WWD*, 40).

This is as far as Yoder travels in his published or unpublished work. Further illumination is available from conversation through the unpublished work of Gayle Koontz. She points out Yoder's reluctance to accept the necessity of ambiguous choice. He is unsympathetic when concerns for enemies and victims are directly opposed. Yet he admits exceptions where he 'can't figure out what to do'. Koontz believes that greater sympathy here would enhance his position, but Yoder fears undercutting the point that Christian ethics should not be determined by hard cases or exceptional circumstances.[66] An exception cannot be predicted. Once prepared for it becomes the determining norm (*KBW*, 62). Christian ethics should not be preoccupied with:

> looking for loopholes and exceptions and limits... before having figured out why the center is the center... If what you want to talk about the most about the law is 'Yes, but where doesn't it apply?' then you haven't yet understood that its center is grace. If you have understood that the center is grace and are committed to living in that grace and believing that there can be victories and miracles and that sacrifices are meaningful, then you'll still have a lot of casuistic crunches... I don't want to avoid dealing with them but I want to avoid needing to resolve them first before people believe that the center is the center.[67]

Yoder, a self-designated 'outvoted theologian', acknowledges 'tragic dilemmas' where it is impossible not to fall short of one's commitment. But terminating someone's life is absolute. Hard cases and crunch decisions are not prototypical, so 'punctualism' sets aside the most fundamental aspects of moral discourse. The position of last resort prepared for in advance ceases to be considered extreme.[68] With Koontz we believe that to leave the question of Christian action open at this point would enhance Yoder's position.[69] With Scriven we believe that to do so would not involve its dismantling.

The difficulty of the limit situation is heightened when Yoder applies to abortion the logic which leads to messianic pacifism. If killing is rejected and suffering preferable to inflicting harm, if God is trusted for a providential deliverance, then even where a mother's life is clearly threatened abortion is to be rejected. Where Protestants are concerned for the mother's welfare and Catholics might allow abortion because of an aggressive threat to the mother's life, the Anabaptist rejects all exceptions.[70]

When Yoder finds a concept of non-violence in Jesus, Stephen Mott faults him for operating in a manner to which he otherwise objects. This concept, Mott argues, is foreign to Jesus' culture. He cannot agree that Jesus represents one social-political-ethical option.[71] By presenting the cross as capable of imitation Yoder neglects its uniqueness, abandonment by God borne vicariously. Jesus' type of action is therefore not necessarily normative. His powerlessness was a matter of timing rather than of ethical choice, not a principle of non-violence but the unique enactment of sacrifice. His servants refused to fight not because violence was the wrong means but because it had the wrong end, preventing Jesus' death.[72] Rejection of violence here no more supports the general rejection of arms than holy war in the Old Testament legitimates ordinary warfare.

Armed defence of one's neighbour, Mott continues, is never discussed in the Bible. But the ethics of conflicting duty involve a multiplicity of claims which cannot all be met simultaneously. One must choose one claim over another. The multilateral situation, of a threat to a person for whom I am responsible, is not directly addressed by Jesus' example.[73] The aggressor, whose life Yoder says is privileged and of no less value, is repelled solely because of his aggression and the unavoidable choice that it presents.[74] Despite this, the Christian will never take life unless the requirements of love in the situation *demand* it and this implies pragmatic pacifism, as Yoder says, since this criterion condemns most wars and most causes of war (*OR*, 87).

The Second Coming is also, according to Mott, part of the politics of Jesus and has both power and violence. The Old Testament approach to power and government includes the imperative to establish justice in the gate with law as its vehicle in association with the king. This is quite removed from Yoder's ambiguity about power and coercion and his opposition to reformation through legislation. There is an absence here of positive, prophetic justice which hinders the seizing of every opportunity to do good.[75] Love and justice are not opposed, rather justice is the order which love requires. Biblically, it has to do with creating and preserving community. It is not restricted to the punitive function but involves vindication and deliverance, expressing as fixed duty and obligation the response of love in certain social situations. Love cannot do less than justice requires but it produces moral actions which cannot be ordered by justice. So love is the greatest factor but justice a necessary instrument.[76]

This is a powerful critique. Yet its weakness is its failure to take seriously Yoder's central point: that discipleship involves conformity to Christ in his death. Unique though it may be, it is also uniquely normative. In the Anabaptist tradition, and arguably in Scripture, the cross is not only an event but a divine principle with prototypical meaning, determining the life and fate of disciples.[77]

The Politics of Resurrection

The key in Yoder's theology is the risk of faith possible for the believer in the God of Jesus Christ. Non-violence grows from an evangelical faith focused on the Spirit, resurrection, the radicality of new birth. It trusts the power of the gospel to bring change.[78] If Christ is Lord to obey him cannot be dysfunctional (*PK*, 37).

Ethics are always in the service of a cosmic commitment. The Christian commitment is found in the imagery of the triumph of the slaughtered Lamb, a code reference to the substance of Jesus' words and works (*PJ*, 233–50). God's triumph does not come through seizing control or assuring survival but through cross and resurrection, through suffering not brute force (*PJ*, 238, 246). The way of the cross means abandonment to the God who vindicates by raising the dead. Objections to this founded upon calculations of cause and effect lose their force in the appeal to faith. The resurrection means that the cross was God's own cause and we are not limited in the face of evil to the available possibilities.[79] By participating doxologically in the Lamb's kingly rule believers contribute to the course of public events.[80] To participate in the work of the Lamb is to share with him who is worthy of all power. It enables the church to accept an ethic of not taking responsibility for the course of events (*STL*, 26–7). Righteousness can be done though the heavens fall (*CAW*, 436). The resurrection gives the courage to do one thing – to follow Christ. As the church alone has this particular faith, the duality by which church and world are distinguished is reinforced.

Eschatology can be used in moral reasoning to justify killing on the basis that death is not the end. Yoder invites us to think differently. The JWT relies upon calculating consequences, assuming that the moral agent has power over events and that effects can be predicted within a closed world. But the resurrection shows that the cosmos is not closed (*CAW*, 437).[81] The one certainty is that the system will not move where we predict. This is the 'irony of history' and lends credence to the ethics of means as the only form of global responsibility (*STL*, 22; *PJ*, 235). There is no basis for preferring management of history to a providential vision of God.[82] Eschatology exposes the pretensions and limitations of the powerful and proclaims that Caesar is not the only mover of history. It denies the Constantinian identification of kingdom and political structures and judges the present order in the light of God's coming order (*OR*, 71). Proclamation of a meaningful future does not turn away from the present but enlightens it (*PJ*, 250). The resurrection of the slain Lamb shows the cross as God's way of advancing history. Those who embrace the cross work with the grain of the universe, partaking in a process in which defeat is part of a wider victory.[83] This conviction is impossible for those who do not believe that Christ is sitting at the right hand of the Father.[84]

This does not exclude concern for effectiveness.[85] The all-or-nothing assumption of Constantinian typology allows no middle-ground between full involvement and full withdrawal. But a minority position has its own effectiveness once it renounces control. Integrity and consistency are good policy in the long run. Dissent maintains awareness of an issue and changes the spectrum, and so the midpoint, of possibilities. It sustains an alternative consciousness, relates an alternative narrative, bequeaths alternative options to future generations and can broker among factions by reason of its minority position.[86]

With the recognition that Yoder, and others inspired by him[87] are articulating a 'politics of resurrection' we complete our exposition.

Summary and Evaluation

In view of Yoder's rejection of calculated effectiveness as an ethical method and the charge of 'evangelical perfectionism',[88] it needs to be shown whether his theology can function as a means of 'translating love into intelligent action'[89] in the complex and ambiguous realities faced by today's church.

Concerning *church* and *world*, Yoder affirms strongly the ontological priority of the church and shows how social theology is affected by it. The state is not in itself a constructive force but is used providentially to balance tensions (*OR*, 74). Not surprisingly, the prophetic task of the church is deemed 'more effective against injustice than getting into the political machinery itself' (*OR*, 78–80). Interpreting the work of God beyond the church risks juxtaposing 'hope for the cumulative results of human achievement with hope in Jahwe who raises the dead'.[90] Change may actually make things worse.[91] Such caution is worth hearing, but Yoder develops inadequately the state's origin in creation and the human capacity for co-operation. To see co-operation rather than domination as the essence of societies might yield a more positive appraisal. If power is the God-given ability to accomplish ends, a more effective account is needed of how it may become the vehicle of redemptive action. Without sacrificing ecclesiocentrism a more affirmative approach is required. Nonetheless, Yoder's analysis prevents that political superficiality which believes the language of legitimation without appreciating the fact of domination and stimulates the search for a compelling communitarian embodiment of God's peace and justice.

Yoder's emphasis on the *normativeness of Jesus* uncovers the ethical distance of the church from him. The church has neglected the scandal which imitation of Christ involves, depriving the world of the newness of resurrection power which faith introduces. If orthodox claims about Christ be true, he shapes and determines all human existence including social and ethical stances and does so by theology and actions which interweave and interpret one another.[92] This raises questions. There are different kinds of norm. It is not clear how to distinguish between that in Christ which is absolutely, presumptively or suggestively binding.[93] Given that some power *is* at the disposal of Christians, how does Jesus' example guide its exercise in situations he was not addressing? If, according to Yoder, everything is derived from the fact of redemption rather than creation, the normative meaning of Jesus for necessary institutions is unclear and needs to be complemented by a fuller doctrine of creation. There remains obscurity about Jesus' mode of relevance and the building of the hermeneutical bridge from his situation to our own.[94]

Yoder combats that dualism which relates Christ's example to the private sphere and which affirms the Old Testament's primacy for the public sphere.[95] He explores the coming of the kingdom as the emergence of a messianic community (*PJ*, 15–25) which mediates faithfully between Christ and the present situation (*PT*, 85). Yet the teachings of Jesus are not invariable laws to be obeyed but concrete, contextual and not necessarily repeatable applications of God's loving demand.[96] Their significance involves recognising the original inspiration behind them while seeking inspiration from the Spirit about how to apply them.[97] The difficulty comes when the principle of love becomes used as a justification for behaviour plainly conflicting with that of Jesus. This was what the Reformers tended to do, 'love' signifying bowing to other interests even when the biblical teaching indicated otherwise.[98]

Jesus was addressing the issue of how an oppressed people responds to its oppression, not giving general direction about how to deal with crimes of violence. Granted that what he taught may be applicable here as well, it is not without a process of interpretative transfer. A form of 'decisionism' seems unavoidable at this point in the commitment as to how this transfer is to be applied.[99] Or else guidance must be sought in the wider framework of the doctrine of God and the nature of its definition at the cross, a search which Yoder deeply suspects.[100]

Gayle Koontz notes that both Richard Niebuhr and Yoder recognise Jesus' non-resistance, but Niebuhr emphasises God's universal determining power whereas Yoder's God persuades and suffers rather than determines; his providence is expressed by redemptive and suffering love rather than through the limitation, sustenance and control of humans. Yoder's failure to attend to God's ordering power raises the question of the ultimate power of a non-resistant God and puts unwarranted emphasis on human freedom.[101] These are cogent points. Is the God revealed in Jesus Christ ultimately non-resistant? Yoder's theology revolves around how God responds to evil and his refusal to violate his creatures' freedom through coercive interventionism.[102] This understanding is made necessary because of the manner of God's self-revelation in the Logos-Christ. It is the pattern of all the divine activity towards humankind (*HPP*, 56, 85). On this is grounded a doctrine of hell as the everlasting capacity of human beings to maintain their rebellion. But this jeopardises the future resolution of the reality of evil if the divine eschatological agency cannot deviate from non-resistance. It raises doubt as to whether the eschaton is significantly different from the present age.[103]

The issue here certainly concerns the nature of divine power and its definition through Christ.[104] Yet to assert the ultimate limit of judgement by the patient God is only to affirm what Christ himself taught. We may therefore agree with Luther that the God whose proper work is redemption is not without his strange work of judgement which sets a limit for human sin. For the social order such an understanding carries the implication that those social structures that limit human sin may be more directly related to God than Yoder indicates.

The state and its violence in Yoder's theology represents the paradox characteristic of Anabaptism and reflects its 'Lutheran' legal positivism. It is a domination structure. Yet there are undeveloped hints of a created ontology, often overlooked by Yoder's critics, which also suggest, in a minor key, the natural law approach. This is part of a wider tension in Yoder. While acknowledging the createdness of the powers the primary emphasis falls on their fallenness (e.g. *PJ*, 195, 203–4). Miller suggests that Yoder is edging towards Marcionism.[105]

Yoder agrees that it is the state's responsibility as God's servant to protect the good and restrain the wrongdoer while suggesting, somewhat ambiguously, that the disciple is excluded from this realm. It may be that the exceptional or borderline case remains unconceded because it leads logically to the legitimation of Christian participation in institutionalised force[106]. Herschberger rejected the distinction between war and policing since both require physical force.[107] The taking of human life is by definition a violation of God's will.[108] Yoder notes pacifists such as Gandhi and Merton who accepted force to defend family or self (*CAW*, 590)[109] but rightly denies the analogy which leads from such limited action to an armaments industry preparing for war (*WWD*, 21–4). Yet the analogy does apply to policing and where this operates with the 'least evil' it is difficult to claim that this conflicts with discipleship. The sword is not *necessarily* 'outside the perfection of Christ'.[110] The duality of belief and unbelief will not *necessarily* be expressed in the refusal to fulfil certain offices but in the manner of their exercise. Military action may be needed as a wider extension of policing, as Yoder indicates (*CWS*, 5), but in this is no justification for war in itself. Small scale and limited self-defence, even in the extreme lethal defence against an aggressor, is no parallel to war (*CAW*, 590).

In Chapter 8 we shall examine further the state's role and address two further crucial and extensive criticisms to Yoder's theology concerning its *lack of Trinitarian depth* and the *wrath of God*. In the meantime our attention turns to Moltmann.

NOTES

1   Zimbelman, 'The Contribution of John Howard Yoder', 370–1.
2   D. W. Dayton, 'Are Jesus' Teachings Normative?', *CT*, 21 December 1973, 29.
3   J. Zimbelman, 'Theological Ethics and Politics in the Thought of Juan Luis Segundo and John Howard Yoder'. PhD Dissertation, University of Virginia, 1986, 191.
4   'That Household We Are'. Address from a conference on 'Is there a Believers' Church Christology?', Bluffton, Ohio, October 1980, 7.
5   'The Authority of the Canon' in W. Swartley (ed.), *Essays on Biblical Interpretation: Anabaptist–Mennonite Perspectives* (Elkhart: Institute of Mennonite Studies, 1984), 277, 284–6, 289; 'The Use of the Bible in Theology', 107, 111.
6   Zimbelman, 'The Contribution of John Howard Yoder', 376–8. Le Masters detects an unresolved tension in Yoder's hermeneutics between biblical realism, insistence on what the text says discovered by scholarly means, and a communal hermeneutic for the interpretation of Scripture: *Discipleship for all Believers*, 56–7, 204, 208–9.

7   'Continental Theology and American Social Action', 228.
8   Ibid., 229; D. A. Shank and J. H. Yoder, 'Biblicism and the Church', *CP* 2 (1955), 27, 31–2, 37.
9   Depending here upon André Trocmé, *Jesus and the Non-violent Revolution* (Scottdale: Herald Press, 1973), 19–76.
10   'Was Jesus a Political Person?', 1.
11   'The Spirit of God and the Politics of Man', 63, 66, 70–1.
12   The significance of the cross is shown in the resurrection. The drawback here is that particular teachings or ways of acting are made absolute when they are better seen in the historical-cultural setting in which Jesus acted. Wogaman prefers to see the character of God as the moral guide: *A Christian Method of Moral Judgment*, 112.
13   'Jesus and Power', EcRev 25 (1973), 450.
14   'The Apostle's Apology Revisited' in W. Klassen (ed.), *The New Way of Jesus* (Newton, Kansas: Faith and Life Press, 1980), 127, 132.
15   'The Social Shape of the Gospel' in W. R. Shenk (ed.), *Exploring Church Growth* (Grand Rapids: Eerdmans, 1983), 283.
16   C. N. Kraus, 'Interpreting the Atonement in the Anabaptist–Mennonite Tradition', *MQR* 66:3 (1992), 305.
17   'The Healing Professions in the Disciples' Church'. Address to the Mennonite Medical Association, Winona Lake, Indiana, 1962, 4.
18   'The Wrath and the Love of God'. Paper delivered to the Puidoux Theological Conference, September 1956, 2, 5.
19   'A "Free Church" Perspective on Baptism, Eucharist, and Ministry', *Midstream* 23 (1984), 273.
20   'Peacemaking Amid Political Revolution'. Seminar lecture presented at Eastern Mennonite College, Harrisonburg, June 1970, 54.
21   'Neither Guerilla nor *Conquista*: The Presence of the Kingdom as Social Ethic' in P. P. Peachey (ed.), *Peace, Politics, and the People of God* (Philadelphia: Fortress Press, 1986), 97–107.
22   'To Serve our God and to Rule the World', 11.
23   'Clearing the Decks for Accountability'. Lecture prior to a Business Ethics Symposium, Notre Dame University, 10 April 1980, 7–10.
24   'That Household We Are', 8.
25   Ibid., 12.
26   'A Fuller Definition of Violence'. Memorandum, 28 March 1973, 3.
27   'The Church and Change: Violence and its Alternatives'. Paper presented at the Annual Conference of the South African Council of Churches, Hammanskraal, South Africa, 24 July 1979, 6.
28   'Helpful and Deceptive Dualisms', 69.
29   'Sacrament as Social Process: Christ the Transformer of Culture', *ThT* 48:1 (1991), 34–6.
30   Ibid., 40–2.
31   'Helpful and Deceptive Dualisms', 71.
32   'The Racial Revolution in Theological Perspective'. Address for a Church Peace Mission Conference on 'Revolution, Non-violence and the Church', Asheville, N. C., 3 December 1963, 15.
33   'Have you ever seen a True Church?'. Methodological Miscellany 2, April 1988, 5.
34   'The Biblical Mandate', 100, 102.

35   Ibid., 101–2.

36   'Neither Guerilla nor *Conquista*', 114.

37   'Discerning the Kingdom of God in the Struggles of the World' *IRM* 68 (1979), 368–9, 372.

38   Capital punishment is illustrative of his approach. In the Old Testament execution was religious rather than civil expiation. Christ having atoned, such expiation is no longer necessary. Its antitype in the New Testament then is not the sword but the cross (*CCP*, 9–10). The sword in Romans 13 is the symbol of judicial authority not of execution. Capital punishment is one of those infringements of the divine will which is not immediately eliminated by the Gospel. Yet the new level of brotherhood in the church works its effect upon the social order. Christ is King, so the line between church and world cannot be impermeable; forgiving ethics must be made relevant to the social order (*CCP*, 10–11) although this will not be immediate or direct. It is erroneous to imagine that Christian positions can be taken to their 'logical conclusion'. The world can at most be challenged one step at a time and the Christian's task is to pull tighter and tighter the limitations on vengeance, keeping violence to a minimum (*CCP*, 11, 16): 'Capital Punishment and the Bible' *CT*, 4 February 1960, 3–6.

39   'The Place of the Peace Message in Missions', Speech delivered to the 1960 Mission Board Meeting, Lansdale, Pennsylvania, 3.

40   'A Summary of the Anabaptist Vision' in C. J. Dyck (ed.), *An Introduction to Mennonite History* (Scottdale: Herald Press, 1967), 106.

41   S. Hauerwas, 'Messianic Pacifism', *Worldview* 16 (1973), 30.

42   Wogaman describes it as 'crypto-pacifist': *A Christian Method of Moral Judgment*, 46.

43   'A Consistent Alternative View within the Just War Family', *FP* 2:2 (1985), 112, 119; 'Military Realities and Teaching the Laws of War' in T. Runyon (ed.), *Theology, Politics and Peace* (Maryknoll: Orbis Books, 1989), 176. Yoder finds a number of positions concealed behind just war language and identifies them as justifiable war, holy war, 'realism', and frenzy or passion: 'Tightening the Grid: Can Just War Thought Be Made Accountable?'. Peace Theology Miscellany 4, January 1988, 4.

44   'Von göttlicher und menschlicher Gerechtigkeit', 168–9.

45   'Surrender: A Moral Imperative', *Review of Politics* 48 (1986), 577, 589.

46   'The Credibility of Ecclesiastical Teaching on the Morality of War' in *Celebrating Peace: Boston University Studies in Philosophy and Religion* II (Notre Dame: University of Notre Dame Press, 1990), 31–51.

47   'Can there be a Just War?', *Radix* 13:2 (1981), 5.

48   'A "Peace Church" Perspective on Covenanting', 319.

49   'A Critique of North American Evangelical Ethics', *Transformation* 2:1 (1985), 29.

50   Mouw acknowledges that ethicists have been stricter about adultery and speculates about how such a doctrine might arise. A hypothetical doctrine would create a tendency to unjustified adultery, especially if people were trained to commit adultery and outstanding adulterers awarded medals! This undergirds Yoder's points: R. J. Mouw, 'Christianity and Pacifism', *FP* 2:2 (1985), 108.

51   'The Church and Change:', 11.

52   Ibid., 12.

53   Ibid., 20–1.

54 Ibid., 14–15.
55 'A Summary of the Anabaptist Vision', 106. Yoder here notes that the Anabaptists had no single word to describe their non-violence. Zimbelman points out that Yoder shifted from the language of non-resistance to non-violent resistance after 1974, showing greater appreciation of how non-violent coercion might effect witness. The use of coercive means by the Christian community is not necessarily considered immoral, although violence is: Zimbelman, 'The Contribution of John Howard Yoder', 388.
56 G. F. Herschberger, *War, Peace and Non-resistance* (Scottdale: Herald Press, 1944 and 1981), 48, 195. This excludes the attempt to pursue social justice through programmes of political pressure (189) questioning the non-violence of Gandhi as a kind of force (193) and therefore unbiblical, 189. The New Testament is entirely unpolitical and the state an instrument of sinful society for cleaning up its own evil: Herschberger, 'Peace and War in the New Testament', *MQR* 17:2 (1943), 67–8; 'Biblical Non-resistance and Modern Pacifism', *MQR* 17:3 (1943), 116, 128, 131, 134. Herschberger changed his mind somewhat about non-violent resistance after closer acquaintance with Luther King: *CAW*, 366, 415.
57 Scriven notes that Yoder's views about power changed from an early contrast between power and servanthood (e.g. *OR*, 29) to seeing servanthood as the Christian form of power: *Transformation*, 212 n. 127. Even political power is legitimate, so long as the search for 'effectiveness' does not compromise discipleship: *STL*, 23, 49. Yoder does not accept that to renounce violence also means the renunciation of power (*PK*, 61) finding in Gandhi and King examples of how a 'sectarian ethic' exercises institution-building pressure. 'Power' is not a univocal, one-dimensional concept: 'Jesus and Power', 454. 'Power in the simplest sense of the word was Jesus' agenda.... Etymologically power is what it takes to make things happen. It usually includes structures to legitimate and obligate, and it distributes the economic and spiritual wherewithal for human fulfilment', 448. In this regard, Jesus was an example of power or authority not tied to the state or to violence – the power of forgiveness, of the pilot experience, of peoplehood, of publicity and 'Jesus did not free His disciples from violence to make them pure and weak, but because He called them to use other, stronger resources', 453.
58 Cf. Rowlands, *Radical Christianity*, 2–33.
59 D. Hill, *The Gospel of Matthew* (London: Marshall, Morgan and Scott, 1972), 127–8.
60 J. Zimbelman, 'Theological Ethics and Politics', 334.
61 'The Basis of Barth's Social Ethics', 4.
62 Under Yoder's influence, Hauerwas recognised non-violence at the heart of the virtuous life embodied in the church: *The Peaceable Kingdom*, xvi–xvii. Through violence humans assert control of their lives and protect their deceptions, hence their need to create enemies. Acceptance by God enables living without these illusions and so without violence, 47–8. This risk is taken because the resurrection gives the church power to be a community of forgiveness, 89–90. Christian ethics calls for behaviour which is impossible except by the miracle of the Holy Spirit, 106. He contends that if a community is truly non-violent then it can no more decide to use violence, even if the situation seems to warrant it, than the courageous can decide, under certain conditions, to be cowardly, 123. Non-violence resists the violent (not to do so abandons them to sin and injustice) but on its own terms, not those of the

evil-doer, 106. This commits the church to the need for imagination and the search for alternatives, 124. It also commits the church to being the most political of all animals, 'exactly because politics understood as the process of discovering the goods we have in common is the only alternative to violence': *Against the Nations*, 7.

63   Zimbelman, 'The Contribution of John Howard Yoder', 387; R. Higginson, Review of *The Peaceable Kingdom* by Stanley Hauerwas in *Anvil* 2:3 (1985), 296. Wogaman criticises Yoder for his absolutism and believes he is evading the fact that failure to use violence may involve a sin of omission. This is the basic dilemma: *A Christian Method of Moral Judgment*, 129. Brian Marshall accepts a strong presumption against violence but finds it difficult to believe that non-violence is *always* the action required. Jesus' act was in an historical situation and is in danger of being made into an abstract universal principle: 'The Ground and Content of Christian Hope'. PhD Dissertation, Nottingham, 1986, 243, 245. Yet the cross opposes violence even as the lesser of two evils and shows its questionable, guilt-incurring nature, 244. He believes that Yoder's position entails renouncing the political power which is the prerequisite for social change. There is no virtue in being powerless *per se*. To exercise power with faith and love means exercising it for others, 247.

64   Scriven, *Transformation*, 189.

65   Ibid., 190–1. Huebner defends Yoder as seeking consistency not legalism and criticises Scriven for working from an apparent fact (that non-violence is not always possible) to the moral prescription that it is sometimes morally justifiable. Yoder works the other way around in seeking for peaceful actions when the only option appears to be violence: H. Huebner, Review of *The Transformation of Culture* in *CGR* 8:1 (1990), 92–3.

66   G. G. Koontz, 'Confessional Theology In A Pluralistic Context: A Study of the Theological Ethics of H. Richard Niebuhr and John H. Yoder'. PhD Dissertation, University of Boston, 1985, 106 citing conversation of 22 December 1980, Elkhart, Indiana.

67   Ibid., 107.

68   'Is an Ethic of Discipleship "Absolute"?'. Methodological Miscellany 1, February 1988, 3, 5–6.

69   Koontz does not deduce that violent action is necessary. She sees it as the duty of holy love to channel all available powers, except dominating and violent power, to restrain and transform evil. In the exceptional situation where no non-violent alternatives are available, this does not mean passively standing by but turning the moment into an act of trust in the power of God which is itself active resistance to the god of violent power: 'The Liberation of Atonement', *MQR* 63:2 (1989), 187.

70   'The Biblical Evaluation of Human Life'. Presentation for a Mennonite Medical Association Study on Abortion in Rosemont, Illinois, 5–6 May, 1973, 10.

71   'The Politics of Jesus and Our Responsibilities', 9.

72   S. C. Mott, *Biblical Ethics and Social Change* (Oxford: Oxford University Press, 1982), 178–81.

73   Ibid., 156, 182–3, 186, 170, 173, 179.

74   Ibid., 185.

75   Mott, 'The Politics of Jesus and Our Responsibilities', 10.

76   *Biblical Ethics*, 53–5, 62–3. See a similar criticism by Stassen that Yoder could

strengthen his case by basing it on the prophetic as well as the jubilee tradition, especially Deuteronomy and Isaiah: 'The Politics of Jesus – Moving Towards Social Ethics', 9, 27.

77   E. Stauffer, 'Täufertum und Märtyrertheologie', *ZfK* 52 (1933), 546–7, 573.

78   'The Contemporary Evangelical Revival and the Peace Churches' in R. L. Ramsmeyer (ed.), *Mission and the Peace Witness: The Gospel and Christian Discipleship* (Scottdale: Herald Press, 1979), 80, 84.

79   'The Christian Answer to Communism', *CP* 10 (1961), 29.

80   'To Serve our God and to Rule the World', 4, 6–7.

81   Ibid., 11.

82   Zimbelman, 'The Contribution of John Howard Yoder', 383.

83   'Clearing the Decks for Accountability', 12–13.

84   'Armaments and Eschatology', *SCE* 1 Part 1 (1988), 46, 53–8.

85   Le Masters criticises Yoder for discounting effectiveness and then suggesting that Christians tailor their political action to a standard of effectiveness. Yoder, he claims, is more concerned with effective political strategising than he admits. The use of middle axioms is such a compromise and a form of dominion. Yoder here embodies important aspects of Constantinianism and resembles Niebuhr in using an approximated version of the demands of love for the sake of playing a role in the governance of the social order: *The Import of Eschatology*, ix; *Discipleship for all Believers*, 155, 166, 176, 181, 205–7. But rejecting the levers of overall control does not preclude specific action to serve justice in relatively powerless ways. Yoder has clarified in discussion that this differs from the idolatrous search for global power. Powerlessness is not the single ultimate principle: Stassen, 'The Politics of Jesus – Moving Towards Social Ethics', 14.

86   'Neither Guerrilla nor *Conquista*', 108–12.

87   Yoder's appeal to the resurrection as determinative for Christian ethics is developed and illuminated by McClendon who discovered his own roots in the Anabaptist (or, his preferred designation, 'baptist') tradition through *PJ: Ethics*, 7. The church's temptation is to deny her starting-point in Jesus, so the church–world distinction is crucial. The church's story is not the world's story and she is called not to betray her particular truth, 17–19. All theology refers to a convictional community and is the task of discovering, understanding and transforming those convictions into the present, 19, 23. It is a self-involving task and for this reason begins chronologically, although not logically, in theological ethics, 35, 41. The church is formed by the story of the life, death and resurrection of Jesus. The radical, baptist vision of the church is also formed by the Anabaptist story but had its agenda set by Calvinism and Arminianism and then by the Enlightenment rather than the Radical Reformation. Baptists have failed to see in their own heritage a guiding vision, so becoming the victims of other ideologies and less themselves, 25–27. What is needed is a recovery of a baptist theological centre which McClendon crystallises as 'shared awareness of the present Christian community as the primitive community and the eschatological community', 31. Ethical reflection is like a three stranded rope comprising the ethics of the body, of culture and community and of the resurrection, that is, the new element of God's possibilities, 64. He selects Yoder, 'the *bête noir* of contemporary moral theology', as the primary representative of this third strand, 73. Hauerwas represents the second strand but is moving towards the third, 69–70. The resurrection strand signifies that when we have reckoned with

those considerations emerging from our sheer bodily existence and from the realities of community formation, there remains a third determining area, that of the radically new, surprising acts of God which cause us not to immerse ourselves in the first and second strands, but to reckon with the cross and resurrection as Jesus' story and our own, 251–257.

88 Wogaman, *A Christian Method of Moral Judgement*, 32–5.

89 Ibid., 35.

90 'Discerning the Kingdom of God', 367.

91 'Peacemaking Amid Political Revolution', 58.

92 E. Arens, 'Jesus' Communicative Actions: The Basis for Christian Faith Praxis, Witnessing, and Confession', *CGR* 3:1 (1985), 72.

93 Zimbelman, 'Theological Ethics and Politics', 334.

94 Cf. Yoder, 'Jesus and Power', 451; Le Masters, *Discipleship for all Believers*, 194. Cranfield argues that opposition to the Zealots does not mean Jesus would have always opposed such action – he may have seen the low probability of success: 'The Christian's Political Responsibility According to the New Testament' *SJT* 15:2 (1962), 188.

95 According to McClendon's parallel analysis, Christ's authority towards the Old Testament is that as the Wisdom of God he understands the Way (Torah) of the Old Testament and sees where its story must go. He therefore gives new overall direction to the Way which means that some practices, and hence some laws which give guidance for them must change: McClendon, *Ethics*, 222. For further support see J. D. G. Dunn, *The Living Word* (London: SCM Press, 1987), 113.

96 P. S. Fiddes, *Past Event and Present Salvation: The Christian Idea of Atonement* (London: Darton, Longman and Todd, 1989), 103.

97 Dunn, *The Living Word*, 125.

98 Yoder, 'Balthasar Hübmaier and the Beginnings of Swiss Anabaptism', 14.

99 So the comment that Yoder's ethic provides no basis for convincing those who do not believe Jesus fully incarnates God's will for the political realm: H. Beckley, Review of *The Priestly Kingdom* in *ThT* 42 (1985), 372.

100 Not all Mennonites are convinced that Jesus is an unambiguous authority for the Mennonite position. He did not decree that 'the sword is a divine order outside the perfection of Christ' and it is doubtful whether he even reflected upon the role of lethal power in the divine ordering of the world: Miller, 'Schleitheim Pacifism and Modernity', 160–1.

101 Koontz, 'Confessional Theology', 111–12.

102 C. Pinches, 'Christian Pacifism and Theodicy: The Free Will Defense in the Thought of John H. Yoder', *MT* 5:3 (1989), 244–5.

103 Ibid., 249–51.

104 'Divine power does not compel even in justice-making activity; it eschews domination and ultimately violence. The redemptive love and holy power visible in Christ takes the form of a servant, not a king, and does not use the sword': Koontz, 'The Liberation of Atonement', 184. G. D. Kaufman conceives of God coercing finite creatures in evolution and the sustaining of the material universe but when free beings emerge God employs power appropriate for evoking and sustaining freedom: *Systematic Theology: A Historicist Perspective* (New York: Scribner's, 1968), 91.

105 Miller, 'Schleitheim Pacifism and Modernity', 159. Miller draws attention to the

way in which Marcion is numbered amongst the restorers of the church to faithfulness in *PT*, 119.

106 'Once you grant Scriven's countercase as legitimate, you have the foundation in place for a just war theory': Huebner, Review of *The Transformation of Culture*, 92.

107 Herschberger, *War*, 164, 175–7. This assumes that physical force and violence are identical.

108 Ibid., 22.

109 Ibid., 24.

110 Miller, 'Schleitheim Pacifism and Modernity', 163.

CHAPTER 6

Moltmann:
The Foundations Of Messianic Theology

In relation to the social order, Moltmann may be said generally to represent a 'natural law' position (as distinguished by Brunk) rooted in the concept of covenant. As this emerges in his theology with some reticence we shall need to trace it with care.

Moltmann describes his theological pilgrimage as 'an existential experience, which must be personally suffered, digested and understood', a kind of 'experimental theology', 'being led by spontaneous inspiration'.[1] For some critics he engages rather in 'Christian poetics', oscillating between exegesis and poetry without sufficient rigour,[2] and exhibits an 'inspired incoherence'[3] (arguably less so in his earlier work where the integrations are clearer).[4] Lack of methodological stringency and attention to the epistemological basis of his assertions is a frequent charge.[5]

In the early trilogy (*TH, CG, CPS*) he viewed the whole of theology successively through the lenses of hope, the cross and the Spirit. Taken together these books were mutually corrective[6] and preparatory to the development from 1980 of a messianic dogmatics with the leading themes of Trinity and the Kingdom of God.[7] The focus in Chapters 6 and 7 is on church and social order within the broader context of Moltmann's complex theology.

Church and World against the Horizon of Hope

Moltmann's earliest writings established him as an interpreter of Bonhoeffer,[8] Reformed federal theology[9] and Protestant mysticism,[10] and of dialectical theology.[11] These concerns emerge in his emphasis on God's faithfulness to his promise and to the world within the processes of human history.[12] *Theology of Hope* (1964) is arguably Moltmann's most original book, hailed as a most influential work of the post-war period,[13] perhaps even the initiator of a new theological era.[14] It restored eschatology from its 'barren existence at the end of Christian dogmatics' to the critical and revolutionary role it fulfilled in the biblical tradition (*TH*, 15). Its thesis has never been abandoned.[15]

The sources for Moltmann's thought, the influence of his Göttingen teachers, Dutch 'apostolate' theology, Barth and from 1957 the Marxist philosopher, Ernst Bloch, have been clarified.[16] The biographical dimensions are alluded to by Moltmann himself (*EG*, 1–18; *FJC*, 9–18; *HTG*, 165–82).[17] From these factors came a 'turn to the future': eschatology was the very medium of theology (*TH*, 16).

THE PRIORITY OF FUTURE HOPE

Moltmann invites new thinking about God, revelation and history. History's significance proceeds from end to beginning. Its end cannot be anticipated from within itself but involves that which is new, which comes to it (*adventus, parousia*), rather than being extrapolated from it (*futurum*),[18] as the 'desirable' not the 'calculable' future (*FH*, 11–15; *FC*, 51). God's transcendence is located in the future: God is before us rather than over or within us and so the world's existence can only be understood from before, from what is yet to be. God has 'future as his essential nature' (*TH*, 16; Revelation 1:4). Theology may speak of the future because of Christ's resurrection but recognises that his future has not yet been realised (*TH*, 17).

Revelation is not *epiphany*, the revelation of the eternal present (*TH*, 41, 46), but *promise* looking to the future for fulfilment (*TH*, 42ff). Otherwise the future is lost by resolving revelation into a self-grounding circle of divine self-revelation (Barth: *TH*, 51–3) or the individual's existential authenticity (Bultmann: *TH*, 69). Such positions reflect a transcendental, Greek eschatology rather than the promise which characterises Israel (*TH*, 40–1). Revelation is construed historically but not so as to synthesise the spirit of the age with theology in a supposed 'progressive revelation' comprehending human culture (*TH*, 75). Rather, Jesus Christ is the apocalypse of the promised future of the truth (*TH*, 84). This future contradicts the present as the resurrection contradicts the cross. The promise announces the coming of a not yet existing reality just as the resurrection goes beyond what is realistically possible or impossible (*TH*, 85). Revelation in eschatological perspective avoids the twin extremes of assimilation to culture and of a ghetto mentality (*TH*, 89–90).

The promise is rooted in God himself and cannot be regarded as a legalistic abstraction. The fulfilment contains an element of unforeseen newness and is open-ended so that the promise takes on new and wider interpretations, an 'overplus of promise' deriving from the inexhaustibility of the God who comes to rest only in a reality that wholly corresponds to himself (*TH*, 102–6). Hope includes an eschatology of 'all things', breaking through all spatial and racial limitations to embrace all peoples and all creation (*TH*, 130–2, 137, 225). This perspective relativises the church–world distinction so determinative for Yoder. The distinction between church and world is not *spatial* (Christians must be in the world) but *temporal*. The church is the world open to the future, the 'eschatological community'[19], distinguished by knowledge and hope of the coming kingdom.

THE DIALECTIC OF CROSS AND RESURRECTION

The dialectic of cross and resurrection encompasses the pain of existence and its transformation by the creative and redemptive activity of God. Cross and resurrection determine history since in them and their proclamation the glory of God's lordship approaches humanity (*TH*, 139). Christ is the 'end of the law' (Romans 10:4) but also the rebirth, liberation and validation of the Old Testament history of promise no longer restricted to Israel but universal and unconditional (*TH*, 145–7). In Christ the incarnation of the coming God and of the future of liberation has taken place. This constitutes his messianic significance (*RRF*, 214). Christ is the mediator and foundation of the new reality (*FH*, 77). In the future of Jesus Christ the promises are yet to be fulfilled within history's arena (*TH*, 154). His lordship is still outstanding but is maintained by seeing the cross as its 'abiding key-signature' in the world (*TH*, 158). History is the realm of suffering and travailing in hope of Christ's future. Where this is neglected distortion of the church into 'an ecstatic form of Hellenistic mystery religion' follows (*TH*, 159).

LATENCY AND TENDENCY

Christ's resurrection introduces a possibility into earthly history which, in Blochian terms, is *latent* in its ongoing course creating a *tendency* towards the future opened up by that resurrection. The resurrection has brought about a necessity and a certainty. Faith must therefore go into the world to benefit it in a worldly faith and hope which do not isolate believers from the world but thrust them into it (*TH*, 196–7). The dialectic enables the acceptance of painful reality while believing in resurrection's universal promise (*TH*, 171). The tendency is towards the abolition of death (*TH*, 165, 194), the victory of life over death and godforsakenness (*TH*, 210). From the resurrection event arises the Spirit, the earnest and pledge of the future of universal resurrection and life (*TH*, 211). It becomes possible to speak of the 'tendencies of the Spirit' pointing to the future into which Christ is risen and spoken of from the historic event of the resurrection which makes history and is its key (*TH*, 212).

A *nova creatio* is hoped for. The Spirit's movement towards this is a *progressus gratiae* because the future comes to pass not by passage of time or dialectic of history since the resurrection stands in contradiction to reality (*TH*, 226), nor by human activity or progressive revelation that enables the spirit of the age to be declared secretly Christian (*TH*, 75), but by the inner necessity of the Christ event. All God has made, including all humanity, will attain to salvation, to what was meant to be (*TH*, 216, 223).

THE EXODUS CHURCH

Eschatology and ecclesiology are intimately related so discussion of Christianity's social shape and ethics becomes inevitable. Moltmann's programme prescribes a future-directed revolution, a self-critical movement of repentance, so that the church may become revolutionary (*RRF*, 134). Under imperial Rome's auspices the church became society's religion and banished eschatology with its critical effects to the margins (*TH*, 15). The millennium was interpreted in terms of the Roman state church.[20] The recovery of hope requires a renewal in which the church becomes a pilgrim community on its way to the universal future in the service of mission. Its people express their hope in their worldly callings. Hope enables resistance to accommodation and a distinctive presence in the world for the world.[21] Christianity can no longer be the *cultus publicus* which since Constantine has fulfilled the traditional role of protector and preserver of the *sacra publica*, the source of religious integration and guarantor through its sacrificial prayers of national stability and favour (*TH*, 304–5; *HP*, 131–2). It cannot accept an alliance with national idol worship (*Man*, 66–7). Neither, despite Pietism, can it accept the other roles which are willingly granted it by modernity – the unprovable but equally irrefutable *cultus privatus* preserving personal, individual and private humanity within industrial society (*TH*, 310–11; *HP*, 130–140), the island of free community in a utilitarian world (*TH*, 320–1) or the protective institution in an exposed cosmos (*TH*, 312–13). These all render it non-worldly, epiphenomenal to, but not intersecting, the public realm (*TH*, 315). It must undergo an exodus from its fixed social roles and temptation to stabilisation as from a Babylonian exile to assume a critical, conflict-laden and therefore fruitful partnership with society (*TH*, 324–5).[22]

The church claims all humanity in mission and works for world transformation, but not to extend its own sovereignty nor to return to its former privileged role of *cultus publicus*. It seeks under estranged conditions that which corresponds to the future and to discern between better and worse correspondences.[23] Mission involves propagating faith and the historic transformation of life, of persons and their relationships and institutions. The Reformation concept of 'callings' intended to indicate this but became distorted into social conservatism when it relied on 'created orders' as a second source of revelation, accepting uncritically the 'stations' determined by the prevailing powers. The challenge is to assert the changeability of the callings and to transform them (*TH*, 321–3, 338), to find a new 'ethic of the hope of faith' as a political theology (*RRF*, 218) and a new political hermeneutic by reading the Bible holding the same intention of liberation as those who originated the biblical traditions.[24]

The hope of new creation gathers up the limited hopes we entertain of an improvement of life. It relativises them, destroying their utopianism and presumption and their uncritical *naïveté* (*RRF*, 121): they do not contain the awaited salvation since hope cannot be reconciled with existence. They remain provisional, precursory and penultimate (*TH*, 37, 75). Christianity must engage in a public struggle for the truth without returning to its Constantinian status (*TH*, 182). Finality can only be realised in the future. When eschatology was lost, the 'temporally final' (*das Endzeitliche*) was replaced through Greek metaphysics by the 'conclusively final' (*das Endgültige*) (*TH*, 157). This shift to a theistic, all-powerful Super-Authority inevitably stifled human freedom. But when God is understood as the power of the future, he becomes the liberator, the foundation of freedom.[25] These divergent understandings give rise either to a community based on answers which are already known or one based upon questions which have yet to be answered because their answer lies in the future (*RRF*, 65; *EH*, 67), to either an absolutist or a dynamic view of truth.[26] Truth can only be provisionally anticipated in our present formulations and this preserves against the absolutism of dogma and its consequences.[27] The difference between these understandings is that between a Constantinian and an eschatological public theology.

RESURRECTION AND REVOLUTION

Meeks has argued that Moltmann's passion is the search for a mediating element which will overcome the modern dualist split between subject and object expressed in the division *inter alia* of self and society, church and world. This element Moltmann locates in the promissory history of God and an overarching eschatology.[28] His approach is profoundly revolutionary (*RRF*, vii) contrasting with that which sees Christianity making up for the 'loss of a centre' in contemporary society.[29] Hope concerns resurrection, the coming of the truly new, not just the eternal return of the same (*RRF*, 14, 21–2). This theology of contradiction undercuts any civil religion that unites institutions and God in a co-operative evolutionary alliance.[30] Christianity's role as state religion meant the denial of eschatology and the delegation of its revolutionary and critical effects to fanatical sects (*TH*, 15, 35; *RRF*, 23, 70–2, 172). Loss of eschatology made possible Christianity's adaptation to its environment (*TH*, 41). Eschatology recovers the revolutionary edge. Whereas for Yoder eschatology enabled the believer to do the one thing that was necessary, to follow Christ, for Moltmann it leads the believer to an infinite number of activities, mainly political, which anticipate the future. The future contradicts the present exposing its negativities and precipitating crisis for it (*TH*, 39, 86, 164, 225–6, 229), dividing it into that which passes away and that which is expected and sought (*TH*, 88, 103). Between the two, as with the dialectic of cross and resurrection, is a *creatio ex nihilo* by the word of God.

Moltmann shows the revolutionary potential in Christianity and calls for a break with sacral politics and sacrifice to the state-gods. Mission is pursued outside of the establishment by disengagement from the civil and political religions in whose name Jesus was crucified (*EH*, 58).[31] Such a revolution must avoid complicity with the world's violence and must depend upon truth not political power.[32] Yet, Moltmann supports the revolutionary urge to gain power and assume authority in order to effect transformation. He considers the problem of violence and non-violence 'illusory' since on occasion not to use violence permits a greater wrong. The use of violence becomes necessary, provided it is sufficiently proportionate and restrained not to jeopardise the revolutionary end through the means (*RRF*, 143–5).

THE REVOLUTIONARY CHURCH AND SOCIAL ORDER

Moltmann has been criticised for so absolutising revolution and stressing contradiction that he ignored secular culture's contribution to the reign of God,[33] for underplaying realised eschatology,[34] not accounting for the continuity of nature and grace[35] and leaving no room for evolutionary development.[36] An alternative revolutionary position questioned whether visions of the future not building upon extrapolations of the objective movement of the politics of freedom remain too futuristic and fail to take account of the operation of freedom in the world.[37] The theology of hope was abstractly critical of the present while offering few concrete alternatives.

Moltmann identified the complaint of a one-sidedness to the detriment of the present as the most common objection to his theology.[38] But his concern was the heretical *loss* of the revolutionary element in Christianity and of the breadth of God's justice. Theology to have saving power must be one-sided, critical and liberating;[39] and yet there is a difference between a dialectic and an antithesis. The theology of hope was aimed at a far-reaching process of revision in the church.[40] Partly under Bloch's influence, he was moving from a theology of being to one of act, from static and spatial metaphors to dynamic and temporal ones.[41] Reality is an historical process moving from the unfinished past toward a future fraught with newness.[42] This does not deny the possibility of continuity, as his distinction between *futurum* (that which is extrapolated out of present possibilities) and *adventus* (that which is other and new but can be *anticipated* in the present) shows. The possibilities of the present are awakened by the coming of the new and other and can only come into being because of it;[43] so the priority remains with the future. He located continuity not in the world but in God's faithfulness and promise and in the coming kingdom.[44]

THE ONTOLOGY OF THE STATE

Here it is appropriate to consider Moltmann's understanding of the state. Distrustful of metaphysics and of definitions that might tie down or betray the future *novum*, he has an 'eschatological resistance to conceptualisation',[45] preferring metaphor and image to discursive reasoning and conceptual analysis. He resists therefore a 'definition' of the state. Yet, as Galloway remarks, 'without responsible metaphysics even the resurrection turns into a metaphor'.[46]

Moltmann's approach reveals consistent aversion to the Lutheran sanctification of 'orders of creation' into an ideology of the *status quo*. In a 1960 article[47] he examined the 'ordinances of creation' in modern expositions. Althaus found divine ordinances within the movements of history and spoke of an 'unconditional essence' of the state, though not an unconditional constitution (cf. *Man*, 83). For Brunner there was within variable historical forms a fundamental structure of human life, communities, ordinances according to which we have to live and act. Künneth and Thielicke emphasised rather the 'ordinances of preservation'; between fall and eschaton are 'interim' or 'emergency' ordinances. This incorporated an historical element yet divided history into three mutations – the orders of creation, preservation and redemption, bracketing off the eschatological to the end. Bonhoeffer developed the 'mandates' as historical functions of God's lordship, places of obedience which continued to the end. This lost the normative character given to the ordinances by tradition and religious glorification, but his selection of 'mandates' could not be grounded biblically or anthropologically but only out of Western history.

In all these variations Moltmann found the concealing of real history and at the bottom of them all a 'timeless foundation under the quicksand of history which is to give a lasting foundation to the house of human society' (*HP*, 117–18). To overcome quasi-naturalistic thinking he argued that humanity does not have nature but history. The lasting is not an eternal reality beneath the flood of change and appearance nor a frame, outline or archetype. It must be an 'influential continuity' within history, grasped in terms of the goal and the end of history. We ask not about the eternal ground but the eschatological goal and historical openness of institutions. Even in its mild form as 'mandates', a theology of ordinances is too much a tool for the reactionary.[48]

Recognising that his scheme raised the opposite problem of lack of continuity, throwing us into a chronic state of alarm because there is no institutional foundation, Moltmann finds continuity in history itself. Ordinances appear as spheres in which God commands and humanity is obedient or disobedient (*HP*, 119–20); the divine command has constancy and continuity. The state is neither naturalistic order nor decisionistic institution but 'a process of the formation of political intention' (Barth) subject to criticism in the light of the coming *shalom* (*HP*, 125).

Moltmann's concern here was to overcome the submissive mentality of German theology and church-life rooted in a 'law mentality'.[49] His political theology was continuous with the Reformed emphasis on Christ's lordship in all dimensions of life (*EH*, 129, 140). His exposition of the state[50] conceives of the Calvinist concern as the search for a just and free social order. Public life, its culture, economy and government, is placed under the divine command, as indicated in Calvin's third use of the law (*EH*, 120–1, 127). The religious covenant originated the momentous theory of the state contract, abolishing the acceptance of hierarchy and requiring new levels of popular political participation. The state exists for the sake of humanity not vice versa (*EH*, 150). The *priesthood* of all believers became translated into their universal *kingship* establishing the people as created for lordship and not subjection. Furthermore, where a ruler failed the contract the people had a legitimate duty of resistance, even of violent resistance, laid upon them (*EH*, 128–9).

Moltmann's exposition of the Calvinist ethic is selective, emphasising its radical impact and potential for a revolutionary stance. We shall return to its significance in Chapter 8.

The Crucified God and Christian Social Existence

Theology of Hope developed the significance of Christ's resurrection while stressing the godforsakenness of the cross (e.g. *TH*, 223). *The Crucified God* shifts attention to a 'critical theology of the cross' after Auschwitz. Where hope heightened the contradiction between God and reality this stage locates contradiction within God himself at the cross.[51] As the theology of hope reflected the liberating mood of the early 1960s so the theology of the cross resonated with the disappointments of the late decade, returning to themes of forsakenness and desolation (*EG*, 14). Moltmann was also at this time developing political theology with Johann-Baptist Metz.[52] Bauckham discerns that in this phase the incarnational emphasis has God so participating in history as almost to make that involvement his whole being, becoming the human rather than the coming God. The stimulus of social criticism moves from hope to the cross.[53] Here is found the criterion of distinct identity, a 'critical theory' of church and society accommodating neither to *status quo* nor revolutionary ideologies and generating self-sacrificing involvement with others (*CG*, 16–18). Theology, even to revolutionising the concept of God, comes under the rubric *crux probat omnia* (CG 4, 7).

THE GOD OF THE CROSS

The question is: Are Christians motivated by the God who was crucified or by the idols of religion, race and class?[54] The true God exists in the event of the cross, revealed as he who suffers and gathers creation's suffering, even death, into himself. This 'breaks the spell of the old philosophical concept of God' (*CG*, 215). Traditional theism, and protest atheism its mirror opposite, are called into question. God is a suffering God (*CG*, 227). God does not change by necessity as the world does but is free to change himself and to subject himself to being changed by others.[55] Triunity, the early church's redefinition of God, is established by the cross as an event in the Spirit between Father and Son in which both are distinguished in separation and perfectly united in will (*CG*, 240–1). Subsequently, Moltmann will argue that the Spirit 'is the presence of God in the absence of the Father' (*HTG*, xvii). The remnant of the philosophical concept of *apatheia*, impassibility, must in the cross's light be removed from a truly Christian theology (*CG*, 243).

Moltmann develops Jewish sources to establish a doctrine of the *pathos* of God (*CG*, 270ff). This takes no further the philosophical understanding of evil but does enable us to find God involved in the world's suffering (*CG*, 229), incorporating himself into the theodicy question (*HP*, 43)[56] and finally transforming suffering into blessedness in his free interaction with the world as Father, Son and Spirit (*CG*, 278). The theodicy question thus remains open until a new creation gives the answer.[57] It is the open wound with which we live and survive (*TKG*, 49).

In Christ God has identified with the godless and abandoned (*CG*, 19). The church's identity is in imitation of him who abandoned himself and found his identity in the cross (*CG*, 16). This complex and speculative[58] theology of the cross also provides criticisms of church and society (*CG*, 41). Before examining these we note more fully the way of Jesus to the cross.

CHRIST ON THE WAY TO THE CROSS

Jesus' way to the cross resulted from conflict with the God of the Jewish law and the political gods of Rome (*CG*, 127). Jesus was crucified as a blasphemer and a rebel: he taught and enacted the belief that God was gracious beyond the law (*CG*, 132–3) and questioned the religious foundations of the *Pax Romana* (*CG*, 136, 143). Crucified in the name of the state gods (a political punishment for rebellion) (*CG*, 139), he is in no sense a non-political figure (*CG*, 144). Despite commonalities, Jesus' teaching on grace distinguished him from the zealous legalism of the Zealots which anticipated the final judgement on the lawless and advanced the kingdom through violence (*CG*, 138–9). Jesus did not impose upon his disciples an absolute principle of non-violence; rather, God's free grace distinguished his politics from the systems of domination and revenge (*CG*, 140).

Jesus anticipated the divine grace destined for the law-breaker. The friend of sinners overcame the pattern of friend and enemy; his company included deadly enemies. He opposed the idolatrous powers but summoned the oppressed to break the patterns of oppression through love rather than vengeance (*CG*, 141). He denied human beings the right to execute vengeance in their own cause, revealing God as incomprehensibly gracious not as a righteous avenger (*CG*, 143). This was a startlingly novel revolution, a 'humane revolt' (*CG*, 142). Grace led in a very different direction from national and imperial political religion.

POLITICAL RELIGION AND THE POLITICS OF THE CROSS

The cross, a political event, makes political theology necessary, provides for it a critical theory and leads to identification with the oppressed.[59] Even before Constantine the church had been adapting its theology to undergird the imperial hierarchy and become the unitive religion of the unitary state (*CG*, 325).[60] It shifted from dissent to persecution. Christianising the state religion, it became politicised by the state (*CG*, 322). Even where there is separation of church and state civic religions have developed to contribute to social integration and undergird the central authority. The church is expected to bear society's religion but imagines itself to be un-political (*CG*, 323). Where this happens the memory of the trial and cross of Jesus is suppressed since he was crucified in the name of political, bourgeois religion. The cross is bound to function critically and to destroy the idols of bourgeois religion (*CG*, 325). It protects theology itself from religion's misuse, the 'false consciousness' that led to the crucifixion.[61]

Political theology interprets 'the dangerous memory of the messianic message of Christ within the conditions of contemporary society in order to free man practically from the coercions of this society' (*EH*, 103). It intends not to reduce theology to a political ideology but to interpret it in terms of political discipleship. This means asking what its function is and what it accomplishes; it must issue in a critical theory (*CG*, 318). Early hierarchical theology foundered on the doctrine of the Trinity, which embraced the crucified Christ, and upon eschatology which prevented identification of *Pax Romana* and *Pax Christi*. Such criticism needs to be radicalised by recalling the trial and cross of Christ (*CG*, 326; *EH*, 107).[62] The cross brings the church into fellowship with the sufferers of its own time, reversing its values so that it becomes critical of the wealthy and powerful and demolishes political domination. God is stateless and classless, the God of the poor, the oppressed and the humiliated (*CG*, 328–9). The cross is inherently iconoclastic: only Christ crucified images the living God. This demands the limitation of political power and stimulates participation in political decisions. Christ was executed by political power so all political theory should seek to criticise the nature, limits and purpose of the state.[63]

God's identification with the rejected and forsaken clarifies how the 'vicious circles of death' found in poverty, violence, racial and cultural alienation, pollution and senselessness may be overcome. Socialism, democracy, emancipation, peace with nature and the discovery of meaning in life (*CG*, 332–5) are the interdependent 'symbols' which point to practice – 'symbols' because they are not ideological idols incapable of further definition or progress (*CG*, 337). They point to life in harmony with him who is revealed in the cross as the gracious God of the outcast.

CHURCH, SOCIETY AND GOD'S ACTIVITY

Moltmann considers two understandings of the relation of the church and the political. The *model of unburdening* (*CG*, 318–19) freed church and politics from each other. This doctrine of the two kingdoms, misunderstood as separating faith and politics, is a proper distinction between the two realms to avoid a state-church or church-state. Yet it risks separation to the point of negligence without bringing theological criteria to bear on political reason. The *model of correspondence* (*CG*, 319–20) sought reflections and correspondences in society of the liberation being realised in the church. Moltmann finds this approach idealising the church as society's model: 'Its liberation is already presupposed, whereas in practice it only becomes free with the society in which it lives' (*CG*, 320). Instead he identifies anticipations and promises in process of realisation in which God is *in* the world and the eschatological *in* the historical. God is present in a history of liberation, in 'transformations of God' whose criterion is identification with the crucified Christ and whose goal is God's indwelling of the new creation towards which the Trinitarian process in history moves (*CG*, 321). Reality becomes a sacrament bearing God's presence and betokening his coming omnipresence parallel to but not replacing God's presence in the sacraments (*CG*, 337).

Meeks' exposition of Moltmann finds here a weak ecclesiology.[64] Political theology requires a community to mediate God's eschatological act, yet Moltmann assimilates the church to mission in a way which makes the church nothing within itself, leaving the mission disincarnate. In responding to the totality of God's mission and its worldly tendencies, Moltmann risks losing sight of the church which cannot be exhaustively construed as mission.[65]

REVOLUTION, THE CROSS AND VIOLENCE

We have noted Moltmann's qualified acceptance of revolutionary violence. His essay 'Racism and the Right to Resist' distinguishes between violence, power and domination (*EH*, 137). *Power* is the means to obtain something by force. It must be used lawfully else it becomes violence: in the political domain power is inevitable and needs public justification. Laws controlling it must be just. *Violence* connotes abuse of power and is not usually applied to its legitimate and legal exercise. However, *justified* 'violence' can be called power whereas the unjustified exercise of 'power' becomes naked violence. The problem of violence is not one of alternatives since all are implicated in its use but of criteria to govern power's justifiable and unjustifiable uses. *Domination* remains unclearly defined by Moltmann but appears to be the unjustified and unaccountable use of power and so akin to violence (*EH*, 138).

For others' sake and without claiming the sanction of a 'just revolution', guilt might sometimes be accepted in taking violent action (*EH*, 142).[66] Those who justify repressive or conserving violence while urging pacifism on the oppressed are imprisoned by ruling class ideology (*EH*, 132, 136). Revolutionary violence cannot be justified but it can be answered for (*EH*, 143). Hunsinger criticises Moltmann for contradicting here his own theology of the cross, indeed of pursuing this discussion without proper reference to the cross. Moltmann argues, following Bonhoeffer, that love risks becoming guilty in order to save and finds in the cross the idea that responsible action requires the assumption of guilt (*EH*, 142). Yet this contradicts the way of the cross as the *refusal* to employ violence, overcoming through suffering endured not inflicted. Hunsinger notes Moltmann's identification of non-violence with non-resistance and the desire for moral purity. He equates revolution with tyrannicide without seeing tyrannicide's qualitative distinction from indiscriminate guerrilla warfare. Non-violence, claims Hunsinger, is the political implication of the cross, not illusory but of fundamental importance. Moltmann makes the cross a formal not material principle, indicating with whom we are to identify without specifying the identification's content.[67] Likewise, Grässer criticises Moltmann for claiming that non-violence is feasible for addressing political problems only in a domination free context (e.g. *EH*, 136). This neglects the possibility of suffering, a remarkable omission when talking of a *theologia crucis*.[68] Jesus' death does not validate violence. It is the end of all ways that search for salvation politically.[69]

Moltmann recognises that discipleship involves non-violence[70] but assumes that where social and political issues are a matter of power this principle is not final. Non-violence is the source of direction and provides criteria for the limiting of force but will be modified by the situation and possibly set aside (*EH*, 136–8).[71] Yet, as Wiebe indicates, the goal of Christian action cannot by-pass Jesus and still lie in the direction of the eschaton he reveals.[72] Wiebe further criticises Moltmann for arguing that without participation in power and economic decision-making the just struggle of the oppressed cannot be achieved (*EH*, 135). Moltmann assumes that change comes from the top down, by what Yoder calls 'gaining the levers of power'.[73] Yet Moltmann is surely correct to point out that whatever the original stimulus to change, the centres of economic and political power must in due course be affected if justice is to be done.

The Church in the Spirit and the Missio Dei

The Crucified God contained a minimal theology of the Spirit, a deficiency Moltmann next sought to remedy. The diminution of the Spirit's personhood is characteristic of Western theology and a concomitant of a mission theology in which Father and Son send the Spirit with no sending by the

Spirit in relation to the Father and the Son. To overcome this he emphases the historical and eschatological glorification by the Spirit of Father and Son.[74] This stage represents the movement to Pentecost via Easter and Good Friday. *The Church in the Power of the Spirit* is radical, missionary and ecumenical 'messianic ecclesiology' (*CPS*, xv; *OC*, 9). Moltmann advocates amidst the decline of the *corpus christianum* (*CPS*, 8–10) the recovery of the *Gemeinde* as the way for the future, the 'fellowship church' and the church's proper form (*CPS*, xvi; *OC*, 9).

THE CHURCH IN THE HISTORY OF THE SPIRIT

The church must be charismatically understood (*CPS*, 36), located in the movement of the Spirit from the Father and the Son through history towards the consummation (*CPS*, 2). Christology forms ecclesiology (*CPS*, 5–6). Early Christianity's 'primal springs' were in Christ (*CPS*, xiii, xv, 5, 8), the church's sole Lord and criterion (*FC*, 106). It is also formed by the future, existing relationally in the Trinitarian history of God, directed messianically in the Spirit towards the unification and glorification of all things (*CPS*, 20, 28).

The church's particularity must be seen within a universal context. The world's salvation will not come through the church but the church's salvation through the salvation of the world. God is an open Trinity, open to humanity, the world and time, whose goal is the eschatological unity of all being within himself (*CPS*, 55–6). He has separated himself from himself to go out into all creation and bring all things to a unity and final glory through his own progress toward becoming one again (*CPS*, 60–2). God himself enters into new experience, making himself vulnerable, taking suffering and death upon himself in order to heal. The church is that community created and 'administered' by the Spirit in fulfilling this mission (*CPS*, 64–5). It is the place where the Spirit's manifestation takes place and has no independent ontology (*CPS*, 69). This actualistic vision preserves the church's particularity while relativising it within the Spirit's saving activities.

THE CHURCH AS THE MESSIANIC COMMUNITY

Jesus Christ is the crucified one, by whom the church's authenticity is tested, and the risen one who has gone before mortals, towards whom it is moving. The church exists between remembrance and hope (*CPS*, 75). There is no definition of the church in itself. It is understood within the Trinitarian movement of God's history (*CPS*, 121). It exists for the world but living between the powers of past oppression and future liberation does so in conflict with society. The 'exodus church' does not emigrate from society but from what is passing away into what is coming, from slavery to freedom (*CPS*, 83–4). Alienated from its environment by following Christ's way, it exists as a sign of promise (*CPS*, 68). It needs rescuing from its self-image as a bulwark against chaos for its revolutionary vocation (*CPS*, 16, 42–7;

FC, 106). This critical stance of the church follows that created by eschatology and the iconoclasm of the cross.

Originating in the crucified Jesus (*CPS*, 86), the church lives his life of grace, loving enemies and repaying evil with good (*CPS*, 88). It is a society of those who share the friendship of Jesus, a circle others may enter (*CPS*, 116ff; *OC*, 50ff). It is inescapably political (*CPS*, 15ff), rejecting the political idolatry which crucified Jesus and taking its place amongst the outcasts (*CPS*, 91). The resurrection frees the church to be a radical, renewing and redeeming alternative to power structures built upon the threat of death (*CPS*, 98). The exaltation of the crucified leads to revaluation of all values (*CPS*, 102), the abolition of all earthly power in favour of the brotherhood of all (*CPS*, 104). So the church becomes a community of liberation and a celebration of the feast without end (*CPS*, 108).

Ubi Christus ibi ecclesia: Christ is present in the church's mission, sacraments and fellowship. Yet he is present also in the poor (Matthew 25). The true church is where Christ is, among the downtrodden, the sick and the captives (*FC*, 57, 106).[75] This double presence is needed if it is to be the church of the crucified Christ whose appearance it awaits (*CPS*, 129, 132).

THE CHURCH AND ITS PARTNERS IN THE KINGDOM

Finding Christ beyond the boundaries of the church requires us to reconceive God's saving activity. The church is not the whole but is related through Christ to the whole (*CPS*, 348–51). God's universal love is not proclaimed through claims to absoluteness but through co-operation and open-minded dialogue, leading not to the lordship of the church but to imitation of the lordship of the Christ who came to serve (*EH*, 177). The church has partners in movement towards the future horizon who are not the church and will never become the church (*CPS*, 134), specifically Israel, the world religions and the 'processes of life'. Hope for these partners may nevertheless be entertained. Enmeshed in life's relationships the church's salvation is finally related to theirs.

Israel is the church's enduring partner and the paradigm for all other partnerships (*CPS*, 135). Moltmann carries this to the point of saying that specific Christian mission to the Jews is inappropriate. Where Israel and her Scriptures are forgotten the church becomes paganised, as in the assimilation to national identity experienced in the Empire and since, and in pretensions to ecclesiastical absoluteness (*CPS*, 139). Israel is the enduring reminder of the church's provisional nature and unfulfilled existence and so renders absolutism or triumphalism impossible in an unredeemed world (*CPS*, 136–7, 138–9, 148, 153). She is both historically and theologically necessary for the church with an independent 'call to salvation' which endures to the *parousia* (*CPS*, 138, 144). Her No to Christ was a consequence of God's hardening and functionally necessary in God's purpose of salvation.[76] Her existence is a paradoxical token of God's judgement, a reminder of the incomplete nature of redemption and an earnest of future hope (*CPS*, 145, 148–9).

This insight stimulates examination of Christian attitudes to other faiths and historical movements. The divine reconciler reconciles those of whatever religion. It is not that there is salvation outside the church but that there is no church outside the salvation which Christ brings to all (*CPS*, 153–4). This is not the sceptical tolerance or disguised absolutism of Enlightenment relativism presupposing some higher watchtower from which the religions might be directed to work to a particular end (*CPS*, 156–7). It is a productive tolerance in which religious traditions convinced of their own truth deal nobly with each other. Yet where relativism and tolerance refer to a relationality from which something beneficial can emerge their truth can be acknowledged. The Christian mission has a quantitative aim to further faith and church growth and a qualitative aim in which through dialogue an alteration in the atmosphere of life may be achieved and common human problems addressed (*CPS*, 152, 159).

Moltmann affirms both that there is salvation outside the church and that there is no salvation outside of Christ.[77] He envisages the emergence of belief in Jesus true to the religious and cultural contexts from which it comes, and the charismatic quickening of different religious gifts and potentialities for God's kingdom (*CPS*, 162). The Christian vocation is to prepare the way for the coming messianic redemption. All culture and religion can be charismatically changed in the Spirit's power. This does not imply the absorption of the religions into the church but their messianic redirection (*CPS*, 163).

The principle we see in Israel is recapitulated in what was previously called the 'secular order' but which because of this term's rigidity and associations with Christendom Moltmann calls the 'world processes'. Here it is a question of economic, political and cultural institutions to which the church adapts as its partners in living relationship (*CPS*, 163–4). The church contributes through its members' secular responsibilities and aims at economic and cultural symbiosis (*CPS*, 169–70), a universal 'socialism' in relations between humans and with the earth (*CPS*, 175) and democratic participation (*CPS*, 177). Christianity encourages forms of government which serve human fellowship, rights and dignity. Historically it contributed to the de-sacralising of the emperor cult, the relegation of the political order at the Reformation to the area of welfare rather than salvation and, through the Puritans, to the abolition of the divine right of kings in favour of a contract or constitution of free citizens. This trend of secularisation, desacralisation and democratisation must be continued. In this sense the secularity of the state (*CPS*, 168), its freeing from surrogate religious and ideological glorification to be what it actually is, is welcomed (HP, 106–7). The state is made for man (*CPS*, 179). It is to serve human rights and duties as a step towards recognising the rights of all humanity and towards world peace (*CPS*, 181–2). Christianity has a duty to help form the political order and not merely to live in it (*CPS*, 178) and states have a duty to enforce human rights (*CPS*, 176, 178, 181).

Through Christ life stands in the sunrise of Christ's new day. Mediations of the kingdom are present, recognised by taking bearings from the history and mission of Jesus (*CPS*, 192, 194–5). Yet there is a limit to messianic activity in the present age, the limit of death, broken in principle but not yet in fact. Till the resurrection Christian faith works to encourage everything which ministers to life and against everything that disseminates death (*CPS*, 195–6).

THE CHURCH, ITS ESSENCE AND ITS PRACTICES

Moltmann's ecclesiology reconceives church life along free church lines. The messianic community exists in the presence and process of the Spirit (*CPS*, 197). The sending of the Spirit is the sacrament of the kingdom. The church lives in the act of proclamation (*CPS*, 206), the happening of which is the presence of the Spirit (*CPS*, 220). It is a free fellowship of persons living messianically and possessing liberating power (*CPS*, 224–6). It witnesses through its social and political form before it utters a word (*PP*, 156–7).

The Constantinian establishment of the church pushed aside the cross of the Christ crucified by the state and suspended the Sermon on the Mount (*CPS*, 92, 325; *PP*, 158). It led to loss of the church's visible form, to the persecution of Jews and dissenters as irreligious destroyers of society (*CPS*, 136). The millennium was no longer the criticism of all government but was identified with the *corpus christianum*. Even the Reformation, despite its rediscovery of the congregation, retained the structure and organisation of the imperial church and simply resolved into state churches operating with the principle *cuius regio, eius religio* (*CPS*, 318–19; *PP*, 79–80). They lost their evangelistic and missionary impetus only to recover it when the *corpus christianum* was beginning to decay (*CPS*, 8–9). The modern German church functions as an institution for the religious care of the people and the passive membership is the basis on which it operates. A personally committed membership would change its character. It only incidentally has anything to do with Christ. It offers cheap grace (*PP*, 159).

The existing church cannot offer itself as a model society because its hierarchical constitution contradicts the kingdom of God. Because every direct intervention by the church in economics, politics and culture has carried the suspicion that it is serving its own interests, the church ought not to claim direct power in secular matters (*CPS*, 166). Yet its character as the messianic community precludes withdrawal (*CPS*, 225). Where the messianic element is neglected the mainstream church itself becomes sectarian. This inevitably evokes the Christianity of reform (*CPS*, 321, 325), yet the sects run the danger of suppressing openness in mission (*CPS*, 318) and live from their conflict with the major churches. A form of the church is needed which is authentic in the present and which is open to the world. A double strategy is advocated by some in which the voluntary minority sets the pace and the majority becomes the means for translating the witness of the minority into social impact (*CPS*, 326). But Moltmann envisages here the committed core being stifled by the silent majority (*CPS*, 333). Recovery of the church as *Gemeinde* provides the impetus for a people's church worthy of the name and for democratic social reconstruction (*CPS*, 261ff, 330; *OC*, 15, 50ff, 60ff). The community of Christians, coming together voluntarily, can become the source of new initiatives for life and living (*PP*, 135). This is the language of Anabaptism.

Since faith comes through response to the word and not family ties, Moltmann rejects infant baptism as a pillar of the *corpus christianum* (*CPS*, 228–229). He advocates confessor baptism (*CPS*, 240–2), the Lord's Supper as an open meal (*CPS*, 245), the charismatic nature of the congregation (*CPS*, 289), a non-hierarchical, non-élitist and representative view of ministry which liberates the people (*CPS*, 302–9) and a consultative, collaborative structure of inter-church relations (*CPS*, 310–11). All of this indicates a shift to an institutionality rooted in covenant and relationship[78] and is evidence of Moltmann's position as a '"free-church person" in the midst of a *Volkskirche*'.[79] The proximity to Anabaptist ecclesiology is striking and becomes explicit:

> [I]t seems to me that the 'future of the Reformation' does not lie on the right wing with its Catholic tendencies but on the so-called left wing of the Reformation, namely, with those who through ever new attempts and under constant persecutions have sought to realize 'the congregation'. They were called 'Schwärmer' and 'baptists' and 'sectarians', and they were rejected. But they sought in truth 'the radical Reformation'... [T]he future of the church of Christ lies in principle on this wing of the Reformation because the widely unknown and uninhabited land of 'the congregation' is found here (*OC*, 117).

Elaborating this claim, and although he at no point displays a detailed knowledge of Anabaptism, Moltmann goes on to specify the principles of believers' baptism, the visible and voluntary assembly of believers, the dissolving of the union of 'throne and altar' particularly expressed by refusal to sanctify military service and weapons, the rejection of all forms of violence, and radical discipleship as the content of this vision.[80] Yet he is also critical of this tradition, seeing that it can function as a religious 'free market' attracting like to like and requiring its pastors to be entertainers of the congregation (*PP*, 160–2). Churches are required which are the subjects of their own history, confessing churches which are liberating and prophetic communities (*PP*, 163–6).

Summary and Reflections

Moltmann's disavowal of *Constantinianism* is clear, cogent and repeated. In addition, he rejects absolutist notions of the church while asserting Christ's uniqueness at every stage. Yet even the claims for Christ are only finally verifiable eschatologically. The church must trust God's truth more than its own representation of it (*TT*, 46).

Despite this, A. R. Eckhardt accuses Moltmann of a pre-1933 attitude to the Jews even in *The Crucified God*. For Eckhardt, the Holocaust was only made possible because of absolute claims and loyalties. In Moltmann that very triumphalism and absolutism continued in the claims made for cross and resurrection.[81] The trinitarianisation of Auschwitz was a blasphemy to those who died and who would have resisted this doctrine to the uttermost. Moltmann is guilty of a 'postponed' or 'proleptic' triumphalism which affects living relations with Jews today. The very symbol of the cross that Moltmann claims as liberating is understood by Jews as a symbol of oppression.[82] So, the historical fate of Christianity has in effect destroyed the possibility of traditional Christian affirmations which now are inextricably captive to ideology. Christians need to be freed from the 'idolatry of triumphing over others' in order that they may accept them. It is not possible to say that Jesus is Messiah without thereby damning the Jews. With Ruether Eckhardt believes that the Christian affirmation must be relativised in order to be freed of religious imperialism. According to Ruether: 'The self-infinitizing of the messianic sect that empowers itself to conquer all mankind in the name of the universal' is essentially 'a false messianism. What Christianity has in Jesus is not the Messiah but a Jew who hoped for the coming of the Kingdom of God and who died in that hope'.[83]

Although Eckhardt's article has been judged exaggerated, in effect claiming that Christianity is inherently anti-Semitic,[84] it illustrates the difficulty of making final claims for Christ in a post-Constantinian context which hears such language as triumphalist imperialism. It will be necessary to return to this issue in the final chapter.

Moltmann is in danger of neglecting the *centrality of the church* by undervaluing its role in mediating Christ sacramentally to the world.[85] Certainly, he relativises the church as God's agent even while acknowledging its necessity.[86] But he also subordinates the church to history in the process of subordinating it to the kingdom. In claiming that the church has no independent ontology and exists in the Spirit on the way to the fulfilment of God's mission, the world assumes priority over the church as the arena of God's activity. Politics becomes the horizon. There is a tension here because he both loses the church in the liberating history of God and presents it in his later theology as a contrast society with a concrete existence.[87]

The question remains whether in rejecting Constantinianism, Moltmann has smuggled it in by the back door, subordinating God's activity in the church to that in the world. There is a proper ecclesiocentricity to the Christian understanding of history which sees the Spirit primarily at work within the church and allows it a determinative and systematic role. Effective mission is made concrete in a congregation which becomes distinct in order to embody the kingdom on its way to becoming world-wide. Particularity is the presupposition for the reign of God reaching all people.[88] The church's upbuilding must therefore remain of primary importance as the embodiment of the kingdom and the means of transformation whereas a Christianity aimed immediately at the transformation of society can become dissipated and secularised.[89]

We have noted Moltmann's resistance to metaphysical thinking and its implications for the *ontology of the state*. Stephen Sykes cites Moltmann as the outstanding example of modern theology's reluctance to talk about power which, Sykes claims, is a *post factum* justification for loss of political power.[90] He argues that throughout Moltmann's work the concept of power almost always connotes domination, with authority and obedience contrasted with consensus and harmony, and calls for a realistic appraisal which reckons with the fact of power in the church and the need for governmental power in the world to enable harmony.[91]

Certainly, Moltmann's discussion of the state has concentrated on its progressive reform. The state is a process rather than a definable reality. This perhaps is one reason why Moltmann attracts the criticism of imprecision in developing his revolutionary praxis. He deals with generalities and limited options without developing a rigorous theological critique of the areas he identifies.[92] All of this is likely to remain vague without greater definition of the state. This need not entail uncritical legitimation of the state, as the 'orders of creation' tended to do, since it could be approached by means of reflection on human and structural fallenness.

Moltmann does not espouse a doctrine of human progress nor does he lack a theology of wrath and atonement.[93] But he believes he follows Christ in asserting that because on the cross Christ took judgement on himself the theme of the 'day of vengeance for our God' must be omitted (*PP*, 74). It is appropriate to ask whether the motif of hope, the almost Hegelian triumph of grace and the history of liberation, and the focus on suffering in explicating the cross may have become so dominant as to mute the themes of sin and fall. Despite all his qualifications and due recognition of the resurrection and the Spirit as its determining powers, there is in Moltmann a sense of inevitability in the progress towards the kingdom of God. This needs to be balanced with, for instance, Yoder's or Reinhold Niebuhr's more cautious approaches. Moltmann contrasts Niebuhr's Protestant pessimism about sin with the 'optimism of grace' (*HTG*, 45).

The following chapter examines further stages of Moltmann's theology and will return to these criticisms and develop others.

NOTES

1   Moltmann, Foreword to R. J. Bauckham, *Moltmann: Messianic Theology in the Making* (Basingstoke: Marshall–Pickering, 1987), vi–vii.

2   A. Fierro, *The Militant Gospel: An Analysis of Contemporary Political Theologies* (London: SCM Press, 1977), 171–2.

3   A. D. Galloway, 'The New Hegelians', *RS* 8:4 (1972), 270.

4   R. J. Bauckham, 'Moltmann's *Theology of Hope* Revisited', *SJT* 42:2 (1989), 199.

5   G. Hunsinger, 'The Crucified God and the Political Theology of Violence: A Critical Survey of Jürgen Moltmann's Thought' Part 1, *THJ* 14:3 (1973), 277–8; A. D. Galloway, Review of *The Church in the Power of the Spirit* in *SJT* 32:1 (1979), 75; P. F. Momose, *Kreuzestheologie: Eine Auseinandersetzung mit Jürgen Moltmann* (Freiburg: Herder, 1978), 6; J. B. Webster, 'Jürgen Moltmann: Trinity and Suffering', *Evangel*, Summer 1985, 4, 6; A. E. McGrath, *The Making of Modern German Christology* (Oxford: Basil Blackwell, 1986), 193.

6   Bauckham, *Moltmann*, ix.

7   'Antwort auf die Kritik an 'Der gekreuzigte Gott' in M. Welker (ed.), *Diskussion über Jürgen Moltmanns Buch 'Der gekreuzigte Gott'* (Munich: Chr. Kaiser Verlag, 1979), 168; Bauckham, *Moltmann*, ix–x.

8   'Herrschaft Christi und soziale Wirklichkeit nach Dietrich Bonhoeffer', *Theologische Existenz Heute* Neue Folge 71 (1959), 5–61; 'Die Wirklichkeit der Welt und Gottes konkretes Gebot nach Dietrich Bonhoeffer' in E. Bethge (ed.), *Die Mündige Welt III* (Munich, 1960), 42–67.

9   'Prädestination und Heilsgeschichte bei Moyse Amyraut: Ein Beitrag zur Geschichte der reformierten Theologie zwischen Orthodoxie und Aufklärung', *ZfK* 65/66 (1953–54), 270–303; 'Zur Bedeutung des Petrus Ramus für Philosophie und Theologie in Calvinismus', *ZfK* 68 (1957), 295–318; 'Jacob Brocard als Vorläufer der Reich-Gottes-Theologie und der symbolisch-prophetischen Schriftauslegung des Johann Coccejus', *ZfK* 71 (1960), 110–29; *Prädestination und Perseveranz* (Neukirchen: Neukirchener Verlag, 1961); Article: 'Perseverance', A. Richardson and J. Bowden (eds.), *A New Dictionary of Christian Theology* (London: SCM Press, 1983), 441–2.

10 'Grundzüge mystischer Theologie bei Gerhard Tersteegen', *EvTh* 16:5 (1956), 205–24; 'Geschichtstheologie und pietistisches Menschenbild bei Johann Coccejus und Theodor Undereyck', *EvTh* 19:8 (1959), 343–61 cp. 'Theology of Mystical Experience', *SJT* 32:6 (1979), 501–20; 'Teresa of Avila and Martin Luther: The Turn to the Mysticism of the Cross', *SIR* 13 (1984), 265–78.

11 J. Moltmann (ed.), *Die Anfänge der Dialektischen Theologie* (Munich: Chr. Kaiser Verlag, 1966 [Teil 1] and 1967 [Teil 2]).

12 Momose, *Kreuzestheologie*, 26–30.

13 Bauckham, *Moltmann*, 3.

14 M. D. Meeks, *Origins of the Theology of Hope* (Philadelphia: Fortress Press, 1974),

xiii.

15 W. J. Hill, *The Three-Personed God: The Trinity as a Mystery of Salvation* (Washington DC: Catholic University Press of America, 1982), 167.

16 See Bauckham, *Moltmann* and (especially) Meeks, *Origins*; F. P. Fiorenza, 'Dialectical Theology and Hope' Part 1, *THJ* 9:2 (1968), 143–63, Part 2, 9:4 (1968), 384–99 and Part 3, 10:1 (1969), 26–42; G. O'Collins, 'The Principle and Theology of Hope' *SJT* 21:2 (1968), 129–44; G. O'Collins, 'Spes Quaerens Intellectum' *Interpretation* 22 (1968), 36–52; Momose, *Kreuzestheologie*, 23–43; G. C. Chapman, 'Jürgen Moltmann and the Christian Dialogue with Marxism', *JES* 18:3 (1981), 435–50; See also Moltmann, 'Ernst Bloch: Messianismus und Marxismus – Einführende Bemerkungen zum "Prinzip Hoffnung"', *Kirche in der Zeit* 15:71 (1959), *EH*, 30–59.

17 See also 'Stations et Signaux: Coup d'oeil retrospectif sur mon cheminement personnel de ces dix dernières années', *Études théologiques et religieuses* 46:4 (1971), 357–63; 'Communities of Faith and Radical Discipleship: An Interview with Jürgen Moltmann' (conducted by Miroslav Volf), *CC* 100 (1983), 246–9.

18 Moltmann, 'The Future as Threat and Opportunity' in D. R. Cutler (ed.), *The Religious Situation* (Boston: Beacon Press, 1969), 940, 926–7.

19 Ibid., 933–994; Meeks, *Origins*, x.

20 Article: 'Hope' in Richardson and Bowden (eds.), *Dictionary*, 271.

21 'The Future as Threat and Opportunity', 934.

22 Moltmann laments the choice made by the German churches after World War II to return to institutional forms as established churches arguing that this created vagueness and loss of identity. It is difficult to become a Christian when through milieu and social pressure you already are one. E.g.: 'The Future as Threat and Opportunity', 923–4.

23 'Die Kirche als Faktor einer kommenden Weltgemeinschaft', *Kirche in der Zeit* 21:7 (1966), 310.

24 M. D. Meeks, 'Foreword' to *EH*, xiii; Bauckham *Moltmann*, 140.

25 'Introduction à la théologie de l'espérance', *Études théologiques et religieuses* 46:4 (1971), 405–6.

26 L. Swidler, 'Foreword' to P. Lapide and J. Moltmann, *Jewish Monotheism and Christian Trinitarian Doctrine* (Philadelphia: Fortress Press, 1981), 9.

27 M. R. Tripole, 'Ecclesiological Developments in Moltmann's Theology of Hope' *TS* 34 (1973), 34–5.

28 Meeks, *Origins*, 8–9.

29 'The Future as Threat and Opportunity', 921.

30 J. A. Irish, 'Moltmann's Theology of Contradiction', *ThT* 32 (1975–76), 21.

31 'Introduction à la théologie de l'espérance', 413–14.

32 'The Theology of Revolution', *New Christian*, 12 December 1968, 9–10.

33 Migliore, 'Biblical Eschatology and Political Hermeneutics', 117–18; L. Gilkey, 'The Contribution of Culture to the Reign of God' in M. Muckenhirn (ed.), *The Future as the Presence of Shared Hope* (New York: Sheed and Ward, 1968), 54; G. C. Chapman, 'Moltmann's Vision of Man', *ATR* 56 (1974), 310–11.

34 O'Collins, 'Spes Quaerens Intellectum', 48. O'Collins points out that the Fourth Gospel is nowhere cited in *TH*.

35 Momose, *Kreuzestheologie*, 144, see also, 156–9.

36 J. Macquarrie, *Christian Hope* (London and Oxford: Mowbrays, 1978), 106; R. J.

Bauckham, 'Jürgen Moltmann' in D. Ford (ed.), *The Modern Theologians* (Oxford: Blackwell, 1989), 308.

37 R. Alves, *A Theology of Human Hope* (Wheathampstead: Anthony Clare Books, 1975), 102; G. C. Chapman, 'Black Theology and Theology of Hope: What have they to say to each other?', *USQR* 29:2 (1974), 112, 118–19.

38 'Antwort auf die Kritik der Theologie der Hoffnung' in W. D. Marsch (ed.), *Diskussion über die 'Theologie der Hoffnung' von Jürgen Moltmann* (Munich: Chr. Kaiser Verlag, 1967), 205.

39 'The Liberation of Oppressors', *JTSA* 26 (1979), 25.

40 'Antwort auf die Kritik der Theologie der Hoffnung', 209, 229.

41 Hunsinger, 'The Crucified God', 278.

42 Chapman, 'Jürgen Moltmann and the Christian Dialogue with Marxism', 439.

43 'Antwort auf die Kritik der Theologie der Hoffnung', 212–13.

44 'Nachwort' to Momose, *Kreuzestheologie*, 181.

45 Chapman, 'Moltmann's Vision of Man', 314, 322, 328; See also Hill, *Three-Personed God*, 168.

46 Galloway, 'Review of *The Church in the Power of the Spirit*', 75.

47 'The Understanding of History in Christian Social Ethics': *HP*, 101–29

48 G. C. Chapman, 'Hope and the ethics of formation: Moltmann as an interpreter of Bonhoeffer' *SJR* 12:4 (1983), 451, 457.

49 Meeks, 'Foreword' to *EH*, xiv.

50 'The Ethic of Calvinism', *EH*, 119–30.

51 J. Niewiadomski, *Die Zweideutigkeit von Gott und Welt in J. Moltmanns Theologien* (Innsbruck-Wien-München: Tyrolia Verlag, 1982), 10.

52 See J.-B. Metz, *Theology of the World* (London: Burns and Oates, 1969).

53 R. J. Bauckham, 'Moltmann's Eschatology of the Cross', *SJT* 30:4 (1977), 310–11.

54 Moltmann, 'The "Crucified God": A Trinitarian Theology of the Cross', *Interpretation* 26 (1972), 278; 'The "Crucified God": God and the Trinity Today', *Concilium 8:6 Church and World* (London: Burns and Oates, 1972), 26.

55 'The "Crucified God": A Trinitarian Theology of the Cross', 287. This is the crucial point in responding to Karl Rahner's comment that it does not help humanity if God is in the same predicament: *HTG*, 122–24.

56 R. J. Bauckham, 'Theodicy from Ivan Karamazov to Moltmann', *MT* 4:1 (1987), 83–97; G. M. Jantzen, 'Christian Hope and Jesus' Despair', *KTR* 5:1 (1982), 1–7.

57 'Theodicy', A. Richardson and J. Bowden (eds.), *Dictionary*, 565. Theology cannot escape the responsibility of also providing a theodicy along traditional lines: P. S. Maitland-Cullen, 'The Theodicy Problem in the Theology of Jürgen Moltmann'. PhD, Edinburgh, 1990, 362–4,

58 R. Strunk, 'Diskussion über *Der Gekreuzigte Gott*', *EvTh* 41:1 (1981), 92.

59 G. Hunsinger, 'The Crucified God and the Political Theology of Violence: A Critical Survey of Jürgen Moltmann's Recent Thought: (2)', *THJ* 14:3 (1973), 379.

60 See also 'The Cross and Civil Religion' in J. Moltmann et al, *Religion and Political Society* (New York and London: Harper and Row, 1974), 18–24.

61 Moltmann, *Umkehr zur Zukunft* (Munich: Chr. Kaiser Verlag, 1970), 20.

62 'The Cross and Civil Religion', 24–7.

63 Ibid., 40.

64 Meeks, *Origins*, 160–1.

65 Ibid., 161–2.

66 *Umkehr zur Zukunft*, 55.
67 Hunsinger, 'The Crucified God (2)', 393–4. Moltmann, while appreciating Hunsinger's articles, objected that he was not seeking to develop a theology of violence, as Hunsinger's title suggests, but to deal with the issue as a question of conscience: 'Antwort auf die Kritik an "Der gekreuzigte Gott"', 189 n. 42.
68 E. Grässer, '"Der politisch gekreuzigte Christus": Kritische Anmerkungen zu einer politischen Hermeneutik des Evangeliums', *ZNW* 62 (1971), 290–1.
69 Ibid., 291.
70 in T. R. Runyon (ed.), *Hope for the Church: Moltmann in Dialogue with Practical Theology* (Nashville: Abingdon, 1979), 132 cited by B. Wiebe 'Revolution as an Issue in Theology: Jürgen Moltmann', *RQ* 26 (1983), 111.
71 Wiebe, 'Revolution as an Issue', 112.
72 Ibid., 118; N. Young, *Creator, Creation and Faith* (London: Collins, 1976), 162–3.
73 Wiebe, 'Revolution', 116, 118. In his later writings Moltmann becomes more critical of social revolutionaries: Chapman 'Black Theology and Theology of Hope', 110, 127.
74 'Antwort auf die Kritik an "Der gekreuzigte Gott"', 186–7.
75 The category of the 'poor' is fundamental for Moltmann. Later he identifies the poor as the true 'anonymous Christians': *HTG*, 122. Yet the term is used in abstraction and simplistically as though there are only two classes of people without regard to the complex patterns of poverty and oppression: Rasmusson, *The Church as Polis*, 77; M. R. Tripole believes the term refers to Jesus' own disciples and not a 'second brotherhood' beyond, and redefining, the church: 'A Church for the Poor and the World: At Issue with Moltmann's Ecclesiology', *TS* 42 (1981), 649–50, 653–4.
76 *Jewish Monotheism and Christian Trinitarian Doctrine*, 78, 88–9.
77 Momose, *Kreuzestheologie*, 136. Cf. H. Küng, 'Die Religionen als Frage an die Theologie des Kreuzes', *EvTh* 33:4 (1973), 401–23.
78 Moltmann, 'Nachwort' to Momose, *Kreuzestheologie*, 182.
79 'The Challenge of Religion in the '80s' in J. M. Wall (ed.), *Theologians in Transition* (New York: Crossroad, 1981), 110.
80 'Communities of Faith and Radical Discipleship', 248.
81 A. R. Eckhardt, 'Jürgen Moltmann, the Jewish People, and the Holocaust', *JAAR* 44:4 (1976), 682–3.
82 Ibid., 684–5, 689.
83 Ibid., 691 referring to R. R. Ruether, *Faith and Fratricide: The Theological Roots of Anti-Semitism* (New York: Seabury Press, 1974), 246. The specific quotation is from 'Christian–Jewish Dialogue: New Interpretations', *ADL Bulletin* 5 (1973), 4.
84 Bauckham, *Moltmann*, 154 n. 16; J. Pawlikowski, 'The Holocaust and Contemporary Christology' in E. S. Fiorenza and D. Tracy (eds.), *Concilium 175: The Holocaust as Interruption* (Edinburgh: T. and T. Clark, 1984), 47.
85 Momose, *Kreuzestheologie*, 163.
86 M. D. Meeks, 'A Handbook for the Church: *The Church in the Power of the Spirit: A Contribution to Messianic Ecclesiology* by Jürgen Moltmann', *Interpretation* 33 (1979), 31.
87 Rasmusson, *The Church as Polis*, 87–8. For 'contrast society' see Lohfink, *Jesus and Community*, 56, 130, 157–63.
88 Vicedom, *The Mission of God*, 39; Lohfink, *Jesus and Community*, 137, 146.

89   Tripole, 'A Church for the Poor', 658.

90   S. Sykes, *The Identity of Christianity* (London: SPCK, 1984), 75.

91   Ibid., 297 n. 61.

92   Chapman, 'Black Theology and Theology of Hope', 129; J. Mark, Review of *The Experiment Hope* in *Theology* 79 (1976), 168; G. M. Newlands 'Review of *The Crucified God*' in *Theology* 78 (1975), 150. Moltmann pointed out that he was not writing theological ethics but a theology of the cross and that his remarks were merely indicative: 'Antwort auf die Kritik an "Der gekreuzigte Gott"', 189.

93   See e.g.: 'Theology of Mystical Experience', 519; 'The "Crucified God": A Trinitarian Theology of the Cross', 291–2; *Jewish Monotheism and Christian Trinitarian Doctrine*, 53; *TKG*, 77.

CHAPTER 7

Moltmann:
The Exposition of Messianic Theology

Moltmann took up from 1980 his 'systematic contributions to theology' (*TKG*, xi) expounding God, creation, christology, eschatology and theological method as 'Messianic Theology' (*GC*, xv).[1] He turns increasingly to 'image thinking' (*WJC*, xv, 4) compounding criticism of his 'inattentiveness to the formal and figural issues of religious imagery and theological language'.[2] This chapter focuses upon the themes of church and society in this stage of writing. Here Moltmann enters into appreciative dialogue with Mennonite theologians, including Yoder.

Foundations: God as Triune Creator

The Trinity and the Kingdom of God sums up Moltmann's previous theology and points to future interests.[3] Trinitarian doctrine is foundational to Moltmann and increasingly modifies eschatology as his framework. Previous expositions implied that God's being was purely future, to the despite of an eternal pre-existent *koinōnia*, and threatened through the 'Trinitarian history of God' to evacuate God into history or historical modalism.[4] The claim that God is constituted as Trinity in the event of the cross (*CG*, 247) is now modified to mean that God is here *revealed* as the 'primordial' yet eternally open Trinity (*CPS*, 95–6; *SL*, 294). The charge of tritheism is countered with the claim that modalism is common in history whereas tritheism is conspicuous by its absence. God's lordship, understood by Barth as divine subjectivity prior to divine triunity, is better conceived *historically* as the constant interplay between Father, Son and Spirit moving to final unity in the *eschaton*.[5] God is no closed circle within an immanent Trinity but open to the world and the future. This image replaces those of circular or triangular Trinities.[6] Reflection has led Moltmann from an exclusively future emphasis to a doctrine of God open both in front and behind.[7] The God within whom history fulfils itself is Trinity both in origin and in eschatological goal (*CPS*, 50–65, *FC*, 74–5).[8]

Trinitarian doctrine has unlimited consequences for humanity, history and the universe and so is crucial for understanding church and society. Moltmann's work draws the criticism of assuming rather than showing that

Christian faith requires a Trinity and that the social doctrine is its appropriate form.[9] His approach is described as overconfident in handling Scripture.[10] His ready identification of Jesus and the second person of the Trinity without clarifying the distinction between Jesus and the Word of God is said to require further justification.[11] However, his exposition is richly suggestive.

THE 'SOCIAL' TRINITY

Moltmann frees Trinitarian doctrine from metaphysics, transcendental subjectivity and monism and develops a social understanding from the biblical narratives (*TKG*, xvi).[12] Economic and immanent Trinities are one and the same (*TKG*, 160). The categories he employs include community, process and relation (*WJC*, xv). When fellowship, participation and receptivity categories replace those of lordship, conquest and production the doctrine of the Trinity contains a power of revolution, liberation and healing (*TKG*, 9). God is no longer the 'Wholly Other' (*Das ganz Andere*) but the 'Wholly Transforming One' (*Das Ganz Ändernde*).

God is constituted by *perichoresis*, the mutual indwelling of the divine persons.[13] This doctrine proceeds from human experience that personhood and society are inseparable: the divine persons are constituted similarly, forming and influencing each other.[14] The consequence of this is not new thinking about God alone, but new thinking (*TKG*, 17–19). God is capable of passion, of entering into the human condition and suffering from, with and for human beings (*TKG*, 4; *HTG*, xvi). This necessitates a self-differentiation in God as the Trinitarian foundation[15] and alters understandings of God's lordship. God rules the world by enduring and participating in its sufferings. His freedom is not that of disposal over property but of being towards the world what he is in himself, the God who loves in the fellowship of Father, Son and Spirit (*TKG*, 56).[16] God is engendering and creative love. The Father loves the Son, but this is love of like for like. He goes out to love also in the Son that which is other than himself, the world which he calls into being (*TKG*, 59).

The sending of the Son and the Spirit clarifies that there is movement in God, a Trinitarian differentiation of the divine unity (*TKG*, 75). The Father sends the Son through the Spirit in the incarnation. Through the resurrection, the Father sends the Spirit through the Son. As the agent of the *eschaton*, the Spirit draws the world through the Son to the Father. In this going out to return to himself drawing the world with him is the history of the kingdom of God. Divine unity consists in union not numerical identity, and this union is open to the world (*TKG*, 95).

CREATION AND REDEMPTION

The creation is understood in Trinitarian terms as mutual interpenetration and participation (*TKG*, 104). The Father is creation's creating origin, the Son its shaping origin, the Spirit its life-giving origin, the 'Spirit of the

Universe', the principle of evolution (*GC*, 14, 98, 100; *WJC*, 96, 104). God's free creation is the product of his freedom to be himself, he in whom freedom and necessity coincide, who loves what is other than himself and wills its free response. Creation is deduced not from God's will therefore but from his essence. It is inherent in the nature of God from eternity. This supposedly avoids residual despotism in the concept of God and is the foundation for 'an ecological doctrine of creation'. It also attracts the criticism that the world has a necessary significance for God, potentially replacing the Son as the object of his love, rendering God finite and humanity infinite by a process of absorption.[17]

Moltmann draws here on Isaac Luria's doctrine of '*zimsum*' and displays his appreciation of Jewish and feminist theology (*TKG*, 162–6; *HTG*, xiii–xvi).[18] God withdraws into himself to make space and time for a finitude other than he yet within and surrounded by himself (*GC*, 86ff; *TKG*, 105ff). This 'panentheism' is not pantheism because creation is in God but not itself God. God creates out of the energies and powers of his own Spirit, so creation exists in close relationship with the creator (*TKG*, 113). *Creatio ex nihilo* means God first 'creating' a *nihil*, a nothingness, literally godforsaken space and so necessarily hell and absolute death (although the nihil only acquires this menace for humans through their self-isolation which we call sin and godlessness). Within this space he lets creation be, maintaining it against the threat of the *nihil* (*GC*, 88–9). So God's limitation of his power is simultaneously a de-limitation of his goodness (*TKG*, 119).

As creation involves preservation from the contradicting power of the *nihil* so redemption is the creative act through which God delivers the world from suffering and fulfils his purpose. Biblical traditions distinguish initial creation (*creatio originalis*), historical or continuing creation (*creatio continua*), and new or eschatological creation (*creatio nova*) (*GC*, 55, 206ff). The divine persons are equally involved in this creative work, the Father as origin, the Son as Logos, the Spirit as energy (*TKG*, 114). The incarnation completes creation-in-the-beginning through the new bond between God and humanity. It is the presupposition for the cross but not simply this (*TKG*, 114–15). Physical redemption from suffering and death was obscured when Augustine and the Latin Fathers traced all suffering back to sin (*TKG*, 50–1). Christ, as bearer of the *imago mundi*, tastes death on behalf of every living thing, entering through resurrection into the glory which is the destiny of all creation. Redemption therefore belongs within continuing creation, the painful labour of God overcoming disaster through participation in suffering (*GC*, 90–1).

Corresponding to God's primordial self-limitation is his eschatological de-restriction, becoming all-in-all in a creation transfigured by the Spirit. Creation's time and space pass away and become the eternal aeon of creation, the cosmic temple of God's indwelling (*WJC*, 329). The teleological movement of evolution finds an eschatological countermovement when 'the divine tempest of the new creation sweeps out of God's future over history's fields of the dead, waking and gathering every last created being' and restoring the ravages of evolution (*WJC*, 303).

COSMIC CHRIST AND CREATOR SPIRIT

Panentheism and the Trinitarian presence of God in creation lead to recapitulation of *perichoresis* as the mystery of creation (*GC*, 1–2, 14). Secularisation and divine transcendence have so been stressed that a pneumatological understanding becomes necessary for the sake of creation's preservation and the rediscovery of its divine mystery in the immanence of God (*GC*, xiii, 98).[19] Messianic or soteriological doctrine understands creation as existing for its future, seeing the present age as *preparatio messianica mundi* (*GC*, 5, 8, 54, 277). This develops previous denials that redemption is merely *restitutio in integrum* (e.g. *CG*, 208, 260–1). A. A. van Ruler's 'messianic intermezzo' (*CPS*, 275) depicted Christ as an 'emergency measure' to remove sin and restore creation. In the judgement Christ's humanity would be discarded.[20] This purportedly Trinitarian position, opposed to Barth's christocentricity, forged a theology of culture based on a theocratic vision of God's kingdom[21] and was conservative and supportive of the *corpus christianum* in inclination. For van Ruler, Christ's mediatorship ceases in the eschaton; for Moltmann, and arguably for the New Testament (Revelation 21:22),[22] it continues as the foundation of the new heaven and new earth, although now with the stress on Christ's *sonship*, his eternal identity (*CG*, 266). The world thus exists for the sake of its completion and fulfilment in the messianic future (*TKG*, 102).

This approach is radicalising. The purpose of creation is understood through Christ who mediates creation and salvation. Yet Moltmann is criticised for reversing the worldview which begins with creation and so failing to affirm creation's ontology or the meaning of the present. By making the future the centre of the gospel rather than the victory of light over darkness and by identifying salvation and creation, he risks fusing creation into fall so ontologically structuralising the sin which is actually a matter of historical existence.[23]

The Trinitarian concept joins divine transcendence and immanence since having created the world God dwells in it and it in him. The Spirit is the principle of creativity on all levels of matter and life and creates possibilities, interactions, harmony, co-operation and community (*GC*, 100). The history of nature and humanity is therefore the history of the divine Spirit. Even in those things which do not accord with God the sighings of the Spirit and God's suffering presence may be discerned (*WJC*, 102). The Spirit functions as divine person, the subject of his own acts towards creation and in glorifying and unifying the Father and the Son (*TKG*, 125–7). He is uniquely personal and no univocal concept of personhood should obscure the concrete differences of Father, Son and Spirit (*GC*, 97).[24] Moltmann points out that

Calvin envisaged the Spirit's presence beyond the church and within creation (*GC*, 96; *CJF*, 57 citing *Institutes* 1:13:14). The Spirit's 'world-sustaining operations' and his messianic, fulfilling presence in the church have long been distinguished, but Moltmann sees these converging (*CPS*, 192; *GC*, 12). The messianic era bestows the Spirit's gifts on persons and awakens the Spirit in the whole enslaved creation (*GC*, 69). The Spirit of Pentecost is the presence of future glory, the glorifying of God among creatures which is the goal of creation (*TKG*, 124–6).

The Spirit proceeds from the origin of time within creation for its preserv- ation (Spirit of God) and from the future into time for its redemption (Spirit of Christ, Holy Spirit). The Spirit of God creates, preserves and develops. The Holy Spirit redeems and sanctifies. The Holy Spirit does not supersede the Spirit of creation but transforms it (*GC*, 263). McIntyre rightly comments that if the Holy Spirit 'transforms' the Spirit of God this implies a distinction between the two, contradicting the fundamental thesis that the Father creates through the Son and by the (one) Spirit. It may be that the distinction is semantic, distinguishing biblical usage of terms while allowing that theology identifies one Spirit.[25]

Analysis of the cosmic Christ corresponds to that of the Spirit. Christ is *Christus evolutor*, Christ in his becoming, and *Christus redemptor*, Christ in his coming (*WJC*, 303). The preserving God endures the self-isolation of his creatures and their contradictions, keeping their future open through his suffering and his silence, granting opportunity for conversion. Preservation is already part of the kingdom of grace and nature and grace are closely interwoven (*WJC*, 291).

TRINITY AND KINGDOM

Joachim of Fiore postulated the ages or kingdoms of Father, Son and Spirit in history to be followed by the kingdom of glory (*TKG*, 202ff; *HTG*, 91–109; *SL* 295–8). The kingdom of the Father concerns creation and preservation, of the Son redemption, of the Spirit rebirth, direct revelation and knowledge. Moltmann's modification posits the three kingdoms as continually present strata and 'qualitative transitions' in history. The divine persons are the subjects of particular aspects of the divine sovereignty, interpenetrating in their work and with history taking place between them (*TKG*, 204).[26] 'God creates all things through his defining and differentiating Word in the primordial vibrancies of his Spirit' (*WJC*, 289). The Spirit is in close proximity to the Logos, the 'Cosmic Christ' securing creation against the chaos. The Son's kingdom presupposes and absorbs the Father's, and the Spirit's kingdom that of the Son in a doctrine of the kingdom differentiated in a Trinitarian sense (*TKG*, 206, 209). The Father's kingdom is not naked power but loving patience preserving the world for glory even as it allows people to enslave themselves (*TKG*, 210). The Son's is the lordship of the crucified consummating the Father's patience and liberating the world for primal openness through vicarious suffering not compulsion. The kingdom becomes Christoform. In the Spirit's presence the freedom of Christ is realised under the conditions of the self-limitation of the Father and the self-emptying of the Son as a pledge of future glory (*TKG*, 211). In the kingdom of glory the world becomes the temple of the triune God (*TKG*, 212).

ECOLOGICAL AND SOCIAL IMPLICATIONS

Moltmann's social doctrine of the Trinity inspires crucial reformulations of creation, society and human nature.[27] The ecological crisis stems from Renaissance and nominalist teaching concerning humanity's dominance over nature legitimated by monotheism and biblical anthropocentrism (*GC*, 1, 23–6; *FC*, 115–30). This was achieved by avoiding the implications of Trinitarian doctrine and ignoring divine immanence as Spirit in creation (GC 9ff). Salvation conceived in overwhelmingly human terms neglects the biblical emphasis on nature's transfiguration and liberation from futility and mortality. Creation understood in Trinitarian terms yields an ecological doctrine of creation because it sees in God's own being the way all things are called to be.

God exists in interpenetration, in the mutuality and reciprocity of love without superiority and subordination. All relationships analogous to God mirror this *perichoresis*, not least creation (*GC*, 17). Human beings live in a perichoretic community of creation[28] developing a life reflecting the participation-in-interdependence of the Trinity. The divine *perichoresis* is possible because of the consubstantiality of the divine persons and Moltmann's perichoretic paradigm may somewhat overlook the difference between God and his creation,[29] although even so it is possible to maintain a broad analogy between the two.[30] *Perichoresis* replaces anthropocentrism with theocentrism, finding the high point of creation not in human beings but in the harmony of all created things represented by the weekly sabbath which points to the sabbath without end (*GC*, 276ff, 290).

The Holy Trinity is also a social programme (*HTG*, xi–xiii).[31] Here Moltmann substantiates familiar themes afresh through the Trinitarian being of God.[32] The thesis that influential political concepts are secularised religious ideas is better understood in terms of mutual interaction (*TKG*, 193).[33] Forms of domination legitimate themselves religiously. Political theology identifies the symmetry between monotheism and imperial rule (*TKG*, 195). Monotheism produced monarchy and patriarchy, and so dependency, helplessness and servitude (*TKG*, 131–2, 163, 191–2).[34] Concepts of 'Father' and 'Lord' became identified,[35] the Constantinian age fusing images of Jupiter father of the gods, in whose name Jesus was crucified, and 'Abba' (*HTG*, 4–10, 20–1; *SL*, 100).[36] Roman concepts of *pater familias* and of the ruler as 'father of the state' (*pater patriae*, *Staatsvater*) were transferred to the Christian God. Correspondingly,

Christian ethics became obedience to the *Haustafeln* rather than the Sermon on the Mount. Luther derived all government (*Obrigkeit*) logically from parental authority, precluding criteria to judge familial and governmental power. By contrast, Calvin insisted on submission to authority 'in the Lord', turning divine fatherhood into a standard of criticism.[37] Fatherhood assumptions founder however on Jesus' antipatriarchalism (Mark 3:31–5; Matthew 10:29–30, 23:9) and his experience of 'Abba' as the nearness and intimacy of God's coming reign (cf. *WJC*, 144; *HTG*, 10–18). The Father is not the father of creation but of the Son whom the merciful and motherly Father begets and brings forth from himself (*TKG*, 162; *HTG*, 22).[38] Through Christ this fatherhood opens to all so that a non-patriarchal expression of fatherhood may be embodied in the church.[39]

When monadic divine sovereignty is made the state's prototype absolutism emerges (*TKG*, 194–7).[40] Only the Trinity safeguards freedom as community without supremacy or subjection (*TKG*, 158).[41] The Trinity, uniting the Father with the crucified Son and the universal Spirit, contradicts the idea of the omnipotent universal ruler. Embracing the suffering of the crucified, it redefines divine fatherhood (*TKG*, 163, 197–8). The Father is not the archetype of the world's mighty ones (*TKG*, 198). Instead the sociality of the divine persons establishes community, personal relations and harmony, fostering social personalism or personal socialism against collectivism and individualism (*TKG*, 199). Political options corresponding to the divine being define people through relationships not power and possession (*TKG*, 198). It conceives divine life in a circulatory, life-imparting fashion (*TKG*, 174) and so ceases to legitimate tyrants (*TKG*, 197).

God's freedom is not freedom of disposal over history, an idea reflecting master–slave relationships, but his loving in a freedom corresponding to himself (*TKG*, 54–5).[42] Human freedom is neither found in domination or independence or rejection of an overbearing God. As in the Trinity it is harmonised personality and sociality, freedom in community and in the love which breaks down barriers (*TKG*, 199, 216–18). The church corresponds to the perichoretic community of Father and Son (John 17:21)[43] and in the Holy Spirit finds a fellowship which liberates without overpowering.[44] Western ecclesiologies emphasised the authority of ministry above the community and charisms of God's people, confining the Spirit and producing passivity. Yet the church is the 'lived' Trinity.[45] This undermines papal and episcopal hierarchies held to correspond to divine monarchy (*TKG*, 200–1). The church corresponding to the Trinity knows fellowship *with* and *in* God (*TKG*, 96), replacing power by concord, authority and obedience by dialogue, consensus and harmony. Ecclesiastical authority yields to faith based on individual insight into the truth of revelation. This implies presbyterial and synodal church order and leadership based on brotherly advice (*TKG*, 202).

Human beings are also *perichoresis*, body and soul in community and harmony. Assumptions of the dominance of the soul have led to alienation from the rhythms and cycles of the body. Understanding the two in mutual interpenetration and differentiated unity brings true individuality and sociality (*GC*, 258–9).

DIALOGUE WITH WORLD RELIGIONS

The doctrine of God as Trinity is distinctively Christian and claims universality. This brings Moltmann back to the nature of Christian truth claims and the question of how relative human beings depict the absolute God while allowing the absolute to remain absolute and the relative, relative. The danger of self-exaltation inherent here is not only a Christian problem (*HTG*, 111). Since Constantine, Christianity in Europe and America has claimed political and cultural absoluteness, understanding itself as the 'soul of the nation' rather than as the body of Christ. In Asia and Africa this was not the case, reliance being upon the non-violent and persuasive mission.[46]

Western toleration after the religious wars reduced the contentious community aspects of religious belief by a 'repressive tolerance'. Relativity was substituted for the absolute of imperial religion, bringing true dialogue to an end because there was no longer anything to talk about (*HTG*, xi).[47] Yet a pluralist theology of religions[48] is no less imperialistic than any other theology. Claims to *absoluteness* are obstructions to the dialogue which is essential for the peace of the world, but the claim to *uniqueness* is dialogue's presupposition.[49] Moltmann's solution avoids identification of church and kingdom so rendering church and world relative. In the age of messianic preparation the church cannot claim universality for itself (*HTG*, 116–18). It must however make its unique witness to the Triune God.

The Way of Jesus Christ

The Way of Jesus Christ corresponds with Anabaptist concentration upon the Synoptic Christ, the concrete humanness of the Messiah.[50] It is a central volume of Moltmann's projected contributions and in structure reflects the way of Christ in cross, resurrection, present cosmic role and parousia.[51]

CHRISTOLOGY IN MESSIANIC PERSPECTIVE

Moltmann seeks to transcend christologies 'from above' and 'from below' by conceiving of Christ 'from before' in the forward movement of God's history. The image of the 'way' connotes progress, implies present limitations and points to the ethical nature of the enquiry concerning Christ (*WJC*, xiv). Christ relates to human history and to the earth. Messianology relates to present soteriological and therapeutic needs, in particular to the ecological crisis (*WJC*, xiii). The Jewish Jesus both overcomes the anti-Judaist bias of Christendom and undergirds the insights of feminist theology (*WJC*, xvi–xvii).

Moltmann moves beyond concentration upon the cross and resurrection to develop a holistic christology. Jesus is not seen in vertical incarnational descent from eternity, as in the creeds, but eschatologically as he who arises by the Spirit from Israel's history as the messianic prophet of the poor (*WJC*, 3–5). This is political since Messiah is an antitype to existing kings (*WJC*, 8–9). Messianic hope arose from the inadequacies of Israel's kingship whose legitimation of its power on a par with the nations conflicted with concern for the poor, humble and oppressed (*WJC*, 8, 21). In power politics God's kind of kingship can hardly be implemented.

Augustine and Constantine internalised salvation, playing down its eschatological and political significance. Because the Christian *imperium* was welcomed as the realisation of Christ's messianic kingdom, the church was delegated internal salvation while the emperor enforced Christianisation externally. Such messianic theocracies cannot tolerate the Jews because they still await the Messiah (*WJC*, 31, 104; *OHD*, 136–8). Losing expectation of the parousia made Christianity a civil religion. The imperial church prayed that the end might be delayed, advancing itself as preserving the state (*WJC*, 313). Where messianic concepts of 'redeemer nations' exist free churches will conflict ideologically with them (*WJC*, 32, 55). For them, premature ecclesiastical or political triumphalism are excluded because Christ is still on his way to becoming the *pantocrator* (*WJC*, 32–3, 54).

Christology cannot be done without *christopraxis*. Following Yoder, Moltmann describes the participation of the community in Christ's mission as 'the politics of Jesus' whose guidelines are the messianic interpretation of the Torah, the Sermon on the Mount (*WJC*, 42). Two-natures christology ignores Christ's actual life, suppressing the intimate relationship of Father and Son by metaphysical categories from the imperial *Sitz im Leben* of the creeds (*WJC*, 53). After Christendom, a christology of the road and beneath the cross embodied in a visible, non-violent community of believers is both possible and necessary (*WJC*, 55).

SPIRIT CHRISTOLOGY

The link between christology and ecclesiology requires the church to reflect its Messiah. It must perceive the humanity of Jesus to understand his divinity and *vice versa* (*WJC*, 69). The challenge is not to *imitatio Christi* (which suggests human effort) but to *conformitas Christi* (*HTG*, 40). The foundation to this approach is Spirit christology. Through the Spirit Jesus brought liberty and healing (*WJC*, 72). He was born of the Spirit, claims the legend of the virgin birth. Mary signifies the motherhood of the Spirit who brought forth Jesus and veneration of Mary is misplaced devotion to the Spirit to whom she witnesses (*WJC*, 83). The Spirit is the source of life, the mother of believers and the co-mediator of salvation (*WJC*, 86).[52] The Spirit constituted the social person of Jesus as Messiah and established the new creation in his acts (*WJC*, 91–2, 94). The Spirit, denying Jesus the economic, political and religious means for a 'seizure of power', led him to the cross, participating in his suffering and becoming indivisibly bound up with his history (*WJC*, 93–4). By the Spirit, Jesus preached to the poor, banished the powers of death and imparted dignity (*WJC*, 99, 101). He proclaimed conversion of all life, established a community of disciples and created a movement of the poor which threatened the Jewish upper class and the Roman occupying force, a conflict which the church would have continued had it not become harmonised with the empire (*WJC*, 100–4). The miracles of Jesus were social acts, removing the impurity of the stigmatised (*WJC*, 107). He even invited 'tax-collectors and sinners' to the messianic banquet (*WJC*, 112ff) demonstrating the justice of grace which comes to make the unjust just and challenges religious and civil morality (*WJC*, 114).

THE MESSIANIC LIFESTYLE

For Moltmann 'an unsolved problem of christology itself' is whether Jesus taught a new ethic and lifestyle. The alternative to a christological foundation for social ethics is natural human ethics such as the 'orders of creation' (*WJC*, 116–17). But in Israel's history of promise the Messiah is always a public person. Without an ethic making public and private demands Jesus would not be the Messiah. He addressed his proclamation of the messianic Torah to God's people and through them to the earth's peoples. Confessing Christ therefore involves following Jesus' messianic path (*WJC*, 118).

Anabaptist and Moravian differences with Lutherans and the Reformed concern whether general responsibility for social 'ordinances' (following Article 16 of the Augsburg Confession)[53] or a more specific ethic of discipleship is required. Following Yoder Moltmann argues:

> It is the justifiable question which Mennonite theology puts to the Protestant doctrine of faith why 'Christ's perfect obedience' should for Protestantism be the yardstick only for saving faith, and not the yardstick for obedience as well. The *solus Christus* of the Reformers cannot be normative merely for the doctrine of faith. It must be the rule for ethics too, for *solus Christus* also means *totus Christus* – the whole Christ for the whole of life as the second thesis of the Barmen Theological Declaration of 1934 says (*WJC*, 118).[54]

This is the issue represented by Anabaptism as Moltmann sees it.[55] *After* the apostolic declaration of salvation through crucifixion and resurrection, the Synoptic Gospels, belonging to the later development of the canon, returned to the way of the earthly Jesus and made it obligatory.[56] Christology and christopraxis unite in ethical christology. According to Denck's dictum, 'No-one is able verily to know Christ except he follow Him in life' (*WJC*, 119).[57] Christian ethics are for Christians and are recommended to the world through being lived in Christian community (*OHD*, 95).[58] They acquire universal significance as they shape the history of humanity or as that history reaches the messianic eschatological horizon (*WJC*, 119, 124–5).

Moltmann follows Trocmé and Yoder in seeing Jesus' radicalisation of the year of Jubilee (Luke 4:18–19; *WJC*, 120) as a programme of social and ecological reform in which indebtedness, enslavement and the exploitation of the earth are done away. Through Jesus people acquire power to act in this messianic reality. A new, corporate and increasingly relevant justice comes into being in the 'contrast-society' of his followers (*WJC*, 122). So the Sermon on the Mount concerns public morality; to regard it as impossible of fulfilment (cf. Bismarck's 'Mit der Bergpredigt kann man keinen Staat regieren') is to mock God, who gives no commandments that cannot be fulfilled (*WJC*, 127). Yet only by orientating ourselves towards the Preacher on the Mount can the Sermon be fulfilled and the *Teufelskreis* of hate overcome.[59] The Sermon is the ethic of a particular community but is directed to the redemption of all and claims universality (*WJC*, 124–125). It is an ethic of unconditional love, the messianic interpretation of the Torah for the Gentile nations (*WJC*, 123–4). It determines whether the church is to be true or whether Christianity exists as a civil religion (*WJC*, 132). The visible community incarnates a messianic alternative (*WJC*, 126). This raises the issue of violence.

MESSIANIC PEACE: THE DISCIPLE AND VIOLENCE

The church is God's work in the world creating peace through justice and is the instrument of this justice (*CJF*, 6).[60] Peace comes by the creation of justice rather than from security (*CJF*, 38). Justice is more than giving each his due, or securing reciprocal recognition and acceptance of other people. It includes the law of mercy, delivering justice to those who are without rights. This divine justice is the creative source of the human legal order (*CJF*, 38–40).

A non-Augustinian reading of the Fall sees the 'violence that leads to death' as humanity's real sin (*WJC*, 127). The story of Cain and Abel, according to the Priestly Writings and Jewish interpretation, marks the beginning of sin. The wickedness of the earth is its being full of violence and rape. After the flood God established himself as the revenger of deeds of violence with the death penalty setting limits to violence without overcoming it (*WJC*, 128). But in Christ comes a peace which both surmounts acts of violence and the retribution and violent resistance used to restrict them. Retaliation is itself declared to be evil (Matthew 5:39–42). Non-violence robs evil of legitimation and puts the perpetrator in the wrong. This describes negatively the overcoming of evil with good (*WJC*, 129; Romans 12:21). Love of enemy responds with creative love, taking responsibility and seeking to remove the causes of enmity (*WJC*, 127–32; *CJF*, 43). It transcends friend–enemy structures of thought. In a nuclear age, it has become the course of reasonable and wise behaviour (*WJC*, 130–32).

Non-violence was characteristic of the pre-Constantinian church but became overlaid first by the myth of *in hoc signo vinces* and then by Augustine's *pax eucharistica* which made peace into a sacramental foretaste of heaven, postponing the 'doing' of the Sermon on the Mount (*WJC*, 134–6). Its realisation in our day requires willingness for martyrdom. Disregard of the martyrs is a sure sign that Christianity has become a civil religion (*WJC*, 155, 196–203). To renounce violence does not mean de-politicisation, the renunciation of power nor exclusion from the struggle for power. It is possible to 'do politics' with the Sermon on the Mount, but only the politics of peace (*CJF*, 44). Here Moltmann reiterates his distinction between power as the just use and violence the unjust use of force. The state has the monopoly on force. The first step in overcoming violence in the public realm assures that all power and every response of force are justified and exercised according to law. The struggle for power is legitimate if it binds power to justice and law (*CJF*, 45). Further steps involve refusing from below to co-operate with the unjust use of power and nations refusing to co-operate with other nations which use violence. The non-violent conquest of violence thus becomes thinkable politically and not only personally, although any such approach may lead to martyrdom. Even here, there is power in vicarious suffering which, on the longer term, can be more convincing than violence (*WJC*, 129–30).

Encounter with Mennonite Theology

The Way of Jesus Christ contains dialogue with Mennonites in general (and Yoder in particular)[61] following visits to two Mennonite seminaries in 1982. The papers then delivered were published (*FJC*), reappearing almost in their entirety in 1984 (*OHD*). The responses of Mennonite theologians at the conference are included in a sequel.[62]

The editors of *Following Jesus Christ* identified a convergence of interests in Moltmann's desire for dialogue with the Historic Peace Church tradition and Mennonite interest in his theology of the cross (*FJC*, 3). They found in him a dual challenge: Mainstream churches are challenged to the discipleship previously obscured by the combination of presumed political neutrality and the JWT, and Mennonites to reject the quietism which has often marked them and to act responsibly and creatively for peace in a threatened world. Moltmann is regarded as evidence that a 'third way' towards the peaceable kingdom is possible. They suggest two 'mild' reformulations of Moltmann's statements: a christology more resolutely based on the gospel record of Christ's life and not the dialectic of cross and resurrection alone, and a clearer distinction between the church and the political orders (*FJC*, 6–7). We have seen evidence of these modifications, the first in direct and explicit statements, the second by stressing the primacy of Jesus' ethic for disciples and its relevance through them to the world. More emphasis than Moltmann has yet achieved upon the church as an identifiable people, the 'visible sacrament and instrument of Christian peace and hope', is appropriate (*FJC*, 7).

The Mennonite theologians' not uncritical responses to Moltmann indicate some convergence.[63] Ecclesiological convergence is by now clear (*FJC*, 13).[64] Moltmann was also involved in declarations in the *Gesellschaft für Evangelische Theologie* and the Reformed Church in Germany against the 'blasphemous heresy' of 'nuclearism' (*FJC*, 16; *OHD*, 128–9; *CJF*, 28–31).[65] The latter raised opposition to the *status confessionis*, not anathematising those who thought differently but inviting them to a change of mind.[66] Moltmann saw a struggle over this issue against the civil religion of the German Federal Republic to which the *Volkskirchen* are expected to give assent[67] and this gives further opportunity for the exploration of church–state relations.

Moltmann envisages continual *Kirchenkampf* against the state and every political religion. The common relationship between religion and state is the struggle for public power by the church and for religious legitimation by the state.[68] Domination seeks religious legitimation since images of God are worshipped with ultimate devotion (*HTG*, 2). But for the Christian, the solidarity of the church is higher than any other loyalty. As with Diognetus, 'every home is foreign and every foreign place is home'.[69] This requires opposition to all messianisms declaring the sacredness of the political. Governments must legitimate themselves through the fulfilment of their promises and the consensus of the people[70] and through commitment to human dignity through the protection of human lives in this and future generations.[71] Present challenges in this area include the drive of 'fundamentalisms' towards the restoration of the unitary religious state or the 'Christian West', and the establishment of the 'Islamic state'. Such states have messianic foundations so political religion and religious imperialism result. When Western modernity threatens to destroy the identity, culture, values and norms of traditional societies these reactions are likely to come.[72] Yet liberation theologies also seek the return of faith to politics, but by the standards of the Sermon on the Mount not the Christian Empire. There are striking parallels and differences between these fundamentalist and liberationist approaches, often found on different sides of the argument but both concerned for a salvation relevant to the world.[73]

As is often the case, Moltmann develops his own theology by first reviewing available options. At the Reformation Roman, Lutheran and Reformed churches developed political theologies which can now be seen to have served the interests of both church and state.[74]

LUTHER AND THE TWO KINGDOMS

Luther's concern was to avoid politics by means of religion and religion by means of politics (*FJC*, 30; *OHD*, 70). Evil was resisted by two 'regiments', the preserving kingdom of the world and the saving kingdom of Christ, each of which had its own justice. In the first, law, the sword, good deeds and reason are valid; in the second grace, the Word, justification and faith without civil pressure or political oppression even of heretics (*OHD*, 68–70). Article 16 of the Augsburg Confession required the practice of love in the ordinances of family and state, perpetuating the impression of an autonomous realm of law in contrast with grace. So Luther criticised Müntzer for translating spiritual ideas into political demands. He neglected criteria for worldly justice and reinforced conformity, as he showed in defining the injustice and terrorism of the princes against the peasants as godly actions.[75] This doctrine provided no basis for resistance to Hitler's perversion of the state (*FJC*, 33; *OHD*, 61, 75). It became an ideology of the politics of force reinforcing the public–private, inner–outer splits of bourgeois religion (*FJC*, 36; *OHD*, 74–5).

Misuse of the two-kingdoms doctrine puts its continuing usefulness in doubt (*FJC*, 35). Understood however within Luther's original apocalyptic context, both regiments are drawn together in their common struggle against evil. The worldly regiment defines the places of Christian action, but the law of those actions is in Christ (*FJC*, 34, 38; *OHD*, 71–3). The worldly ordinances are thus to be re-shaped in accord with Christ. They do more than repress evil. They are processes open to the future justice and peace of God's kingdom (*OHD*, 76) with transformative as well as preservative potential. Luther's theological error was to subordinate Christ to an apocalyptic eschatology rather than viewing history from the perspective of the resurrection. The link between orthodoxy and orthopraxis means that the freedom of the gospel, of faith and of the church requires freedom of speech, conscience and religion, a free church in a free state.[76] Luther and Müntzer, justification and liberation, the grace which justifies and which executes justice, are in fact fellow warriors (*HTG*, 46–8).

BARTH'S CHRISTOLOGICAL POLITICS

The Reformed tradition has also maintained a doctrine of two kingdoms to distinguish church and state while affirming the call to discipleship in civic affairs (*FJC*, 43; *OHD*, 13, 81). This position found expression in the Barmen Declaration and its paradigm in the Confessing Church's resistance to Hitler's totalitarianism. Christ's lordship cannot be restricted to spiritual, churchly or private realms (*OHD*, 82). Barth's theology of church and state, foundational to the Barmen Declaration, affirms a christological eschatology in which Christ has become Lord of all creation. Christ is Lord of the state, so theological thought proceeds from Christ to church and from church to politics (*FJC*, 45–6). The state is an earthly and temporary vessel for the good founded on justice not force alone (*OHD*, 90–1). Romans 13 offers not a metaphysic[77] of the state but counsel for Christians responding to evil, including in the political sphere (*FJC*, 47). Yet the Bible describes the new creation politically (*basileia, polis, politeuma*), so hope includes the coming of a heavenly 'state'. State and society are unfinished and are orientated towards God's coming lordship (*FJC*, 47). Church and state are two communities, one united by confessing Christ, the second by a legal order protected by force and aimed at securing relative freedom and peace (*FJC*, 48–9). The church shapes the civil community indirectly by being itself, making God's coming lordship apparent by its own consciously political existence in the freedom and peace of Christ (*OHD*, 85). It resists the state's hubris, points to its provisional character, and rejects both demonisation and divinisation of the political. Without erecting a Christian doctrine of the state it holds the political processes accountable (*FJC*, 51). The civil community is within Christ's kingdom, so there can be no apolitical Christianity. Without sanctifying imperfect politics the church looks for parables of the kingdom, correspondences and analogies in the civil community to the criteria of God's justice and its own life (*OHD*, 12, 19–35, 89; *HTG*, 55). In summary, democratic socialism is the best available correspondence to the kingdom of God (*OHD*, 91).[78] The true state has its model and example in the true church (*OHD*, 90).

Here, Moltmann finds the difficulty. The real church is compromised, not the forerunner but the 'tail-light of cultural development' (*OHD*, 92). Barth's 'enthusiasm', overemphasis on Christ's victory over the powers, neglects the fact that Christ's rule is the rule of the crucified who conquers through weakness, not might (*FJC*, 58).

MODELS FOR CHURCH AND STATE: POLITICAL THEOLOGY

The political theology of Moltmann and Metz grew out of dissatisfaction with the repression of Confessing Church insights. Instead of a free church in a free state the period of German reconstruction opted for a new institutional partnership of church and state (*FJC*, 61; *OHD*, 97). Political theology began with criticism of the social function of the church in these new circumstances. With Bonhoeffer it saw secularisation more positively than those who saw it as the abandonment of God. Secularisation represented the de-divinisation and de-demonisation of the world in favour of its true worldliness, true historicity and orientation to the future. It focused on *praxis*, the function of religion (*TT*, 16–18, 93), criticising religious legitimation of society.[79]

Since Constantine the subject of salvation history was no longer the Christian church but the Christian state. This false messianism turned Christian universality into a state mission of imperial and cultural expansion. The church became part of the public order, its hierarchy part of the political rule, church participation a civic duty. Friend–foe schemes of thought and enemy images proved necessary for the projection of self-anxiety, and national security assumed the characteristics of the unconditional. Civil religions bind themselves to particular societies whereas ecumenical Christianity represents the universal within individual societies. The God of the poor establishes communities of the unlike on the edges of society.[80] There is therefore a choice between the heresy of 'millennium politics' (equating the political empire with the kingdom of God and the Christian nation with the people of God) and political discipleship of a crucified Lord who reveals the fatal disharmony and necessary choice between Christ and Caesar. All false messianisms of the West which threaten human dignity, whether the cultural unity of church and state, the ambivalent messianism of the American dream, the idolatrous messianism of Olympic religion, the atheistic messianism of Bloch, or messianic Zionism conflict with the suffering Messiah (*OHD*, xiv, 135–216).

Political theology employs the Marxist criticism of religion not against the content of faith but to expose whether doctrines are used to liberate or oppress. It aims to awaken the political consciousness of Christian theology, to expose the fact that no theology is apolitical, least of all that which claims so to be but actually co-operates with the *status quo* (*OHD*, 99).[81] The theology of hope provided the conceptual tool to turn the church from a backward and inward orientation into a messianic faith orientated to the future and serving liberation and transformation (*OHD*, 100).[82] Jesus is the sign of resistance to a world that resists God and is closed to the future. His resurrection anticipates the *eschaton* and initiates the resurrection process and the new creation (*OHD*, 102–3).

Against Luther political theology insists on salvation's public nature; against Barth it believes that the crucified one is still on his way to overall lordship (*OHD*, 104). Moltmann's concern here is to avoid any suggestion of a premature christocracy. Political theology insists that the Bible is only understood through political involvement in history's liberating processes. Theology aims to transform the world not merely to reflect upon it. This requires identification with the poor, oppressed and guilty and consequently is a common theology for the active lay-person rather than a specialised one for priests and pastors (*OHD*, 107–8).

Political theology seeks sacramental mediations of the coming kingdom within history and at this point does not appear to be very far from Barth's position. Church and society are seen critically and hopefully against the future horizon. That the church is not yet the true church does not jeopardise the pattern of thought. It too is the human sphere in which the future is manifested by the Spirit. The state, while accepted as a given reality, is that which is passing away under the pressure of the coming kingdom (*OHD*, 109).

MODELS FOR CHURCH AND STATE: ANABAPTISM

European humanism, after the wars of religion, secured religious freedom but was joined by free churches which asserted the right to voluntary community and developed democracy (*OHD*, 140–1). Anabaptism, about which despite his positive comments Moltmann does not seem to have detailed knowledge, belongs to this tradition. State and national churches do not create an atmosphere friendly to democracy. When churches become free from the state, the state becomes free from the church. So, for Moltmann the future lies in a free church way of life and its correspondence in a free state with freedoms of religion, belief, conscience, association and indeed of theology being theologically grounded (*OHD*, 143, 156; *TT*, 24–5). Secularisation of the *corpus christianum* therefore provides the opportunity to develop the open and ecumenical church of Christ to replace bourgeois religion (*TT*, 10, 26, 40, 87).

Article 16 of the Augsburg Confession was written *contra* Article 6 of the Schleitheim Confession.[83] The Anabaptists also adopted a two-kingdoms doctrine but insisted on one ethical norm: Christ. As the worldly regiment required sub-Christian standards, they refused activity in ordinances that would compromise their witness. The disagreement concerns support *of* the world orders or undivided discipleship *in* those orders (*OHD*, 113). Undivided discipleship prevented Anabaptists from committing acts of violence even to impede or punish others doing violent acts. Executioners and soldiers could not be in 'holy station' so the Anabaptists chose defencelessness, suffering and martyrdom supported by their voluntary communities (*OHD*, 114–15).[84] The Augsburg position affirmed that participation in worldly ordinances cannot be considered sinful since they are ordinances of God. Civil authority is created by God and equipped with a monopoly of force to preserve social peace and establish political justice. Christian responsibility requires participation. But so formulated distinctive discipleship is lost (*OHD*, 117). Lutherans risk co-operating uncritically without perspectives for the transformation of the structures, but only for 'love' within them. It is true that Article 16 adds the qualifier '*nisi cum jubent peccare*', but this is done without more exact formulation (*OHD*, 72, 116, 118). Conversely Anabaptism risks setting the church and world in exclusive opposition, not recognising this world with all its violence and inhumanity as God's world (*OHD*, 5, 116).

These positions are reconcilable, according to Moltmann, by affirming that the worldly ordinances are themselves to be transformed along the lines of the Sermon on the Mount and, to the degree to which they are, disciples may participate in them (*TH*, 329ff). How Anabaptist 'principled pacifism' is to view those acts of violence by which violence is to be prevented remains unclear (*OHD*, 119). To advocate defencelessness as a political proposal involves others in the consequences of that risk (*OHD*, 124). Nevertheless, the Anabaptist refusal of violence is considered realism in the light of today's apocalyptic 'universal context'.[85] The potential for mass destruction reveals the sinfully irresponsible and unjustifiable nature of all war (*OHD*, 129). Creative love for the enemy is needed which overcomes the friend–foe thinking which leads to war. The witness of the peace churches is thus essential for the whole church (*OHD*, 131). A *Volkskirche* can never truly be a Confessing Church (*bekennende Kirche*) since civil religion must always represent the interests of the ruling classes.[86] The church must first *become* the church of Christ before it can *remain* the church in its witness to the world. The lesson of Barmen was that a confessing church exists where Christ alone is followed.[87]

This exposition brings Moltmann in principle close to an Anabaptist position.[88] Yet the distinction between violence and the 'just use of force' (*WJC*, 129–30; *CJF*, 44–5) remains unclear about the relation of discipleship and force (e.g. *OHD*, 115). Our previous chapter noted that revolutionary violence was given limited legitimation, but this is now declared to have been 'renounced from the beginning' by the political theology he and Metz developed.[89] State use of force is viewed pragmatically, every exercise of power being tied to law, which is the intention of the JWT (*OHD*, 119) (although Moltmann disclaims representing this theory).[90] The duty of resistance to the illegal and illegitimate use of power against human rights follows. 'The principle of "non-violence" does not exclude the struggle for power when this struggle is involved in binding power to justice' (*CJF*, 45; *WJC*, 130). If Moltmann's definition of Anabaptism as renouncing violence 'even to impede or punish others doing violent acts' stands, he has not declared his principled response to this possibility.

Moltmann's earlier declarations on revolution cast doubt on whether his theological pacifism is rooted in the being of God and the mission of Christ or is strategic in view of the nuclear threat (*OHD*, 118ff).[91] The contention that nuclear war reveals the nature of all war indicates that his position can be extended (*OHD*, 129). Yet the question of the 'border-line case' troubles him, particularly, as with Bonhoeffer, the possible conscious assumption of guilt in tyrannicide.[92] He can also advocate intervention (presumably military) in the affairs of other countries when human rights are trampled underfoot (*JCT*, 26). When tyrannical injustice is substituted for law, resistants are obliged to use counter-violence. As resistance to a tyrant is the legitimate fulfilment of the contract with rulers who become tyrannical, 'violent' resistance in this border-line case is as justifiable as the normal exercise of power by the state. Those who approve of the latter cannot but approve of the former. Unavoidable killing incurs guilt but can be answered for.[93] This suggests that killing in the pursuit of the 'normal' exercise of power also renders guilty. How this may be reconciled with his statements about the non-violence of Jesus and the commitment to follow him remains unclear.

For Willard Swartley, Moltmann's challenge to Mennonites concerns the existence of the 'extreme case' whereas the corresponding challenge to Moltmann concerns the paradigmatic nature of Bonhoeffer's actions in the light of Jesus.[94] Yoder has pointed out that the July plot against Hitler's life resulted only in further loss of life and the regime's increased paranoid determination to fight to the last.[95] Perhaps this indicates that the risk of following Jesus in the non-violent way applies even in the extreme case. Both Yoder and Moltmann acknowledge that there is an open space concerning extreme cases. Yoder does this reluctantly not to exalt the hard case into the normative instance and out of his persuasion that discipleship cannot be reduced to a form of 'punctiliar' ethical reasoning. Moltmann is less wary, but the exceptional case is precisely that, theologically unreconciled within the logic of his argument, perhaps necessarily so to prevent the extreme case determining the argument.

The Universal Spirit of Life

Moltmann's fourth contribution to systematic theology in fact develops his pneumatology. As much of his social theology depends upon God's presence in the world this is appropriate. It elucidates the Spirit's personhood as 'the loving, self-communicating, out-fanning and out-pouring presence of the eternal life of the triune God' (*SL*, 289) and his relative independence from the persons and efficacies of Father and Son. The relation between Word and Spirit is mutual. The Spirit precedes and goes beyond the workings of the Son and is recognised in everything which ministers to life and resists its destruction (*SL*, x–xi, 3). The book is a sustained attempt therefore to demonstrate the closeness between the human spirit and the divine Spirit without confusing the two. It takes the breadth of human experience seriously in a 'holistic pneumatology' (*SL*, xiii, 35, 42). It must return inevitably to the continuity and discontinuity between the Spirit of God and the Spirit of Christ already referred to. This is in fact the same question as that of the creative and redemptive works of God in general.

Moltmann presupposes that the redeeming Spirit of Christ and the creative Spirit of God are one and the same in a way which brings the church into community with all creation (*SL*, 9–10). The Spirit is identified with the *Shekinah*, the presence of God accompanying and suffering with his people. Through the *Shekinah* dwelling in Jesus the Spirit has bound itself to Jesus' fate without becoming identical with him. So the Spirit of God has become definitively the Spirit of Christ and Christ the determining subject of the Spirit (*SL*, 62, 68). In the history of the Holy Spirit a different kind of divine presence is made known from that in the original creation. People in their corporeality and then the new heaven and new earth become the 'temple' in which God himself dwells.[96]

Recognising the Spirit as liberating and revolutionary and the church as the pneumatological community questions, as so much else, the clerical hierarchy which denies freedom to the church. Remembering their tradition makes Christians into radicals (*SL*, 107–9). Liberation theology reminds us that eschatological redemption is linked to historical liberation and that salvation is finitely healing and holistic (*SL*, 113). The Spirit is concerned with the rebirth of all things, for which reason he has been poured out on all flesh. Cultural experiences and movements can also be shot through with the Spirit, church and culture being interwoven in the interplay of the spiritual. This makes the relationship between church and world reciprocal with the church gaining new impulses from outside and *vice versa*.

The line of baptism and membership exists between Christian and non-Christians, but the church is wrongly described (Barth) as 'prototype', 'example' or 'model' for the world. This strains the church, makes it incapable of learning and sets up a clerical claim to domination in society. The church's distinctiveness consists in its redeeming experiences of the Spirit which influence the surrounding communities (*SL*, 230–31, 294). This leads again to the call that the 'gathered congregation' or community church should emerge. Traditional feudalist and centrist forms need to be transcended in a world in which the centralist and non-contractualist state no longer functions (*SL*, 247, 252). Personal and voluntary commitment and the participatory congregation come to the fore with the Spirit enabling Christians to take responsibility and shape their own lives (*SL*, 234–5).

Summary and Critical Reflections

Moltmann's development in a *social Trinitarian* direction must be identified as of primary significance. This and the christological shift to *totus Christus*, in which we have traced Mennonite influence, and his *Spirit-christology* strengthen his already well-established free church ecclesiology. Yet comprehending all humanity and creation within the scope of redemption roots this ecclesiology in love for the world and preserves it from sectarianism. The political theology which flows from this enables a non-Constantinian understanding of church and society.

Moltmann is not immune to the charge of *ideology*,[97] propounding theological judgements which reinforce an already determined social commitment. This is clearest in his development of the social Trinity. It is true that all theology takes place in social context and the relation between politics and theology is dialectical.[98] Yet because Moltmann's approach is highly contextual and seeks to mediate or correlate theology to the modern world by showing its therapeutic relevance (*TT*, ix, 94), his understanding and his theological methods change with the context. This is evident in the shift in his theology from the concerns of modernity with its stress on the primacy of history to those of 'post-materialism' or postmodernity, the apparent arbitrariness and non-foundational nature of his constructions and the 'dangerously unclear' nature of his hermeneutical principles.[99] He is therefore led into incoherence, as for instance in his treatment of human rights, a characteristic concern of modernity, where he both asserts the universal priority of human rights over particular traditions, including the Sermon on the Mount, and their importance for the relevance of the church to the world (*OHD*, 7)[100] and the priority and universal relevance of the Sermon. Moltmann is less successful than Barth in keeping socio-political reality under the control of the christological norm.[101]

In a penetrating criticism, Rasmusson turns back upon Moltmann his functional critique of religion and asks what interests his theology serves. He draws attention to the new social movements and the emergence after World War II of a new 'knowledge class' élite within the upper middle classes concerned with the production of symbolic knowledge and conflicting with the business class dealing with the production of goods. The knowledge class is characterised by an anti-bourgeois 'adversary culture' and values the antinomian self, tolerance and liberation. Moltmann's theology is concerned to mediate with this culture and to provide theological legitimation for its concerns accepted uncritically and simplistically as givens. What he omits from his agenda is here as significant as what he includes, and we draw attention to his reluctance to provide a theology of the state in this regard. Even his form of free church ecclesiology corresponds with the values of this culture. Appeal to the abstract poor is part of this culture's legitimation of its concerns as justice for the marginalised and oppressed. Rasmusson concludes that despite his disavowal Moltmann is *actually propounding a Constantinian theology* by identifying the new social movements with the Spirit and allowing the context of the knowledge class élite to determine the content of theology as previously it was determined by the ruling class.[102] Perhaps this is the ground of the never-explicitly-owned natural theology which Ayres detects.[103]

A further concern is *the marginalisation of the themes of sin and judgement.* Redemption becomes healing from mortality and suffering through divine participation on the cross. The theology of atonement develops in personal and relational terms. Abelard is right, not Anselm. The wrath of God is his love repulsed and wounded, assuming this form that it may remain love. The pain of God's love for sinners is borne by God in Christ on the cross (*HTG*, 51–2). This is a crucial part of the matter but surely not all. Without *some* concept of retribution the judgement which sin brings upon itself becomes something for which God bears no responsibility. Moltmann presupposes universal salvation and envisions the ravages of evolution and of history being diachronically healed by the Spirit. The element of the tragic is excluded from final judgement since judgement makes righteousness prevail even among the unjust (*WJC*, 315). Jesus rejected the law of retribution in favour of the law of unconditioned grace and the Christ who is to come will not act in contradiction to Jesus (*WJC*, 336ff). In Christ divine judgement is replaced by divine love (e.g. *CG*, 128–35).

Moltmann elevates this to the point of contradiction, to the extent that he must choose one against the other, eschatological against apocalyptic Christianity (*WJC*, 336–8) even while recreating an apocalyptic out of the nuclear crises of the present (e.g. *CJF*, 1–15). A 'hopeful' universalism which neither counts upon the salvation of all nor rules out the possibility that all may be saved (and indeed hopes for it) is a theological possibility,[104] living faithfully within the 'magnetic field' set up by the amazing grace of God and the appalling sin of the world.[105] Moltmann offers however a dogmatic universalism and so lays insufficient emphasis upon human resistance and sin and upon the drama and risk of history. Does his God, then, ruling by suffering rather than by his word, lose the capacity to say No to the rebellion of his creatures by being assimilated to the evolutionary process?

Mennonite theologian Ted Koontz asks whether Moltmann's theology leads to an unwarranted optimism in what may be expected from the world. Koontz is inclined to see the activity of God as a dramatic and discontinuous breaking into the world rather than a process of continuity. This leads him to a more pessimistic stance in which conversion from the world and so the church assume higher profiles.[106] Moltmann rejects the charge of optimism, confessing his hope to be in God rather than human possibilities,[107] but there is here a point which has consequences. Moltmann emphasises process and evolutionary movement towards a goal which is sure and the drama of redemption yields to the history of creation's liberation. Opposing patriarchal notions of domination, he denies that God exercises freedom *over* history. Furthermore his failure to do justice to the complex nature of power, defining it in such a way as to oppose power and love in God and emphasising the powerlessness of Jesus, obscures the fact that God does exercise power, but in the name of love. This suspicion of power stands in unresolved paradox with his view of the need to struggle for power. Yet power is not intrinsically evil.[108] Moltmann's Trinitarian theology of history must surely retain the sense of God's freedom over history if God is to be its Lord and not its victim.

Here we draw connections with the much reduced *theology of the state*. He repeatedly assumes that there is some agency which will enforce human rights and take the kind of action democratic socialism requires, even speaking of the need for 'political will' to achieve ecological reforms (*CJF*, 14) and of a needed 'world organisation' (*CJF*, 22), yet he is reluctant to grant the state an ontology within Cod's creation. He has little to say about the institutional form of the world order he desires, making power into something bad and failing to depict how it actually works in church and society. Rasmusson argues that this is the perilous weakness of the socialist tradition Moltmann supports. Moltmann's language is rhetorical rather than analytical and he fails to develop the potential of his theology for a better understanding. He divests God, church and political powers of power without rethinking the concept of power from within his theology. At the same time he is advocating measures which confirm modernity's presumption of unlimited power.[109]

Moltmann therefore undercuts the theological materials he requires for a theology of the state. God's revelation in Jesus does not require us to avoid the notion of divine judgement, of which Jesus himself spoke in word and parable in ways that cannot be rejected as unreconstructed apocalyptic. This suggests that while sacrificial love is the preferred and primary mode of God's creative and redeeming activity, he sets limits to the freedom of creatures to resist his long-suffering mercy, and this is judgement. Although it inclines against the direction of his thought, Moltmann acknowledges that to affirm this does not jeopardise the confidence about the judgement he wishes to engender (*WJC*, 338). It does however enable us to carry through the thought to the activity of God in history. For the sake of his creatures, he sets a limit to the chaos he will endure. The judgement of God manifests his mercy in preserving a world awaiting redemption. Moltmann's idea of judgement as the prevailing of divine righteousness and the ending of injust-ice (*WJC*, 315; *SL*, 272) still requires a process whereby sin will be recognised as sin and judged. In this sense some concept of retribution is still required since proportionality is involved. In turn the state may be seen to function at least in part as an agent of the recognition and condemnation of injustice without detriment to those fuller understandings of justice which look for the redemption of the wrongdoer by means of judgement.

Despite these criticisms, Moltmann's allusions to the *covenant* suggests a direction in which the state may be conceived which corresponds to what we have previously called, following Brunk's specific definition of the term, 'natural law'. We shall consider this further in the next chapter in which we construct from the materials Yoder and Moltmann offer us and in the context of wider Anabaptist–Reformed interaction the elements of a theology of messianic community, social order and state.

NOTES

1   This series has now grown to six volumes after the inclusion of *SL*. The volume on eschatology, *The Coming of God* was published in 1996. The volume on theological method is anticipated.

2   G. Loughlin, Review of *History and the Triune God* in *Theology* 96 (1993), 60. Ayres refers to a 'ballet of theological terms and biblical phrases which defies comprehension': L. Ayres, Review of *History and the Triune God*, *SJT* 46:4 (1993), 575.

3   J. J. O'Donnell, 'The Doctrine of the Trinity in Recent German Theology', *THJ* 23:2 (1982), 153.

4   Hill, *Three-Personed God*, 173.

5   'Antwort auf die Kritik an *Der gekreuzigte Gott*', 184.

6   'The Unity of the Triune God: Remarks on the Comprehensibility of the Doctrine of the Trinity and its Foundation in the History of Salvation', *SVTQ* 28:3 (1984), 169.

7   R. J. Bauckham, 'Jürgen Moltmann' in Toon and J. D. Spiceland (eds.), *One God in Trinity* (London: Samuel Bagster, 1980), 114, 125–6. See also Moltmann, 'Schöpfung, Bund und Herrlichkeit: Zur Diskussion über Karl Barths Schöpfungslehre', *EvTh* 48:2 (1988), 109–10.

8   Bauckham, *Moltmann*, 111–12; Hill, *Three-Personed God*, 174.

9   J., Mackey, *The Christian Experience of God as Trinity* (London: SCM Press, 1983), 205.

10   R. Page, 'Review of *The Trinity and the Kingdom of God*' in *SJT* 37:1 (1984), 98; K. Blaser, 'Les enjeux d'une doctrine Trinitarian social', *Revue de Théologie et de Philosophie* 113 (1981), 163.

11   J. B. Cobb, 'Reply to Jürgen Moltmann's, "The Unity of the Triune God"', *SVTQ* 28:3 (1984), 174–6.

12   'The Unity of the Triune God', 159–60, 171.

13   Ibid., 164–5.

14   MacKey, *God as Trinity*, 206–7.

15   Ibid., 205.

16   See also E. Moltmann-Wendel and J. Moltmann, *Humanity in God* (London: SCM Press, 1984), 55–69.

17   S. W. Sykes et al, Review of *The Trinity and the Kingdom of God* in *Theology* 85 (1982), 209.

18   Moltmann takes account increasingly of feminist concerns. See e.g. 'The Motherly Father: Is Trinitarian Patripassianism Replacing Theological Patriarchalism?' in E. Schillebeeckx and J. B. Metz (eds.), *Concilium 143: God as Father?* (1981), 74–84; 'Die Bibel und das Patriarchat: Offene Fragen zur Diskussion über "Feministische Theologie" ', *EvTh* 42:5 (1982), 480–4; (with Elisabeth Moltmann) 'Menschwerden in einer neuen Gemeinschaft von Frauen und Männern' *EvTh* 42:1 (1982), 80–92.

19   'The Scope of Renewal in the Spirit', *EcRev* 42:2 (1990), 100.

20   R. A. Muller, 'Christ in the Eschaton: Calvin and Moltmann on the Duration of the *Munus Regium*', *HTR* 74:1 (1981), 32.

21   J. F. Jansen, '1 Cor. 15: 24–28 and the Future of Jesus Christ', *SJT* 40:4 (1987), 562–3, 565–6.

22   Ibid., 569–70.

23   B. J. Walsh, 'Theology of Hope and the Doctrine of Creation: An Appraisal of Jürgen Moltmann', *EQ* 59:1 (1987), 54, 58–9, 63–4, 65.

24   'Theological Proposals Towards the Resolution of the Filioque Controversy' in L. Vischer (ed.), *Spirit of God, Spirit of Christ* (London: SPCK, and Geneva: World Council of Churches, 1981), 172; 'The Unity of the Triune God', 170.

25   J. McIntyre, 'Review of *God in Creation* by Jürgen Moltmann' in *SJT* 41:2 (1988), 269, 270.

26   'The Inviting Unity of the Triune God' in C. Jeffré and J-P. Jossue (eds.), *Concilium 177: Monotheism* (Edinburgh: T. and T. Clark, 1985), 55.

27   Blaser, 'Les enjeux', 163.

28   'The Inviting Unity of the Triune God', 57.

29   MacIntyre, Review of *God in Creation*, 271; Forster, Review of *The Way of Jesus Christ* in *Anvil* 8:2 (1991), 171.

30   Marshall, 'The Ground and Content', 235.

31   *Humanity in God*, 104–6.

32   Blaser, 'Les enjeux', 166; Moltmann indicates an alliance between patriarchalism and Constantinianism with the consequent depressing of Christianity's liberating potential. Conversely, rejection of a church constructed paternalistically from above requires one in which community enables people to be the subjects of their own lives and initiatives and where the Holy Spirit gains a new prominence: 'Menschwerden in einer neuen Gemeinschaft von Frauen und Männern', 83.

33   'Christian Theology and Political Religion' in L. Rouner (ed.), *Civil Religion and Political Theology* (Notre Dame: Notre Dame Press, 1986), 43.

34   'The Inviting Unity of the Triune God', 51; *Humanity in God*, 92–4.

35   'The Inviting Unity of the Triune God', 54, 55.

36   E. Moltmann-Wendell and J. Moltmann, *God: His and Hers* (London: SCM Press, 1991), 75–6.

37   'Ich glaube an Gott den Vater: Patriarchalische oder nichtpatriarchalische Rede von Gott', *EvTh* 43:5 (1983), 403–5.

38   See also 'The Motherly Father: Is Trinitarian Patripassianism Replacing Theological Patriarchalism?', 52; 'Theological Proposals Towards the Resolution of the Filioque Controversy', 167; 'Ich glaube an Gott den Vater', 411; *Humanity in God*, 89.

39   Ibid., 410–14.

40   Sykes makes the criticism that Moltmann treats all power as dominative: Sykes et al, Review of *The Trinity and the Kingdom of God*, 209.

41   Colin Gunton sees in this a clear attempt to defend the faith from justified criticism by reappropriating a more truly Christian doctrine of God: *The Promise of Trinitarian Theology* (Edinburgh: T. and T. Clark, 1991), 22. The doctrine also serves to criticise illusory notions of freedom as autonomy.

42   See also '"Dialektik, die umschlägt in Identität" – was ist das? Zu Befürchtungen Walter Kaspers' in Welker (ed.), *Diskussion über Jürgen Moltmanns Buch 'Der gekreuzigte Gott'*, 155.

43   'The Inviting Unity of the Triune God', 56.

44   'The Fellowship of the Holy Spirit: Trinitarian Pneumatology', *SJT* 37:3 (1984), 287–9.

45   Ibid., 293–4.

46   'Dient die "pluralistische Theologie" dem Dialog der Weltreligionen?', *EvTh* 49:6 (1989), 530.

47   Ibid., 531.

48   Moltmann has in view J. Hick and, F. Knitter (eds.), *The Myth of Christian Uniqueness* (London: SCM Press, 1987).

49   'Dient die "pluralistische Theologie" dem Dialog der Weltreligionen', 535.

50   Kaufman points out that for the 'left-wing' of the Reformation the Synoptic Jesus is the canon in the canon: *Systematic Theology*, 66.

51   R. J. Bauckham, 'Moltmann's Messianic Christology', *SJT* 44:4 (1991), 519, 525.

52   'Editorial: Can there be an Ecumenical Mariology?' in H. Küng and J. Moltmann

(eds.) *Concilium 168: Mary in the Churches* (Edinburgh: T. and T. Clark, 1983), xv; Moltmann-Wendell and Moltmann, *God: His and Hers*, 33–8.

53 See Appendix 2.

54 On p. 357 n. 357 he cites Yoder's essay, 'The Prophetic Dissent of the Anabaptists', 99. For the Barmen Declaration see Appendix 3.

55 This was confirmed by Professor Moltmann in a personal conversation on 9 July 1991: cf. Bauckham, 'Moltmann's Messianic Christology', 527–8.

56 'Vorwort' to Yoder, *Die Politik Jesu: Der Weg des Kreuzes* (Maxdorf: Agape Verlag, 1981), 6.

57 Moltmann draws the Denck citation from Yoder, 'The Prophetic Dissent of the Anabaptists', 95.

58 Bauckham, 'Moltmann's Messianic Christology', 528.

59 'Liebet eure Feinde' in V. Hochgrebe (ed.), *Provokation Bergpredigt* (Stuttgart: Kreuz Verlag, 1982), 64, 67–8, 76.

60 'Justice creates peace' in S. Tunnicliffe (ed.), *Towards a Theology of Peace* (London: European Nuclear Disarmament, 1989), 267.

61 See Moltmann 'Vorwort' to Yoder, *Die Politik Jesu*, 5–7.

62 W. Swartley (ed.), *Dialogue Sequel to Jürgen Moltmann's 'Following Jesus Christ in the World Today'*, Occasional Paper No 8 (Elkhart and Winnipeg: Institute of Mennonite Studies and CMBC Publications, 1984).

63 See e.g. the editorial preface in *Dialogue Sequel*, 4.

64 Moltmann's article, 'Religion and State in Germany: West and East' in *Annals of the American Academy of Political and Social Science* 483 (1986), 110–18 outlines the German shift from a state church in 1919 in which the churches functioned as part of the state order to a *Volkskirche* in which the churches remained privileged public organisations which negotiated 'concordats' with the state. The abandonment of a state church meant that the state had to legitimate itself secularly through democratic consensus, although even this situation can give rise to 'civil religion'. This situation prevailed to 1933 when Hitlerian totalitarianism sought to overcome an autonomous church but was restored in 1945, leaving the churches with a system of involuntary church affiliation. By contrast in East Germany after 1961 the church became self-reliant. Although church affiliation then dropped to 30% compared to the 90% in the West, Moltmann argues that this *Gemeindekirche* exercised a more distinctly recognisable influence and has neither accommodated itself to socialism nor retreated into the ghetto.

65 'Foreword' to G. C. Chapman, *Facing the Nuclear Heresy* (Elgin, Illinois: Brethren Press, 1986), x–xi.

66 'Dient die "pluralistische Theologie" dem Dialog der Weltreligionen', 529.

67 'Religion and State in Germany: West and East', 116–17.

68 Ibid., 111.

69 'Christian Theology and Political Religion', 41.

70 Ibid., 42.

71 'Human Rights, the Rights of Humanity and the Rights of Nature' in H. Küng and J. Moltmann (eds.), *Concilium: The Ethics of World Religion and Human Rights* (London: SCM Press, 1990/2), 127.

72 'Fundamentalism and Modernity' in *Concilium: Fundamentalism as an Ecumenical Challenge* (London: SCM Press, 1992/3), 112.

73 Ibid., 115.

74 'Reformation and Revolution' in M. Hoffman (ed.), *Martin Luther and the Modern Mind: Freedom, Conscience, Toleration, Rights*, Toronto Studies in Theology 22 (New York and Toronto: Edwin Mellen Press, 1985), 180–2.

75 Ibid., 177–80, 182.

76 Ibid., 186.

77 See also *Bekennende Kirche Wagen: Barmen 1934–1984* (Munich: Chr. Kaiser Verlag, 1984), 272; H.-J. Kraus and J. Moltmann, 'Bekennende Kirche Werden: Barmen 1934–1984' in *Junge Kirche* 45:5 (1984), 263.

78 On this see F. W. Marquhardt, 'Socialism in the Theology of Karl Barth' in G. Hunsinger (ed.), *Karl Barth and Radical Politics* (Philadelphia: Westminster Press, 1976), 47–76 and *Theologie und Sozialismus: Das Beispiel Karl Barths* (Munich: Chr. Kaiser Verlag, 1972).

79 'Christian Theology and Political Religion', 43.

80 Ibid., 42–57 cf. also 'Die Entdeckung der Anderen: Zur Theorie des kommunikativen Erkennens', *EvTh* 50:5 (1990), 400–14.

81 'Political Theology and the Ethics of Peace' in T. Runyon (ed.), *Theology, Politics and Peace* (Maryknoll: Orbis Books, 1989), 35.

82 Continuity with C. F. Blumhardt can be found here: J. Bentley, 'Christoph Blumhardt: Preacher of Hope', *Theology* 78 (1975), 582.

83 Appendix 1.

84 Meeks describes the freedom from violence which Anabaptism proclaimed as an 'eschatological realism' in contrast to the paradoxical realism of Lutheranism and the triumphalist realism of the Reformed ethic: 'Introduction' to *OHD*, xiii–xiv.

85 Bauckham, 'Moltmann's Messianic Christology', 523.

86 'The Challenge of Religion in the '80s', 111.

87 *Bekennende Kirche Wagen: Barmen 1934–1984*, 18–19, 21. 'The Church Must Remain the Church' was the motto of the Confessing Church: 'Religion and State in Germany: East and West', 112.

88 Cf. *Dialogue Sequel*, 5.

89 Ibid., 55.

90 Ibid., 61.

91 Ibid., 45–7.

92 Ibid., 60–2. This reiterates Moltmann's previous position.

93 'Commentary on "To Bear Arms"' in R. A. Evans and A. F. Evans (eds.), *Human Rights: A Dialogue Between the First and Third Worlds* (Maryknoll: Orbis Books, and Guildford: Lutterworth Press, 1983), 50–1.

94 *Dialogue Sequel*, 6.

95 *WWD*, 15. Yoder's words should be read as comment on the irony of Bonhoeffer's decision rather than as an argument from pragmatic considerations.

96 'Theology of Mystical Experience', 518.

97 Hill, *Three-Personed God*, 174.

98 Marshall, 'The Ground and Content of Christian Hope', 236–7.

99 Rasmusson, *The Church as Polis*, 26–9, 39, 42–5; Bauckham, 'Jürgen Moltmann' in Ford (ed.), *Modern Theologians*, 308–9.

100 'Human Rights, the Rights of Humanity and the Rights of Nature', 121, 133–4; Rasmusson, *The Church as Polis*, 114–17.

101 G. A. Butler, 'Karl Barth and Political Theology' *SJT* 27:4, 459.

102 Rasmusson, *The Church as Polis*, 164–7.

103 Ayres, Review of *History and the Triune God*, 574.
104 Marshall, 'The Ground and Content', 193.
105 Newbigin, *The Gospel in a Pluralist Society*, 88, 175–6.
106 *Dialogue Sequel*, 49–53.
107 Ibid., 61.
108 Marshall, 'The Ground and Content', 234–5, 238.
109 Rasmusson, *The Church as Polis*, 113–14, 133.

CHAPTER 8

Church and Social Order:
A Reformed–Anabaptist Dialogue

Yoder's Anabaptist and Moltmann's political theologies hold much in common. The practical and social nature of Christian discipleship, a strong eschatology, the messianic and missionary thrust, the Bible as critical subversive memory, social criticism and the need for a post-Constantinian church, the church's visibility in committed communities as signs of God's kingdom are all shared themes.[1] However the convergence ought not to obscure their differences. This chapter evaluates their discussions of church and world, the state, the Trinity and the wrath of God, all of which bear on a theology of the social order, and then places these discussions within the context of wider Reformed and Anabaptist debate.

Yoder and Moltmann in Dialogue

CHURCH AND WORLD

The primary, and instructive, contrast to arise between Yoder and Moltmann concerns the centrality of the church. We have followed Rasmusson in arguing that Moltmann does not escape a form of Constantinianism in that his theology articulates the characteristic concerns of the new social movements and exhibits in this way its own form of élitism. Moltmann certainly warns against accommodation to the spirit of the age, but on reflection he appears to have in mind its conservative rather than its progressive tendencies. Although his intention is to write orthodox Christian theology, his contextual method of making that theology 'relevant' maintains inadequate control in discriminating the concerns of these 'progressive' movements. Their agendas are accepted uncritically, their difficulties and complexities underestimated, and the theological tradition manipulated to validate their interests. Redemptive action takes place primarily in the world, and the role of the church is to serve this process. Christianity is fitted into a wider history of liberation from oppression, the fundamental category of salvation Moltmann employs, and becomes subservient to it in a way which conflicts with his Barthian-Barmen tradition.[2] Incoherence results from this,

compounded by Moltmann's shift from an early Marxist socialism to a
'green' socialism without clarifying the relation between the two.[3]

In this analysis, we have suggested, Moltmann gives insufficient weight to
the church as the locus of salvation. To this extent his political theology is in
tension with the Radical Reformation elements also present in his theology.
These are made to serve the former. Rasmusson's nodal criticism of
Moltmann, by contrast with Hauerwas, is that the political struggle for
emancipation is the horizon against which the church's theology is
interpreted whereas for Hauerwas the church's story is the 'counter story'
that interprets the world's politics.[4] The same may be said in relation to
Yoder who firmly maintains the independence of the church over against the
majority opinions of the day. It exists in distinction from both conservative
and liberal trends, legitimating neither and subjecting both to scrutiny from
the base-point of its own convictions. Dominant opinion of whatever kind is
seen as simply one more subculture, not as a privileged source of truth (by
definition the same for everyone) which can take precedence over the
church's own story and claim the power to validate it.[5]

For Moltmann the struggle over the processes of social change is primary
and the church assessed in relation to it. But he neglects the church as that
disciplined community in which good and free people are formed, as though
it were self-evident what form of society is desirable and where the people
are to be found who might populate it. He deals with liberation but not with
the substance of what liberated people are to be or how they are formed.[6] He
has surprisingly little to say of the implications of the church's existence as a
contrast society, his interest being largely confined to defining the church as
an arena free of oppression and to acquiring freedom for the individual. Yet
for the church to fulfil its function as a formative community requires not the
renunciation of power but its exercise in alternative forms, including the
recognition of shaping authorities. Moltmann adds little to this discussion.
By contrast, we judge Yoder's insistence on the primacy of the church and
his systematic attention to the nature of its life to demonstrate a more
consistent 'disavowal of Constantine'.

This said, we are not convinced that Yoder reckons adequately with the
'world' as an arena in which God is active and may be found. Although he
advocates a dialectical relationship with culture, his analysis inadequately
recognises the degree to which the church is dependent upon its environment
and bound up constructively with other formative communities than itself.
We judge the reason for this to be that his Mennonite inheritance involves an
element of sociological, rather than simply theological, separatism. The
world is felt in this tradition to be another, and cancerous, place. Yoder
certainly recognises that the healing resources of Christ reach beyond those
who know his name and that the 'adversary' is part of the truth finding
process and so needs to be heard (*BP*, 69). Yet the public realm is more than

an arena towards which a witness is to be borne. Alongside a theology of the church is required a theology of the world which values all in it which is worthy of love and care. Yoder's 'Anabaptist enthusiasm' attracts criticism from within his own tradition from those for whom the radical particularism of resident aliens within a holy colony in a hostile world is 'ontologically impossible, aesthetically undesirable and socially irresponsible'.[7] Yoder's self-referential ecclesiology, operating from a stance of epistemological privilege, is judged to neglect both the sheer delights of the public square and its existence as a source of theological constructions holding out the possibilities of mutual transformation.[8] In these respects Moltmann expects to encounter the presence of God in the world in ways Yoder appears not to anticipate. An adequate theology between Yoder and Moltmann will need to maintain a positive theology of the world without surrendering the critical centrality of the church. It may be that a theology is possible which combines Moltmann's concern for liberation from oppression as an imperative for government with Yoder's emphasis upon the disciplined community producing persons able to sustain a free and just society.[9]

THE STATE

Yoder offers here a strong theology which becomes a point of ostensible disagreement with Moltmann. Moltmann is uncomfortable with talk of a 'fallen world' and finds Yoder's exposition of the powers, Christ's lordship over them and their redemption excessively mythological and enthusiastic. Christ is still on his way to victory.[10] Moltmann anticipates a cessation rather than a redemption of the state.[11]

It is questionable here whether Moltmann understands Yoder. The mythological language of the powers' creation and fall describes not a metaphysical event but the fall of human institution-building capacities in and with humanity and their divorce from human control.[12] Moltmann develops a similar perspective of human-made structures which through persistent sin lead to social syndromes dominating and pressurising humans. Those in these structures want the good but comply with evil. They are formed by structures, although he also points out that just structures do not automatically make good persons (*HTG*, 54–5). Likewise he recognises that the biblical symbolism of evil, which is 'exploratory' rather than explanatory, points to a quasi-objective violence of enslaving structures (*Teufelskreise*) over humans.[13] This indicates that Yoder and Moltmann are not far from each other. The fallen powers which shape Yoder's view of the state have their echo in Moltmann's caution about power and fundamental suspicion of its present distributions.

Moltmann's hesitations reflect his dislike of metaphysics, undoubtedly because of the use of the concept 'order of creation' in pre-Nazi Germany to give the nation-state an immutable 'special, original and fundamental status'[14] – to bitter effect. He refers to the 'order of preservation'[15] but prefers the more fluid notions of 'processes of life', 'influential continuities' or 'spheres for the divine command' which deny the state ontological autonomy. It is doubtful whether this position recognises with sufficient seriousness the state's powerful actuality and this deprives Moltmann of a tool of analysis. He would benefit here from Yoder's 'legal positivism' to provide a sharper focus. Moltmann, nevertheless, assumes the necessity of state action to safeguard rights. He endorses Reformed pressure towards a contractual social philosophy and follows the Reformed tradition of just revolution. His characteristic concern, in keeping with his affinity for the adversary culture, is for forms of *resistance* to the state and he capitalises on Calvinism's potential in this area. This is most clearly seen in a recent article which clarifies his previous thought and develops the argument of this work.

Moltmann's concern for resistance leads him to favour not the coercive theocratic elements in Calvin (although he embraces Calvin's concern for the totality of life) but those which support resistance against rulers. The transition from absolutism to the democratisation of the right of resistance is a transition to an alternative form of government in which the key element is that of covenant or federalism.[16] Federal theology[17] originates not with Calvin but with Bullinger and presupposes that humans can form covenants with God and with each other. People, and their politics, are symbiotic and social. This is the foundation of the state as a covenant of free citizens based upon the created disposition of humankind and the anticipation of heavenly citizenship. *In this sense*, he argues, the state belongs as such to the essence and not the alienation of humankind, whatever the perversions of human sin. The state is not merely a phenomenon of sin. War belongs to the *status corruptionis* not the *status naturalis* of humanity.[18] This position clarifies Moltmann's previous negative comment on the state's future. The state of *legal positivism* will cease but as *covenant* (natural law) recovers in principle the intention of creation and has a future in redemption.

This 'covenant' position stands in contrast to Thomas Hobbes' 'Leviathan', in which also there is a contract, not *between* people but rather with the ruler for protection against hostile nature. The ruler's will is the law. Leviathan is intended to tame the wolf nature of human beings but becomes a superwolf.[19] There is a clear echo here of the legal positivism/natural law distinction. Moltmann comes down on the side of the latter as the safeguard against the former. The freedom of church from state is the best guarantee against totalitarianism. Political theology's task is to Christianise the churches' political existence 'according to the criteria of the discipleship of Christ which are to be found in the Sermon on the Mount: the culture of non-violence'.[20] He clearly points therefore to the possibilities of the state and finds the view he advocates to originate in the 'church covenant of free congregations'.[21] We conclude from this that his underlying theology is

Reformed but in the more radical, less 'theocratic', more contractual mode of this tradition. This particular emphasis also indicates that the boundaries between Anabaptist and Reformed theologies are more porous than has sometimes been assumed.

Yoder's theology is communitarian, seeking the embodiment of virtue within the Christian community and pursuing social justice not by political advocacy but through an alternative community governed by love and compassion.[22] He constructs a theology of the state, allowing it ontological reality, but emerges with a predominantly negative formulation. Although affirming the creation and fall of the powers and their subjugation under the lordship of Christ, the emphasis falls upon their fallenness. The state is a domination structure which is providentially overruled but which cannot become a vehicle of redemptive action. The church relates to it in disjunction.

Certainly, Yoder sees an aspect of state power with great clarity. The state's legitimacy is severely qualified. It is below the Christian level[23]. He comes close to Marx's theory of the state as an organ of the ruling class for compelling the exploited to fall into line.[24] Yoder agrees that, even so, state monopoly of force is a providential safeguard against unbridled violence. Yet the state also integrates the power of the whole community, mobilising it to accomplish higher ends. It is 'society acting as a whole with the ultimate power to compel compliance within its own jurisdiction'.[25] The state can undergird the weak with the collective power of the whole community.[26] Our contention is that within the state as a *fallen* power is a *created* structure necessary for human life and recoverable on analogy with the church's covenantal existence.

An adequate theology of the state needs to blend together themes of creation, fall, redemptive process and hope for the new age.[27] Social institutions influence social relationships and so Christians have responsibility strenuously to seek institutions that embody caring relationships and allow opportunity for human development.[28] This is stewardship, not the desire to control history. If God's redemptive purposes remain to some degree dependent upon the state's order-maintaining functions it is difficult to claim a vocational exemption from participation in them. Granted that Yoder's concern is with the *manner* of this participation, it nonetheless appears that his eschatology dominates the doctrine of creation despite the fact that his exousiology stresses creation and redemption in addition to fall and permits a more nuanced approach.[29] Moltmann's covenant emphasis, echoes of which are not failing in Yoder, suggests what is to be retrieved and shows how the life of the church can function as a redemptive stimulus. A realistic estimate of the state will hold in tension Yoder's awareness of its fallenness and Moltmann's hope for its recovery.

According to Friesen the doctrine of creation is the framework for affirming institutional structure.[30] Social beings create symbols and culture and express this through institutional relationships. Coercion belongs *intrinsically* to social existence, shaping, pressing together and structuring co-ordinated behaviour. But there is a distinction between violent coercion and that which orders human behaviour without exploiting.[31] Socio-historical structures are not as such sinful, but their absolutisation is. War is one of the forms this takes as nations advance and protect their own interests.[32] But *institutional* resources are required which can solve problems of conflict and injustice.[33]

Yoder certainly hints that created reality, obscured by the fall, contains pressures and sanctions necessary for life. It becomes impossible then to reject the powers on the basis that they are coercive: some coercion belongs to life as created. The challenge is to distinguish between this and its distortions. Yoder's theology with its stress on redemption and eschatology eclipses the theology of creation which is necessary if evil is to be combated not by evil but by a vigorous defence of the good. The natural law approach indicates how the social order can be viewed, fashioning a moral consensus out of which law can properly emerge. It points to the creative role of the church in helping to shape the social order. God's redemptive purpose expressed in the church thus assists the recovery of his original intention in creation.

Without viewing the state as *invariably* evil Yoder gives minimal encouragement to appreciating its role in protecting the innocent and enhancing the life of the weak through forms of power that may appear coercive.[34] His refusal to seek for *effectiveness* must surely be qualified. To be faithful within history involves concern for the likely effects of our actions.[35] Concern to fulfil the cultural mandate should not be construed as an arrogant attempt to manage history. Yoder's pessimism about the state is credible but is not the whole truth. Beneath the idolatrous distortions a created framework for corporate, institutional existence waits to be retrieved and must be retrieved if the co-operative essence of humanity is to triumph over its propensity for violence. It needs to be taken seriously since *shalom* flows from a just social order.[36]

Moltmann is right to find the categories of 'orders' too limiting. Creation, preservation and redemption are interwoven and interactive. The distinction between Moltmann and Yoder and, we now contend, the traditions they represent, is with the relative *continuity* or *discontinuity* of human social arrangements with divine action. Yoder stresses the discontinuity created by sin and fall. Moltmann's theology initially shared this, not by stressing fallenness but by contrasting historical and future reality. His fuller theology came to assert more the continuity of divine, liberating action and human social progression, although with some reluctance to claim this of government. Beneath the distinction between the state as covenant or Leviathan, he argues, lie contrasting positive and negative anthropologies. The positive anthropology is grounded theologically in the experience of God's *proximity*. To stress the *distance* of God leads to hierarchical structures of state and church as mediators but if the life-giving Spirit is poured out on all flesh then the 'covenant of free citizens and their agreement' which we call democracy becomes realisable.[37] This leads us to consider that proximity of God which is expressed by the doctrine of the Trinity.

The Trinity

Yoder's general neglect of creation is attributable to the paucity of his Trinitarian theology. Moltmann's theology is here immeasurably richer than Yoder's 'unitarianism of the Son'. Yoder's criticisms of Richard Niebuhr demonstrate his concern not to cancel out Jesus with the Father and the Spirit (*PJ*, 103–4; *BP*, 45). But Niebuhr's concern was rather, quite validly, to consider the ways in which the God made known in Christ acts and rules in the world and to discover a synthesis in the doctrine of God which comprehends the partial emphases, not merely ethical, of different traditions.[38] To construct a full Trinitarian doctrine in the light of Jesus Christ is an essential task. Yet Yoder disparages a plural or social doctrine of the Trinity and allows the doctrine only a formal role. Trinitarian doctrine merely undergirds the normativeness of Jesus. He has a clear place for the pre-existent Logos and the glory of the risen Christ and there are assertions of God's providentially controlling the course of history (*OR*, 59–60): but Father and Spirit are minimally displayed. We contend that only a balanced doctrine of God will yield an adequate political theology which 'combines order with justice, power with love, authority with service, triumph with suffering, grace with action, law with freedom'.[39]

Moltmann and Yoder are distinguished by the narrative frameworks within which they do their theology. Constantinian theology locates the church within a narrative of 'God and Country'. The church thus loses its distinctiveness and those holding to faithfulness over compromise appear sectarian.[40] Yoder's narrative is christological and places history between resurrection and parousia. The resurrection begins a new age, the source of all creation's hope for a future consummation which is the reign of the God incarnate in Jesus.[41] The church foreshadows the future guaranteed by Jesus' resurrection. It produces and sustains disciples and is the proleptic social location of God's kingdom,[42] performing practices which challenge the dominant structures of the world. Through bread, wine and baptism, it focuses on Jesus' eschatological significance. It is the social space in which faithfulness to God is possible.[43]

Within this storied context is located the discussion of justice. From within the story of Jesus Yoder has difficulty in conceiving the just use of violence.[44] Entering the discussion of the social order at the point of redemption shapes his treatment. Obedience to the non-resistant way of Jesus is a controlling norm over notions of effectiveness.[45] He rejects as Promethean moral 'engineering' that form of consequentialist reasoning that is not shaped by the confession that Jesus is Lord and Redeemer of history.[46] The christological narrative decisive for Yoder determines his conception of justice and explains his reluctance to concede the typical objections of his critics. Yoder is unclear on the possibility of exceptions because he relies almost exclusively on discipleship language without showing how this integrates with theology proper.[47] His christological ethic focuses on fall and redemption before creation. Since Christ is also the agent of creation it cannot neglect creation altogether, but Yoder does not follow Bonhoeffer in finding in the incarnation the ground of a new worldliness.[48] Our concern at this point is not with this framework as such but with its completeness.

This narrative of resurrection and parousia approximates to Moltmann's approach in *Theology of Hope* which gave rise to similar criticisms of neglect of creation, culture and continuity. It was later corrected by a Trinitarian framework which offered greater possibilities of holding together the total demands of the theological enterprise. Moltmann engaged in this task by stressing the Trinitarian history of God, the narrative unfolding of God's being through the dramas of history and the interplay between the kingdoms of Father, Son and Spirit. The mutual indwelling of self-giving persons became the grammar for conceiving the nature of human being and community within the community of creation, undergirding the democratic socialism which continually re-emerges in Moltmann's social thought. The doctrine embraces the whole of reality. Although Yoder argues that it is only Jesus' cross that Christians are called to imitate, it is clear that the 'non-resistance' of the cross was Jesus' response to the reaction awakened by the 'non-violent resistance' of his ministry.[49] If then the moment of the cross is understood within the narrative of Christ's life, that life and death can only be understood within the Trinitarian narrative of God's ultimate resistance to evil.

Valid though Yoder's insights are, they will always be lacking unless they are transposed into a Trinitarian framework. This will be most clearly the case in the neglect of creation[50]. Yoder's approach is fundamentally historical and ethical, and so anti-metaphysical and anti-ontological with an inclination to politicise the biblical message at the expense of other dimensions (e.g. *PT*, 226).[51] Paradoxically, its historicism accords with the modern western spirit of which Radical Reformation thought was both a product and ally. With the Anabaptist–Mennonite tradition generally it requires a fuller Trinitarianism the basis of all theology, both to embrace the universal element and to resist the currents of the day.[52] This is clearly difficult for some for whom the Trinity belongs to the products of Christendom.[53] Yet it is to do no more than locate ourselves in the unfolding story that supplied identity to Jesus himself. If Christ is the norm this involves embracing his faith in the Father and his reliance on the Spirit as well as imitating his actions. This leads us to locate ourselves, as he did, within the Old Testament story. The Christ story alone, with its focus on redemption, could mean we overlook vital aspects.[54] Equally the admission of the Spirit as with Calvin or Moltmann into the first article of the creed finds God at work in the whole of life and allows fuller expression to the truth beyond the walls of the church, perhaps even to the recognition of *charismata* bestowed in the secular realm. In the light of the Spirit the world is not a quasi-godless vacuum.[55]

Yoder's valid concern remains, however, the relating of Trinitarian activity throughout history to the revelation given in Jesus Christ, particularly to his non-resistant death. How does Christ define God and his activity towards human beings? It would be true to say that Christianity has never collectively resolved the question of whether, if the incarnation is a radically inventive moment which constitutes a claim to finality in the revelation of God and is not an incidentally chosen path, it is possible that the God so revealed will at some later stage intervene with coercive force.[56] The cross is the paradigmatic instance of God's action.[57]

We noted some difficulty in determining *in what sense* Christ is the norm. Potential light is given on this in Randall Bush's work on conflict in Moltmann and Tillich. Human growth to maturity comes through conflict and its integration. There are here, he argues, two types of conflict: Type A is the way to spiritual realisation of meaning which sees God as 'inspiring ideal'; Type B involves the struggle of human groups and sees God as 'directing principle'. Yet God is ontologically both,[58] immanent to and distinct from creation, revealed but hidden. He is hidden to allow those tensions to exist which make it possible for human beings to engage in a voluntary process of spiritual transformation.[59] But the type A conflict through which this comes has a diabolical manifestation, the projection of its shadow side on to others, creating injustice. So the tension is created between letting creatures be and overcoming the diabolical effects of their injustice. God exists therefore in a dialectic of hiddenness and revealedness. In revealedness he overcomes injustice by judging it in history, so keeping type A conflict in check. But the end of this action is the keeping open of the context in which the utmost freedom is possible and creatures may realise the good through voluntary acts of community. When this principle is taken too far it leads to the attempt to achieve justice through coercion.[60] At the cross God acts in kenosis and hiddenness. The two kinds of conflict are here worked through. Christ comes to maturity without deception and projected injustice, achieving justice not

through violence and coercion but through justifying grace. His Spirit
continues to elicit from creation its voluntary realisation of the good as
creativity and justice.[61] The church is one context in which destructive
libidinal and coercive power are being overcome and raised to a higher
level.[62]

Bush enables us to conceive how divine activity in history may be
directed to judging and limiting human injustice in order to keep open that
space wherein human beings come to maturity by free response to God.
Coercion cannot achieve the higher purposes of human existence but may
serve to preserve the context in which those purposes are realised. In this
way it is not inconsistent to conceive of the Christ-like God acting in
coercive judgement. Such action is directed towards the higher end but
cannot of itself achieve that end. For this the redemptive work of Christ and
the Spirit are necessary and the church expresses this invitation to voluntary
spiritual realisation. This also means that all coercive actions need to be
accountable to the end of redemption and consistent with it. We may agree
with Yoder that non-resistance is part of the essential nature of *agapē* (*PT*,
227) in the sense that his higher purposes can only be realised in this way;
but not that this is the only form God's love can take. A fuller Trinitarian
approach makes this clear. This leads us to reassess God's wrath.

THE WRATH OF GOD

We here find fault with both Moltmann and Yoder. Moltmann transposes sin
into transience and suffering, in which God savingly participates, while
leaving some room for the 'double soteriological significance' of the cross as
salvation from past guilt and mortality.[63] Yet the note of judgement is muted.
Yoder expounds atonement as restoration of communion through one who
suffers death rather than defend self. Moltmann does not neglect the role of
the Father in the cross: this is where God's triune nature is revealed in the
grief of the Father, the suffering of the Son and the outflow of the Spirit.
Yoder finds no place for the Father in the cross, other than as he is subsumed
by the Son in his expression of non-violent agape absorbing human hostility,
or for the personhood of Father and Spirit. Neither Moltmann's nor Yoder's
approach has room for wrath as an active expression of God's opposition to
sin. Moltmann's history of God makes anti-despotism and the realisation of
freedom the controlling factors, to the detriment of God's power and
authority, and shapes his social theology accordingly.[64] Yoder denies that
wrath is an attitude or attribute of God (*PT*, 236) but sees it, following
Hanson, as an impersonal process of cause and effect. Accordingly, the role
of the state is not to serve God as an agent of *God's* wrath but to channel
human vengeance (*PT*, 229).

Before offering an alternative perspective we consider the place of anger
in human penal systems. We sympathise with the aversion to a forensic

theory of atonement, of calculated wrath. Yet even human wrath is not entirely sinful or vengeful. Biblically, wrath and judgement concern the restoration of a community in which relationships have been ruptured. Anger reflects injury caused. By punishing or demanding contrition of the perpetrator the community asserts that the injury and the person injured matter.[65] Without such anger it is doubtful whether a community would be truly human and forgiveness would be in danger of being trivialised. Yet retribution without concern for restoration overlooks the dehumanisation of the criminal which has led to the injury.[66] A community restoration model of criminal justice does not exclude retribution but does exclude the rejection of any offender as a person. Yoder is correct to see that through the state human wrath is channelled to regulate its expression and restrain revenge. He overlooks the fact that in addition to this limitation of wrath being good in itself there is within it that expression of anger which is intrinsically necessary for the maintenance of humane community. This cannot be called evil. It is incorrect to distinguish sharply between wrath and redemption as though the Christian may serve the latter but not the former. Wrath is a necessary step on the way to redemption because it awakens the recognition of wrong-doing and the need for contrition. Wogaman asserts what Yoder denies, that it is possible to do the negative act in a redemptive way, not least in the policing function.[67]

It is appropriate to speak of God's wrath in two ways. It is expressed in that process whereby sin reaps its own reward. Human beings bring wrath upon themselves. This cannot be reduced to an autonomous, impersonal process from which God remains detached. It was established and is sustained by him and so must be rooted in God's active opposition to what opposes him. God does not here act non-resistantly but remains actively faithful to his creation through judgement upon sin, preserving the world from chaos and granting it order. It is not necessary to prove divine non-resistance in order to establish Christian non-violence. God has power to destroy both soul and body in hell (Matthew 10:28) but this is his prerogative alone. Christians forego 'vengeance' because they know that ultimate justice is assured, guaranteed by God (Romans 12:19). This expresses God's love for his creation. But the fullest extent of God's love is that his justice is not only retributive and preservative but redemptive and transformative, *justitia evangelica*.[68] In God human sin is eternally endured and eternally overcome and this eternal atonement outcrops savingly into time at the cross.[69] He forgives and restores in a way which keeps faith with creation. The state may be understood ontologically, if not always existentially, as in part a means of God's preservation of order and the visitation of his wrath rooted in justice and flowing from love. The cross indicates that God's forgiveness passes through and does not deny his own wrath. God's judgement is itself a manifestation of mercy.

It is therefore appropriate to speak also of wrath in personal terms as God's own experience. Kraus places the cross within a total work of liberation.[70] Guilt is the shameful betrayal of covenant or familial trust rather than a legal trespass. God is not bound by a law of justice to demand retributive payment to satisfy his own moral nature. The fundamental problem is alienation. The wrath to be overcome is the humiliation, disgrace, resentment and scandal caused by disloyalty. Sin is an offence against love not law, against the Father. Wrath is love's anguish, not juridical. Roman and Germanic legal theory has obscured this primary personal-moral focus. Sin destroys the ground of personal relationship and atonement must not condone but deal with it objectively. Christ's was a representative not a penal substitution, freeing us through an act of God's solidarity with us and giving us new identity. The atonement is the personal process of painful reconciliation which reconciles self-alienated humanity, the vicarious reconciling action of God's holy love which overcomes love's wrath without indulging human sin.[71] Moltmann, we have seen, comes close to such a formulation. The cross anticipates the final judgement on what contradicts God (*FH*, 32–3; *Man*, 115). Yet he neglects the continuing nature of that judgement.

The effect of our analysis is to relate God more directly to the justice-maintaining role of the state. Within its inadequate human justice there is some correspondence to divine justice without which this function would be theologically untenable. The divine No exists now and at the final judgement. Yoder and Moltmann neglect the strong biblical theme of God's *implacable judgement*. The greater wisdom is to see that this No serves and is swallowed up by the divine Yes. In this sense even the judgmental role of the state can *in principle* be turned to a redemptive purpose.

CONCLUSION

From this discussion emerges a primary concern over the dialectic between creation, fall and redemption or the nature and application of Reformed theology's 'cultural mandate', God's command to humankind to develop creation's potential.[72] Yoder's theology lacks the Trinitarian narrative which would provide the fullness his theology needs. Moltmann has this foundation but neglects the fallenness of creation and categories of sin and judgement. In an illuminating analogy John Milbank conceives of Christianity seeking

> to recover the concealed text of an original peaceful creation beneath the palimpsest of the negative distortion of *dominium*, through the superimposition of a third redemptive template which corrects these distortions by means of forgiveness and atonement.

The task is complicated by the persistence of the second text and the way the church compromises with it and continues to write it. This is an unresolved matter for Christianity.[73] Here is the core of the issue. Further exploration must relate to the disentangling of the state as created, fallen and redeemable.

A Reformed–Anabaptist Dialogue

A theology of socio-political structures is complex and may be construed from God's creating, preserving or redeeming activity.[74] We increase the complexity by suggesting that the order of preservation may be conceived in its *continuity* or *discontinuity* with divine action, as directly willed or providentially overruled. This accounts for much of the Reformed–Anabaptist debate over this issue.

In conversation with Richard Mouw, Yoder has identified the alleged Anabaptist rejection of the 'cultural mandate' and the state as significant for Reformed–Anabaptist debate.[75] Anabaptist scepticism over the derivability of ethics from nature, reason or the orders of creation was an extension of the Reformed doctrine of the fallenness of reason. Reformed and Anabaptists are therefore carrying on a conversation in the same league (cf. *TRS*, 160–1).

The Reformed argument assumes: (1) That *the cultural mandate is univocal* with no serious debate as to the substance of moral obligation; to do something different is thus to reject the mandate. (2) *The cultural mandate is monolithic.* Ethical selectivity is therefore culpable inconsistency. (3) *The civil order is the quintessence of the cultural mandate.* All other aspects of culture depend upon the civil order. (4) *The sword is the quintessence of the civil order.* A civil order without the sword is defective. There is no controversy with Anabaptists concerning the cultural mandate or civil order understood as social contract, public welfare, dialogical formulation of public policies, or the execution of policies serving the common weal. The sword is the point of debate. (5) In identifying sword and civil order Reformed theology is in effect *fusing creation and fall.* Unfallen society would need civil order but not sword. Only here did Anabaptists deny the call to administer the 'created order'. (6) *The sword is available to believers* because of (7) a *divine act of institution of government* after the flood. (8) All this is *known by way of revelation.*

The key issue here concerns the degree to which the 'sword' can belong to creation or redemption. Social order is a created mandate but the claim that it must wield the sword fuses creation and fall. For Yoder the 'order of nature' beneath the structure of fallenness is compromised to the point of being lost[76] and so his scepticism about the knowledge of creation is clear.

Mouw responds that under certain conditions it is legitimate for disciples to participate in governmentally sanctioned lethal violence. In that governments are vested by God with legitimate authority to police internally and defend from external enemies, it is permissible and even obligatory for

Christians to participate. On occasion God did in the Old Testament endorse the use of violence.[77] Yet if God has in some sense instituted the sword Mouw speculates, without answer, on how its exercise is altered by the work of the Lamb.[78] He finds room for a new Reformed–Anabaptist front involving a vocational pacifism which does not stand in judgement on fellow believers who judge differently.[79]

We wish to develop this suggestion of a new front which combines Anabaptist and Reformed positions.[80] The Mouw–Yoder conversation narrows down the contentious issues: (1) Yoder affirms civil order, but the sword is legitimate only as divine accommodation to sin and so is *discontinuous* with discipleship. He does not discuss how far coercion belongs to creation. Creation is obscured by fall. (2) For Mouw the sword belongs to fallenness but is mandated by God to preserve justice. This establishes its *continuity* with discipleship. Yet its function is to be scrutinised and transformed in the light of redemption. These positions express responsible and morally accountable positions. They correspond closely to the distinction between Anabaptist social theology and the relatively more positive and Reformed English Baptist approach identified in Chapter 3. It might however be more accurate for Yoder to describe the Reformed position not only as fusing creation and fall but (from Yoder's perspective) as combining *fall* and *redemption* since the permission or institution of the sword by God rather than its root in creation is what makes it acceptable.

Walter Wink's extensive analysis of the biblical language of the powers can clarify here our discussion. All reality is comprised of inner and outer dimensions. The inner dimension he calls 'interiority' and sees as the spirituality which is constellated within any human institution. What the New Testament knows as 'the world', human society in defiance of God, Wink calls 'the System'.[81] The biblical language of angels, demons and the devil does not refer to metaphysical ontologies but expresses the interiority of alienated social structures. 'Satan', therefore, is the collective weight of human fallenness, the spirituality constellated by the alienated human race in its entirety or by a society that idolatrously pursues its own enhancement.[82]

The System involves domination kept in place by violence. It is a network of systems hell-bent on control, a satanic parody of God.[83] The history of human states is a history of domination and violence in which the states change but the underlying, beastly reality abides (Revelation 13), successively riding the winners of history.[84] This is the nature of political power. Still, there is abundant evidence that human beings can live peaceably and are not themselves 'genetically wired for warfare'.[85] In contrast to the System stands the reign of God revealed in Christ.[86] Christ's kingdom is not of this world. He is the small scale fluctuation which will lead to large-scale transformation.[87] The church is to act in liberating continuity with him but pressure from the System has forced it progressively towards the hierarchical and violence-based system that Jesus rejected. 'The dream of the New Reality of Jesus has long since turned into the nightmare, first of Christendom, then of our more recent secular totalitarianisms'.[88]

So far, Wink argues on the side of an 'anarchic' view of the 'powers', but this requires qualification. The powers are good, fallen and to be redeemed. It is idolatry and not intrinsic evil which accounts for the System.[89] Furthermore, these three realities concerning the powers are to be understood *simultaneously* rather than *consecutively*:

> God at one and the same time *upholds* a given political or economic system... required to support human life; *condemns* that system insofar as it is destructive of full human actualization; and *presses for its transformation* into a more humane order. Conservatives stress the first, revolutionaries the second, reformers the third. The Christian is expected to hold together all three.[90]

We have identified a tension between the Reformed and Anabaptist understandings of the state. Reformed approaches take seriously the created nature of the powers, their preserving role and the possibility of redemption. Anabaptist approaches focus upon the fallenness of the system to the detriment of its creation. The Anabaptists were right to express their understanding paradoxically and so concede the fallenness and yet the necessity of the powers.

> It is precisely this simultaneity of Creation, Fall, and Redemption, freed from literalistic temporalizing, that delivers us from naiveté regarding our personal or social powers for transformation. It liberates us from the illusion that at least some institutions are 'good' and viable and within human direction, or can be rendered so by discipline or reform or revolution or displacement. The Powers are at one and the same time ordained by God and in the power of Satan. They can, to some degree, be humanized, but they are still fallen. They can be open to transcendence, but they will still do evil. They may be benign, but within a Domination System of general malignancy.[91]

This enables Wink to

> negotiate a truce between two camps long at odds. The one argues that all governmental, economic, educational, and cultural systems are intrinsically evil, though capable of some limited good. This position is held by some Amish, Mennonites and others from the Anabaptist tradition. The other insists that governments and other public institutions are not just post-Fall phenomena but intrinsic elements of God's creation, and therefore capable not only of reform but even of being 'christianized'. This position is associated with the Calvinist tradition... [T]he invidious

'either/or' of the debate leaves us either abandoning the Powers to secularity or installing an establishment Christianity: either withdrawal or theocracy... Instead of these two extremes, the New Testament view of the Powers gives us a broad continuum of possible emphases, adaptable to every situation. There are no pre-packaged answers to tell us how Christians should engage the powers... all live in a paradox of 'as if not', as being in but not of the Domination System. 'Come out of her, my people' (Rev. 18:4) may be our marching orders but so may be the call to assume secular office (as with Joseph and Daniel). Spiritual discernment takes the place of fixed rules.[92]

A critical stance implies both the disavowal of Constantinianism and the retrieval of a more subversive critique of the state. Otherwise the distinction between church and state remains a matter merely of divine delegation rather than addressing the radical fallenness of the world recognised by radical Augustinianism and Anabaptism alike. Moltmann's Trinitarian theology provides every reason for rediscovering the doctrine of creation but failing to reckon fully with sin and fall it requires Yoder's more critical analysis to complement and sharpen it. Yet it is more confident about present redemption and finds in the covenant a direction in which this may be achieved. This differs from the theocratic strands of Augustinianism and Calvinism which are a false assimilation of redemption to fall. Instead it challenges the fallen structures in the light of redemption in order to retrieve more adequately the ontological reality of social co-operation. It does not uncritically baptise the sword into the order of redemption and this is a primary Anabaptist concern.

Conclusion: The State and Paradox

As with King Saul, the state is both a rejection of divine kingship and a gracious divine accommodation to human autonomy. It is both rooted in creation and added as a remedy for fallenness. It is unsurprising that Anabaptists and Reformed have stressed first one side and then the other of the paradox. To overlook the fallenness of the state draws it inappropriately into the church or assimilates the church to its idolatrous demands. Constantinianism succumbs to this error. It is also erroneous to neglect God's gifts in creation and providence. A fully Trinitarian theology, informed by God's revelation in Christ, which recognises the divine proximity within the world guards against this.

This analysis enables us now to move beyond a paradoxical formulation of the state since it clarifies the points of apparent contradiction. However, it leaves us with an unmistakable ambivalence in our formulation. To summarise:

(1) Christian theology will be conscious of *the corporate nature of human society as created by God*. This createdness includes regional, national[93] and cultural identity, the potential for institutions to support, shape and discipline human society, and a *nurturing* 'dominion' over creation (the 'cultural mandate'). It involves *Gemeinschaft* rather than *Gesellschaft*. This allows room for the 'state' as co-ordinated co-operation in achieving common ends and voluntary justice. Such action is both protective, in that it shields weaker members of the community, and 'coercive' in that corporate action creates an unstoppable force which it is difficult to resist. This coercion is not oppressive since it grows out of agreement and consensus. Political service of the community is a noble task involving the disposition of power and of decisions which affect others, but such power is willingly accorded by the 'governed' and remains accountable to them. It has great potential for good.

(2) Christian theology will be conscious of *the actual fallenness of all human corporate existence and its resolute resistance to God*. Being estranged from God the political sphere resists God and serves individual and group self-interest. Legitimate and accountable dominion is transformed into individual and group domination maintained by violence. Institutions and nations behave idolatrously and seek religious legitimation to maintain their power. Political service is used as a means of self-advancement for cynical purposes. Nevertheless, obscured within this fallen reality but not abolished there remains the created ontology necessary for human existence. The dialectic of creation and fall means that the state and politics will remain an ambiguous affair. The fact and extent of the fall is revealed in the cross of Christ at which human institutions and persons alike were revealed in their hostility to God.

(3) Christian theology will be conscious of *the possibility of redemption* which both awaits the consummation and takes form within the boundaries of history in the messianic and covenantal community through Christ and the Spirit. Here there is a provisional restoration of created ontology, of truly personal and truly corporate existence. The church points to and stimulates renewal in the civil community but cannot join itself without compromise to the fallen and dominating structures of society and state. Its civil task is to seek the recovery of created ontology, 'the concealed text of an original peaceful creation beneath the palimpsest of the negative distortion of *dominium*' (Milbank). It must do this 'through the superimposition of a third redemptive template which corrects these distortions by means of forgiveness and atonement'. The church's life in Christ by the Spirit constitutes this template. Yet 'the persistence of the second text and the way the church compromises with it and continues to write it' remains the chief obstacle. Disentanglement from complicity with the fallen powers is necessary. This entails the rejection of the idolatry of nationhood and of war, which proceeds from national idolatries, but raises questions about that

defence of the peace and the civil order which we have called 'policing' and for which a biblical mandate exists. Non-violent policing can be declared an extension of the protective and legitimately coercive functions of the created (rather than fallen) order and is *in principle* unproblematic. 'Violent' policing might be considered complicity with the 'second text' or in extreme circumstances as the least evil *because it is mandated by God in this limited circumstance* as permissible. Whether wrath is understood in the redemptive manner outlined above, and the degree of openness of police functions to the 'order of redemption' will be crucial elements in the process of discrimination between these elements. The church neither endorses nor condones violence but embodies peace in its common life. It recognises supportively both the freedom and the dilemmas of conscience faced by its individual members. There are ambiguities where the most that can be required is responsible and accountable action.[94]

NOTES

1   Cf. Rasmusson, *The Church as Polis*, 27.
2   Ibid., 376.
3   Ibid., 126.
4   Ibid., 188, 215, 225, 260.
5   Yoder, 'On Not Being Ashamed of the Gospel: Particularity, Pluralism, and Validation', *FP* 9:3 (1992), 286–7, 289.
6   Rasmusson, *The Church as Polis*, 282–4.
7   S. J. Holland, 'Preaching with Prophets, Musing with Mystics, Dancing with Strangers: Anabaptism as Public Theology'. Address delivered at the 'Whither the Anabaptist Vision?' Conference, Elizabethtown, USA, 14 June 1994.
8   Ibid., 5–6.
9   Cf. T. Koontz, 'Mennonites and "Postmodernity"', *MQR* 63:4 (1989), 421, 424.
10 Moltmann's approach overlooks the degree to which the NT presents the incarnate Christ as having accomplished the 'end' of creation: A König, *The Eclipse of Christ in Eschatology* (Grand Rapids: Eerdmans, 1989), 73.
11 See the exchange in *Dialogue Sequel*, 27 and, 57–8.
12 Cf. K. Barth, 'The Lordless Powers', *The Christian Life: Church Dogmatics* IV/4 (Edinburgh: T. and T. Clark, 1981), 213–32.
13 'Zwölf Bemerkungen zur Symbolik des Bösen', *EvTh* 52:5 (1992), 2, 6.
14 K. W. Clements, *A Patriotism For Today* (London: Collins, 1986), 46–9.
15 According to Moltmann, 'order of preservation' (*Erhaltungsordnung*) was coined by Bonhoeffer. 'Order of creation' (*Schöpfungsordnung*) implies that institutions derive intrinsic worth from their supralapsarian creation. 'Order of preservation' implies an institution preserved by God's grace or wrath and so of temporary value. Bonhoeffer later adopted the more fluid language of the 'mandates' and discerned four: marriage and family, culture, government and church. These were to exist until

the eschaton: 'The Lordship of Christ and Human Society' in *Two Studies in the Theology of Bonhoeffer* (New York: Charles Scribner's Sons, 1967), 76, 79–80 ; Clements, *Patriotism*, 48–9.

16 'Covenant or Leviathan? Political Theology for Modern Times', *SJT* 47:1 (1994), 21–3.

17 This is a particular and enduring element in Moltmann's early thought to which Meeks does not draw attention despite *Origins*, 21–3. 'The federal theology potentially provided an adequate base for the reconstruction of northern European Protestant society and culture': D. A. Weir, *The Origins of the Federal Theology in Sixteenth-Century Reformation Thought* (Oxford: Clarendon Press, 1990), 7.

18 'Covenant or Leviathan?', 30, 34.

19 Ibid., 28–9, 31.

20 Ibid., 40.

21 Ibid., 26.

22 Koontz, 'Mennonites and "Postmodernity"', 421, 426.

23 Wogaman, *Christian Perspectives on Politics*, 43, 46.

24 K. Marx and F. Engels, *The Communist Manifesto* (Harmondsworth: Penguin, 1967), 82. Engels: 'The state is nothing but a machine for the oppression of one class by another, in the democratic state no less than in the monarchy': *Karl Marx Selected Works Volume II* (New York: International Publishers, 1939), 459–60 .

25 Wogaman, *Christian Perspectives on Politics*, 13.

26 Ibid., 233.

27 D. K. Friesen, *Christian Peacemaking and International Conflict: A Realist Pacifist Perspective* (Scottdale: Herald Press, 1986), 53.

28 Wogaman, *Christian Perspectives on Politics*, 231.

29 Ibid., 128.

30 Friesen, *Christian Peacemaking*, 99.

31 Milbank argues that coercion is sometimes necessary to protect people from self-damage. The risk of promoting resentment is offset by the possibility that the recipient may later consent to the measures taken. This redeems the action by retrospective acceptance: Milbank, *Theology and Social Theory*, 418.

32 Friesen, *Christian Peacemaking*, 72–94.

33 Ibid., 55–61.

34 Hauerwas, 'Messianic Pacifism', 33.

35 Friesen, *Christian Peacemaking*, 156.

36 P. B. Yoder, 'Toward a Shalom Biblical Theology', *CGR* 1:3 (1983), 49.

37 'Covenant or Leviathan?', 34–5.

38 H. R. Niebuhr, 'The Doctrine of the Trinity and the Unity of the Church', *ThT* 3 (1946), 383; Stassen, 'The Politics of Jesus – Moving Towards Social Ethics', 18–23.

39 J. Corrie, 'Towards a "Trinitarian Political Theology"', *Anvil* 6:1 (1989), 35.

40 Le Masters, *Discipleship for all Believers*, 110.

41 Ibid., 31, 37, 39.

42 Ibid., 19, 41, 51–77.

43 Ibid., 59, 74.

44 Ibid., 96.

45 Ibid., 84–5.

46 Ibid., 81–3.

47   Huebner, Review of *The Transformation of Culture*, 92. See also on the limitations of discipleship language: S. F. Dintaman, 'The Spiritual Poverty of the Anabaptist Vision', *CGR* 10:2 (1992), 205–8.

48   'Via the narrow christocentric defile, Bonhoeffer attains to a new panorama of the world as the place which God has made and reconciled to himself through the incarnation, cross and resurrection of Jesus Christ': Clements, *Patriotism*, 57.

49   Le Masters, *Discipleship For All Believers*, 184–5, 204.

50   Similarly G. G. Koontz considers Yoder's christocentrism preserves the concreteness of the biblical story but that a more theocentric vision is needed in inter-religious dialogue: 'Confessional Theology in a Pluralistic Context', 295–6.

51   A. J. Reimer, 'The Nature and Possibility of a Mennonite Theology', *CGR* 1:1 (1983), 40, 43.

52   Ibid., 36, 44–5, 54.

53   J. D. Weaver, 'Perspectives on a Mennonite Theology', *CGR* 2:3 (1984), 208.

54   T. R. Y. Neufeld, 'Christian Counterculture: Ecclesia and Establishment', *MQR* 63:2 (1989), 202.

55   M. Beintker, 'Creator Spiritus: Zu einem unerledigten Problem der Pneumatologie', *EvTh* 46:1 (1986), 24–6.

56   Milbank, *Theology and Social Theory*, 384. Cf. Pawlikowski's distinction between the 'commanding God' and the 'compelling God' who wins by the attractiveness of his nature rather than by domination: 'The Holocaust and Contemporary Christology', 45.

57   Marshall, 'The Ground and Content', 238.

58   R. D. Bush, 'Recent Ideas of Divine Conflict. The Influence of Psychological and Sociological Theories of Conflict upon the Trinitarian Theology of Paul Tillich and Jürgen Moltmann'. DPhil Dissertation, Oxford, 1990, 369.

59   Ibid., 372.

60   Ibid., 373–75.

61   Ibid., 377.

62   Ibid., 382.

63   R. J. Bauckham, 'In Defence of the Crucified God' in N. M. De S. Cameron (ed.), *The Power and the Weakness of God* (Edinburgh: Rutherford House Books, 1990), 98.

64   Corrie, 'Towards a "Trinitarian Political Theology"', 44.

65   Wogaman, *Christian Perspectives on Politics*, 254–6.

66   Ibid., 256.

67   Ibid., 129.

68   E. Brunner, *Justice and the Social Order* (London: Lutterworth Press, 1945), 102–3.

69   D. M. Baillie, *God was in Christ: An Essay on Incarnation and Atonement* (London: Faber and Faber, 1956 and 1968), 198–200.

70   J. D. Weaver argues that the *Christus Victor* motif is the proper motif of a minority church, fell out of use after Constantine and is once more needed: 'Atonement for the Nonconstantinian Church', *MT* 6:4 (1990), 307–23.

71   Kraus, 'Interpreting the Atonement in the Anabaptist–Mennonite Tradition', 307–311, *Jesus Christ Our Lord* (Scottdale: Herald Press, 1990), 159–68; T. N. Finger, *Christian Theology: An Eschatological Approach* I (Scottdale: Herald Press, 1985), 329–30, 340–1.

72 H. Dooyeweerd: 'The story of creation itself indicates that the cultural mode of formative activity is grounded in God's creation order. God immediately gave man the great cultural mandate: subdue the earth and have dominion over it. God placed this cultural command in the midst of the other creational ordinances. It touches only the historical aspect of creation. Through this aspect, creation itself is subject to cultural development': *Roots of Western Culture: Pagan, Secular, and Christian Options* (Toronto: Wedge Publishing Foundation, 1979), 64–5.

73 Milbank, *Theology and Social Theory*, 417.

74 Hauerwas, 'The Non-resistant Church', 197; W. Herberg, 'The Social Philosophy of Karl Barth' in Barth, *Community, State and Church*, 26–7.

75 'Reformed Versus Anabaptist Social Strategies: An Inadequate Typology', *TSF Bulletin* 8 (1985), 2–7.

76 Ibid., 5–6.

77 Mouw, 'Christianity and Pacifism', 105–6.

78 R. J. Mouw, 'Abandoning the Typology: A Reformed Assist', *TSF Bulletin* 8 (1985), 10.

79 'Christianity and Pacifism', 109.

80 See also Loewen, 'Church and State in the Anabaptist–Mennonite Tradition', 160.

81 Wink, *Engaging the Powers*, 52.

82 W. Wink, *Unmasking the Powers: The Invisible Forces That Determine Human Existence* (Philadelphia: Fortress Press, 1986), 25.

83 *Engaging the Powers*, 49.

84 Ibid., 90–2.

85 Ibid., 36–7.

86 Ibid., 46–9.

87 Ibid., 55, 58.

88 Ibid., 45–6.

89 Ibid., 65.

90 Ibid., 67.

91 Ibid., 70.

92 Ibid., 84.

93 Nationalism renders the status of the modern nation state questionable but biological continuity through time and some common regional and historical identity appear essential: K. W. Clements, *Patriotism* and 'Nationalism and Internationalism: A Theological Critique' in R. J. Bauckham and R. J. Elford (eds.), *The Nuclear Weapons Debate* (London: SCM Press, 1989), 65–79.

94 In Chapter 9 I develop a programmatic statement of the relation of church, social order and state out of the more detailed analysis of this dissertation.

Towards a Politics of Resurrection

This chapter draws together some of the diverse threads of this dissertation and develops them in twenty-one unfolding theses. The aim is to produce a constructive theology which goes beyond the more precise discussions of the dissertation itself and illustrates the uses to which its enquiries may be put. The main text reflects the argument of previous chapters with supplementary comment largely contained in the footnotes.

The Trinity: Fountainhead of Theology

Thesis 1: *The doctrine of the Trinity is the fountainhead of all Christian theology, including of the church and the social order.*

Here the doctrine is understood in the social and historical way expounded by Moltmann. The God who has his being in independence from the world has opened himself to it so that it exists in dependence upon and interaction with Father, Son and Holy Spirit. There are no autonomous realms of reality separate from Christ's lordship but there is a complementarity of divine action in creation, preservation and redemption whose intention is revealed in the total career of Christ.

Thesis 2: *The doctrine of the Trinity is the source in particular of the theology of mission and constitutes a claim upon all creation.*

Christian mission flows from the prior mission and self-giving of God through Christ in the Spirit. Christian faith cannot be dissolved into general religious consciousness. God's universal and loving mission has taken form in a particular human being, in particular events and in a particular community – but with universal intent.[1] The humble mode of God's self-revelation in Christ indicates that the mission is pursued by the declaration of truth not the quest for power, by persuasion and regeneration not imposition.[2]

The Church as Communion and Mission

Thesis 3: *The church is that community of believers which participates by the Spirit in the fellowship and mission of the triune God.*

The being of God as communion is the ontological basis for the church which is that being's echo within history.[3] Through the Son and by the Spirit believers are drawn into the communion of God's own being and become partakers of the divine nature. The word preached evokes response and participation in the Spirit. Inevitably therefore the church is a confessing or believers' church constituted by the Spirit from those gathered into communion. As God's being has stability and form, so the church has stability of relationships and takes form as a community of equally valued persons each giving and receiving, each serving and being served within the body of Christ. The church is an *icon* of the Trinity.[4]

The being of God is dynamic. He moves outwards to embrace the world he has made. This is the *missio Dei* and to be gathered into God's being is to share his mission. The church is therefore a missionary, messianic community sharing in the earthly mission of the Messiah and the manner of its fulfilment. Only in this way can the church be the agent of God's redemption. Tragically, the church has frequently forsaken this vocation. Yet the church is not so much the *agent* of mission as its *locus*. Without claiming masterful control of history it is the place where the powers of the kingdom are present as the Spirit's firstfruits. It rehearses and re-enacts the story which has given it birth.[5] It shapes and forms its members so that Christ is formed within them. In mission the church changes and learns through its missionary encounters (John 16:13; Acts 10: 24–48). Its central concern is the disclosure through its life as the new humanity of the meaning of history in which individuals find their meaning.[6] The church is only authorised to represent the reign of God in the way Jesus did, challenging the powers of evil and bearing in its own life the cost of the challenge.[7]

Thesis 4: *This missionary and messianic concept of the church requires a free church ecclesiology.*

This is implied in the previous thesis and is substantiated throughout the previous chapters. Existence as a freely-choosing and disciplined community is the authentic form of the church's life. This requires the reformation of existing ecclesial bodies and the renewal of congregational life in a decentralised direction in which power is commonly owned by the church's members. Only so can the church adequately act as an evangelistic, socially transforming community which confronts the patterns of control and domination of the political community. This does not imply the rejection of power relations but their refashioning along alternative lines. Salvation has an ecclesial character and has from the beginning been a form of political existence. The radical distinction between church and political community is implied in this fact. Where this is lost sight of the church's potential as a transformative community is diminished.

The Social Order and the State

Thesis 5: *The social order must also be seen within the context of Trinitarian action in creation, preservation and redemption.*

Life is lived in the framework of God's gracious upholding of existence. Social existence belongs intrinsically to creation and reflects the divine image and community. Human personhood depends upon community. By the grace of God such community is preserved for the sake of humane existence. God's saving activity, revealed through Christ and the Spirit, is directed through the church towards the recovery of *shalom*. The cultural mandate is to be taken seriously as the restoration of all human experience to its intended goals. Creation is to be respected and celebrated and the redeemed life includes a deeper penetration into its intrinsic meaning and worth. This includes its social dimensions, its institutional constellations and the particularities of ethnic identity. These are *created* realities and so all idolatry or partisanship are to be resisted, but theology is concerned for the recovery and fulfilment of God's intended creation from beneath the distortions of human fallenness.

Thesis 6: *The state is properly understood as a 'secular' entity.*

The state as we currently know it, a centralised agency disposing of the monopoly of force within a given territory, is a temporary expedient which God ordains or allows as a means of restraining chaos and anarchy while the world waits to be redeemed. This is a doctrine of a limited state. The state cannot be the means of redemption nor should it claim divine honours or messianic significance. All human realities are relativised in the light of the transcendent Lord and ultimate loyalty is due only to him. The state belongs to this world and to this age. It is secular as distinct from sacral, that is, free to fulfil its function without clothing itself with specifically religious symbolism or manipulating religions to mask injustice or structural inequity.[8] The secularising[9] and demythologising power of the gospel becomes evident in unmasking pretensions to divinity. This is the effect of the declaration in Romans 13:4 that rulers are 'God's servant to do you good', not objects of ultimate concern and devotion. The 'secular state' is a Christian notion when it implies rejection of theocratic attempts to impose norms and values dictated by an established church. The state is governed by laws drawn from the collective wisdom of its people. The paradox of these claims is that although they imply the disestablishment of religion, where there is no shared sense of accountability to a transcendent reality within the general population the state is inclined to forsake its mere secularity, fall prey to other ideologies and become idolatrous.

✻ Thesis 7: *The state is a permissive ordinance.*

The state is an alternative to that direct rule of God which can alone safeguard a perfect balance of justice and compassion. Israelite kingship is the ambiguous model, a permissive ordinance of divine accommodation to human unwillingness to submit to divine kingship which nonetheless was taken up into the divine purpose. It remained a flawed and intrinsically unstable instrument employing domination and exploitation (1 Samuel 8: 11–22). This is the background to Romans 13, an ambiguous legitimation which questions at the same time as it permits. This subverts Calvin's enthusiastic legitimation of rulers as vicars of God.

Thesis 8: *Each state represents a particular 'configuration' or 'constellation' of the human potential for organisation and institutionalisation.*

There is no state 'as such', no metaphysical entity of independent existence outside the people who compose it.[10] Actual states are rooted in and develop from the human capacity for corporate and co-operative organisation and are the particular forms assumed under the conditions of sin and fall from this potential. They are malleable, capable of reconfiguration. The created energies and substructures that give rise to the state are capable of redemption and transfiguration, but the particular configurations we call states are absorbed and superseded in the consummated kingdom by the direct rule of God.

Thesis 9: *Despite the role assigned to them the state and all systems of human government are intrinsically flawed, although providentially overruled.*

All systems of government, however stable and peaceful in the present, have
❦ their proximate origin in violence and the lust for power and are ultimately maintained by violence. There is an intensification of fallenness when it comes to structures as opposed to persons. Being constellated from human potential they are inherently fallen. They tend to serve the purposes of the ruling élite. Religious significance given to states is therefore always corrosive of true religion.

It is significant to the Christian that the Roman state perceived Jesus as a political offender and insurrectionist and crucified him. A faith which has the cross at its heart cannot take a naive attitude towards political authorities but will be aware of the discontinuity between divine and state action. It is to the credit of Anabaptism that this discontinuity was recognised. Christianity is
an eschatological faith with a future hope that subverts present pretensions. But the cross which judges human states also indicates that they are

providentially determined. Against their will they are required to do God's will to the extent that a limited justice and peace are maintained.

Thesis 10: *The limited, temporal role of the state involves the maintenance of justice, peace and freedom.*

Whatever the state does it will do imperfectly. It is inevitably tainted by the self-interest of the powerful. The role assigned to it by God is to reward the good and punish the evil-doer. It is the providentially ordered framework within which human beings may live out their lives peacefully, freely and fairly. However, as a fallen structure it will only ever deliver a limited justice, peace and freedom and does even this by the grace of God. Only God can bring about the full reality.

The distinction between policing and making war holds good. Policing is directed to the maintenance of order and peace and can be directed with precision against evil-doers. It aims to thwart and restrain wrongdoing. The state's judicial function regulates and channels public anger and to achieve this needs to be effective and just. It serves also to safeguard community values. It is not necessary to oppose wrath to redemption as the former can serve the latter. War is undertaken between nations and by its very nature destroys the peace and afflicts the innocent. Romans 13 does not mandate such action. Questions remain about the legitimacy of defence of the civil order on which internal peace depends and an impartial policing function between nations in conflict. In these areas violence is not, however, the only option.

Thesis 11: *In matters of religion the state is called to be 'neutral' and to respect plurality.*

No state or society can be value-neutral but 'neutrality' in this proposition refers to the value of *impartiality* which is a fundamental biblical requirement of rulers. The state provides the historical framework within which religious faiths might argue and persuade. The maintenance of religious liberty is therefore a duty of the state and is arguably the liberty from which all others derive.[11] True faith cannot be coerced.[12] Thesis 11 is a theological implicate of this conviction and its concept of the impartial state a product of a particular religious vision.[13] Free church Christianity supports plurality without endorsing pluralism.[14] It hopes for a 'covenantalism' or 'chartered pluralism' as a way of holding together social unity and diversity.[15]

The doctrine of election, which stresses the freedom of divine grace, implies that faith in Christ is not a matter of human legislation but of free divine action. To anticipate the divine decision is a form of blasphemy. Constantinianism created a hybrid of Christianity and coercive power which is a denial of the essential aspects of the freedom of God and the freedom of humanity. Persecution and privilege are to be rejected. State impartiality towards religion does not of necessity imply indifference. Religious traditions and living faiths shape lives and foster personal and civic virtues in a manner essential to the social order. Politics is a function of culture and culture has religion at its heart.[16] So the effort to secure tolerance by denying the reality of religion is bizarre.[17]

We do not deny the need for societies to derive their fundamental values from a religious source. Impartiality is a religious value. It is entirely consistent that Christianity both seek to propagate itself and evangelise culture and that it refuse to do this through imposition but only through persuasion. The moral consensus will inevitably express itself eventually through the collective, and to that extent coercive, legislation of the civil community. As this use of power is based upon consensus it does not *in principle* conflict with the Christian criticism of domination.[18]

Thesis 12: *Within the fallen structures of human states is a created ontology awaiting redemption.*

This is a crucial balancing statement. In that the purpose and goal of creation is *covenant* and that humans are ontologically capable of harmonious relationship with God and each other, symbiosis, community and cooperation are essential elements of their existence. Christian action towards the state is directed towards qualifying its nature as domination in the direction of covenant. This task is only ever fragmentarily accomplished.

Thesis 13: *The theology of the state is, in summary, ambivalent.*

This conclusion is implied in the analysis of the powers as created, fallen and to be redeemed. The ambivalence is evident in biblical attitudes to the state in Old Testament and New Testament. It is characteristic of the church before Constantine and of Anabaptism which recognised the necessity of government while rejecting its invasive and violent methods and its consequent discontinuity with divine or ecclesial action. What we there described as paradox, suggesting an apparent conflict owing to inadequate understanding, we are now able to call 'ambivalence' because our analysis has clarified its nature. The ambivalence is evident in Yoder. The Reformed, theocratic tradition perceived it with less clarity and accommodated redemption to fall by overestimating the continuity between divine and state action. In the federal tradition retrieved by Moltmann we have discovered an alternative Reformed approach more consonant with Anabaptism and supplementing its neglect of creation. The covenant of redemption enables recovery of creation's ontology and points to an area of greater continuity with divine, redemptive action. The divine proximity heightens the hope for its redemption. We cannot therefore close off the possibility that the powers may find themselves fulfilling redemptive purposes.

Here then is the element of ambivalence when we regard the state, an ineliminable tension between any political allegiance and discipleship.[19] To stress the createdness of the powers at the expense of their fallenness leads us to fall prey to them. This is the element of truth in those conservative positions which would separate the spiritual and the political.[20] To stress their fallenness at the expense of their createdness might lead us to negate the necessary good they can do. Only in maintaining the ambivalence do we judge with sound judgement. Our contention is however that first of all we must recognise the fallen nature of the powers and their severe inability. Only thus are we freed from illusion to recognise within them the ontology of God's creation and the relative possibilities of restoration.

The Relationship of Church and Social Order

How in the light of our discussion does the church relate to the social order?

Thesis 14: *It is essential to maintain the church–world distinction.*

The language of 'church and state' already implies a distinction and a potential conflict between two centres of loyalty. From the beginning, Christianity, whatever the variations, has insisted that there is a dialogue between church and rulers. This acted as a stimulus towards a more open society. Yet Constantinianism confused the distinction between two radically different determinations and overestimated the fallen state's capacity to be congruous or continuous with the redeeming activity of God. God's rule over the church is immediate but over the state it is permissive and by providential overruling.[21] The church's task is to seek first God's kingdom and apply itself to conformity to God in Christ through the Spirit. Rightly enterprised this is a political service in that it relativises the state and enables it to assume its appropriate place. The church must concern itself therefore with its primary duty and although it can accomplish a variety of things must not seek them apart from this duty.[22]

Thesis 15: *The cause of Christ will never be advanced by means of worldly power or alliances with the state.*

This was the Constantinian error and it stands in direct contrast to the way of cross and resurrection embraced by Jesus. Worldly power is attractive and in each generation its temptations need to be faced and resisted anew. The temptation is to seek power in order to do good things. Yet the fallenness of the powers needs to be taken into account. Those who seek to bend the powers to their will eventually find themselves being bent. In this sense Christians are 'anarchists'; they are suspicious of worldly power and do not believe that God's purposes are achieved by entering into the domination system and using it for supposedly good ends. In keeping with Jesus' mission, the church is to remain detached from partisan power struggles and to concern itself with truth rather than propaganda. For it to fulfil its task a distance of church from state is necessary which is jeopardised by establishment, implicit concordat or holy alliance.[23]

This implies that the church should reject any unqualified form of alignment with political and governmental authorities nor should it be capturable by partisan programmes. Its transcendent dimensions make mandatory a critical distancing from all temporal movements.[24] This is traditionally known as the 'separation of church and state' and is a fundamental free church axiom. It stands in contrast to the idea of an established church or a state religion. Its rationale lies in the perception that because the powers are fallen any form of alignment of the church with them is bound to be corrupting and the distinction between church and world eroded. The powers of state seek to use religion for narrow political ends, to legitimate their own status or policies. The church is tempted to pursue its ends by the illegitimate means of power, privilege and imposition.[25] This is an unholy alliance and a wrong understanding of mission. It is a form of sectarianism since it identifies the church with national, localised identities rather than allowing it to be the new humanity which transcends all earthly loyalties.[26] It also suffers from the illusion of establishing 'premature absolutes'[27] within the always provisional circumstances of humanity, emphasising the 'divinity' of the church and a premature universality rather than its continuing humanity.[28] Because it is faith in the crucified and looks for the coming of 'the kingdom of our God and of his Christ' to replace the kingdoms of this world, Christianity makes an inherently unstable and unpredictable state religion.

Sociologically speaking there can be no absolute separation of church and state since all institutions benefit from the stability of other institutions, especially that of the state.[29] It is preferable therefore to speak of the 'disestablishment of religion'.[30] Establishment hinders the potential of religion to express its genius.[31] For the church to embrace its minority, pilgrim existence is to liberate itself for mission.[32]

A challenge to free church ecclesiology exists in that it is historically indebted for its vitality and definition to the very state religion against which it protests. Yoder recognises that the free church is historically and theologically dependent upon the unreformed mother church and radicalises an incomplete reformation, piggybacking intellectually and institutionally upon it and posing the challenge of a non-dependent non-post-establishment form of the believers' church.[33] The free church provides a radical stimulus to formal religion[34] whereas state religion provides both the Christianised mass from which it recruits and the means of wider social impact.

An established church arguably obviates a merely private religion and maintains the tradition of social responsibility.[35] The most persuasive argument in its favour within the English context is that, provided it undergoes some reform to obviate erastianism and fulfils increasingly an ecumenical and representative function within a religiously plural society, a weak establishment such as now exists maintains sufficient distance from the state to be a symbol of a transcendent dimension in a way which checks the monistic tendencies of the secular.[36] Paradoxically this could serve precisely the opposite, critical purpose from the monism which has been the weakness of establishment in the past. On the other hand, for the church to divest itself of institutional power and privilege could open up the possibility of a truer dialogue with minority religious communities.[37] The two ecclesial forms of the church as inclusive institution and as believing community can arguably be seen as the *yin* and the *yang* of the church, opposite but complementary forces which mitigate each other's risks.[38] In actuality they are symbiotic, but the free church form has the future potential and is justified in pressing for consistent change in the direction it represents.[39]

Thesis 16: *The disestablishment of religion does not imply the separation of church from society.*

Christians live in society and follow the example of their Lord in so doing. They are concerned to affirm the accountability of all aspects of human existence and culture to him, to witness to his meaning for the public square[40] and to see public affairs shaped, as much as is feasible in the present age, by Christian perspectives. They seek to ensure that the state remains properly secular (avoiding idolatry), impartial in matters of religion (while respecting the place and importance of religious faith among its citizens) and committed to justice, peace and freedom. The existence of such a state is a blessing and its absence or distortion a potential tragedy. However, the state is a human enterprise which is not predicated upon faith in God but is an accommodation by God to human unbelief. While Christians are determined by faith in God and their opinions are informed by their faith and values, in the political realm they are bound to argue for solutions and remedies which operate with what is humanly possible for a given society at a given time. They will operate with a constellation of engagement models.[41]

Thesis 17: *The church moulds society wherever possible according to its own pattern of social existence in Christ.*

The church recognises the fallenness of all political powers and their limitations. All come under judgement. It guards itself against delusion and false hope and refuses to locate final hope for humanity in any human ideology or political system but only in the Messiah. Its detachment is a form of engagement freeing it to distinguish between relative goods. Because the powers are rooted in created reality they are however capable of redemptive improvement and the Christian duty is to seek for this. This is done by:

(a) *Faithfully being the church.* In remaining true to their vocation Christians collectively resist encroachments and develop values which can be offered in time to the public arena. The justice, peace and freedom which are the responsibility of the state receive definition and are protected from distortion, in part, through the witness of the church. From within its own life the church is able to offer ways of relating in social organisms which may be translated into the wider community. This is particularly so in the common ownership and exercise of power distinctive of the free church[42] and in the practice of reconciling forgiveness. Messianic communities have innovative potential for all humanity.

(b) *Participating constructively in the social order and the intermediate structures of society.* The maintenance of liberty depends on these as buffers between the state and the unbridled use of power on the one hand and the unaccountable market on the other. They offer maximum opportunity for involvement and allow the values of the church to be translated into the wider community in the development of a moral consensus and practice out of which social legislation ultimately grows. Civic society and culture provide space for uncoerced human association in ways which enable both government and market to function less coercively.[43]

(c) *Political participation.* The power of government to affect the whole of a society means that redemptive change must in time reach this dimension, not however by imposition but by regeneration. Concern for this impact should not be considered an arrogant 'seizing of the levers of power' but as the proper use of God-given power. The state exists as the outer limit and framework of society and is a legitimate sphere of involvement to the degree that it entails no basic compromise of Christian principle. The distinction between 'positive law' and 'natural law' is helpful here. All states are *de facto* based upon the power of the ruling classes. The Christian aims to develop as a check and bridle against this that rule of law which emerges from the corporately owned moral consensus and is akin to the church's own covenant and self-regulation. This certainly involves shaping the community's intentional use of its powers within an accountable framework in the direction of non-violence, co-operation and common welfare.

Each of these above spheres makes vital contributions to political life. They are to be seen interactively with the impulses of the Spirit arising primarily and repeatedly within the church without being confined to it. The church does not receive the Spirit as a static possession but only dynamically so within the missionary dialogue with the world, a dialogue which is full of surprises and holds open the possibilities of change for both church and world. The legislation of social change and the nurture of just and humane institutions is a necessary task but can only happen because of the wider process of cultural formation. For this reason the political sphere is no more an arena of social responsibility than the others. It is one avenue of social change among others, although it is to be recognised that the breakdown or corruption of the organs of state can wreak great havoc. Excessive dependence upon political action as the principal thrust against social evil neglects the fact that the political is dependent upon vital forces nurtured elsewhere.[44] Private, public and political realms are interrelated and interdependent. The evangelization of culture can produce major paradigm shifts in the public consensus which ultimately have power to shape official, political and economic structures.[45]

Thesis 18: *The church is called to non-violence in imitation of Christ.*

This needs to be asserted unambiguously. God's redemptive purposes are not achieved through violence. Violence, including state violence, is an extensive problem. Within the fallen world system it is inevitably the case that certain actions are deemed *necessary* for the preservation of the system. As systems carry with them their own logic and rationality, within the terms of such rationality they may indeed be necessary. However, Christians who live by faith in the God of resurrection are not bound by human necessity or the false rationality of fallen systems. This freedom is made known in Christ. The call to peacemaking is not a call to 'legalistic' obedience but to proclamation of and witness to the gospel. The issue concerns whether violence is a way of carrying out the witness.[46]

Although Jesus' death was an example of willing self-sacrifice we doubt that this can be used to legitimate passive non-resistance. Jesus practised a third way between violence and resignation to injustice: non-violent resistance. This was an active form of resistance which did not mirror the evil of the evil-doer but sought creative ways of awakening a consciousness of injustice. The instances he gave included prophetic actions and humour.[47] Evil is certainly to be resisted, but not by recycling the injustices involved. By their nature Jesus' actions are not repeatable. Non-violence is not therefore a new law, but a new freedom from the vicious circle of necessity. Without claiming there can never be exceptions we *can* say that non-violence is at the heart of the gospel and of the church's task.[48] Only the rejection of violence creates the pressure to develop creative alternatives.[49] The church should never legitimise the violence of war. But it is also wise not to judge those who take up violence out of desperation.[50]

Thesis 19: *The state holds the monopoly of force but its use remains always morally ambiguous and questionable.*

Here we re-encounter the paradox to which the study of Anabaptism calls attention. State-sanctioned force is necessary but questionable. We advocate here a more pragmatic, 'realist pacifist'[51] approach than Yoder's. We have indicated that coercion can belong to creation and not necessarily to fall. We have also developed understandings of the wrath of God which perceive it as serving merciful and redemptive purposes. We do not define *physical force* as necessarily violent but as possibly restraining violence.[52] We are therefore more confident that coercion and force *may* be used properly *in extremis* in societies where social and political power is commonly owned and accountable to the moral consensus. We see here a greater continuity with the preserving activity of the Triune God than Yoder allows. In other states the difficulties will be greater and possibly insuperable, the discontinuity with divine action greater. However, any use of force and coercion remains questionable because of its dangers and risks.

The normativeness of Jesus for the Christian is applied to these functions not as their necessary rejection but as their modification. Here we believe there to be a tenable distinction between the 'orders of creation' as an *epistemological* and as an *ontological* category. With Moltmann and Yoder we reject the category as an independent norm for knowledge or action. But there is an ontological dimension which concerns the givenness of existence and the harmony of life with life, which makes its legitimate demands but which is only truly known in the light of revelation. The responsibility to nurture and protect belongs to created social existence. To neglect this responsibility at whatever level of human social existence is unacceptable and it must be reckoned with theologically. The manner, but not the fact, of its exercise will be modified in the light of Christ. The example of Jesus cannot be made into a *principle* of absolute non-violence. It does however embody the imperative of love of enemy and concern for *redemption*. Killing is hard to reconcile with this imperative. We are not willing to dismiss border-line situations where there is a conflict of responsibilities but do not believe that these should determine the debate.

The state monopoly of force is itself a measure to bring violence under control and must be in each case justified and accountable. Unlike Yoder we argue here that in that it is mandated by God it becomes a possible sphere of individual Christian obedience, especially so when non-violent restraint is the norm. Even so, some lethal force may prove necessary in the policing function as a limited and reluctant concession within an overall commitment to non-violence. We resist the logic that extends a concession at one point into a legitimation of violence at any point. If violence is evil primarily because it usurps the divine prerogative over life, this limited divine permission changes its moral nature, as is shown by the divine command to Israel in particular circumstances. But this permissive ordinance is a temporary concession to a world which is passing away.[53] It will always remain a questionable, boundary area in which accountable action will be required, not sinless perfection. We believe that there is a tenable distinction at this point between individual, conscientious Christian action and the peaceful way embodied in the Christian community as a whole. It is never the church's calling to give religious legitimation to killing. Furthermore there is, despite Yoder, a differentiation of behaviour, even of moral behaviour, according to the social office occupied. The duality between church and society is not only a distinction between faith and unbelief but concerns that which is *entrusted* to responsible individuals by society and the fact that such individuals act on behalf of the whole of society and not only of a segment within it. It is conceivable therefore that the same responsible disciple may face differing moral imperatives even while judging them in the light of the one norm, Jesus Christ. This is the truth in Luther's concept of the two kingdoms which both Yoder and Moltmann criticise, and rightly so in so far as it appeals to an independent norm.

The position here espoused differs from Yoder in that it understands the state's use of force, which in itself Yoder accepts, to be a possible sphere of Christian action, which Yoder doubts. It comes close to the positions indicated by Moltmann,[54] yet because Moltmann is reluctant to substantiate the preserving functions of the state he lacks the theological construct to undergird his position. Consequently his concessions to the use of force appear as deviations from his main line of thought and therefore as arbitrary and uncontrolled. The position we have developed allows control to be maintained.

Thesis 20: *It is the duty of the Christian to work for the reduction and minimisation of all forms of violence and coercion.*

A Trinitarian vision of the social order envisages its formation to correspond wherever possible with the divine purpose. This includes qualifying the powers of state in the light of God's purpose of redemption. Fallen society will never correspond with the kingdom of God. A realistic strategy aims to lessen its violence and should produce a position on which many could agree 'beyond just war and pacifism'.[55] The distinction between war and policing is one such step. That between force and violence, although questionable, discriminates between socially authorised protection of the innocent and morally illegitimate violence. The advocacy of non-lethal force and of non-violent restraint wherever possible captures both the need to maintain order and the imperative to leave open for the offender space for repentance and amendment. Our previous analysis of the wrath of God and refusal to oppose this of necessity to redemption indicates that the demands of the order of preservation can to a degree be co-ordinated with that of redemption.

Thesis 21: *The resurrection is both the sign of hope for the world and the assurance that risky imitation of Christ's way has ultimately redemptive power.*

In the Trinitarian activity of God, the life, death and resurrection of Christ are the means of redemption. This is the ground of a universal Christian hope and is the point and means of reconciliation. In so far as Christian action in the Spirit corresponds to the self-giving way of Jesus it participates in his ministry of reconciliation. To follow Christ at these points is risky in that it conflicts with fallen rationality. The resurrection is the sign that in the providence of God such action is never wasted whatever its short term cost. The church shares in the redeeming work of Christ to the extent that, inspired by him, it risks its life.

Conclusion

We set out in the foregoing work to develop in conversation with Yoder and Moltmann a non-Constantinian theology of church and social order to guide the church in its messianic mission. The summary of findings attempted in this chapter can be seen to be closely in line with what Burkholder describes[56] as 'witnessing non-violence' and to incorporate aspects of each view of government he indicates. It asserts that in principle the way of Christ applies to governments while accepting that this ideal will need to be translated into the realm of the possible, given that the way of Christ is not universally embraced. It accepts critically the place of government in creation and the mandate of government to use force in protecting the innocent, but only when applied justly and at a minimal level. It characterises this reality as neutral rather than sinful and hopes for a closer identification of the orders of preservation and redemption. This basic view is mixed with the pragmatism of the dialectical standpoint which is not afraid of ambiguity, a degree of compromise and the art of the possible in the struggle to modify and harness governmental powers in a redemptive direction.

In Chapter 3 we noted that the English Baptists assumed a position between Anabaptism and Reformed Christianity with an inclination to the Reformed. The position we have arrived at here is similarly situated, with the difference that its more critical estimate of the state inclines it towards Anabaptism. We hold that this social and political theology provides a consistent and workable approach to serve the church in its transforming mission.

<h2 style="text-align:center">NOTES</h2>

1   Certain elements in Christianity, its monotheism, its use of military imagery, the language of sovereignty and its universal claims, made it viable as an imperial religion. Yet these themes are subject to constant reinterpretation through the crucified Messiah so that, with closer acquaintance, Christianity has often proven to be an awkward and ambiguous partner for the powerful and to involve a uncongenial form of universality.

   Alasdair MacIntyre has analysed how modernity has rejected teleology and reduced morality to an assortment of conceptual fragments from the past. Moral consensus has become impossible. Politics has become civil war carried on by other means: *After Virtue: A Study in Moral Theory* (London: Duckworth, 1981 and 1985), 253–256. His analysis undergirds Newbigin's thesis that the missionary task of Christianity includes, as it did for the ancient world, the provision of a narrative which makes universal sense. The church does not possess absolute truth but knows where guidance is found for the common search for truth: Newbigin, *The Gospel in a Pluralist Society*, 47, 64, 126, 163. If MacIntyre is correct in arguing that there is no universal rationality distinguishable from particular traditions, the doctrine of election suggests that it is impossible to have universal impact except through a particular tradition, 87. Newbigin rightly claims that the idea of a secular society free of value commitments is a myth, 217–20. The church must claim the 'high ground of public truth' but dogma has been rejected because it became entangled with coercion. The gospel is negated if the freedom in which alone it can be believed is denied, 10, 223. His general thesis is supported by Milbank's argument that social theories are theologies or anti-theologies in disguise, offering a new metaphysics as a totalising representation of finitude: *Theology and Social Theory*, 3, 105, 259, 280. Secular reason cannot be argued against or refuted because it is only a *mythos*. It is only by out-narrating it that people will be persuaded that Christianity offers a better story, 330. Similarly, McFadyen argues that in God's singularity and universality the world's plurality achieves a unity. Yet his position differs from the 'Enlightenment-Christendom' model which allows only one account of truth and rationality. The real public realm has to do not with the enforcement of truth but with a communication between different frames of thought in which truth is to be *communicated* and *found*. This follows from the missionary relationship of Christianity to the world. Dialogical communication, following Jesus, allows freedom to the other to make response and as an overflow of loving mutuality rejects totalitarian politics or epistemological frameworks: A. McFadyen, 'Truth as Mission: The Christian Claim to Universal Truth in a Pluralist Public World', *SJT* 46:4 (1993), 437–56. This captures more effectively than Newbigin the fact that since Christian truth is *self-involving*, it cannot be 'public' in the way that other 'facts' are.

2   In a searching Appendix to Hauerwas' *After Christendom*, David Toole asks whether there is an *implicit* violence in the conviction that one possesses the truth and describes Newbigin's language as 'condescending', 'violent' and 'exclusionary', 158–9. This takes up the issue of whether Christianity must be *inherently* imperialistic because of its 'exclusive' claims. The discussion needs to disentangle truth and power. Claims to truth are bound to seek universal acceptance but this should be by means of persuasion not compulsion. Hans Küng asserts: (a) People can find salvation outside the church in the religions in spite of the untruth they contain. (b) Christianity's *uniqueness* is inevitable in view of the cross of Christ but is not *exclusiveness*. (c) Generous Christian service in a spirit of openness which does not deny its own convictions but also does not compel specific answers is appropriate towards other religions. This means dialectical acceptance and rejection of what is valuable in other religions, honouring and accepting this without absolutism or eclecticism. This is the spirit of the cross and is more concerned with people than systems: 'Die Religionen als Frage an die Theologie des Kreuzes', 401–23.

3   Gunton, *The Actuality of Atonement*, 199 and *The Promise of Trinitarian Theology*, 72.

4   Only recently has the potential of the doctrine of the Trinity for congregational ecclesiology been developed. Western models of the Trinity beginning with the unity of deity have undergirded hierarchical and institutional views of the church whereas Eastern theologies locating divinity in the communion of the persons provide a better basis for the church's form as community: Gunton *The Promise of Trinitarian Theology*, 61–4. Miroslav Volf illustrates the possibilities: As the one God is a fellowship of divine persons so the church is a fellowship of particular persons and the universal church of particular churches. The Spirit's distribution of the *charismata* suggests the church as the pneumatological community – decentralised, sharing common responsibility for the life of the church in a mutual submission in which charismatic gifting is integrated for the common good through the ministry of

those recognised and ordained by the congregation. The church's ecclesiality consists in the reality of Christ's presence among his people only after which come ordination and the sacraments. The *communio sanctorum* is visible only to the degree that the church lives as the *imago trinitatis*. The full experience of the church's integration into the life of God awaits the eschaton but is reflected and illustrated by the present reality of this integration in the church's life: 'Kirche als Gemeinschaft: Ekklesiologische Überlegungen aus freikirchlicher Perspektive' *EvTh* 49:1 (1989), 72.

This raises the issue of institution. Volf understands this to mean the stable structure of social interaction without which nothing is possible. In this sense, the Trinity is an institution since there is a stable structure of interaction between the divine persons. For the church, therefore, the question is not whether it exists as an institution but what kind of institution it should be, 73. This concerns both the distribution of power and whether the cohesion of the institution is externally or internally guaranteed. The distribution of power may be distinguished as between *symmetrical-decentralised* and *asymmetrical-monocentric* institutional forms. Cohesion may be *guaranteed by external forces* or *by free, internal affirmation*. All institutions exist somewhere in the matrix created between asymmetrical-monocentric/externally guaranteed and freely affirmed/symmetrical-decentralised poles. As a fellowship of love the Trinity exists according to the latter institutional model. Consequently, to the degree to which the church exists as an hierarchical institution it fails to represent the Trinity. The more the church is characterised by symmetrical-decentralised forms and by freely affirmed integration, the more it corresponds to the Trinitarian communion. It is possible for a human social entity to achieve stable integration by freely affirmed interaction only by clearly defining the obligations, rights and tasks of a collectivity, and by recognising that such definitions will always be open to improvement, 74–5.

5   Newbigin, *The Gospel in a Pluralist Society*, 119–20.
6   Ibid., 124–5, 136.
7   Ibid., 134.
8   Littell, 'The New Shape of the Church–State Issue', 184.
9   Shiner indicates the variety of uses of this term and suggests its avoidance unless it is specifically identified as referring neutrally to desacralisation, differentiation (recognition of the altered role of the religious community in a changing society) or transposition (the migration of certain 'religious' functions into the 'non-religious' sphere): L. Shiner, 'The Concept of Secularization in Empirical Research', *Journal for the Scientific Study of Religion* 6:2 (1967), 219.
10 E. Yoder, 'Christianity and the State', *MQR* 1:3 (1937), 174.
11 Brunner, *Justice and the Social Order*, 56.
12 The Christian claim to universal significance does not at first sight offer a basis for tolerance and has often been used to deny it. But if free and self-engaging response implies the freedom to withhold that response, tolerance becomes unavoidable. In addition, to be intolerant ignores our limited understanding and overlooks fallibility. This is not to render Christianity doubtful but to distinguish between the *original truth of the person of Christ* and the derivative *human attempt to encapsulate that in doctrine* which is always mutable. The dialogical context provided by tolerance permits the latter to come under scrutiny and so to improve itself: Tinder, *The*

Political Meaning of Christianity, 125–30. This is Moltmann's 'productive tolerance'.

13 The 'naked public square' is better remaining religiously naked than being 'loaded with the one-sided values of those who do not know how to coexist with others who are different in a pluralistic society': C. C. Goen, 'Remembering Who We Are: Some Baptist Perspectives on Church–State Issues', *ABQ* 10:4 (1991), 284–5.

14 Newbigin, *The Gospel in a Pluralist Society*, 14, 243–4.

15 O. Guinness, 'Tribespeople, Idiots or Citizens?: Religious Liberty and the Reforging of the American Public Philosophy', *Spectrum* 23:1 (1991), 40.

16 Neuhaus, *Naked Public Square*, 27.

17 Ibid., 163. The position developed here argues that pluralism is not dependent upon the liberalism with which it is often associated, indeed, liberalism attempts covertly to impose individualism by undervaluing the communal dimensions of religion and developing a homogeneously liberal society. A position which respects the public dimensions of religion is more likely to build a stable political structure:, Marshall, 'Liberalism, Pluralism and Christianity: A Reconceptualisation', *Fides et Historia* 23:3 (1989), 4–17. Faith has the metaphysical and moral vision to make the world safe for pluralism: D. Keyes 'Pluralism, Relativism and Tolerance', *Third Way* 15:10 (1992–93), 33.

18 It should be clear from this that we do not regard a society which has been shaped by an agreed Christian consensus as therefore Constantinian in the way that term has been interpreted in this dissertation.

19 J. J. Haldane, 'Christianity and Politics: Another View', *SJT* 40:2 (1987), 259, 273.

20 Ibid., 265.

21 E. Yoder, 'Christianity and the State', 178.

22 Vicedom, *The Mission of God*, 46. Without an independent common life loyalty to the state would become an absolute. This would be destructive in making loyalty to the instrument higher than the purpose it serves: Lindsay, *Democracy*, 67. This is the foundation of the separation of church and state. There must be room for necessary divided loyalties, 72–3. On the same basis the fostering of the distinction between state and society by developing loyalties beyond the state is necessary. Transcendence is that which makes valuable and makes relative and enables discrimination, 74, 78.

23 Hastings, *Church and State*, 1–15, 54–6.

24 Neuhaus, *Naked Public Square*, 7; Moltmann: 'The real God is an iconoclastic word against man': *Man*, 108–10.

25 Neuhaus, *Naked Public Square*, 165.

26 There is an occasional Baptist disposition to be tolerant towards established religion as an expression of the national spirit and as state recognition of the supremacy of God: e.g. H. Martin, 'Protestantism and the State', *BQ* 12 (1946–48), 316–17. Others find the trend towards civil religion as the merging of consensus religious sentiments with nationalistic aspirations (USA): General Board of the ABC/USA 'American Baptist Policy Statement on Church and State', *ABQ* 6:4 (1987), 206.

27 Mott, *Biblical Ethics and Social Change*, 191–2.

28 Gunton, *The Promise of Trinitarian Theology*, 68.

29 G. Zahn, 'The Religious Basis of Dissent', *MQR* 41:2, 136.

30 Mott, *Biblical Ethics*, 195. Even this requires further definition. Many forms of religion are recognised and protected in law but this does not constitute

'establishment' as we are using the term. Rather it refers to the granting of privileged status to one form of religion in return for certain religious services to the state. Rejection of this form of establishment does not preclude the recognition of a certain tradition as having had historical significance in the formation of a culture and consequently its prominent place within society, provided this tradition is not exclusively privileged. Debates about 'establishment' routinely overlook this distinction between state and society as though disengaging from state links also implies withdrawal from society.

31   Disestablishment of a religion, its deliverance from concerns of country and nation, stimulates greater creativity and fidelity within it. Hans Jonas cited three moments in history to illustrate how political uprooting can lead to a liberation of spiritual substance: the exile of the Jews to Babylonia leading to the creativity of a Second Isaiah, the overthrow of Babylonia by Persia requiring the Babylonian religion to rely on its own spiritual content alone, and, with the collapse of the Persian empire, the transformation of Mazdaism into a rational theological system freed from the negatives of its imperial past: *The Gnostic Religion* (Beacon Press, Boston, 1958), 15–17. Kee cites the further example of the emergence of primitive Christianity from the state cult of Judaism into the Hellenistic world with enriched and liberated potential. These examples suggest both that the disestablishment of religion tends to the flowering of true religious potential and, conversely, that the establishment of religion hinders it, possibly diverting its energy into art as a substitute for the prophetic and away from the establishment of justice and peace: Kee *Christ versus Constantine*, 171–4. Without detracting from the value of the aesthetic, this imbalance needs to be rectified.

32   D. J. Bosch, *Witness to the World: The Christian Mission in Theological Perspective* (London: Marshall, Morgan and Scott, 1980), 248.

33   Yoder, 'The Believers' Church: Global Perspectives', 9–11.

34   J. G. G. Norman believes that while asserting absolute truth the sect-type can acknowledge the relativity of its own understanding. Its values safeguard against spiritual tyranny and encourage toleration, preserving individualism: 'The Relevance and Vitality of the Sect-Idea', *BQ* 27:6 (1978), 252–5. A fruitful tension and interaction is therefore possible between sect-type and church-type (256–7).

35   A. Hastings, 'Church and State in a Pluralist Society', *Theology* 95 (1992), 170.

36   Hastings, *Church and State*, 63–6.

37   P. Weller, 'Freedom and Witness in a Multi-Religious Society: A Baptist Perspective: Part 1', *BQ* 33:6 (1990), 260 and 'Part 2' 33:7, 304.

38   Marty, 'Baptistification Takes Over', 33, 36.

39   Adrian Hastings finds the arguments for disestablishment of the Church of England attractive but believes that both Christianity and English society would be weakened by it without any compensating advantage. The Church would be repudiating too much of its past history in a time of weakness and that would not be wise: *A History of English Christianity*, 664.

40   The 'naked public square' is the result of political doctrine excluding religiously grounded values from the conduct of public business. But the public square cannot remain naked and clothes itself with new 'meanings' imposed by the ambitions of the modern state: Neuhaus, *Naked Public Square*, ix. Now the secular Enlightenment is in collapse alternatives, including those derived from Christian history, can be given serious consideration (175).

41 Neuhaus, *Naked Public Square*, 7.

42 The congregation forms rules which provide the framework for the richness and spontaneity of the common life. By analogy, the state serves the community by regulation in the service of freedom: Lindsay, *Democracy*, 57–8, 65. Compulsion can mean failure in that the state has to make happen what should be achieved freely, but it can also achieve unified action in areas where anarchy and freedom are mutually exclusive and so provide more liberty than would exist without it (45, 53, 58). The state offers means for the peaceful settlement of disputes, can make perpetual war against war and enforce a minimum standard of external conduct in order to maximise liberty. For the same reason it maintains a minimum standard of economic life. A healthy society always therefore maintains a certain amount of regulation and compulsion (59–62).

43 Rasmusson, *The Church as Polis*, 360–7.

44 Mott, *Biblical Ethics*, 197.

45 Holland, 'God in Public', 46–7.

46 H.-W. Bartsch, 'The Foundation and Meaning of Christian Pacifism', in M. E. Marty and D. G. Peerman (eds.) *New Theology No. 6: On Revolution and Non-Revolution, Violence and Non-Violence, Peace and Power* (London: Collier–Macmillan, 1969), 187, 190.

47 Wink, *Engaging the Powers*, 175–82.

48 Ibid., 218.

49 Ibid., 209.

50 Ibid., 240.

51 Friesen's, *Christian Peacemaking* develops this position constructively.

52 Friesen, *Christian Peacemaking*, 152.

53 Wink, *Engaging the Powers*, 239.

54 Moltmann: 'As long as we are still on the way to peace we cannot abolish force altogether, but we can control and limit its use': *EH*, 176.

55 Ibid., 227–9.

56 See above, 44ff.

The Schleitheim Confession, 1527

Brotherly Union of a Number of Children of God Concerning Seven Articles

The articles we have dealt with, and in which we have been united, are these: baptism, ban, the breaking of bread, separation from abomination, shepherds in the congregation, the sword, the oath.

I.   Notice concerning baptism. Baptism shall be given to all those who have been taught repentance and the amendment of life and [who] believe truly that their sins are taken away through Christ, and to all those who desire to walk in the resurrection of Jesus Christ and be buried with Him in death, so that they might rise with Him; to all who with such an understanding themselves desire and request it from us; hereby is excluded all infant baptism, the greatest and first abomination of the pope. For all this you have the reasons and the testimony of the writings and the practice of the apostles. We wish simply yet resolutely and with all assurance to hold to the same.

II. We have been united as follows concerning the ban. The ban shall be employed with all those who have given themselves over to the Lord, to walk after [Him] in His commandments; those who have been baptized into the one body of Christ, and let themselves be called brothers or sisters, and still somehow slip and fall into error and sin, being inadvertently overtaken. The same [shall] be warned twice privately and the third time be publicly admonished before the entire congregation according to the commandment of Christ (Mt. 18). But this shall be done according to the ordering of the Spirit of God before the breaking of bread so that we may all in one spirit and in one love break and eat from one bread and drink from one cup.

III. Concerning the breaking of bread, we have become one and agree thus: all those who desire to break the one bread in remembrance of the shed blood of Christ, they must beforehand be united in the one body of Christ, that is the congregation of God, whose head is Christ, and that by baptism. For as Paul indicates, we cannot be partakers at the same time of the table of the Lord and the table of devils. Nor can we at the same time partake and drink of the cup of the Lord and the cup of devils. That is: all those who have fellowship with the dead works of darkness have no part in the light.

Thus all who follow the devil and the world, have no part with those who have been called out of the world unto God. All those who lie in evil have no part in the good.

So it shall and must be, that whoever does not share the calling of the one God to one faith, one baptism, to one spirit, to one body together with all the children of God, may not be made one loaf together with them, as must be true if one wished truly to break bread according to the command of Christ.

IV. We have been united concerning the separation that shall take place from the evil and the wickedness which the devil has planted in the world, simply in this; that we have no fellowship with them, and do not run with them in the confusion of their abominations. So it is; since all who have not entered into the obedience of faith and have not united themselves with God so that they will do His will, are a great abomination before God, therefore nothing else can or really will grow or spring forth from them than abominable things. Now there is nothing else in the world and all creation than good or evil, believing and unbelieving, darkness and light, the world and those who are [come] out of the world, God's temple and idols, Christ and Belial, and none will have part with the other.

To us, then, the commandment of the Lord is also obvious, whereby He orders us to be and to become separated from the evil one, and thus He will be our God and we shall be his sons and daughters.

Further, He admonishes us therefore to go out from Babylon and from the earthly Egypt, that we may not be partakers in their torment and suffering which the Lord will bring upon them.

From all this we should learn that everything which has not been united with our God in Christ is nothing but an abomination which we should shun. By this are meant all popish and repopish works and idolatry, gatherings, church attendance, winehouses, guarantees and commitments of unbelief, and other things of the kind, which the world regards highly, and yet which are carnal or flatly counter to the command of God, after the pattern of all iniquity which is in the world. From all this we shall be separated and have no part with such, for they are nothing but abominations, which cause us to be hated before our Christ Jesus, who has freed us from the servitude of the flesh and fitted us for the service of God and the Spirit whom He has given us.

Thereby shall also fall away from us the diabolical weapons of violence – such as sword, armor, and the like, and all of their use to protect friends or against enemies – by virtue of the word of Christ: 'you shall not resist evil'.

V. We have been united as follows concerning shepherds in the church of God. The shepherd in the church shall be a person according to the rule of Paul, fully and completely, who has a good report of those who are outside the faith. the office of such a person shall be to read and exhort and teach, warn, admonish, or ban in the congregation and properly to preside among the sisters and brothers in prayer, and in the breaking of bread, and in all things to take care of the body of Christ, that it may be built up and developed, so that the name of God might be praised and honored through us, and the mouth of the mocker be stopped. He shall be supported, wherein he has need, by the congregation which has chosen him, so that he who serves the gospel can also live therefrom, as the Lord has ordered. But should a shepherd do something worthy of reprimand, nothing shall be done without the voice of two or three witnesses. If they sin they shall be publicly reprimanded, so that others might fear.

But if the shepherd should be driven away or led to the Lord by the cross, at the same hour another shall be ordained to his place, so that the little folk and the little flock of God may not be destroyed, but be preserved by warning and be consoled.

VI. We have been united as follows concerning the sword. The sword is an ordering of God outside the perfection of Christ. It punishes and kills the wicked, and guards and protects the good. In the law the sword is established over the wicked for punishment and for death, and the secular rulers are established to wield the same.

But within the perfection of Christ only the ban is used for the admonition and exclusion of the one who has sinned, without the death of the flesh, simply the warning and the command to sin no more.

Now many, who do not understand Christ's will for us, will ask: whether a Christian may or should use the sword against the wicked for the protection of the good, or for the sake of love.

The answer is unanimously revealed: Christ teaches and commands us to learn from Him, for He is meek and lowly of heart and thus we shall find rest for our souls. Now Christ says to the woman who was taken in adultery, not that she should be stoned according to the law of His Father (and yet He says, 'what the Father commanded me, that I do') but with mercy and forgiveness and the warning to sin no more, says: 'Go, sin no more'. Exactly thus should we also proceed, according to the rule of the ban.

Second, is asked concerning the sword: whether a Christian shall pass sentence in disputes and strife about worldly matters, such as the unbelievers have with one another. The answer: Christ did not wish to decide or pass judgement between brother and brother concerning inheritance, but refused to do so. So should we also do.

Third, is asked concerning the sword: whether the Christian should be a magistrate if he is chosen thereto. This is answered thus: Christ was to be made a king, but He fled and did not discern the ordinance of His Father. This we should also do as He did and follow after Him, and we shall not walk in darkness. For He Himself says: 'Whoever would come after me, let him deny himself and take up his cross and follow me'. He Himself further forbids the violence of the sword when He says: 'the princes of this world lord it over them etc., but among you it shall not be so'. Further Paul says, 'Whom God has foreknown, the same he has also predestined to be conformed to the image of his Son', etc. Peter also says, 'Christ has suffered (not ruled) and has left us an example, that you should follow after in his steps'.

Lastly one can see in the following points that it does not befit a Christian to be a magistrate: the rule of the government is according to the flesh, that of the Christians according to the Spirit. Their houses and dwelling remain in this world, that of the Christians is in heaven. Their citizenship is in this world, that of the Christians is in heaven. The weapons of their battle and warfare are carnal and only against the flesh, but the weapons of Christians are spiritual, against the fornication of the devil. The worldly are armed with steel and iron, but Christians are armed with the armor of God, with truth, righteousness, peace, faith, salvation and with the Word of God. In sum: as Christ our Head is minded, so also must be minded the members of the body of Christ through Him, so that there be no division in the body, through which it would be destroyed.

VII. We have been united as follows concerning the oath. The oath is a confirmation among those who are quarrelling or making promises. In the law it is commanded that it should be done only in the name of God, truthfully and not falsely. Christ, who teaches the perfection of the law, forbids His [followers] all swearing, whether true nor false; neither by heaven nor by earth, neither by Jerusalem not by our head; and that for the reason which He goes on to give: 'For you cannot make one hair white or black'. You cannot perform what is promised in swearing, for we are not able to change the smallest part of ourselves.

Now there are some who do not believe the simple commandment of God and who say, 'But God swore by Himself to Abraham, because He was God (as He promised him that He would do good to him and would be his God if he kept His commandments). Why then should I not swear if I promise something to someone?' The answer: hear what Scripture says: 'God, since he wished to prove overabundantly to the heirs of His promise that His will did not change, inserted an oath so that by two immutable things we might have a stronger consolation (for it is impossible that God should lie)'. Notice the meaning of the passage: God has the power to do what He forbids you, for everything is possible to Him. God swore an oath to Abraham, Scripture says, in order to prove that His counsel is immutable. That means: no one can withstand and thwart His will; thus He can keep His oath. But we cannot, as Christ said above, hold or perform our oath, and therefore we should not swear.

Others say that swearing cannot be forbidden by God in the New Testament when it was commanded in the Old, but that it is forbidden only to swear by heaven, earth, Jerusalem, and our head. Answer: hear the Scripture. He who swears by heaven, swears by God's throne and by Him who sits thereon. Observe: swearing by heaven is forbidden, which is only God's throne; how much more is it forbidden to swear by God Himself. You blind fools, what is greater, the throne or He who sits upon it?

Others say, if it is then wrong to use God for truth, then the apostles Peter and Paul also swore. Answer: Peter and Paul only testify to that which God had promised Abraham, whom we long after have received. But when one testifies, one testifies concerning that which is present, whether it be good or evil. Thus Simeon spoke of Christ to Mary and testified: "Behold: this one is ordained for the falling and rising of many in Israel and to be a sign which will be spoken against'.

Christ taught us similarly when He says: Your speech shall be yea, yea, and nay, nay; for what is more than that comes of evil. He says, your speech or your word shall be yes and no, so that no one might understand that He had permitted it. Christ is simply yea and nay, and all those who seek Him simply will understand His Word. Amen.

From *The Schleitheim Confession* translated and edited by John Howard Yoder, Herald Press, Scottdale, PA 15683, USA. Used by permission.

The Augsburg Confession, 1530 (Extract)

Article 16: Civil Government

It is taught among us that all government in the world and all established rule and laws were instituted and ordained by God for the sake of good order, and that Christians may now without sin occupy civil offices or serve as princes and judges, render decisions and pass sentence according to imperial and other existing laws, punish evildoers with the sword, engage in just wars, serves as soldiers, buy and sell, take required oaths, possess property, be married, etc...

Condemned here are the Anabaptists who teach that none of these things indicated above is Christian.

Also condemned are those who teach that Christian perfection requires the forsaking of house and home, wife and child, and the renunciation of such activities as are mentioned above. Actually, true perfection consists alone of proper fear of God and real faith in God, for the Gospel does not teach an outward and temporal but an inward and eternal mode of existence and righteousness of the heart. The Gospel does not overthrow civil authority, the state, and marriage but requires that all these be kept as true orders of God and that everyone, each according to his own calling, manifest Christian love and genuine good works in his station of life. Accordingly Christians are obliged to be subject to civil authority and obey its commands and laws in all that can be done without sin. But when commands of the civil authority cannot be obeyed without sin, we must obey God rather than men (Acts 5:29)

Source: T. G. Tappert (ed.), *The Book of Concord* (Philadelphia: Fortress Press, 1959).

The Barmen Declaration, 1934

In view of the errors of the 'German Christians' and of the present Reich Church Administration, which are ravaging the Church and at the same time also shattering the unity of the German Evangelical Church, we confess the following evangelical truths:

1. 'I am the way the Truth and the Life; no one comes to the Father except through me.' (Jn. 14:6)
    'Truly, truly I say to you, he who does not enter the sheep-fold through the door but climbs in somewhere else, he is a thief and a robber. I am the Door; if anyone enters through me, he will be saved.' (Jn. 10:1, 9)

    Jesus Christ, as he is attested to us in Holy Scripture, is the one Word of God which we have to hear, and which we have to trust and obey in life and in death.

    We reject the false doctrine that the Church could and should recognise as a source of its proclamation, beyond and besides this one Word of God, yet other events, powers, historic figures, and truths as God's revelation.

2. 'Jesus Christ has been made wisdom and righteousness and sanctification and redemption for us by God.' (1 Cor. 1:30)

    As Jesus Christ is God's comforting pronouncement of the forgiveness of all our sins, so, and with equal seriousness, he is also God's vigorous announcement of his claim upon our whole life. Through him there comes to us joyful liberation from the godless ties of this world for free, grateful service to his creatures.

    We reject the false doctrine that there could be areas of our life in which we would belong not to Jesus Christ but to other lords, areas in which we would not need justification and sanctification through him.

3. 'Let us, however, speak the truth in love, and in every respect grow into him who is the head, into Christ, from whom the whole body is joined together.' (Eph. 4: 15-16)

    The Christian Church is the community of brethren in which, in Word and sacrament, through the Holy Spirit, Jesus Christ acts in the

present as Lord. **With both its faith and its obedience, with both its message and its order, it has to testify in the midst of the sinful world, as the Church of pardoned sinners, that it belongs to him alone and lives and may live by his comfort and under his direction alone, in expectation of his appearing.**

We reject the false doctrine that the Church could have permission to hand over the form of its message and of its order to whatever it itself might wish or to the vicissitudes of the prevailing ideological and political convictions of the day.

4.   'You know that the rulers of the Gentiles exercise authority over them and those in high position lord it over them. So shall it not be among you; but if anyone would have authority among you, let him be your servant' (Matt. 20: 25-26)

The various offices in the Church do not provide a basis for some to exercise authority over others but for the ministry with which the whole community has been entrusted and charged to be carried out.

We reject the false doctrine that, apart from this ministry, the Church could, and could have permission to, give itself or allow itself to be given special leaders (Führer) vested with ruling authority

5.   'Fear God, honour the King!' (1 Pet. 2: 17)

Scripture tells us that by divine appointment the State, in this still unredeemed world in which also the Church is situated, has the task of maintaining justice and peace, so far as human discernment and human ability make this possible, by means of the threat and use of force. The Church acknowledges with gratitude and reverence toward God the benefit of this, his appointment. It draws attention to God's Kingdom (Reich), God's commandment and justice and with these the responsibility of those who rule and those who are ruled. It trusts and obeys the power of the Word, by which God upholds all things.

We reject the false doctrine that beyond its special commission the State should and could become the sole and total order of human life and so fulfil the vocation of the Church as well.

We reject the false doctrine that beyond its special commission the Church should and could take on the nature, tasks and dignity which belong to the State and thus become itself an organ of the State.

6. 'See, I am with you always, to the end of the age.' (Matt. 28:20)
   'God's Word is not fettered.' (II Tim. 2:9)

The Church's commission, which is the foundation of its freedom, consists in this: in Christ's stead, and so in the service of his own Word and work, to deliver to all people, through preaching and sacrament, the message of the free grace of God.

We reject the false doctrine that with human vainglory the Church could place the Word and work of the Lord in the service of self-chosen desires, purposes and plans.

The Confessional Synod of the German Evangelical Church declares that it sees in the acknowledgement of these truths and in the rejection of these errors the indispensable theological basis of the German Evangelical Church as a confederation of Confessional Churches. It calls upon all who stand in solidarity with its Declaration to be mindful of these theological findings in all their decisions concerning Church and State. It appeals to all concerned to return to unity in faith, hope and love.

Verbum Dei manet in aeternum

Source: Douglas S. Bax, 'The Barmen Theological Declaration: A New Translation', *Journal of Theology for Southern Africa* 47 Special Issue: In Celebration of the Barmen Declaration (Cape Town, 1984), 12–20. Used by permission.

Bibliography

Works by Jürgen Moltmann

a) Books

Prädestination and Perseveranz: Geschichte und Bedeutung der reformierten Lehre 'de perseverentia sanctorum' (Neukirchen: Neukirchener Verlag, 1961)

The Theology of Hope: On the Ground and the Implications of a Christian Eschatology, translated by J. W. Leitch (London: SCM Press, 1967)

Religion, Revolution and the Future, translated by M. Douglas Meeks (New York: Charles Scribner's Sons, 1969)

Hope and Planning, translated by Margaret Clarkson (London: SCM Press, 1971)

The Gospel of Liberation, translated by H. Wayne Pipkin (Waco, Texas: Word Books, 1973)

Theology and Joy, translated by Reinhard Ulrich and with an extended introduction by David Jenkins (London: SCM Press, 1973)

The Crucified God: The Cross of Christ as the Foundation and Criticism of Christian Theology, translated by R. A. Wilson and John Bowden (London: SCM Press, 1974)

Man: Christian Anthropology in the Conflicts of the Present, translated by John Sturfdy (London: SPCK, 1974)

The Experiment Hope, edited and translated by M. Douglas Meeks (London: SCM Press, 1975)

The Church in the Power of the Spirit: A Contribution to Messianic Ecclesiology, translated by Margaret Kohl (London: SCM Press, 1977)

The Open Church: Invitation to a Messianic Lifestyle, translated with an introduction by M. Douglas Meeks (London: SCM Press, 1978). Published in the USA as *The Passion for Life: A Messianic Lifestyle* (Philadelphia: Fortress Press, 1978)

The Future of Creation, translated by Margaret Kohl (London: SCM Press, 1979)

Experiences of God, translated by Margaret Kohl (London: SCM Press, 1980)

Jewish Monotheism and Christian Trinitarian Doctrine: A Dialogue by Pichas Lapide and Jürgen Moltmann, translated by Leonard Swidler (Philadelphia: Fortress Press, 1981)

The Trinity and the Kingdom of God: The Doctrine of God, translated by Margaret Kohl (London: SCM Press, 1981)

Following Jesus Christ in the World Today: Responsibility for the World and Christian Discipleship (Elkhart: Occasional Paper No 4 of the Institute of Mennonite Studies, 1983)

The Power of the Powerless, translated by Margaret Kohl (London: SCM Press, 1983)

Bekennende Kirche Wagen: Barmen 1934–1984 Herausgegeben von Jürgen Moltmann mit Beiträgen von Jürgen Moltmann, Martin Rohrkrämer, Bertold Klappert, Ulrich Duchrow, Helmut Simon, Joachim Beckman, Wilhelm Niesel, Kurt Scharf, Hans-Joachim Kraus (München: Kaiser Traktate, Chr. Kaiser Varlag, 1984)

God in Creation: An Ecological Doctrine of God. The Gifford Lectures, 1984–85 translated by Margaret Kohl (London: SCM Press, 1985)

On Human Dignity: Political Theology and Ethics, translated M. D. Meeks, O. C. Dean and S. Gehlert and with an introduction by M. Douglas Meeks (Philadelphia: Fortress Press, 1985)

Theology Today: Two Contributions towards Making Theology Present, translated by John Bowden (London: SCM Press, 1988)

Creating a Just Future: The Politics of Peace and the Ethics of Creation in a Threatened World translated by John Bowden (London: SCM Press, 1989)

The Way of Jesus Christ: Christology in Messianic Dimensions, translated by Margaret Kohl (London: SCM Press, 1990)

History and the Triune God : Contributions to Trinitarian Theology, translated by John Bowden (London: SCM Press, 1991)

The Spirit of Life: A Universal Affirmation, translated by Margaret Kohl (London: SCM Press, 1992)

The Coming of God: Christian Eschatology, translated by Margaret Kohl (London: SCM Press, 1996)

With Jürgen Weissbach, *Two Studies in the Theology of Bonhoeffer* (New York: Charles Scribner's Sons, 1967) translated by R. H. and I. Fuller and with an Introduction by R. H. Fuller)

With Harvey Cox, Langdon Gilkey, Van A. Harvey and John Macquarrie and edited by by Frederick Herzog, *The Future of Hope: Theology as Eschatology* (New York: Herder and Herder, 1970)

With Herbert W. Richardson, Johann Baptist Metz, Wili Oelmüller and M. Darrol Bryant, *Religion and Political Society*, edited and Translated (in part) in The Institute of Christian Thought (New York: Harper and Row, 1974)

With Elisabeth Moltmann-Wendell, *God: His and Hers*, translated by John Bowden (London: SCM Press, 1991)

With Elisabeth Moltmann-Wendell (eds.), *Humanity in God* (London: SCM Press, 1984)

b) Articles

'Prädestination und Heilsgeschichte bei Moise Amyraut: Ein Beitrag zur Geschichte der reformierten Theologie zwischen Orthodoxie und Aufklärung', *ZfK* 65/66 (1953–54), 270–303

'Zur Bedeutung des Petrus Ramus für Philosophie und Theologie im Calvinismus', *ZfK* 68 (1957), 295–318

'Herrschaft Christi und soziale Wirklichkeit nach Dietrich Bonhoeffer', *Theologische Existenz Heute* Neue Folge 71 (1959), 5–61

'Ernst Bloch: Messianismus und Marxismus: Einführende Bemerkungen zum "Prinzip Hoffnung"', *Kirche in der Zeit: Evangelische Kirchenzeitung* 15:9 (1960), 291–295

'Jacob Brocard als Vorläufer der Reich-Gottes-Theologie und der symbolisch-prophetischen Schriftauslegung des Johann-Coccejus', *ZfK* 71 (1960), 110–129

'Die Wirklichkeit der Welt und Gottes konkretes Gebot nach Dietrich Bonhoeffer' in Eberhard Bethge (ed.), *Die Mündige Welt III* (Munich, 1960), 42–67

'Die Kirche als Faktor einer kommenden Weltgemeinschaft', *Kirche in der Zeit: Evangelische Kirchenzeitung* 21:7 (1966), 307–310

'Antwort auf die Kritik der Theologie der Hoffnung' in W-D Marsch (ed.), *Diskussion über die 'Theologie der Hoffnung' von Jürgen Moltmann* (Munich: Chr Kaiser Verlag, 1967), 201–238

'The Theology of Revolution', *New Christian* (12 December 1968), 9–10

'The Future as Threat and Opportunity' in D. R. Cutler (ed.), *The Religious Situation* (Boston: Beacon Press 1969), 921–941

'Toward a Political Hermeneutics of the Gospel' in M. E. Marty and D. G. Peerman (eds.), *New Theology No 6: On Revolution and Non-Revolution, Violence and Non-Violence, Peace and Power* (London: Collier–Macmillan, 1969), 66–90

'Stations et Signaux: Coup d'oeil retrospectif sur mon cheminement personnel de ces dix dernières années', 'Introduction à la théologie de l'espérance' and 'La religion de l'espérance', *Études théologiques et religieuses* 46:4 (1971), 357–363, 399–414 and, 385–398 respectively

'Theological Basis of Human Rights and of the Liberation of Man' in *Reformed World* 31:8 (1971), 348–357

'The "Crucified God": A Trinitarian Theology of the Cross', *Interpretation* 26 (1972), 278–299

'The "Crucified God": God and the Trinity Today' in *Concilium 8:6 Church and World* (1972), 26–37 (London: Burns and Oates, 1972)

'Response to the Opening Presentations' and 'Hope and the Biomedical Future of Man' in E. H. Cousins (ed.), *Hope and the Future of Man* (Philadelphia: Fortress Press, 1972), 55–59 and, 89–105

'Gesichtspunkte der Kreuzestheologie heute', *EvTh* 33:4 (1973), 346–365

'The Cross and Civil Religion' in J. Moltmann et al., *Religion and Political Society* (New York and London: Harper and Row, 1974)

'Foreword' to M. D. Meeks The Origins of the Theology of Hope (Philadelphia: Fortress Press, 1974), ix–xii

'Freedom in the Light of Hope', *JTSA* 6 (1974), 23–33

'The Liberating Feast' in H. Schmidt and D. Power (eds.), *Concilium 2:10: Politics and Liturgy* (London: Burns and Oates, 1974)

'Warum "Schwarze Theologie"?', *EvTh* 34:1 (1974), 1–3

'The Trinitarian History of God', *Theology* 78 (1975), 632–46

'Creation and Redemption' in R. W. A. McKinney (ed.), *Creation, Christ and Culture: Studies in Honour of T. F. Torrance* (Edinburgh: T. and T. Clark, 1976), 119–134

'God's Kingdom as the Meaning of Life for the World' in H. Küng and J. Moltmann (eds.), *Concilium 117: Why Did God Make Me?* (New York: Seabury Press, 1978), 97–103

'Nachwort' to P. F. Momose, *Kreuzestheologie: Eine Auseinandersetzung mit Jürgen Moltmann* (Freiburg: Herder, 1978), 174–183

'Théologie et Droits de L'Homme', *Revue des Sciences Religieuses* 52 (1978), 299–314

'The Confession of Jesus Christ: A Biblical Theological Consideration' in H. Küng and J. Moltmann (eds.), *Concilium 118: An Ecumenical Confession of Faith?* (New York: Seabury Press, 1979), 13–19

'"Dialektik, die umschlägt in Identität" – was ist das? Zu Befürchtungen Walter Kaspers' and 'Antwort an die Kritik an "Der gekreuzigte Gott"' in M. Welker (ed.), *Diskussion über Jürgen Moltmanns Buch 'Der gekreuzigte Gott'* (Munich: Chr. Kaiser Verlag, 1979), 149–156 and, 165–190

'The Liberation of Oppressors', *JTSA* 26 (1979), 24–38

'Theology of Mystical Experience', *SJT* 32:6 (1979), 501–20

'The Challenge of Religion in the '80s' in J. M. Wall (ed.), *Theologians in Transition: The Christian Century 'How My Mind Has Changed' Series* with an introduction by Martin E. Marty (New York: Crossroad, 1981), 107–12

'The Motherly Father. Is Trinitarian Patripassianism Replacing Theological Patriarchalism?' in E. Schillebeeckx and J. B. Metz (eds.), *Concilium 143: God As Father?* (1981), 74–84

'Theological Proposals towards the Resolution of the Filioque Controversy' in L. Vischer (ed.), *Spirit of God, Spirit of Christ: Ecumenical Reflections on the 'Filioque' Controversy* (London: SPCK and Geneva: World Council of Churches, 1981), 164–73

'Vorwort' in John Howard Yoder, *Die Politik Jesu: Der Weg des Kreuzes* (Maxdorf: Agape Verlag, 1981), 5–7

'Die Bibel und das Patriarchat: Offene Fragen zur Diskussion über "Feministische Theologie"', *EvTh* 42:5 (1982), 480–4

'Liebet Eure Feinde' in V. Hochgrebe (ed.), *Provokation Bergpredigt* (Stuttgart: Kreuz Verlag, 1982), 63–74 also published as 'Feindeliebe', *Evangelische Kommentare* 15 (1982), 503–5

'Politisierung der Religion', *Evangelische Kommentare* 15 (1982), 276

Articles: 'Cross, Theology of' 'Hope', 'Perseverance' and 'Theodicy' in Alan Richardson and John Bowden (eds.), *A New Dictionary of Christian Theology* (London: SCM Press, 1983), 135–7, 270–2, 441–2, 564–6 respectively

'Editorial: Can there be an Ecumenical Mariology?' in H. Küng and J. Moltmann (eds.), *Concilium 168: Mary in the Churches* (Edinburgh: T. and T. Clark, 1983), xii–xv

'Commentary on "To Bear Arms"' in R. A. Evans and A. F. Evans (eds.), *Human Rights: A Dialogue Between the First and Third Worlds* (Maryknoll: Orbis Books and Guildford: Lutterworth Press, 1983), 48–52

'Communities of Faith and Radical Discipleship: An Interview with Jürgen Moltmann' (conducted by Miroslav Volf), *The Christian Century* 100 (1983), 246–9

'Ich glaube an Gott den Vater: Patriarchalische oder nichtpatriarchalische Rede von Gott?', *EvTh* 43. 5 (1983), 397–415

'Alienation and Liberation of Nature' in L. Rouner (ed.), *On Nature* (Notre Dame: University of Notre Dame Press, 1984), 133–44

'Teresa of Avila and Martin Luther: The Turn to the Mysticism of the Cross', *Studies in Religion* 13 (1984), 265–78

'The Unity of the Triune God: Remarks on the Comprehensibility of the Doctrine of the Trinity and its Foundation in the History of Salvation', *SVTQ* 28:3 (1984), 157–71

'The Fellowship of the Holy Spirit: Trinitarian Pneumatology', *SJT* 37:3 (1984), 287–300

'Verschränkte Zeiten der Geschichte: Notwendige Differenzierungen und Begrenzungen des Geschichtsbegriffs', *EvTh* 44. 4 (1984), 213–27

'Reformation and Revolution' in M. Hoffmann (ed.), *Martin Luther and the Modern Mind: Freedom, Conscience, Toleration, Rights*, Toronto Studies in Theology 22 (New York and Toronto: Edwin Mellen Press, 1985), 163–90

'The Inviting Unity of the Triune God' in J-P. Jossue (ed.), *Concilium 177: Monotheism* (Edinburgh: T. and T. Clark, 1985), 50–8

'The Expectation of His Coming', *Theology* 88 (1985), 425–8

'Christian Theology and Political Religion' in L. Rouner (ed.), *Civil Religion and Political Theology* (Notre Dame: Notre Dame Press, 1986), 41–58

'Foreword' to G. C. Chapman, *Facing the Nuclear Heresy: A Call to Reformation* (Elgin: Brethren Press, 1986), ix–xii

'Religion and State in Germany – West and East', *Annals of the American Academy of Political and Social Science* 483 (1986), 110–18

'Die atomare Katastrophe: Wo bleibt Gott?', *EvTh* 47:1 (1987), 50–60

'Foreword' to R. J. Bauckham, *Moltmann: Messianic Theology in the Making* (Basingstoke: Marshall–Pickering, 1987), vii–x

'Peace and the Fruit of Justice' in H. Küng and J. Moltmann (eds.), *Concilium 195: A Council for Peace* (Edinburgh: T. and T. Clark, 1988), 109–20

'Schöpfung, Bund und Herrlichkeit: Zur Diskussion über Karl Barths Schöpfungslehre', *EvTh* 48:2 (1988), 108–27

'Dient die "pluralistische Theologie" dem Dialog der Weltreligionen?', *EvTh* 49:6 (1989), 528–36

'The Nuclear Catastrophe and Where is God?' and 'Justice Creates Peace' in S. Tunnicliffe (ed.), *Towards a Theology of Peace: A Symposium* (London: European Nuclear Disarmament, 1989), 24–34 and, 266–74

'Political Theology and the Ethics of Peace' in T. Runyon (ed.), *Theology, Politics and Peace* (Maryknoll: Orbis Books, 1989), 31–42

'Come Holy Spirit – Renew the Whole of Creation', *EcRev* 40:2 (1990), 98–107

'Die Entdeckung der Anderen: Zur Theorie des kommunikativen Erkennens', *EvTh* 50:5 (1990), 400–14

'Human Rights, The Rights of Humanity and the Rights of Nature' in H. Küng and J. Moltmann (eds.), *Concilium: The Ethics of World Religion and Human Rights* (London: SCM Press, 1990/2), 120–35

'The Scope of Renewal in the Spirit', *EcRev* 42:2 (1990), 98–106

'Fundamentalism and Modernity' in H. Küng and J. Moltmann (eds.), *Concilium: Fundamentalism as an Ecumenical Challenge* (London: SCM Press, 1992/3), 109–115

'Zwölf Bemerkungen zur Symbolik des Bösen', *EvTh* 52:1 (1992), 2–6

'The Church as Communion' in W. Beicken, S. Freyne and A. Weiler (eds.), *Concilium: Messianism Through History* (London: SCM Press, 1993/1), 136ff

'Covenant or Leviathan? Political Theology for Modern Times', *SJT* 47:1 (1994), 19–41

With Elisabeth Moltmann-Wendel, 'Menschwerden in einer neuen Gemeinschaft von Frauen und Männern', *EvTh* 42:1 (1982), 80–92

With Hans-Joachim Kraus, 'Bekennende Kirche werden: Barmen 1934–1984', *Junge Kirche* 45:5 (1984), 260–3

With Elisabeth Giesser, 'Menschenrechte, Rechte der Menschheit und Rechte der Natur', *EvTh* 50:5 (1990), 437–44

Works by John Howard Yoder

a) Books

The Ecumenical Movement and the Faithful Church Focal Pamphlet Series No 3 (Scottdale: Mennonite Publishing House, 1958)

As You Go: The Old Mission in A New Day Focal Pamphlet Series No 5 (Mennonite Publishing House, 1961)

The Christian and Capital Punishment (Newton, Kansas: Faith and Life Press, 1961)

Täufertum und Reformation in der Schweiz: 1. Die Gespräche zwischen Täufern und Reformatoren in der Schweiz, Schriftenreihe des Mennonitischen Geschichtsvereins 6 (Karlsruhe: Buchdrückerei und Verlag H. Schneider, 1962)

The Christian Witness to the State (Newton, Kansas: Faith and Life Press, 1964)

The Pacifism of Karl Barth (Scottdale: Herald Press, 1968)

Täufertum und Reformation in Gespräch: Dogmengeschichtliche Untersuchungen der frühen Schweizerischen Täufern und Reformatoren Basler Studien zur Historischen und Systematischen Theologie 13 (Zurich: EVZ-Verlag, 1968)

Karl Barth and the Problem of War (Nashville: Abingdon Press, 1970)

Nevertheless: The Varieties and Shortcomings of Christian Pacifism (Scottdale: Herald Press, 1971)

The Politics of Jesus: Vicit Agnus Noster (Grand Rapids: Eerdmans, 1972)

The Original Revolution: Essays on Christian Pacifism (Scottdale: Herald Press, 1972)

The Legacy of Michael Sattler (Scottdale: Herald Press, 1973)

Preface to Theology: Christology and Theological Method (Elkhart: Co-op Bookstore, 1981)

Christian Attitudes To War, Peace and Revolution: A Companion to Bainton (Elkhart: Co-op Bookstore, 1983)

What Would You Do?: A Serious Answer To A Standard Question (Scottdale: Herald Press, 1983)

The Priestly Kingdom: Social Ethics as Gospel (Notre Dame: University of Notre Dame Press, 1984)

When War is Unjust: Being Honest in Just-War Thinking (Minneapolis: Augsburg Publishing House, 1984)

He Came Preaching Peace (Scottdale: Herald Press, 1985)

The Fullness of Christ (Elgin, Illinois: Brethren Press, 1987)

The Royal Priesthood: Essays Ecclesiological and Eccumenical, compiled by Michael Cartwright (Grand Rapids: Eerdmans, 1994)

For the Nations: Essays Public and Evangelical (Grand Rapids: Eerdmans, 1997)

With Douglas Gwyn, George Hunsinger and Eugene F. Roop, *A Declaration on Peace: In God's People the World's Renewal Has Begun* (Scottdale: Herald Press, 1991)

With Glen H. Stassen and D. M. Yeager, *Authentic Transformation: A New Vision of Christ and Culture* (Nashville: Abingdon, 1996)

The Schleitheim Confession, translated and edited by John H. Yoder (Scottdale: Herald Press, 1973)

Balthasar Hübmaier: Theologian of Anabaptism, translated and edited by John H. Yoder and H. Wayne Pipkin (Scottdale: Herald Press, 1989)

b) Articles

'Caesar and the Meidung', *MQR* 23:2 (1949), 76–98

Review of *La Guerre et l'Évangile* by Jean Lasserre in *MQR* 28:1 (1954), 76–7

'Reinhold Niebuhr and Christian Pacifism', *MQR* 29:2 (1955), 101–17

Article: 'France', *ME* 2 (Scottdale: Mennonite Publishing House, 1956), 359–62

'Epistolary: An Exchange by Letter' and 'What are our Concerns?', *CP* 4 (1957), 4–9, 20–32

'The Prophetic Dissent of the Anabaptists' in G. F. Herschberger (ed.), *The Recovery of the Anabaptist Vision* (Scottdale: Herald Press, 1957), 93–104

'A Review and Discussion of "Kirchenzucht bei Zwingli" by Roger Ley', *MQR* 31:1 (1957), 63–71

'The Turning Point in the Zwinglian Reformation', *MQR* 32:2 (1958), 128–40

'Balthasar Hubmaier and the Beginnings of Swiss Anabaptism', *MQR* 33:1 (1959), 5–17

With Heinold Fast, 'How to Deal with Anabaptists: An Unpublished Letter of Heinrich Bullinger', *MQR* 33:2 (1959), 83–94

'Marginalia', *CP* 7 (1959), 56–63

Article: 'Zwingli', *ME* 4, 1052–4

'The Two Kingdoms', *Christus Victor* 106 (1959), 3–9

'Capital Punishment and the Bible', *CT*, 4 February 1960, 3–6

'Marginalia', *CP* 8 (1960), 44–9

'A Light to the Nations' and 'Marginalia', *CP* 9 (1961), 14–18 and 44–8

'Continental Theology and American Social Action', *RIL* 30:2 (1961), 225–30

'The Christian Answer to Communism' and 'Marginalia', *CP* 10 (1961), 26–31 and, 32–39

'The Otherness of the Church', *MQR* 35:4 (1961), 286–296

'A Review and Discussion', *MQR* 35:1 (1961), 79–88

'Translator's Preface' and 'Translator's Epilogue' in H. Berkhof, *Christ and the Powers* (Scottdale: Herald Press, 1962 and 1977), 5–7 and 69–70

'Von göttlicher und menschlicher Gerechtigkeit', *ZEE* 6 (1962), 166–81

'Marginalia', *CP* 11 (1963), 59

'A Review and Discussion', *MQR* 37:1 (1963), 133–8

'And On Earth Peace…', *Mennonite Life* 20:3 (1965), 108–10

'Marginalia – A Syllabus of Issues', *CP* 12 (1966), 51–6

'Anabaptist Origins in Switzerland', 'Persecution and Consolidation' and 'A Summary of the Anabaptist Vision' in C. J. Dyck (ed.) *An Introduction to Mennonite History* (Scottdale: Herald Press, 1967), 26–35, 36–43 and 103–11 respectively

'Binding and Loosing', *CP* 14 (1967) and also published as an appendix to John White and Ken Blue, *Healing the Wounded: The Costly Love of Church Discipline* (Leicester: IVP, 1985), 211–34

'Is There Historical Development of Theological Thought' in C. J. Dyck (ed.), *The Witness of the Holy Spirit: Proceedings of the Eighth Mennonite World Conference* (Nappanee: Evangel Press, 1967), 379–88

'On the Meaning of Christmas', *CP* 16 (1968), 14–19

'The Evolution of the Zwinglian Reformation', *MQR* 43:1 (1969), 95–122

'The Fullness of Christ: Perspectives on Ministries in Renewal', *CP* 17 (1969), 33–93

'A People in the World: Theological Interpretation' in J.L. Garrett Jr (ed.), *The Concept of the Believers' Church: Addresses from the 1967 Louisville Conference* (Scottdale: Herald Press, 1969), 250–83.

'The Way of the Peacemaker' in J. A. Lapp (ed.), *Peacemakers in a Broken World* (Scottdale: Herald Press, 1969), 111–25

'Anabaptist Vision and Mennonite Reality' in A. J. Klassen (ed.) *Consultation on Anabaptist–Mennonite Theology: Papers Read at the 1969 Aspen Conference* (Fresno: Council of Mennonite Seminaries, 1970), 1–46

'A Non-Baptist View of Southern Baptists', *Review and Expositor* 67 (1970), 219–28

'Reformation and Missions: A Literature Review', *Occasional Bulletin of the Missionary Research Library* (1971), 1–9; also published in revised form in W. R. Shenk (ed.), *Anabaptism and Mission* (Scottdale: Herald Press, 1984), 40–50

'Der Kristallisationspunkt des Täufertums', *MG* Neue Folge 24 (1972), 35–47

'Church Growth Issues in Theological Perspective' in W. R. Shenk (ed.), *The Challenge of Church Growth: A Symposium* (Elkhart: Institute of Mennonite Studies, 1973), 25–47

'Exodus and Exile: The Two Faces of Liberation', *Crosscurrents* (1973), 297–309

'Jesus and Power', *EcRev* 25 (1973), 447–54

'*Anabaptists and the Sword* Revisited: Systematic Historiography and Undogmatic Nonresistants', *ZfK* 85 (1974), 126–39

'The Biblical Mandate' in R. J. Sider (ed.), *The Chicago Declaration* (Carol Streams: Creation House, 1974), 88–116

'Evangelicals at Chicago', *Christianity and Crisis* 34:2 (February 18, 1974), 23–5

'Anabaptism and History: "Restitution" and the Possibility of Renewal' in H-J. Goertz (ed.), *Umstrittenes Täufertum, 1525–1975, Neue Forschungen* (Göttingen: Vandenhoeck und Ruprecht, 1975), 144–258

'The Disavowal of Constantine: An Alternative Perspective on Interfaith Dialogue' in *Tantur Yearbook of the Ecumenical Institute for Advanced Theological Studies* (Jerusalem: Tantur, 1975/76), 47–68

'The "Constantinian" Sources of Western Social Ethics', *Missionalia* 4:3 (1976), 98–108 (also *PK*, 135–47)

'What Would You Do If? An Exercise in Situation Ethics', *JTSA* 17 (1976), 3–24

'The Christian Case for Democracy', *JRE* 5:2 (1977), 209–223 (also, in rewritten form, *PK*, 151–71)

'Introduction' to *The Origins and Characteristics of Anabaptism: Proceedings of the Colloquium organized by the Faculty of Protestant Theology of Strasbourg, 20–22 February 1975* (The Hague: Martinus Nijhoff, 1977), 3–9

'The Schleitheim Brotherly Union', *GH*, 22 February 1977, 165–66

'Power and the Powerless', *CQ*:36 (1978), 29–35

'The Theological Basis of the Christian Witness to the State', 'On Divine and Human Justice', 'Church and State According to a Free Church Tradition' and 'Epilogue: The Way Ahead' in D.F. Durnbaugh (ed.), *On Earth Peace: Discussions on War/Peace Issues between Friends, Mennonites, Brethren and European Churches 1935–1975* (Elgin: Brethren Press, 1978), 136–43, 197–210, 279–88 and 390–93 respectively

'Radical Reformation Ethics in Ecumenical Perspective', *JES* 15:4 (1978), 647–661 (also *PK*, 105–22)

'"Spirit" and the Varieties of Reformation Radicalism' in *De Geest in het Gedin: opstellen aangeboden aan J.A. Osterbaan* (Willink: H.D. Tjeenk, 1978), 301–6

'The Believers' Church: Global Perspectives' in J.K. Zeman (ed.), *The Believers' Church in Canada: Addresses and Papers from the Study Conference in Winnipeg, May 1978* (Baptist Federation of Canada and Mennonite Central Committee [Canada] 1979), 3–15

'The Contemporary Evangelical Revival and the Peace Churches' in R. L. Ramsmeyer (ed.), *Mission and the Peace Witness: The Gospel and Christian Discipleship* (Scottdale: Herald Press, 1979), 68–103

'Discerning the Kingdom of God in the Stuggles of the World', *IRM*, 68 (1979), 366–72

'The Enthusiasts and the Reformation' in H. Küng and J. Moltmann (eds.), *Concilium 128: Conflicts about the Holy Spirit* (New York: Seabury Press, 1979), 41–7

'The Spirit of God and the Politics of Man', *JTSA* 29 (1979), 62–71

'Theological Perspectives on "Growth with Equity"' in M. E. Jegen and C. K. Wilber (eds.), *Growth With Equity: Strategies For Meeting Human Needs* (New York: Paulist Press, 1979), 9–16

'Another "Free Church" Perspective on Baptist Ecumenism', *JES* 17:2 (1980), 149–59

'The Apostle's Apology Revisited' in W. Klassen (ed.), *The New Way of Jesus: Essays Presented to Howard Charles* (Newton, Kansas: Faith and Life Press, 1980), 115–34

'Could There Be a Baptist Bishop?', *Ecumenical Trends* (Graymoor) 9:7 (1980), 104–7

'Mennonite Political Conservatism: Paradox or Contradiction' in H. Loewen (ed.), *Mennonite Images: Historical, Cultural and Literary Essays Dealing with Mennonite Issues* (Winnipeg: Hyparion Press, 1980), 7–16

'Can there be a Just War?', *Radix* 13:2 (1981), 3–9

'The Hermeneutics of Peoplehood', *JRE* 10:1 (1982), 40–67 (also *PK*, 15–45)

'Living the Disarmed Life: Christ's Strategy for Peace' in J. Wallis (ed.), *Waging Peace: A Handbook for the Struggle to Abolish Nuclear Weapons* (San Francisco and Sydney: Harper and Row, 1982), 126–34

'But We Do See Jesus' in L. S. Rouner (ed.), *Foundations of Ethics* (University of Notre Dame: Notre Dame Press, 1983), 57–75 (also *PK*, 46–62)

'Evangelization is the Test of our Ethical Vocation', *IRM* 72 (1983), 610

'The Experiential Etiology of Evangelical Dualism', *Missiology: An International Review 11* (1983), 449–59

'The Social Shape of the Gospel' in W. R. Shenk (ed.), *Exploring Church Growth* (Grand Rapids: Eerdmans, 1983), 277–84

'Sometimes the Truth Surprises', *GH*, 13 September 1983, 633–4

'A Free Church Perspective on Baptism, Eucharist and Ministry', *Midstream* 23 (1984), 270–7

'The Hermeneutics of the Anabaptists' and 'The Authority of the Canon' in W. Swartley (ed.), *Essays on Biblical Interpretation: Anabaptist–Mennonite Perspectives* (Elkhart: Institute of Mennonite Studies, 1984), 11–28 and 265–90

'Introduction' to *God's Revolution: The Witness of Eberhard Arnold* Edited by the Hutterian Society of Brothers and John Howard Yoder (New York: Paulist Press, 1984), 5–22

'A Consistent Alternative View Within the Just War Family', *FP* 2:2 (1985), 112–20

'A Critique of North American Evangelical Ethics', *Transformation: An International Dialogue on Evangelical Social Ethics* 2:1 (1985), 28–31

'Reformed Versus Anabaptist Social Strategies: An Inadequate Typology', *TSF Bulletin* 8 (1985), 2–7

'The Use of the Bible in Theology' in R. K. Johnston (ed.), *The Use of the Bible in Theology: Evangelical Options* (Atlanta: John Knox Press, 1985), 103–20

'Calling a Council for Peace', *Ecumenical Trends* 15:10 (1986), 157–60

'Karl Barth: How His Mind Kept Changing' in D. K. McKim (ed.), *How Karl Barth Changed My Mind* (Grand Rapids: Eerdmans, 1986), 166–171

'A "Peace Church" Perspective on Covenanting', *EcRev* 38 (1986), 318–321

'Neither Guerilla nor *Conquista*: The Presence of the Kingdom as Social Ethic' in P. P. Peachey (ed.), *Peace, Politics, and the People of God* (Philadelphia: Fortress Press, 1986), 95–116

'Surrender: A Moral Imperative', *Review of Politics* 48 (1986), 576–95

Review of *Unmasking the Powers: The Invisible Forces That Determine Human Existence* by Walter Wink in *TSF Bulletin* 10 (1987), 34–5

'The Anabaptist Shape of Liberation' in H. Loewen (ed.), *Why I am a Mennonite: Essays on Mennonite Identity* (Scottdale: Herald Press, 1988), 338–48

'Armaments and Eschatology', *SCE* 1:1 (1988), 43–61

'Helpful and Deceptive Dualisms', *HBT* 10 (1988), 67–82

'To Serve Our God and to Rule the World', *ASCE* (1988), 3–14

'Military Realities and Teaching the Laws of War' in T. Runyon (ed.), *Theology, Politics and Peace* (Maryknoll: Orbis Books, 1989), 176–80

'Withdrawal and Diaspora: The Two Faces of Liberation' and 'Orientation in Midstream: A Response to the Responses' in D. S. Schipani (ed.), *Freedom and Discipleship: Liberation Theology in Anabaptist Perspective* (Maryknoll: Orbis Books, 1989), 76–84 and, 159–69

'The Credibility of Ecclesiastical Teaching on the Morality of War' in *Celebrating Peace: Boston University Studies in Philosophy and Religion II* (University of Notre Dame: Notre Dame Press, 1990), 31–51

'Sacrament as Social Process: Christ the Transformer of Culture', *ThT* 48:1 (1991), 33–44

'The Believers' Church Conferences in Historical Perspective', *MQR* 65:1 (1991), 5–19

With David A. Shank, 'Biblicism and the Church', *CP* 2 (1955), 26–69

With Alan Kreider, 'The Anabaptists' and 'Christians and War' in T. Dowley (ed.), *The History of Christianity* (Berkhamsted: Lion, 1977), 24–7 and, 399–403

c) Unpublished papers

The following unpublished papers are available as indicated in the libraries of the Associated Mennonite Biblical Seminaries, Elkhart, Indiana (AMBS) or the London Mennonite Centre (LMC), Highgate, London

'The Wrath and the Love of God'. Paper delivered to the Puidoux Theological Conference, September 1956 (AMBS)

'The Place of the Peace Message in Missions'. Speech delivered to the 1960 Mission Board Meeting, Lansdale, Pennsylvania (LMC)

'The Healing Professions in the Disciples' Church'. Address to the Mennonite Medical Association, Winona Lake, Indiana, 1962 (AMBS)

'The Racial Revolution in Theological Perspective'. Address for a Church Peace Mission conference on 'Revolution, Nonviolence and the Church', Asheville, N. C., 3 December 1963 (AMBS)

'"Christ and Culture": A Critique of H. Richard Niebuhr' Drafted in 1964 and revised in 1976 (AMBS)

'The Message of the Bible on its own Terms'. Paper presented at the Mennonite Student Services Summer Seminar, August 1964 (AMBS)

'The Christian View of Other Religions'. A paper prepared for a forum on this topic by The Canadian Mennonite, 1966 (AMBS)

'Concepts of Evangelism in Current Debate'. Lecture delivered at AMBS, 13 February 1967 (AMBS)

'Christian Unity within a divided North American Protestantism'. Memorandum, 1 March 1967 (AMBS)

'Checklist of the functions of the church'. Address delivered to the Commission on Church Organization, 10 April 1967 (LMC)

'Condemnation and Reconciliation'. Paper presented at a Malone College Consultation, Canton, Ohio, July 1967 (AMBS)

'Theses on the Definition of the Free Church Vision', Second Draft, 30 May 1968 (AMBS)

'Exploration of the Issue of Evangelism in Contemporary Debate'. Memorandum of the Mennonite Board of Missions and Charities, 2 September 1968 (AMBS)

'A Clarification of Views of the Church'. Paper presented at a Mennonite Board of Missions Study Meeting, Brussels, Belgium, 1–2 January 1969 (AMBS)

'Anabaptist Vision and Mennonite Reality' Lecture presented at Goshen Seminary Forum, 6 February 1969 (AMBS)

'Peacemaking Amid Political Revolution'. Seminar lecture presented at Eastern Mennonite College, Harrisonburg, June 1970 (AMBS)

'The Heritage – Anabaptist Origins and Theology'. Address delivered to the Inter-Seminaries Consultation, Elkhart, 28–31 January 1971 (AMBS)

'The Third World and Christian Mission'. Address to the Theological Conference of the International Federation of Free Evangelical Churches, North Park Seminary, Chicago, 3 September 1971 (AMBS)

'A Fuller Definition of Violence'. Memorandum, 28 March 1973 (AMBS)

'The Biblical Evaluation of Human Life'. Presentation for a Mennonite Medical Association Study on Abortion in Rosemont, Illinois, 5–6 May 1973 (AMBS)

'Was Jesus a Political Person?'. Address delivered at Goshen College, 22 October 1973 (AMBS)

'The Apriori Difficulty of "Reformed–Anabaptist Conversation"'. Memorandum, 27 January 1977 (AMBS)

'Tertium Datur: Refocusing the Jewish–Christian Schism'. Address to the Notre Dame Graduate Union, 23 October 1977 (AMBS)

'The Limits of Obedience to Caesar: The Shape of the Problem'. Address delivered to the Study Conference of the Commission on Home Ministries, June 1978 (LMC)

'The Basis of Barth's Social Ethics'. Extempore lecture at the Midwestern Section of the Karl Barth Society, Elmhurst, Illinois, 29–30 September 1978 (AMBS)

'The Church and Change: Violence and its Alternatives'. Paper presented at the annual conference of the South African Council of Churches, Hammanskraal, South Africa, 24 July 1979 (AMBS)

'The Stone Lectures', presented at Princeton Theological Seminary in 1979 and as the Jaynes Morgan Lectures at Fuller Theological Seminary also in 1979 (LMC)

'Clearing the Decks for Accountability'. Lecture prior to a Business Ethics Symposium, Notre Dame University, 10 April 1980 (AMBS)

'That Household We Are'. Address from a conference on 'Is there a Believers' Church Christology?', Bluffton, Ohio, October 1980 (AMBS)

'Judaism as a Non-non-Christian Religion'. Lecture in 'The Theology of the Christian World Mission' course, AMBS 1964–73, transcribed February 1981 (AMBS)

'The Finality of Jesus Christ and Other Faiths'. Manuscript prepared as background for the course 'Ecclesiology in Missional Perspective', AMBS, Fall 1983 (AMBS)

'Tightening the Grid: Can Just War Thought Be Made Accountable?'. Peace Theology Miscellany 4, January 1988 (AMBS)

'Is an Ethic of Discipleship "Absolute"?'. Methodological Miscellany 1, February 1988 (AMBS)

'Have you ever seen a True Church?'. Methodological Miscellany 2, April 1988 (AMBS)

'Salvation through Mothering?'. Feminist Theology Miscellany 1, April 1988 (AMBS)

'Is not the Relaxation of the Restraints Upon War Justified when the Stakes are Especially Great?'. Peace Theology Miscellany 9, August 1988 (AMBS)

General Works

1) Books and Articles

Aagaard, A. M., 'Missio Dei in katholischer Sicht: Missionstheologische Tendenzen', *EvTh* 34:5 (1974), 420–33

Alves, R. A., *A Theology of Human Hope* (Wheathampstead: Anthony Clare Books, 1975)

Ambler, R., Review of *Creating a Just Future* by Jürgen Moltmann in *SJT* 43:4 (1990), 503–4

Arens, A., 'Jesus' Communicative Actions: The Basis for Christian Faith Praxis, Witnessing, and Confessing', *CGR* 3:1 (1985), 67–85

Atherton, J. (ed.), *Social Christianity: A Reader* (London: SPCK, 1994)

Attfield, D. G., 'Can God Be Crucified? A Discussion of J. Moltmann', *SJT* 30:1 (1977), 47–57

Augustine, *City of God* (Harmondsworth: Penguin, 1984)

Austed, T., 'Attitudes towards the State in Western Theological Thinking', *Themelios* 16:1 (1990), 18–22

Avis, P. D. L., '"The True Church" in Reformation Theology', *SJT* 30:4 (1977), 319–45

Ayres, L., Review of *History and the Triune God* by Jürgen Moltmann in *SJT* 46:4 (1993), 574–5

Baelz, P., Review of *The Peaceable Kingdom: A Primer in Christian Ethics* by Stanley Hauerwas in *Theology* 88 (1985), 65–7

Baillie, D. M., *God was in Christ: An Essay on Incarnation and Atonement* (London: Faber and Faber, 1956 and 1968)

Bainton, R. H., 'The Left Wing of the Reformation', *JR* 21 (1941), 124–34

— 'The Struggle for Religious Liberty', *CH* 10 (1941), 95–124

— *Christian Attitudes to War and Peace: A Historical Survey and Critical Re-evaluation* (Nashville: Abingdon Press, 1960 and 1986)

Baltke, W., *Calvin and the Anabaptist Radicals* (Grand Rapids: Eerdmans, 1981)

Barclay, O. R., 'The Theology of Social Ethics: A Survey of Current Positions', *EQ* 62:1 (1990), 63–86

Barnes, I. J., 'Church and State. An Examination of Dr Karl Barth's Treatise "Christengemeinde und Bürgergemeinde"', *BQ* 12 (1946–48), 245–317

Barnes, T. D., *Constantine and Eusebius* (Cambridge, Mass. and London: Harvard University Press, 1981)

Barth, K., 'Volkskirche, Freikirche, Bekenntniskirche', *EvTh* 3 (1936), 411–22

— *Church and State* (London: SCM Press, 1939)

— *The Church and the Political Problem of Our Day* (London: Hodder and Stoughton, 1939)

— *The Teaching of the Church Regarding Baptism* (London: SCM Press, 1948)

— *Church Dogmatics* Volumes I–IV. Translation editors G. W. Bromiley and T. F. Torrance (Edinburgh: T. and T. Clark, 1956–75)

— 'Basic Problems of Christian Social Ethics: A Discussion with Paul Althaus' in J. M. Robinson (ed.), *The Beginnings of Dialectical Theology* (Richmond: John Knox Press, 1968)

— *Community, State and Church: Three Essays*. Edited and with an Introduction by Will Herberg (Gloucester, Mass: Peter Smith, 1968)

— *The Christian Life: Church Dogmatics* IV/4. Translated by G. W. Bromiley (Edinburgh: T. and T. Clark, 1981)

Bartsch, H-W., 'The Foundation and Meaning of Christian Pacifism' in M. E. Marty and D. G. Peerman (eds.), *New Theology No. 6: (On Revolution and Non-Revolution, Violence and Non-Violence, Peace and Power* (London: Collier–Macmillan, 1969), 185–98

Basset, J-C., 'Croix et Dialogue des Religions', *Revue d'histoire et de philosophie religieuses* 56 (1976), 545–58

Bauckham, R. J., 'Moltmann's Eschatology of the Cross', *SJT* 30:4 (1977), 301–11

— 'Jürgen Moltmann' in P. Toon and J. D. Spiceland (eds.), *One God in Trinity: An Analysis of the Primary Dogma of Christianity* (London: Samuel Bagster, 1980), 111–32

— 'Theology after Hiroshima', *SJT* 38:6 (1985), 583–601

— 'Bibliography: Jürgen Moltmann', *MC* 28:2 (1986), 55–60

— *Moltmann: Messianic Theology in the Making* (Basingstoke: Marshall-Pickering, 1987)

— 'Theodicy from Ivan Karamazov to Moltmann', *MT* 4:1 (1987), 83–97

— *The Bible in Politics: How to Read the Bible Politically* (London: SPCK, 1989)

— Article: 'Jürgen Moltmann' in David F. Ford (ed.), *The Modern Theologians: An Introduction to Christian Theology in the Twentieth Century* 1 (Oxford: Blackwell, 1989), 293–310

— 'Moltmann's Theology of Hope Revisited', *SJT* 42:2 (1989), 199–214

— 'In Defence of "The Crucified God"' in Nigel M. de S. Cameron (ed.), *The Power and the Weakness of God* (Edinburgh: Rutherford House Books, 1990), 93–118

— 'Moltmann's Messianic Christology', *SJT* 44:4 (1991), 519–31

— Review of *The Way of Jesus Christ: Christology in Messianic Dimensions* by Jürgen Moltmann in *Theology* 94 (1991), 296–8

Bauman, C., 'The Theology of the "Two Kingdoms": A Comparison of Luther and the Anabaptists', *MQR* 38:1 (1964), 37–49 and 60

Bax, D. S., 'The Barmen Declaration: A New Translation', *JTSA* 47 (1984), 12–20

Baxter, A., Review of *God in Creation: An Ecological Doctrine of Creation* by Jürgen Moltmann in *Theology* 90 (1987), 51–3

Baylor, M. G. (ed.), *The Radical Reformation*, Cambridge Texts in the History of Political Thought (Cambridge: Cambridge University Press, 1991)

Baynes, N. H., *Constantine the Great and the Christian Church* (London: Oxford University Press, 1934 and 1972)

— *Byzantine Studies and Other Essays* (London: Athlone Press, 1955)

Beaver, R. P., 'The Peace Witness in the Christian Mission', *MQR* 37:2 (1963), 96–112

Bebbington, D. W., *The Nonconformist Conscience: Chapel and Politics 1870–1914* (London: George Allen and Unwin, 1982)

— 'The Baptist Conscience in the Nineteenth Century', *BQ* 34:1 (1991), 13–24

Beckley, H., Review of *The Priestly Kingdom* by John H. Yoder in *ThT* 42 (1985), 371–2

Beintker, M., 'Creator Spiritus: Zu einem unerledigten Problem der Pneumatologie', *EvTh* 46:1, 12–26

Begbie, J., 'The Confessing Church and the Nazis: A Struggle for Theological Truth', *Anvil* 2:2 (1985), 117–30

Bender, H. S., 'Church and State in Mennonite History', *MQR* 13:2 (1939), 83–103

— 'The Anabaptists and Religious Liberty in the 16th Century', *ARf* 44 (1953), 32–51 and *MQR* 29:2 (1955), 83–100

— 'The Pacifism of the 16th Century Anabaptists', *CH* 24 (1955), 119–131 and *MQR* 30:1 (1956), 5–18

— Article: 'Evangelism', *ME* 2, 269–73

— Article: 'Historiography: Anabaptist General', *ME* 2, 751–6

— 'The Anabaptist Vision' in G. F. Herschberger (ed.), *The Recovery of the Anabaptist Vision* (Scottdale: Herald Press, 1957), 29–54

— 'The Zwickau Prophets, Thomas Müntzer and the Peasants' War' in James M. Stayer and Werner O. Packull (eds.), *The Anabaptists and Thomas Müntzer* (Dubuque and Toronto: Kendall/Hunt Publishing, 1980), 145–51

— *Menno Simmons' Life and Writings: A Quadricentennial Tribute 1536–1936* with writings selected and translated from the Dutch by John Horsch (Moundridge, Kansas: Gospel Publishers, 1983)

— et al (eds.), *The Mennonite Encyclopaedia* Vols 1–4 (Scottdale: Herald Press, 1955–9)

Bentley, J., 'Karl Barth as a Christian Socialist', *Theology* 76 (1973), 349–56

— 'Christoph Blumhardt: Preacher of Hope', *Theology* 78 (1975), 577–82

— *Between Marx and Christ: The Dialogue in German-Speaking Europe 1870–1970* (London: Verso Press, 1982)

Bergsten, T., *Balthasar Hübmaier: Seine Stellung zu Reformation und Täufertum 1521–1528* (Kassel: J. G. Oncken Verlag, 1961)

Berkhof, H., *Christ and the Powers*. Translated from the Dutch by John H. Yoder (Scottdale: Herald Press, 1962 and 1977)

Bettis, J., 'Political Theology and Social Ethics: The Socialist Humanism of Karl Barth', *SJT* 27:3 (1974), 287–305

Blanchy, A., 'Lire Moltmann', *Études théologiques et religieuses* 46:4 (1971), 365–83

— 'Théologie Trinitaire et éthique sociale chez J. Moltmann', *Études théologiques et religieuses* 57:2 (1982), 245–54

Blanke, F., *Brothers in Christ: The History of the Oldest Anabaptist Congregation, Zollikon, near Zurich, Switzerland* (Scottdale: Herald Press, 1961)

Blaser, K., 'Les enjeux d'une doctrine trinitaire sociale: À propos du dernier libre de Jürgen Moltmann', *Revue de Théologie et de Philosophie* 113 (1981), 155–66

Boff, L., *Church, Charism and Power: Liberation Theology and the Institutional Church* (London: SCM Press, 1985)

— *Ecclesiogenesis: The Base Communities Reinvent the Church* (Glasgow: Collins, 1986)

— *Trinity and Society* (Tunbridge Wells: Burns and Oates, 1988)

— and C. Boff, *Introducing Liberation Theology* (Tunbridge Wells: Burns and Oates, 1987)

Bonhoeffer, D., *Ethics* (London: SCM Press, 1955)

— *The Cost of Discipleship* (London: SCM Press, 1959)

Borg, M. J., *Conflict, Holiness and Politics in the Teaching of Jesus* (New York and Toronto: The Edwin Mellen Press, 1984)

Bosch, D. J., *Witness to the World: The Christian Mission in Theological Perspective* (London: Marshall, Morgan and Scott, 1980)

— 'The Scope of Mission', *IRM* 83 (1984), 27–9

— *Transforming Mission: Paradigm Shifts in Theology of Mission* (Maryknoll: Orbis Books, 1991)

Braaten, C. E., 'The Triune God: The Source and Model of Christian Unity and Mission', *Missiology: An International Review* 18:4 (1990), 415–27

Brackney, W. H. and Burke R. J. (eds.), *Faith, Life and Witness: The Papers of the Study and Research Division of the Baptist World Alliance 1986–1990* (Birmingham, Alabama: Samford University Press, 1990)

Bradshaw, T., *The Olive Branch: An Evangelical Anglican Doctrine of the Church* (Carlisle: Paternoster Press, 1992)

Briggs, J. H. Y., *Freedom: A Baptist View* (London: Baptist Publications, 1978)

British Council of Churches, *The Forgotten Trinity 1: The Report of the BCC Study Commission on Trinitarian Doctrine Today* (London: British Council of Churches, 1989)

British Council of Churches, *The Forgotten Trinity 3: A Selection of Papers presented to the BCC Study Commission on Trinitarian Doctrine Today* (London: BCC/CCBI, 1991)

Brown, D. W., 'The Radical Reformation: Then and Now', *MQR* 45:3 (1971), 250–63

— Review of *Karl Barth and the Problem of War* by John Howard Yoder in *MQR* 46:2 (1972), 168–70

— 'Communal Ecclesiology: The Power of the Anabaptist Vision' *ThT* 36 (1979), 22–9

Brown, K., Review of *What Would You Do?* by John Howard Yoder *in Evangelical Review of Theology* 10 (1986), 190–1

Brown, M., 'Jesus: Messiah not God', *CGR* 5:3 (1987), 233–52

Brown, P., *Augustine of Hippo: A Biography* (London: Faber and Faber, 1967)

Brunk, C. G., 'Reflections on the Anabaptist View of Law and Morality' *CGR* 1:2 (1983), 1–20

Brunner, E., *The Divine Imperative: A Study in Christian Ethics* (London: Lutterworth Press, 1937)

— *Justice and the Social Order* (London: Lutterworth Press, 1945)

— *The Christian Doctrine of Creation aud Redemption: Dogmatics Vol II* (London: Lutterworth Press, 1952)

Buchanan, C., 'Mission and Establishment' in P. Turner and F. Sugeno (eds.), *Crossroads Are For Meeting: Essays on the Mission and Common Life of the Church in a Global Society* (Sewanee: SPCK/USA, 1986), 187–204

Bühler, P., *Kreuz und Eschatologie: Eine Auseinandersetzung mit der politischen Theologie im Anschluss an Luthers theologia crucis* (Tübingen: J. C. B. Mohr, 1981)

— 'Existence et Histoire: Quelques éléments de réponse à Jean-Pierre Thévenaz', *Revue de Théologie et de Philosophie* 115 (1983), 209–14

Burchard, C., Review of *Die Politik Jesu: Der Weg des Kreuzes* by John H. Yoder (aus dem Amerikanischen von Wolfgang Krauss mit einem Vorwort von Jürgen Moltmann) in *TZ* 40 (1984), 87–9

Burkholder, J. L., 'The Church in a Brave New World' in J. A. Lapp (ed.), *Peacemakers in a Broken World* (Scottdale: Herald Press, 1969), 144–54

— *The Problem of Social Responsibility from the Perspective of the Mennonite Church* (Elkhart: Institute of Mennonite Studies, 1989)

— 'Mennonites on the Way to Peace', *GH*, 19 February 1991, 1–4, 8

Busch, E., *Karl Barth: His Life from Letters and Autobiographical Texts* (London: SCM Press, 1976)

Butler, G. A., 'Karl Barth and Political Theology', *SJT* 27:4 (1974), 441–59

Calvin, J., *Institutes of the Christian Religion*. Edited in two volumes by J. T. McNeill (Philadelphia: Westminster Press, 1960)

— *Treatises Against the Anabaptists And Against the Libertines*. Edited by B. W. Farley (Grand Rapids: Baker Book House, 1982)

Capps, W. H., *Hope Against Hope: Moltmann to Merton in One Theological Decade* (Philadlephia: Fortress Press, 1976)

Chadwick, H., 'The Emperor as Antichrist', *TLS*, 28 May 1982

Chapman G. C., 'Black Theology and Theology of Hope: What have they to say to each other?', *USQR* 29:2 (1974), 107–29

— 'Moltmann's Vision of Man', *ATR* 56 (1974), 310–30

— 'Jürgen Moltmann and the Christian Dialogue with Marxism', *JES* 18:3 (1981), 435–50

— 'Hope and the ethics of formation: Moltmann as interpreter of Bonhoeffer', *STR* 12:4 (1983), 449–60

Chappus, J-M., 'Who Are the Reformed Today?' in H. G. Vom Berg et al (eds.), *Mennonites and Reformed in Dialogue: Studies from the World Alliance of Ref ormed Churches No 7* (Geneva: WARC; Lombard: Mennonite World Conference, 1986), 33–40

Child, R. L., Ekklesia and Koinonia: An Essay in Understanding', *BQ* 17 (1957–58), 351–61

Clements, K. W., 'Moltmann on the Congregation', *BQ* 28:3 (1979), 101–9

— *A Patriotism for Today: Dialogue with Dietrich Bonhoeffer* (Bristol: Bristol Baptist College, 1984)

— 'Nationalism and Internationalism: A Theological Critique' in R. J. Bauckham and R. J. Elford (eds.), *The Nuclear Weapons Debate: Theological and Ethical Issues* (London: SCM Press, 1989), 65–79

— *What Freedom?: The Persistent Challenge of Dietrich Bonhoeffer* (Bristol: Bristol Baptist College, 1990)

Clifford, P. R., *Politics and the Christian Vision* (London: SCM Press, 1984)

Cobb, J. B., 'Reply to Jürgen Moltmann's "The Unity of the Triune God"', *SVTQ* 28:3 (1984), 173–7

Cochrane, A. C., *The Church's Confession Under Hitler* (Philadelphia: Westminster Press, 1962)

— *Reformed Confessions of the Sixteenth Century*. Edited with historical introductions by Arthur C. Cochrane (London: SCM Press, 1966)

Coggins, J. R., 'Toward a Definition of Sixteenth-Century Anabaptism: Twentieth-Century Historiography of the Radical Reformation', *JMS* 4 (1986), 183–207

— *John Smyth's Congregation: English Separatism, Mennonite Influence and the Elect Nation* (Scottdale: Herald Press, 1991)

Cole, R. C. and Moody, M. E. (eds.), *The Dissenting Tradition: Essays for Leland H. Carson* (Athens: Ohio University Press, 1975)

Colwell, J. E., 'A Radical Church? A Reappraisal of Anabaptist Ecclesiology', *TB* 38 (1987), 119–41

Connell, J. C., Review of *Theology of Hope* by Jürgen Moltmann in *Vox Evangelica* 6 (1969), 72–7

Cornwell, P., *Church and Nation* (Oxford: Basil Blackwell, 1983)

Corrie, J., 'Towards a "Trinitarian Political Theology"', *Anvil* 6:1 (1989), 33–44

Cranfield, C. E. B., 'The Christian's Political Responsibility According to the New Testament', *SJT* 15 (1962), 176–92

Cullmann, O., *The State in the New Testament* (London: SCM Press, 1957)

Dakin A., *The Baptist View of the Church and Ministry* (London: Baptist Union, 1944)

Davis, K. R., *Anabaptism and Asceticism: A Study in Intellectual Origins* (Scottdale: Herald Press, 1974)

Davis, K. R. 'Anabaptism as a Charismatic Movement', *MQR* 53:3 (1979), 219–34

Dayton, D., 'Are Jesus' Teachings Normative?', *CT*, 21 December 1973, 29

de Gruchy, J., 'Radical Peace-Making: The Challenge of some Anabaptists' in C. Villa-Vicencio (ed.), *Theology and Violence: The South African Debate* (Grand Rapids: Eerdmans, 1988), 173–85

Dekar, P. R., 'Baptists and Peace' in J. K. Zeman and W. Klaassen (eds.), *The Believers' Church in Canada: Addresses and Papers from the Study Conference in Winnipeg, May 1978* (Baptist Federation of Canada and Mennonite Central Committee [Canada 1979), 325–32

— 'Baptist Peacemakers in the Nineteenth Century Peace Societies', *BQ* 34:1 (1991), 3–12

de Lavalette, H., 'Ambiguïtés de la Théologie Politique', *Recherches de Science Religieuse* 59 (1971), 545–62

Desroche, H., *The Sociology of Hope* (London: Routledge and Kegan Paul, 1979)

Dillistone, F. W., 'The Theology of Jürgen Moltmann', *MC* 18:4 (1975), 145–50

Dintaman, S. F., 'The Spiritual Poverty of the Anabaptist Vision', *CGR* 10:2 (1992), 205–8

Dooyeweerd, H., *Roots of Western Culture: Pagan, Secular, and Christian Options* (Toronto: Wedge Publishing Foundation, 1979)

Dorries, H., *Constantine and Religious Liberty* (New Haven: Yale University Press, 1960)

Dulles, A., *Models of the Church: A Critical Assessment of the Church in all its Aspects* (Dublin: Gill and Macmillan, 1974)

Dunn, J. D. G., *The Living Word* (London: SCM Press, 1987)

Durnbaugh, D. F., *The Believers' Church: The History and Character of Radical Protestantism* (London and New York: Macmillan, 1968)

— 'Theories of Free Church Origins', *MQR* 42:2 (1968), 83–95

— 'Free Churches, Baptists, and Ecumenism: Origins and Implications', *JES* 17 (1980), 3–20

Dyck, C. J. (ed.), *An Introduction to Mennonite History* (Scottdale: Herald Press, 1967)

— and Martin, D. D. (eds.), *The Mennonite Encyclopaedia* 5 (Scottdale: Herald Press, 1990)

Ecclestone, A., 'Mystique and Politique', *Theology* 79 (1976), 29–35

Eckhardt, A. R., 'Jürgen Moltmann, the Jewish People and the Holocaust', *JAAR* 44:4 (1976), 675–91

Eller, V., Review of *The Politics of Jesus* by John Howard Yoder in *BLT* 18 (1973), 107–8

— *Christian Anarchy: Jesus' Primacy over the Powers* (Grand Rapids: Eerdmans, 1987)

Ellul, J., *The Ethics of Freedom* (Grand Rapids: Eerdmans, 1976)

— *Violence: Reflections from a Christian Perspective* (London and Oxford: Mowbrays, 1978)

— *Anarchy and Christianity* (Grand Rapids: Eerdmans, 1988)

Elton, G. R., *Reformation Europe 1517–1559* (London and Glasgow: Collins, 1963)

Estep, W. R., *The Anabaptist Story* (Grand Rapids: Eerdmans, 1975)

Evangelical Church in Germany, 'Violence and the Use of Violence in Society: Theological Theses on Social Conflict' with Commentary by Martin Honecker, *EcRev* 25:4 (1973), 455–67

Farrer, A. J. D., 'The Relation between English Baptists and the Anabaptists of the Continent', *BQ* 2 (1924–25), 30–6

Fiddes, P. S., *Past Event and Present Salvation: The Christian Idea of Atonement* (London: Darton, Longman and Todd, 1989)

Fierro, A., *The Militant Gospel: An Analysis of Contemporary Political Theologies* (London: SCM Press, 1977)

Finger, T. N., 'The Way to Nicea: Reflections from a Mennonite Perspective', *CGR* 3:3 (1985), 231–49

— *Christian Theology: An Eschatological Approach Volumes I and II* (Scottdale: Herald Press, 1985 and 1989)

Fiorenza, F. P., 'Dialectical Theology and Hope' Part 1, *THJ* 9:2 (1968), 143–163, Part 2, *THJ* 9:4 (1968) 384–399 and Part 3, *THJ* 10:1 (1969), 26–42

Flannery, A. (ed.), *Vatican Council II: The Conciliar and Post-Conciliar Documents* (Dublin: Dominican Publications, 1975)

Ford, S. H., 'Perichoresis and Interpenetration: Samuel Taylor Coleridge's Trinitarian Conception of Unity', *Theology* 89 (1986), 20–4

Forrester, D. B., *Theology and Politics* (Oxford: Basil Blackwell, 1988)

— *Beliefs, Values and Policies: Conviction Politics in a Secular Age*, The Hensley Henson Lectures, 1987–1988 (Oxford: Clarendon Press, 1989)

Forster, P., Review of *The Way of Jesus Christ: Christology in Messianic Dimensions* by Jürgen Moltmann in *Anvil* 8:2 (1991), 171–2

Forsyth, P. T., *Faith, Freedom and the Future* (London: Hodder and Stoughton, 1912)

Fowler, R. B., *A New Engagement: Evangelical Political Thought 1966–1976* (Grand Rapids: Eerdmans, 1982)

Friedmann, R., 'The Nicolsburg Articles: A Problem of Early Anabaptist History', *CH* 36:4 (1967), 391–409

Friesen, D. K., 'Normative Factors in Troeltsch's Typology of Religious Association', *JRE* 3:2 (1975), 271–83

— *Christian Peacemaking and International Conflict: A Realist Pacifist Perspective* (Scottdale: Herald Press, 1986)

— 'An Anabaptist Theology of Culture for a New Century'. Address delivered at the 'Whither the Anabaptist Vision?' Conference, Elizabethtown, USA, 15 June 1994

Galloway, A. D., 'The New Hegelians', *RS* 8:4 (1972), 367–71

— Review of *The Church in the Power of the Spirit* by Jürgen Moltmann in *SJT* 32:1 (1979), 73–75

Garrett, J. L., 'The Nature of the Church According to the Radical Continental Reformation', *MQR* 32:2 (1958), 111–27

Gaustad, E. S., 'Religious Liberty: Baptists and Some Fine Distinctions', *ABQ* 6:4 (1987), 215–25

General Board of the American Baptist Churches/USA, 'American Baptist Policy Statements', *ABQ* 5 Nos 2 and 3 (June and September 1986), 92–161

— 'American Baptist Policy Statement on Church and State', *ABQ* 6:4 (1987), 204–14

George, T., 'Between Pacifism and Coercion: The English Baptist Doctrine of Religious Toleration', *MQR* 58:1 (1984), 30–49

Gerth, H. H. and Mills, C. W. (eds.), *From Max Weber: Essays in Sociology* (London and Boston: Routledge and Kegan Paul, 1948)

Gilkey, L., 'The Contribution of Culture to the Reign of God' in M. Muckenhirn (ed.), *The Future as the Presence of Shared Hope* (New York: Sheed and Ward, 1968)

Gill, R., Review of *Against the Nations: War and Survival in a Liberal Society* by Stanley Hauerwas in *SJT* 39:4 (1986), 571–74

Gilmore, A., *The Pattern of the Church: A Baptist View* (London: Lutterworth Press, 1963)

— (ed.), *Christian Baptism: A Fresh Attempt to Understand the Rite in Terms of Scripture, History and Theology* with an Introductory Chapter by E. A. Payne (London: Lutterworth Press, 1959)

Gladwin, J., Review of *Creating a Just Future: The Politics of Peace and the Ethics of Creation in a Threatened World* by Jürgen Moltmann in *Anvil* 7:3 (1990), 277

Goen, C. C., 'Remembering Who We Are: Some Baptist Perspectives on Church–State Issues', *ABQ* 10:4 (1991), 280–87

Goudzwaard, B., *Idols Of Our Time* (Downers Grove: InterVarsity Press, 1984)

Grässer, E., 'Der politisch gekreuzigte Christus: Anmerkungen zu einer politischen Hermeneutik des Evangeliums', *ZNW* 62 (1971), 260–94

Greenslade, S. L., *Church and State from Constantine to Theodosius* (London: SCM Press, 1954)

Grenz, S. J., 'Isaac Backus and the English Baptist Tradition', *BQ* 30:5 (1984), 221–31

Gross, L. 'Recasting the Anabaptist Vision: The Longer View', *MQR* 60:3 (1986), 352–63

Guiness, O., 'Tribespeople, Idiots or Citizens? Religious Liberty and the Reforging of the American Public Philosophy', *Spectrum* 23:1 (1991), 29–50

Gunton, C. E., Review of *Man: Christian Anthropology in the Conflicts of the Present* and *The Experiment Hope* by Jürgen Moltmann in *RS* 13:2 (1977), 259

— 'The Political Christ: Some Reflections on Mr Cupitt's Thesis', SJT 32:6 (1979), 521–40

— *Yesterday and Today: A Study of Continuities in Christology* (London: Darton, Longman and Todd, 1983)

— 'Barth, The Trinity, and Human Freedom', *ThT* 43:3 (1986), 316–30

— 'Reinhold Niebuhr: A Treatise of Human Nature', *MT* 4:1 (1987), 71–81

— *The Actuality of Atonement: A Study of Metaphor, Rationality and the Christian Tradition* (Edinburgh: T. and T. Clark, 1988)

— 'Augustine, the Trinity and the Theological Crisis of the West', *SJT* 43:1 (1990), 33–58

— 'The Idea of Dissent and the Character of Christianity', *Reformed Quarterly* 1:5 (1990), 2–6

— 'Using and Being Used: Scripture and Systematic Theology', *ThT* 47:3 (1990), 248–59

— *The Promise of Trinitarian Theology* (Edinburgh: T. and T. Clark, 1991)

— and Hardy, D. W. (eds.), *On Being the Church: Essays on the Christian Community* (Edinburgh: T. and T. Clark, 1989)

Gustafson, J. M. 'A Theocentric Interpretation of Life' in James M. Wall (ed.), *Theologians in Transition: The Christian Century 'How My Mind Has Changed Series'* with an introduction by Martin E. Marty (New York: Crossroad, 1981), 82–92

— *Ethics from a Theocentric Perspective Volume I: Theology and Ethics* (Chicago: University of Chicago Press, 1981) and *Volume II: Ethics and Theology* (Chicago: University of Chicago Press, 1984)

— 'The Sectarian Temptation: Reflections on Theology, the Church and the University', *PCTS* 40 (1985), 83–94

Gustafson, S. W., 'From Theodicy to Discipleship: Dostoevsky's Contribution to the Pastoral Task in "The Brothers Karamazov", *SJT* 45:2 (1992), 209–22

Gutiérrez, G., *A Theology of Liberation: History, Politics and Salvation* (London: SCM Press, 1974)

Habegger, D., '"Non-resistance and Responsibility" – A Critical Analysis', *CP* 7 (1959), 33–40

Habgood, J., *Church and Nation in a Secular Age* (London: Darton, Longman and Todd, 1983)

Haldane, J. J., 'Christianity and Politics: Another View', *SJT* 40:2 (1987), 259–86

Hanson, A. T., *The Wrath of the Lamb* (London: SPCK, 1957)

Harries, R., 'Reinhold Niebuhr's Critique of Pacifism and his Pacifist Critics' in Richard Harries (ed.), *Reinheld Niebuhr and the Issues of our Time* (London and Oxford: Mowbrays, 1986)

Harrington, S. P., 'Im Kampf der Kulturen', *Die Zeit* 33 (13 August 1993)

Harrison, P. M., *Authority and Power in the Free Church Tradition: A Social Case Study of the American Baptist Convention* (Princeton: Princeton University Press, 1959)

Harvey, D., *The Condition of Postmodernity: An Enquiry into the Origins of Cultural Change* (Oxford: Blackwell, 1989)

Hastings, A., *A History of Christianity: 1920–1985* (London: Collins, 1986)

— *Church and State: The English Experience. The Prideaux Lectures for 1990* (Exeter: University of Exeter, 1991)

— 'Church and State in a Pluralist Society', *Theology* 95 (1992), 165–76

Hauerwas, S., 'Messianic Pacifism', *Worldview* 16 (1973), 29–33

— 'The Non-resistant Church: The Theological Ethics of John Howard Yoder' in Hauerwas, *Vision and Virtue: Essays in Christian Ethical Reflection* (Notre Dame: University of Notre Dame Press, 1981)

— *The Peaceable Kingdom: A Primer in Christian Ethics* (London: SCM Press, 1984)

— *Should War Be Eliminated?: Philosophical and Theological Investigations* (Milwaukee: Marquette University Press, 1984)

— *Against the Nations: War and Survival in a Liberal Society* (Minneapolis: Winston Press, 1985)

— 'Pacifism: Some Philosophical Considerations', *FP* 2:2 (1985), 99–104

— 'Will the Real Sectarian Stand Up?', *ThT* 44:1 (1987), 87–96

— *Christian Existence Today* (Durham, North Carolina: Labyrinth Press, 1988)

— 'Epilogue: A Pacifist Response to the Bishops' in Paul Ramsey, *Speak Up for Just War or Pacifism: A Critique of the United Methodist Bishops' Pastoral Letter 'In Defense of Creation'* (University Park and London: Pennsylvania State University Press, 1988), 149–82

— 'The Sermon on the Mount, Just War and the Quest for Peace' in H Küng and J. Moltmann (eds.), *Concilium 195: A Council for Peace* (Edinburgh: T. and T. Clark, 1988), 36–43

— *After Christendom? How the Church Is to Behave If Freedom, Justice, and a Christian Nation Are Bad Ideas* (Nashville: Abingdon Press, 1991)

— 'Living the Proclaimed Reign of God: A Sermon on the Sermon on the Mount', *Interpretation* 47:2 (1993), 152–58

— and Willimon, W. H., *Resident Aliens: Life in the Christian Colony* (Nashville: Abingdon Press, 1989)

— and Chris K. Huebner, Harry J. Huebner and Mark Thiessen Nation, (eds.), *The Wisdom of the Cross: Essays in Honor of John Howard Yoder* (Grand Rapids: Eerdmans, 1999)

Hayden, R. (ed.), *Baptist Union Documents 1948–1977* (London: Baptist Historical Society, 1980)

Haymes, B., *A Question of Identity: Reflections on Baptist Principles and Practice* (Leeds: Yorkshire Baptist Association, 1986)

Hedinger, U., 'Glaube und Hoffnung bei Ernst Fuchs and Jürgen Moltmann', *EvTh* 27:1 (1967), 36–51

Herberg, W., 'The Social Philosophy of Karl Barth' in K. Barth, *Community, State and Church* (Gloucester, Mass.: Peter Smith, 1968), 11–67

Heriot, D. B., 'Anabaptism in England during the 16th and 17th Centuries', *Transactions of the Congregational Historical Society* 12 (1933–36), 256–71, 312–20

Herschberger, G. F., 'Peace and War in the Old Testament', *MQR* 17:1 (1943), 5–22

— 'Peace and War in the New Testament', *MQR* 17:2 (1943), 59–72

— 'Biblical Non-resistance and Modern Pacifism', *MQR* 17:3 (1943), 115–35

— *War, Peace and Non-resistance* (Scottdale: Herald Press, 1944 and 1981)

— 'Christian Non-resistance: Its Foundation and its Outreach', *MQR* 29:2 (1955), 156–62

— Review of *The Politics of Jesus* by John Howard Yoder in *MQR* 48:4 (1974), 534–8

— (ed.), *The Recovery of the Anabaptist Vision* (Scottdale: Herald Press, 1957)

Hick, J. and Knitter P. F. (eds.), *The Myth of Christian Uniqueness* (London: SCM Press, 1987)

Higginson, R., Review of *The Peaceable Kingdom: A Primer in Christian Ethics* by Stanley Hauerwas in *Anvil* 2:3 (1985), 295–6

Hill, C., *The World Turned Upside Down: Radical Ideas During the English Revolution* (London: Temple Smith, 1972)

Hill, D., *The Gospel of Matthew* (London: Marshall, Morgan and Scott, 1972)

Hill, W. J., *The Three-Personed God: The Trinity as a Mystery of Salvation* (Washington DC: Catholic University Press of America, 1982)

Hillerbrand, H. J., 'An Early Anabaptist Treatise on the Christian and the State', *MQR* 32:1 (1958), 28–47

— 'The Anabaptist View of the State', *MQR* 32:2 (1958), 83–127

— 'Anabaptism and History', *MQR* 45:2 (1971), 107–22

Hodgson, P. C., 'Ecclesia of Freedom', *THT* 44:2 (1987), 222–34

Hoitenga, D., Review of *Karl Barth and the Problem of War* by John Howard Yoder in *TRJ* 23 (1973), 29–30

Holl, K., 'Luther und die Schwärmer' in *Gesammelte Aufsätze zur Kirchengeschichte I: Luther* (Tübingen: J. C. B. Mohr, 1932), 420–67

Holland, S. J., 'God in Public: A Modest Proposal for a Quest for a Contemporary North American Anabaptist Paradigm', *CGR* 4:1 (1986), 43–55

— 'The Problems and Prospects of a "Sectarian Ethic": A Critique of the Hauerwas Reading of the Jesus Story', *CGR* 10 No 2 (1992), 157–68

— 'Preaching with Prophets, Musing with Mystics, Dancing with Strangers: Anabaptism as Public Theology'. Address delivered at the 'Whither the Anabaptist Vision?' Conference, Elizabethtown, USA, 14 June 1994

Hood, R. E., 'Karl Barth's Christological Basis for the State and Political Praxis', *SJT* 33:3 (1980), 223–38

— *Contemporary Political Orders and Christ: Karl Barth's Christology and Political Praxis* (Pennsylvania: Pickwick Publications, 1985)

Hornus, J-P, *It Is Not Lawful For Me to Fight: Early Christian Attitudes Toward War, Violence and the State* (Scottdale: Herald Press, 1980)

Horsch, J., 'Is Dr Kuehler's Conception of Early Dutch Anabaptism Historically Sound?' Part 1, *MQR* 7:1 (1933), 48–60 and Part 2, *MQR* 7:2 (1933), 97–126

Horst, I. B., *The Radical Brethren: Anabaptism and the English Reformation to 1558* (Nieuwkoop: B. De Graaf, 1972)

Hostetler, B. S., 'Non-resistance and Social Responsibility: Mennonites and Mainline Peace Emphasis, ca 1950 to 1985', *MQR* 64:1 (1990), 49–73

Hryniewicz, W., 'Le Dieu Souffrant? Réflexions sur la notion chrétienne de Dieu', *Église et Théologie* 12 (1981), 333–56

Hudson, W. S., 'Who were the Baptists?', *BQ* 16 (1955–56), 303–12

— 'John Locke: Heir of Puritan Political Theorists' in G. L. Hunt (ed.), *Calvinism and the Political Order* (Philadelphia: Westminster Press, 1965), 108–74

Huebner, H., Review of *The Transformtion of Culture: Christian Social Ethics After H. Richard Niebuhr* by Charles Scriven in *CGR* 8:1 (1990), 91–3

Hunsinger, G., 'The Crucified God and the Political Theology of Violence: A Critical Survey of Jürgen Moltmann's Thought' Part 1, *THJ* 14:3 (1973), 266–79 and Part 2, *THJ* 14:4 (1973), 379–95

Hunt, G. L., 'Our Calvinist Heritage in Church and State' in G. L. Hunt (ed.), *Calvinism and the Political Order* (Philadelphia: Westminster Press, 1965), 175–91

Irish, J. A., 'Moltmann's Theology of Contradiction', *ThT* 32 (1975–6), 21–31

Jansen, J. F., '1 Cor. 15:24–28 and the Future of Jesus Christ', *SJT* 40:4 (1987), 543–70

Jantzen G. M., 'Christian Hope and Jesus' Despair', *KTR* 5:1 (1982), 1–7

Jenkins, D. T., *The Church Meeting and Democracy* (London: Independent Press, 1944)

— *The British: Their Identity and Their Religion* (London: SCM Press, 1975)

Jenson, R. W., 'The Hauerwas Project', *MT* 8:3 (1992) 285–95

Jonas, H., *The Gnostic Religion* (Boston: Beacon Press, 1958)

Jones, A. H. M., *Constantine and the Conversion of Europe* (Harmondsworth: Pelican, 1972)

Jordan, W. K., *The Development of Religious Toleration in England: From the Accession of James I to the Convention of the Long Parliament (1603–1640)* (London: George Allen and Unwin, 1936)

Jüngel, E., *Christ, Justice and Peace: Toward a Theology of the State in Dialogue with the Barmen Declaration* (Edinburgh: T. and T. Clark, 1992)

Kaufman, G. D., *Systematic Theology: A Historicist Perspective* (New York: Scribner's, 1968)

— Review of *The Priestly Kingdom: Social Ethics as Gospel by John Howard Yoder* in *CGR* 4:1 (1986) 78–80

Kee, A., *Constantine versus Christ: The Triumph of Ideology* (London: SCM Press, 1982)

— Review of *On Human Dignity: Political Theology and Ethics* by Jürgen Moltmann in *RS* 24:4 (1985), 615–17

— 'Marx's Messianic Faith', in W. Beicken, S. Freyne and A. Weiler (eds.), *Concilium: Messianism Through History* (London: SCM Press, 1993/1), 101–13

— (ed.), *A Reader in Political Theology* (London: SCM Press, 1974)

Keim, A. N., 'The Anabaptist Vision: Reassurance and a Rallying Point for the Church', *GH*, 19 April 1994, 1–3, 8

Kerstiens, F., 'The Theology of Hope in Germany Today' in *Concilium 9:6 Hope* (London: Burns and Oates, 1970), 101–11

Keyes, D., 'Pluralism, Relativism and Tolerance', *Third Way* 15:10 (December 1992 / January 1993), 30–33

King, N. Q., *The Emperor Theodosius and the Establishment of Christianity* (London: SCM Press, 1961)

Klaassen, W., 'The Nature of Anabaptist Protest', *MQR* 45:4 (1971), 291–311

— *Anabaptism in Outline: Selected Primary Sources* (Scottdale: Herald Press, 1981)

— 'The Anabaptist Critique of Constantinian Christendom', *MQR* 55:3 (1981), 218–30

— Review of *Constantine Versus Christ: The Triumph of Ideology* by Alistair Kee in *MQR* 57:4 (1983), 399–401

— 'Sixteenth-Century Anabaptism: A Vision Valid for the Twentieth Century?', *CGR* 7:3 (1989), 241–52

— '"Of Divine and Human Justice": The Early Swiss Brethren and Government', *CGR* 10:2 (1992), 169–85

— 'Anabaptist Hermeneutics: The Letter and the Spirit', *MQR* 40:2 (1966), 83–96

Klassen, W., 'The Limits of Political Authority as seen by Pilgram Marpeck', *MQR* 56:4 (1982), 342–64

Klassen, William and Klaassen Walter (eds.), *The Writings of Pilgram Marpeck* (Scottdale: Herald Press, 1978)

Kliever, L. D., 'Baptist Origins: The Question of Anabaptist Influence', *MQR* 36:4 (1962), 291–348

König, A., *The Eclipse of Christ in Eschatology: Toward a Christ-Centred Approach* (Grand Rapids: Eerdmans, 1989)

Koontz, G. G., 'A Confessional Theology in a Pluralistic Context: A Study of the Theological Ethics of H. Richard Niebuhr and John H. Yoder', *MQR* 61:4 (1987), 413–18

— 'The Liberation of Atonement', *MQR* 63:2 (1989), 171–91

Koontz, T., 'Mennonites and "Postmodernity"', *MQR* 63:4 (1989), 401–27

Kraus, C. N., 'Anabaptist Influence on English Separatism as seen in Robert Browne', *MQR* 34:1 (1960), 5–19

— *Jesus Christ Our Lord: Christology from a Disciple's Perspective* (Scottdale: Herald Press, Revised Edition 1990)

— *God Our Saviour: Theology in a Christological Mode* (Scottdale: Herald Press, 1991)

— 'Interpreting the Atonement in the Anabaptist–Mennonite Tradition', *MQR* 66:3 (1992), 290–311

— *The Community of the Spirit: How the Church is in the World* (Scottdale: Herald Press, 1993)

Küng, H., *The Church* (London: Burns and Oates, 1967)

— 'Die Religionen als Frage an die Theologie des Kreuzes', *EvTh* 33:4 (1973), 401–23

LaCugna, C. M. and McDonnell K., 'Returning from "the Far Country": Theses for a Contemporary Trinitarian Theology', *SJT* 41:2 (1988), 191–215

Latourette, K. S., *A History of the Expansion of Christianity: Volume 3: Three Centuries of Advance 1500–1800 AD* (New York: Harper and Row, 1939)

Le Masters, P., *The Import of Eschatology in John Howard Yoder's Critique of Constantinianism* (San Fransisco: Mellen Research University Press, 1992)

— *Discipleship for all Believers: Christian Ethics and the Kingdom of God* (Scottdale: Herald Press, 1992)

Liechty, D., 'Christian Freedom and Political Freedom', *CGR* 4:2 (1986), 101–23

Lindbeck, G. A., 'The Sectarian Future of the Church' in J. P. Whelan S. J. (ed.), *The God Experience: Essays in Hope* (New York: Newman Press, 1971)

Lindsay, A. D., *The Churches and Democracy* (London: Epworth Press, 1934)

Littell, F. H., 'Church and Sect', *EcRev* 6 (1954), 262–76

— 'The Work of the Holy Spirit in Group Decisions', *MQR* 34:2 (1960), 75–96

— *From State Church to Pluralism: A Protestant Interpretation of Religion in American History* (New York: Doubleday, 1962)

— *The Origins of Sectarian Protestantism: A Study of the Anabaptist View of the Church* (London and New York: Macmillan, 1964)

— 'The New Shape of the Church–State Issue', *MQR* 40:3 (1966), 179–89

— 'The Concept of the Believers' Church' in J. L. Garrett (ed.), *The Concept of the Believers' Church* (Scottdale: Herald Press, 1969)

— Review of *Täufertum und Reformation in Gespräch* by John Howard Yoder in *MQR* 44:4 (1970), 400–1

— 'The Anabaptist Theology of Mission' in W. R. Shenk (ed.), *Anabaptism and Mission* (Scottdale: Herald Press, 1984), 13–23

Loewen, H. J., 'Peace in the Mennonite Tradition: Toward a Theological Understanding of a Regulative Concept' in R. T. Bender and A. P. F. Sell (eds.), *Baptism, Peace and the State in the Reformed and Mennonite Traditions* (Waterloo: Wilfrid Laurier University Press, 1991), 87–121

— 'Church and State in the Anabaptist–Mennonite Tradition: Christ Versus Caesar?' in R. T. Bender and A. P. F. Sell (eds.), *Baptism, Peace and the State in the Reformed and Mennonite Traditions* (Waterloo: Wilfrid Laurier University Press, 1991), 145–165

— (ed.), *One Lord, One Church, One Hope, One God: Mennonite Confessions of Faith* (Elkhart: Institute of Mennonite Studies, 1985)

Lohfink, G., *Jesus and Community: The Social Dimension of Christian Faith* (London: SPCK, 1985)

Long, E. L. Jr., *A Survey of Recent Christian Ethics* (Oxford: Oxford University Press, 1982)

— Article: 'Modern Protestant Ethics' in John Macquarrie and James Childress (eds.), *A New Dictionary of Christian Ethics* (London: SCM Press, 1986), 383–8

Longbottom, D., Review of *Systematic Theology: Ethics Vol 1* by James McClendon in *CGR* 6:3 (1988), 271–3

Lorenzen, T., 'Introduction: Human Rights and Baptists', *ABQ* 9:4 (1990), 198–204

Loserth, J., Article: 'Hübmaier, Balthasar', *ME* 2, 826–34

Loughlin, G., Review of *History and the Triune God: Contributions to Trinitarian Theology* by Jürgen Moltmann in *Theology* 96 (1993), 59–60

Louth, A., Review of *Constantine versus Christ: The Triumph of Ideology* by Alistair Kee in *Theology* 86 (1983), 139–41

Lumpkin, W. L. (ed.), *Baptist Confessions of Faith* (Valley Forge: Judson Press, 1959)

McBeth H. L. (ed.), *A Sourcebook for Baptist Heritage* (Nashville: Broadman Press, 1990)

McClendon, J. Wm. Jr., 'What Is A "baptist" Theology?', *ABQ* 1:1 (1982), 16–39

— *Systematic Theology: Ethics* (Nashville: Abingdon Press, 1986)

— 'Balthasar Hübmaier, Catholic Anabaptist', *MQR* 65:1 (1991), 20–33

McFadyen, A., 'Truth as Mission: The Christian Claim to Universal Truth in a Pluralist Public World', *SJT* 46:4 (1993), 437–56

McGrath, A. E., *The Making of Modern German Christology: From the Enlightenment to Pannenberg* (Oxford: Basil Blackwell, 1986)

— 'Pluralism and the Decade of Evangelism', *Anvil* 9:2 (1992), 101–14

MacIntyre, A., *After Virtue: A Study in Moral Theory* (Notre Dame: University of Notre Dame Press, 1981 and 1984)

McIntyre, J., Review of *God in Creation* by Jürgen Moltmann in *SJT* 41:2 (1988), 267–73

Mackey, J. P., *The Christian Experience of God as Trinity* (London: SCM Press, 1983)

MacKinnon, D. M., Review of *Constantine versus Christ: The Triumph of Ideology* by Alistair Kee in *SJT* 36:2 (1983), 261–3

MacLoughlin, D., Review of *Moltmann: Messianic Theology in the Making* by Richard Bauckham in *SJT* 44:2 (1991), 267–9

MacMullen, R., *Christianizing the Roman Empire: AD 100–400* (New Haven and London: Yale University Press, 1984)

McNeill, J. T., 'John Calvin on Civil Government' in G. L. Hunt (ed.), *Calvinism and the Political Order* (Philadelphia: Westminster Press, 1965), 23–45

Macquarrie, J., *Christian Hope* (London and Oxford: Mowbrays, 1978)

— 'Today's Word for Today 1: Jürgen Moltmann', *The Expository Times* 92:1 (1980), 4–7

McWilliams, W., 'Divine Suffering in Contemporary Theology', *SJT* 33:1 (1980), 35–53

Manley, K. R., 'Origins of the Baptists: The Case for Development from Puritanism–Separatism' in W. H. Brackney and R. J. Burke (eds.), *Faith, Life and Witness: The Papers of the Study and Research Division of the Baptist World Alliance 1986–1990* (Birmingham, Alabama: Samford University Press, 1990), 56–69

Mark, J., Review of *The Experiment Hope* by Jürgen Moltmann in *Theology* 79 (1976), 165–9

Marquhardt, F. W., Theologie und Sozialismus: Des Beispiel Karl Barths (Munich: Chr. Kaiser Verlag, 1972)

— 'Socialism in the Theology of Karl Barth' in G. Hunsinger (ed.), *Karl Barth and Radical Politics* (Philadelphia: Westminster Press, 1976), 47–76

Marsch, W-D (ed.), *Diskussion über die 'Theologie der Hoffnung' von Jürgen Moltmann* (Munich: Chr. Kaiser Verlag, 1967)

Marshall, P., *Thine is the Kingdom: A Biblical Perspective on the Nature of Government and Politics Today* (Basingstoke: Marshalls, 1984)

— 'Liberalism, Pluralism and Christianity: A Reconceptualisation', *Fides et Historia* 23:3 (1989), 4–17

— *A Calvinist Political Theory* (South Africa: Institute for Reformational Studies, 1991)

Martin, E., 'Making Peace with Hell: An Agenda for Reconciling the Doctrine of Hell with Mennonite Pacifism', *CGR* 8:1 (1990), 23–33

Martin, G. W., *The Church: A Baptist View* (London: Baptist Publications, 1976)

Martin, H., 'Protestantism and the State', *BQ* 12 (1946–48), 309–17

Martin, M., 'The Pure Church: The Burden of Anabaptism' *CGR* 1:2 (1983), 29–41

Marty, M. E., 'Baptistification Takes Over', *CT*, 2 September 1983, 32–6

Marx, K., *Karl Marx Selected Works II* (New York: International Publishers, 1939)

Marx, K. and Engels, F., *The Communist Manifesto* (Harmondsworth: Penguin, 1967)

Mayhew, P., *A Theology of Force and Violence* (London: SCM Press, 1989)

Medhurst, K. N. and Moyser G. H., *Church and Politics in a Secular Age* (Oxford: Clarendon Press, 1988)

Meeks, M. D., *Origins of the Theology of Hope* (Philadelphia: Fortress Press, 1974)

— 'A Handbook for the Church: *The Church in the Power of the Spirit: A Contribution to Messianic Ecclesiology* by Jürgen Moltmann', *Interpretation* 33 (1979), 301–4

— 'Trinitarian Theology: A Review Article', *ThT* 38:4 (1982), 472–7

— 'Introduction' to J. Moltmann, *On Human Dignity: Political Theology and Ethics* (Philadelphia: Fortress Press, 1985), ix–xiv

Meihuizen, H. W., 'The Concept of Restitution in the Anabaptism of Northwestern Europe', *MQR* 44:2 (1970), 141–58

Metz, J. B., *Theology of the World* (London: Burns and Oates / Herder and Herder, 1968)

Meyendorff, J., 'Reply to Jürgen Moltmann's "The Unity of the Triune God"', *SVTQ* 28:3 (1984), 183–8

Migliore, D. L., 'Biblical Eschatology and Political Hermeneutics', *ThT* 26 (1969–70), 116–32

— 'The Trinity and Human Liberty', *ThT* 36:4 (1980), 488–97
— Review of *The Power of the Powerless: The Word of Liberation for Today* by Jürgen Moltmann in *ThT* 41:2 (1984), 223–26
Milbank, J., 'The Second Difference: For a Trinitarianism Without Reserve', *MT* 2:3 (1986), 213–33
— 'An Essay Against Secular Order', *JRE* (1987), 199–233
— *Theology and Social Theory: Beyond Secular Reason* (Oxford: Blackwell, 1990)
Miller, G. T., 'Religious Liberty', *ABQ* 2:3 (1983), 188–99
Miller, J. W., 'Schleitheim Pacifism and Modernity: Notes Toward the Construction of a Contemporary Mennonite Pacifist Apologetic', *CGR* 3:2 (1985), 155–63
Miller, L., 'The Church as Messianic Society: Creation and Instrument of Transfigured Mission' in W. R. Shenk (ed.), *The Transfiguration of Mission: Biblical, Theological and Historical Foundations* (Scottdale: Herald Press, 1993), 130–52
Miscamble, W. D., 'Sectarian Passivism?', *ThT* 44,:1 (1987), 69–77
Momose, P. F., *Kreuzestheologie: Eine Auseinandersetzung mit Jürgen Moltmann* (Freiburg: Herder, 1978)
Mondin, B., 'Theology of Hope and the Christian Message', *Biblical Theology Bulletin* 2:1 (1972), 43–63
Morse, C., *The Logic of Promise in Moltmann's Theology* (Philadelphia: Fortress Press, 1979)
Mott, S. C., 'The Politics of Jesus and Our Responsibilities', *TRJ* 26 (1976), 7–10
— *Biblical Ethics and Social Change* (Oxford: Oxford University Press, 1982)
Mouw, R. J., 'Abandoning the Typology: A Reformed Assist', *TSF Bulletin* 8 (1985), 7–10
— 'Christianity and Pacifism', *FP* 2:2 (1985), 105–11
— Review of *When War Is Unjust: Being Honest in Just War Thinking* by John Howard Yoder in *MQR* 59:4 (1985), 415–16
Muller, R. A., 'Christ in the Eschaton: Calvin and Moltmann on the Duration of the *Munus Regium*', *HTR* 74:1 (1981), 31–50
Mullins, E. Y., *The Axioms of Religion: A New Interpretation of the Baptist Faith* (Philadelphia: Judson Press, 1908)
Munson, J., *The Nonconformists: In Search of a Lost Culture* (London: SPCK, 1991)
Nation, Mark Thiessen, *A Comprehensive Bibliography of the Writings of John Howard Yoder* (Goshen: Mennonite Historical Society / Goshen College, 1997)
Neff, W. F., Article: 'Denk, Hans', *ME* 2, 32–5
Neufeld, T. R. Y., 'Christian Counterculture: Ecclesia and Establishment', *MQR* 63:2 (1989), 193–209
— 'Romans 13 in Our Day', *CGR* 9:3 (1991), 315–20
Neuhaus, R. J., Review of *The Politics of Jesus* by John Howard Yoder in *Commonweal*, 22 February 1974, 516–17
— *The Naked Public Square: Religion and Democracy in America* (Grand Rapids: Eerdmans, 1984 and 1988)
Newbigin, L., 'Christ and the Cultures', *SJT* 31:1 (1978), 1–22
— *The Other Side of 1984: Questions for the Churches* (Geneva: World Council of Churches, 1983)
— *Foolishness to the Greeks: The Gospel and Western Culture* (Geneva: World Council of Churches, 1986)
— *The Gospel in a Pluralist Society* (London: SPCK, 1989)

Newlands, G. M., Review of *The Crucified God* by Jürgen Moltmann in *Theology* 78 (1975), 148–50

Nicholls, D. (ed.), *Church and State in Britain Since 1820* (London: Routledge and Kegan Paul, 1967)

Nicholson, J. F. V., 'Towards a Theology of Episcope Among Baptists', *BQ* 30:6 (1984), 265–281 and 30:7 (1984), 319–31

Nicol, I. G., 'Church and State in the Calvinist Reformed Tradition' in R. T. Bender and A. P. F. Sell (eds.), *Baptism, Peace and the State in the Reformed and Mennonite Traditions* (Waterloo, Wilfrid Laurier University Press, 1991), 123–43

Niebuhr, H. R., 'The Grace of Doing Nothing', *CC*, 23 March 1932, 378–80

— 'The Doctrine of the Trinity and the Unity of the Church', *ThT* 3 (1946), 371–84 reprinted as 'Theological Unitarianisms', *ThT* 40:2 (1983), 150–7

— *Christ and Culture* (New York and London: Harper and Row, 1951 and 1975)

Niebuhr, R. R., *Leaves from the Notebook of a Tamed Cynic* (San Franciso and London: Harper and Row, 1929 and 1957)

— 'Must We Do Nothing?', *CC*, 30 March 1932, 415–17

— *An Interpretation of Christian Ethics* (London: SCM Press, 1936)

— *Why the Christian Church is not Pacifist* (London: SCM Press, 1940)

— *The Children of Light and the Children of Darkness* (London: Nisbet and Co, 1945)

— *Moral Man and Immoral Society: A Study in Ethics and Politics* (London: SCM Press, 1963)

— *The Nature and Destiny of Man* Vols 1 and 2 (New York: Scribner's, 1964)

Norman, J. G. G. 'The Relevance and Vitality of the Sect–Idea', BQ 27:6 (1978), 248–58

Niewiadomski, J., *Die Zweideutigkeit von Gott und Welt in J. Moltmanns Theologien*: Innsbrucker Theologische Studien 9 (Innsbruck-Wien-München: Tyrolia Verlag, 1982)

Novak, M., *The Open Church: Vatican II Act II* (London: Darton, Longman and Todd, 1964)

O'Collins, G., 'Spes Quaerens Intellectum', *Interpretation* 22 (1968), 36–52

— 'The Principle and Theology of Hope', *SJT* 21:2 (1969), 129–44

O'Donnell, J. J., 'The Doctrine of the Trinity in Recent German Theology', *THJ* 23:2 (1982), 153–67

— 'The Trinity as Divine Community: A Critical Reflection Upon Recent Theological Developments', *Gregorianum* 69:1 (1988), 5–34

Olson, R., 'Trinity and Eschatology: The Historical Being of God in Jürgen Moltmann and Wolfhart Pannenberg', *SJT* 36 (1983), 213–27

Oyer, J., 'Luther and the Anabaptists', *BQ* 30:4 (1983), 162–72

Packull, W. O., 'Between Paradigms: Anabaptist Studies at the Crossroads', *CGR* 8:1 (1990), 1–22

Page, R., Review of *The Trinity and the Kingdom of God* by Jürgen Moltmann in *SJT* 37:1 (1984), 97–8

Pauls, P., '"A Pestiferous Sect": The Anabaptists in England from 1530–1660', *JMS* 3 (1985), 60–72

Pawlikowski, J., 'The Holocaust and Contemporary Christology' in E. S. Fiorenza and D. Tracy (eds.), *Concilium 175: The Holocaust as Interruption* (Edinburgh: T. and T. Clark, 1984), 43–9

Payne, E. A., *The Fellowship of Believers* (London: Carey Kingsgate Press, 1944)

— 'The Anabaptists of the 16th Century and their Influence in the Modern World' The Dr Williams's Trust Lecture at the Presbyterian College, Carmarthen, 5 October 1948
— 'Michael Sattler and the Schleitheim Confession, 1527', *BQ* 14 (1951), 337–44
— *The Free Churches and the State* (London: Carey Kingsgate Press, 1952)
— 'Who were the Baptists?', *BQ* 16 (1955–56), 339–342
— 'Contacts Between Mennonites and Baptists', *Foundations* 4:1 (1961), 3–19
— *The Free Church Tradition in the Life of England* (London: Hodder and Stoughton, 1965)
— *The Free Churches: Today's Challenges* (London: Free Church Federal Council, 1973)
Peachey, P. P., 'Marxist Historiography of the Radical Reformation: Causality or Covariation?' in C. S. Meyer (ed.), *Sixteenth Century Essays and Studies* (Saint Louis: The Foundation for Reformation Research, no date), 1–16
— *Die Soziale Herkunft der Schweizer Täufer in der Reformationszeit: Eine Religionssoziologische Untersuchung* (Karlsruhe: Buchdrückerei und Verlag Heinrich Schneider, 1954)
— 'Spirit and Form in the Church of Christ', *CP* 2 (1955), 15–25
— 'Anabaptism and Church Organization', *MQR* 30:3 (1956), 213–28
— 'What is Concern?', *CP* 4 (1957), 14–19
— 'The End of Christendom', *CP* 9 (1961), 19–23
— 'Church and Nation in Western History' in P. P. Peachey (ed.), *Biblical Realism Confronts the Nation* (Scottdale: Fellowship Publications and Herald Press, 1963), 11–32
— 'New Ethical Possibility: The Task of "Post-Christendom" Ethics', *Interpretation* 19 (1965), 26–38
— 'The Radical Reformation, Political Pluralism and the Corpus Christianum' in *The Origins and Characteristics of Anabaptism: Proceedings of the Colloquium organized by the Faculty of Protestant Theology of Strasbourg, 20–22 February 1975* (The Hague: Martinus Nijhoff, 1977), 10–26
— 'Constantinian Christendom and the Marx–Engels Phenomenon', *MQR* 55:3 (1981), 184–97
— 'The "Free Church": A Time Whose Idea Has Not Come' in W. Klaassen (ed.), *Anabaptism Revisited: Essays on Anabaptist/Mennonite Studies in Honor of C. J. Dyck* (Scottdale: Herald Press, 1992), 173–88
Péguy, C., 'Notre Jeunesse' in A. Suarès (ed.), *Oeuvres Complètes de Charles Péguy 1873–1914* (Paris: Éditions de la Nouvelle Revue Française, 1916)
Pinches, C., 'Christian Pacifism and Theodicy: The Free Will Defense in the Thought of John Howard Yoder', *MT* 5:3 (1989), 239–55
Pipkin, H. W. and Yoder J. H. (ed.), *Balthasar Hübmaier: Theologian of Anabaptism* (Scottdale: Herald Press, 1989)
Pipkin, H. W., 'The Baptismal Theology of Balthasar Hübmaier', *MQR* 65:1 (1991), 34–53
Plant, R., 'The Anglican Church and the Secular State' in G. Moyser (ed.), *Church and Politics Today: The Role of the Church of England in Contemporary Politics* (Edinburgh: T. and T. Clark, 1985), 313–36
Preston, R. H., 'Reflections on Theologies of Social Change' in R. H. Preston (ed.), *Theology and Change: Essays in Memory of Alan Richardson* (London: SCM Press, 1975), 148–66

Quainton, C. E., 'The Anabaptists in England during the Commonwealth', *MQR* 6:1 (1932), 30–42

Quirk, M. J., 'Beyond Sectarianism?', *ThT* 44:1 (1987), 78–86

Rahner, K., *The Shape of the Church to Come* (London: SPCK, 1974)

Rainbow, J. H., '"Confessor Baptism': The Baptismal Doctrine of the Early Anabaptists', *ABQ* 8:4 (1989), 276–90

Rasmusson, A., *The Church as Polis: From Political Theology to Theological Politics as Exemplified by Jürgen Moltmann and Stanley Hauerwas* (Lund: Lund University Press, 1994)

Redekop, C., 'The Community of Scholars and the Essence of Anabaptism', *MQR* 67:4 (1993), 429–50

Reimer, A. J., 'The Nature and Possibility of a Mennonite Theology', *CGR* 1:1 (1983), 33–55

Rideman, P., *Confession of Faith: Account of Our Religion, Doctrine and Faith Given By Peter Rideman of the Brothers Whom Men Call Hutterians* (London: Hodder and Stoughton/Plough Publishing House, 1950)

Roberts, R. H., 'Transcendental Sociology? A Critique of John Milbank' s Theology and Social Theory: Beyond Secular Reason', *SJT* 46:4 (1993), 527–35

Robinson, H. W., *The Life and Faith of the Baptists* (London: Methuen and Co, 1927)

Rordorf, W., 'Tertullians Beurteilung des Soldatenstandes', *Vigiliae Christianae* 23 (1969), 105–41

Rowland, C., *Radical Christianity: A Reading of Recovery* (Oxford: Polity Press, 1988)

Ruether, R. R., 'The Free Church Movement in Contemporary Catholicism' in M. E. Marty and D. G. Peerman (eds.), *New Theology No. 6: On Revolution and Non-Revolution, Violence and Non-Violence, Peace and Power* (London: Collier–Macmillan, 1969), 269–87

— 'Augustine and Christian Political Theology', *Interpretation* 29 (1975), 252–65

Rumscheidt, M., Review of *Der gekreuzigte Gott: Des Kreuz als Grund und Kritik christlicher Theologie* by Jürgen Moltmann in *SJT* 27:3 (1974), 354–56

Rutschman, L. A., 'Anabaptism and Liberation Theology', *MQR* 55:3 (1981), 255–70

Ruth, J. L., 'America's Anabaptists: Who They Are', *CT*, 22 October 1990, 52–6

Sanneh, L., 'Pluralism and Christian Commitment', *ThT* 45:1 (1988), 21–33

— 'Particularity, Pluralism and Commitment' Review of *The Gospel in a Pluralist Society* by Lesslie Newbigin in *CC*, 31 January 1990, 103–5

Sawatsky, R. J., Review of *The Problem of Social Responsibility from the Perspective of the Mennonite Church* by J. Lawrence Burkholder in *CGR* 8:2 (1990), 223–6

Schaller, L. E., 'The Use of Power and Social Change', *Review and Expositor* 68 (1971), 327–37

Schäufele, W., *Des Missionarische Bewusstsein und Wirken der Täufer* (Neukirchen-Vluyn: Verlag des Erziehungsvereins, 1966)

— 'The Missionary Vision and Activity of the Anabaptist Laity' in W. R. Shenk (ed.), *Anabaptism and Mission* (Scottdale: Herald Press, 1984), 70–87

Schluter, M. and Clements, R., 'Jubilee Institutional Norms: A Middle Way between Creation Ethics and Kingdom Ethics', *EQ* 62:1 (1990), 37–62

Scriven, C., *The Transformation of Culture: Christian Social Ethics After H. Richard Niebuhr* (Scottdale: Herald Press, 1988)

— 'The Reformation Radicals Ride Again', *CT*, 5 March 1990), 13–19

Sell, A. P. F., 'Anabaptist–Congregational Relations and Current Mennonite–Reformed Dialogue', *MQR* 61:3 (1987), 321–34

Sellers, I., 'Edwardians, Anabaptists and the Problem of Baptist Origins', *BQ* 29 (1981–82), 97–112

Shank, D. A., 'Jesus the Messiah: Messianic Foundation of Mission' in W. R. Shenk (ed.), *The Transfiguration of Mission: Biblical, Theological and Historical Foundations* (Scottdale: Herald Press, 1993), 37–82

Shank, D. R., 'Anabaptists and Mission' in W. R. Shenk (ed.), *Anabaptism and Mission* (Scottdale: Herald Press, 1984), 202–28

— Review of *The Priestly Kingdom: Social Ethics as Gospel* by John Howard Yoder in *MQR* 60:2 (1986), 202–28

Shenk, W. R. (ed.), *The Transfiguration of Mission: Biblical, Theological and Historical Foundations* (Scottdale: Herald Press, 1993)

Shiner, L., 'The Concept of Secularization in Empirical Research', *Journal for the Scientific Study of Religion* 6:2 (1967), 207–20

Shurden, W. B., *The Baptist Identity: Four Fragile Freedoms* (Macon, Georgia: Smith and Helwys Publishing, 1993)

Simon, U., Review of *Theology of Hope* by Jürgen Moltmann in *Theology* 72 (1969), 128–9

Simon, U., Review of *Moltmann: Messianic Theology in the Making* by Richard J. Bauckham in *Theology* 92 (1989), 47–8

Smucker, D. E., 'The Theological Triumph of the Early Anabaptist–Mennonites', *MQR* 19:1 (1945), 5–26

— 'A Mennonite Critique of the Pacifist Movement', *MQR* 20:1 (1946), 81–8

Snyder, A., 'The Influence of the Schleitheim Articles on the Anabaptist Movement: An Historical Evaluation', *MQR* 63:4 (1989), 323–344

— 'The Monastic Origins of Swiss Anabaptist Sectarianism', *MQR* 57:1 (1983), 5–26

Stanley, B., 'Evangelical Social and Political Ethics: An Historic Perspective', *EQ* 62:1 (1990), 19–36

Stassen, G. H., 'Anabaptist Influence in the Origin of Particular Baptists', *MQR* 36:4 (1962), 322–48

— 'The Politics of Jesus – Moving Towards Social Ethics' (An unpublished address to the Mennonite Peace Theology Colloquium, Kansas City, 8 October 1976 deposited in the library, LMC)

— 'A Social Theory Model for Religious Social Ethics', *JRE* 5 (1977), 9–37

Stauffer, E., 'Täufertum und Märtyrertheologie', *ZfK* 52 (1933), 545–98

Stayer, J. M., 'Anabaptist Non-resistance and the Rewriting of History: Or, Is John Yoder's Conception of Anabaptist Non-resistance Historically Sound?' (Unpublished and undated paper deposited in the library, LMC)

— 'Hans Hut's Doctrine of the Sword: An Attempted Solution', *MQR* 39:3 (1965), 181–91

— 'The Doctrine of the Sword in the First Decade of Anabaptism', *MQR* 41:2 (1967), 165–6

— 'The Munsterite Rationalization of Bernhard Rothmann', *JHI* 28:2 (1967), 179–92

— 'Eine fanatische Täuferbewegung in Esslingen und Reutlingen?', *Blätter für Württembergische Kirchengeschichte* (1968), 53–9

— 'Anabaptists and the Sword' *MQR* 44:4 (1970), 371–5

— *Anabaptists and the Sword* (Lawrence, Kansas: Coronado Press, 1972)

— 'Reflections and Retractions on *Anabaptists and the Sword*', *MQR* 51:3 (1977), 196–212

— 'Reublin and Brötli: The Revolutionary Beginnings of Swiss Anabaptism' in *The Origins and Characteristics of Anabaptism: Proceedings of the Colloquium organized by the Faculty of Protestant Theology of Strasbourg, 20–22 February 1975* (The Hague: Martinus Nijhoff, 1977), 83–102

— 'The Swiss Brethren: An Exercise in Historical Definition', *CH* 47:2 (1978), 174–95

— 'Was Dr Kuehler's Conception of Early Dutch Anabaptism Historically Sound? The Historical Discussion of Munster 450 Years Later', *MQR* 60:3 (1986), 261–88

— *The German Peasants' War and Anabaptist Community of Goods* (Montreal: McGill-Queen's University Press, 1991)

— W. O. Packull, and K. Deppermann, 'From Monogenesis to Polygenesis: The Historical Discussion of Anabaptist Origins' *MQR* 49:2 (1975), 83–121

— and W. O. Packull (eds.), *The Anabaptists and Thomas Müntzer* (Dubuque and Toronto: Kendall/Hunt Publishing, 1980)

Strunk, R., 'Diskussion über *Der gekreuzigte Gott*', *EvTh* 41:1, 89–94

Swartley, W., *Sabbath, Slavery, War and Women* (Scottdale: Herald Press, 1983)

— (ed.) *Dialogue Sequel to Jürgen Moltmann's 'Following Jesus Christ in the World Today'* Occasional Paper 8 (Elkhart and Winnipeg: Institute of Mennonite Studies and CMBC Publications, 1984)

Swidler, L., 'Foreword' to P. Lapide and J. Moltmann, *Jewish Monotheism and Christian Trinitarian Doctrine* (Philadlephia: Fortress Press, 1981)

Sykes, S., Review of *The Trinity and the Kingdom of God* by Jürgen Moltmann in *Theology* 85 (1982), 207–9

— *The Identity of Christianity: Theologians and the Essence of Christianity from Schleiermacher to Barth* (London: SPCK, 1984)

Tappert, T. G. (ed.), *The Book of Concord* (Philadelphia: Fortress Press, 1959)

Tawney, R. H., *The Acquisitive Society* (London and Glasgow: Collins, 1961)

Temple, W., *Christianity and the Social Order* (London: SCM Press, 1950)

Thévenaz, J-P.,'Vérité d'espérance ou vérité de connaisance? Les enjeux théoriques et politiques de la théologie de Jürgen Moltmann', *Études théologiques et religieuses* 49:2 (1974), 225–47

— 'Le Dieu Crucifié N'a-t-il Plus D'Histoire?', *Revue de Théologie et de Philosophie* 115 (1983), 199–208

Thils, G., '"Soyez riches d'espérance par la vertu du Saint-Esprit" (Rom. 15:13). La Théologie de L'Espérance de J. Moltmann', *Ephemerides Theologicae Lovanienses* 47 (1971), 495–503

Thistlethwaite, S. B., 'Comments on Jürgen Moltmann's "The Unity of the Triune God"', *SVTQ* 28:3 (1984), 179–82

Tinder, G., *The Political Meaning of Christianity: An Interpretation* (Baton Rouge: Louisiana State University Press, 1989)

Torrance, A. J., 'Introductory Essay' in E. Jüngel, *Christ, Justice and Peace: Towards a Theology of the State in Dialogue with the Barmen Declaration* (Edinburgh: T. and T. Clark, 1992), ix–xx

Tripole, M. R., 'Ecclesiological Developments in Moltmann's Theology of Hope', *TS* 34 (1973), 19–35

— 'A Church for the Poor and the World: At Issue with Moltmann's Ecclesiology', *TS* 42 (1981), 645–59

Trocmé, A., *Jesus and the Non-violent Revolution*. Translated from the French by Michael H. Shank and Marlin E. Miller (Scottdale: Herald Press, 1973)

Troeltsch, E., *Protestantism and Progress: A Historical Study of the Relation of Protestantism to the Modern World* (London: Williams and Norgate, 1912)

— *The Social Teaching of the Christian Churches* Vols 1 and 2 (London: George Allen and Unwin, 1931)

Trulson, R. S., 'Baptist Pacifism: A Heritage of Non-violence', *ABQ* 10:3 (1991), 199–217

Tschäbitz, G., 'The Position of Anabaptism on the Continuum of the Early Bourgeois Revolution in Germany' in J. M. Stayer and W. O. Packull (eds.), *The Anabaptists and Thomas Müntzer* (Dubuque and Toronto: Kendall/Hunt Publishing, 1980), 28–39

Tecker, R. W., 'Revolutionary Faithfulness' in M. E. Marty and D. G. Peerman (eds.), *New Theology No. 6: On Revolution and Non-Revolution, Violence and Non-Violence, Peace and Power* (London: Collier–Macmillan, 1969), 199–228

Verduin, L., *The Reformers and Their Stepchildren* (Exeter: Paternoster Press, 1965)

— *The Anatomy of a Hybrid: A Study in Church–State Relationships* (Grand Rapids: Eerdmans, 1976)

Vicedom, G. R., *The Mission of God: An Introduction to a Theology of Mission* (St Louis: Concordia Publishing House, 1965)

Villa-Vicencio C., *Between Christ and Caesar: Classic and Contemporary Texts on Church and State* (Grand Rapids: Eerdmans, 1986)

Volf, M., 'Kirche als Gemeinschaft: Ekklesiologische Überlegungen aus freikirchlicher Perspektive', *EvTh* 49:1 (1989), 52–76

Vose, H. M., 'Attitudes Toward War and Peace Reflected by some Puritan–Separatist Spiritual Descendants – The Baptists', *MQR* 64:4 (1990), 371–84

Walker, M., 'The Atonement and Justice', *Theology* 91 (1988), 180–6

Walsh, B. J., 'Theology of Hope and the Doctrine of Creation: An Appraisal of Jürgen Moltmann', *EQ* 59:1 (1987), 53–76

— 'The Transformation of Culture: A Review Essay', *CGR* 7:3 (1989), 252–67

— 'Liberal Tyranny', *Third Way* 15:6 (1992), 26–30

Walton, R. C., *The Gathered Community* (London: Carey Kingsgate Press, 1946)

— 'Was there a Turning Point of the Zwinglian Revolution?', *MQR* 42:1 (1968), 45–56

Walzer, M., *The Revolution of the Saints: A Study in the Origins of Radical Politics* (New York: Atheneum, 1968)

Watts, M. R., *The Dissenters: From the Reformation to the French Revolution* (Oxford: Clarendon Press, 1978)

Weaver, J. D., 'The Anabaptist Vision from Recovery to Reform', *Mennonite Life*, September 1982, 14–16

— 'A Believers' Church Christology', *MQR* 57:2 (1983), 112–31

— 'Perspectives on a Mennonite Theology', *CGR* 2:3 (1984), 189–210

— 'Becoming Anabaptist–Mennonite: The Contemporary Relevance of Sixteenth-Century Anabaptism', *JMS* 4 (1986), 162–82

— 'Atonement for the Nonconstantinian Church', *MT* 6:4 (1990), 207–323

Weber, M., 'Politics as a Vocation' in H. H. Garth and C. W. Mills (eds.), *From Max Weber: Essays in Sociology* (London and Boston: Routledge and Kegan Paul, 1948)

Weber, O., *Versammelte Gemeinde: Beiträge zum Gespräch über Kirche und Gottesdienst* (Giessen: von Munschowsche Universitäts-Drückerei, 1949)

Webster, J. B., 'Jürgen Moltmann: Trinity and Suffering', *Evangel: A Quarterly Review of Biblical, Practical and Contemporary Theology* (1985), 4–6

Wedderburn, A. J. M., 'A New Testament Church Today?', *SJT* 31:6 (1978), 517–32

Weir, D. A., *The Origins of the Federal Theology in Sixteenth-Century Reformation Thought* (Oxford: Clarendon Press, 1990)

Welker, M. (ed.), *Diskussion über Jürgen Moltmanns Buch 'Der Gekreuzigte Gott'* (Munich: Chr. Kaiser Verlag, 1979)

Weller, P., 'Freedom and Witness in a Multi-Religious Society: A Baptist Perspective' Part 1, *BQ* 33:6 (1990), 252–264 and Part 2, *BQ* 32:7 (1990), 302–15

Wenger, J. C. (ed.), *The Complete Writings of Menno Simons c. 1496–1561* (Scottdale: Herald Press, 1956)

West, C. C., *Communism and the Theologians: Study of an Encounter* (London: SCM Press, 1958)

West, W. M. S., 'The Anabaptists and the Rise of the Baptist Movement' in A. Gilmore (ed.), *Christian Baptism: A Fresh Attempt to Understand the Rite in Terms of Scripture, History, and Theology* (London: Lutterworth Press, 1959), 223–72

White, B. R., *The English Separatist Tradition* (Oxford: Oxford University Press, 1971)

— *Authority: A Baptist View* (London: Baptist Publications, 1976)

— 'Anabaptist Studies: A Review Article', *BQ* 34:2 (1991), 88–91

Whitley, W. T., *A History of British Baptists* (London: Charles Griffin and Co., 1923)

— 'Continental Anabaptists and Early English Baptists', *BQ* 2 (1924–25), 24–30

Widmer, G-P., 'Le Nouveau et le Possible: Notes sur les théologies de l'esperance', *Revue d'histoire et de philosophie religieuses* 55 (1975)

Wiebe, B., 'Interpretation and Historical Criticism: Jürgen Moltmann', *RQ* 24 (1981), 155–66

— 'Revolution as an Issue in Theology: Jürgen Moltmann', *RQ* 26 (1983), 105–20

— *Messianic Ethics: Jesus' Proclamation of the Kingdom of God and the Church in Response* (Scottdale: Herald Press, 1992)

Wilder, A. N., 'Kerygma, Eschatology and Social Ethics' in W. D. Davies and D. Daube (eds.), *The Background of the NT and its Eschatology: Studies in Honour of C. H. Dodd* (Cambridge: Cambridge University Press, 1956), 509–36

Wilkinson, A., *Dissent or Conform?: War, Peace and the English Churches 1900–1945* (London: SCM Press, 1986)

Williams, G. H., 'Christology and Church–State Relations in the Fourth Century', *CH* 20:4 (1951), 3–26

Williams G. H. and Mergal, A. M. (eds.), *Spiritual and Anabaptist Writers: Documents Illustrative of the Radical Reformation* (Philadelphia: Westminster Press, 1957)

Williams, G. H., *The Radical Reformation* (Philadelphia: Westminster Press, 1962)

Williams, G. W., 'The Anabaptists in the Sixteenth Century' in M. John (ed.), *Welsh Baptist Studies* (Cardiff: South Wales Baptist College, 1976), 9–34

Williams, R., 'Trinity and Revelation', *MT* 2:3 (1986), 197–212

— 'Politics and the Soul: A Reading of the *City of God*', *Milltown Studies* 19 and 20 (1987), 55–72

Williams, S. N., *Jürgen Moltmann: A Critical Introduction* with a foreword by R. J. Bauckham (Leicester: Theological Students' Fellowship, 1987)

Williams, T. S. M., Review of *On Human Dignity: Political Theology and Ethics* by Jürgen Moltmann in *Theology* 88 (1985), 400–2

Wink, W., *Naming the Powers: The Language of Power in the New Testament* (Philadelphia: Fortress Press, 1984)

— *Unmasking the Powers: The Invisible Forces That Determine Human Existence* (Philadelphia: Fortress Press, 1986)

— *Engaging the Powers: Discernment and Resistance in a World of Domination* (Minneapolis: Fortress Press, 1992)

Winter, S. F., 'Michael Sattler and the Schleitheim Articles: A Study in the Background to the first Anabaptist Confession of Faith', *BQ* 34:2 (1991), 52–66

Wogaman, J. P., *A Christian Method of Moral Judgement* (London: SCM Press, 1976)

— *Christian Perspectives on Politics* (London: SCM Press, 1988)

Wolterstorff, N., *Until Justice and Peace Embrace* (Grand Rapids: Eerdmans, 1983)

Wood, J. E. Jr., 'Toward a Theology of Human Rights: A Baptist Perspective', *ABQ* 9:4 (1990), 205–23

Wray, F., 'The Anabaptist Doctrine of the Restitution of the Church', *MQR* 28:3 (1954), 189–96

Wright, C. J. H., *The People of God and the State: An Old Testament Perspective* (Bramcote: Grove Ethical Studies 77, 1990)

— 'The People of God and the State in the Old Testament', *Themelios* 16:1 (1990), 4–10

— 'The Ethical Authority of the Old Testament: A Survey of Approaches' Part 1, *TB* 43.1 (1992), 101–120 and Part 2, *TB* 43.2 (1992), 203–31

Wright, N. G., *The Radical Kingdom: Restoration in Theory and Practice* (Eastbourne: Kingsway, 1986)

— *The Fair Face of Evil: Putting the Power of Darkness in its Place* (London: Marshall–Pickering, 1988)

— *Challenge to Change: A Radical Agenda for Baptists* (Eastbourne: Kingsway, 1991)

— 'Mission, the Shape of the Church and Ecumenism' in P. Beasley-Murray (ed.), *Mission to the World: Essays to Celebrate the 50th Year of the Ordination of George Raymond Beasley-Murray to the Christian Ministry* (Didcot: Baptist Historical Society, 1991), 52–6

— 'Catching the Bell Rope', *Anabaptism Today* 1 (1992), 17–20

— *Makt och lärjungaskap: En frikyrklig teologi om förhållandet församling–samhälle* (Orebro: Orebro Missionskolas Skriftserie 8, 1993)

— 'Disestablishment: A Contemporary View from the Free Churches', *Anvil* 12:2 (1995), 121–35

— '"The Sword": An Example of Anabaptist Diversity', *BQ* 36:6 (1996), 264–79

— 'Baptist and Anabaptist Attitudes to the State: A Contrast', *BQ* 36:7 (1996), 349–57

— *The Radical Evangelical: Seeking a Place to Stand* (London: SPCK, 1996)

— *Power and Discipleship: Towards a Baptist Theology of the State* (Oxford: Whitley Publications, 1996)

Wright, N. T., 'The New Testament and the "State"', *Themelios* 16:1 (1990), 11–17

— 'How can the Bible be Authoritative?', *Vox Evangelica* 21 (1991), 7–32

Yoder, E. and Herschberger, G. F., 'The Christian's Relation to the State in Time of War', *MQR* 9:1 (1935), 5–36

Yoder, E., 'Christianity and the State', *MQR* 11:3 (1937), 171–95

— 'The Obligation of the Christian to the State and Community – "Render to Caesar"', *MQR* 13:2 (1939), 104–22

Yoder, P. B., 'Toward a Shalom Biblical Theology', *CGR* 1:3 (1983), 39–49

Young, F., 'The Early Church: Military Service, War and Peace', *Theology* 92 (1989), 491–503

Young, N., *Creator, Creation and Faith* (London: Collins, 1976)

Zahn, G., 'The Religious Basis of Dissent', *MQR* 41:2 (1968), 132–43

Zimbelman, J., 'The Contribution of John Howard Yoder to Recent Discussion in Christian Social Ethics', *SJT* 45:3 (1992), 367–99

Zizioulas, J., *Being as Communion: Studies in Personhood and the Church* (London: Darton Longman and Todd, 1985)

— 'The Doctrine of God the Trinity Today: Suggestions for an Ecumenical Study' in *The Forgotten Trinity: 3 A Selection of Papers presented to the BCC Study Commission on Trinitarian Doctrine Today* (London: British Council of Churches, 1991)

2) Dissertations

Bristow, M. E. A., 'The Church in the Theology of Jürgen Moltmann'. MPhil Dissertation, University of Manchester, 1988

Bush, R. B., 'Recent Ideas of Divine Conflict: The Influences of Psychological Theories of Conflict upon the Trinitarian Theology of Paul Tillich and Jürgen Moltmann'. DPhil Dissertation, University of Oxford, 1990

Fitz-Gibbon, A. L., 'A Study in Church–State Relations in the Writings and Teaching of the Anabaptists of the Sixteenth Century'. MLitt Dissertation, University of Newcastle-upon-Tyne, 1992

Giles, R. S., 'The Church as a Counter-culture Before Constantine'. MLitt Dissertation, University of Newcastle-upon-Tyne, 1987

Hughes, D. H., 'The Ethical Use of Power: A Discussion with the Christian Perspectives of Reinhold Niebuhr, John Howard Yoder and Richard J. Barnet'. PhD Dissertation, Southern Baptist Theological Seminary, 1984

Jennings, B. K., 'A Critical Appraisal of Typologies of Religious Orientation in the Theology of Ernst Troeltsch and H. Richard Niebuhr'. MPhil Dissertation, Open University, 1988

Koontz, G. G., 'Confessional Theology In A Pluralistic Context: A Study of the Theological Ethics of H. Richard Niebuhr and John H. Yoder'. PhD Dissertation, University of Boston, 1985

McEntyre, J. E., 'The Increasing Significance of Symbolic Resistance in Selected Fiction from "War and Peace" to "Mila 18"'. PhD Dissertation, Graduate Theological Union, 1981

Maitland-Cullen, P. S., 'The Theodicy Problem in the Theology of Jürgen Moltmann'. PhD Dissertation, University of Edinburgh, 1990

Marshall, B., 'The Ground and Content of Christian Hope'. PhD Dissertation, University of Nottingham, 1986

Parham, R. M. III, 'An Ethical Analysis of the Christian Social Strategies in the Writings of John C. Bennett, Jacques Ellul and John Howard Yoder'. PhD Dissertation, Baylor University, 1984

Van Gerwen, J. M. L., 'The Church in the Theological Ethics of Stanley Hauerwas (Sociology, Comparative, Morality)'. PhD Dissertation, Graduate Theological Union, 1984

Wright, N. G., 'Karl Barth and Evangelicalism: A Study of the Relationship between Karl Barth and the Evangelical Tradition with Particular Reference to the Concept of "Nothingness"'. MTh Dissertation, University of Glasgow, 1987

Zimbelman, J. A., 'Theological Ethics and Politics in the Thought of Juan Luis Segundo and John Howard Yoder'. PhD Dissertation, University of Virginia, 1986

Index

Paternoster Biblical and Theological Monographs

(Uniform with this Volume)

Eve: Accused or Acquitted?

An Analysis of Feminist Readings of the
Creation Narrative Texts in Genesis 1–3

Joseph Abraham

Two contrary views dominate contemporary feminist biblical scholarship. One finds in the Bible an unequivocal equality between the sexes from the very creation of humanity, whilst the other sees the biblical text as irredeemably patriarchal and androcentric. Dr. Abraham enters into dialogue with both camps as well as introducing his own method of approach. An invaluable tool for anyone who is interested in this contemporary debate.

2000 / 0-85364-971-5

Deification in Eastern Orthodox Theology

An Evaluation and Critique of the Theology of Dumitru Staniloae

Emil Bartos

Bartos studies a fundamental yet neglected aspect of Orthodox theology: deification. By examining the doctrines of anthropology, Christology, soteriology and ecclesiology as they relate to deification, he provides an important contribution to contemporary dialogue between Eastern and Western theologians.

1999 / 0-85364-956-1 / 386pp

The Weakness of the Law

Jonathan F. Bayes

A study of the four New Testament books which refer to the law as weak (Acts, Romans, Galatians, Hebrews) leads to a defence of the third use in the Reformed debate about the law in the life of the believer.

2000 / 0-85364-957-X

The Priesthood of Some Believers

Developments in the Christian Literature of the First Three Centuries

Colin J. Bulley

The first in-depth treatment of early Christian texts on the priesthood of all believers shows that the developing priesthood of the ordained related closely to the division between laity and clergy and had deleterious effects on the practice of the general priesthood.

2000 / 0-85364-958-8

Paul as Apostle to the Gentiles
His Apostolic Self-awareness and its Influence
on the Soteriological Argument in Romans
Daniel J-S Chae

Opposing 'the post-Holocaust interpretation of Romans', Daniel Chae competently demonstrates that Paul argues for the equality of Jew and Gentile in Romans. Chae's fresh exegetical interpretation is academically outstanding and spiritually encouraging.

1997 / 0-85364-829-8 / 392pp

Parallel Lives
The Relation of Paul to the Apostles in the Lucan Perspective
Andrew C. Clark

This study of the Peter-Paul parallels in Acts argues that their purpose was to emphasize the themes of continuity in salvation history and the unity of the Jewish and Gentile missions. New light is shed on Luke's literary techniques, partly through a comparison with Plutarch.

2000 / 085364-979-0

Baptism and the Baptists
Theology and Practice in the Twentieth Century
Anthony R. Cross

At a time of renewed interest in baptism, *Baptism and the Baptists* is a detailed study of twentieth-century baptismal theology and practice and the factors which have influenced its development.

1999 / 0-85364-959-6

The Crisis and the Quest
A Kierkegaardian Reading of Charles Williams
Stephen M. Dunning

Employing Kierkegaardian categories and analysis, this study investigates both the central crisis in Charles Williams's authorship between hermeticism and Christianity (Kierkegaard's Religions A and B), and the quest to resolve this crisis, a quest that ultimately presses the bounds of orthodoxy.

1999 / 0-85364-985-5 / 278pp

The Triumph of Christ in African Perspective
A Study of Demonology and Redemption in the African Context
Keith Ferdinando

This book explores the implications for the gospel of traditional African fears of occult aggression. It analyses such traditional approaches to suffering and biblical responses to fears of demonic evil, concluding with an evaluation of African beliefs from the perspective of the gospel.

1999 / 0-85364-830-1 / 439pp

Suffering and Ministry in the Spirit
Paul's Defence of His Ministry in 2 Corinthians 2:14 – 3:3
Scott J. Hafemann

Shedding new light on the way Paul defended his apostleship, the author offers a careful, detailed study of 2 Corinthians 2:14 – 3:3 linked with other key passages throughout 1 and 2 Corinthians. Demonstrating the unity and coherence of Paul's argument in this passage, the author shows that Paul's suffering served as the vehicle for revealing God's power and glory through the Spirit.

1999 / 0-85364-967-7 / 276pp

The Words of our Lips
Language-Use in Free Church Worship
David Hilborn

Studies of liturgical language have tended to focus on the written canons of Roman Catholic and Anglican communities. By contrast, David Hilborn analyses the more extemporary approach of English Nonconformity. Drawing on recent developments in linguistic pragmatics, he explores similarities and differences between 'fixed' and 'free' worship, and argues for the interdependence of each.

2001 / 0-85364-977-4

One God, One People
The Differentiated Unity of the People of God
in the Theology of Jürgen Moltmann
John G. Kelly

The author expounds and critiques Moltmann's doctrine of God and highlights the systematic connections between it and Moltmann's influential discussion of Israel. He then proposes a fresh approach to Jewish–Christian relations, building on Moltmann's work and using insights from Habermas and Rawls.

2000 / 0-85346-969-3

Calvin and English Calvinism to 1649
R.T. Kendall

The author's thesis is that those who formed the Westminster Confession of Faith, which is regarded as Calvinism, in fact departed from John Calvin on two points: (1) the extent of the Atonement and (2) the ground of assurance of salvation. 'No student of the period can ignore this work' – *J.I. Packer.*

1997 / 0-85364-827-1 / 224pp

Karl Barth and the Strange New World within the Bible
Neil B. MacDonald

Barth's discovery of the strange new world within the Bible is examined in the context of Kant, Hume, Overbeck, and, most importantly, Wittgenstein. Covers some fundamental issues in theology today; epistemology, the final form of the text and biblical truth-claims.

2000 / 0-85364-970-7

Attributes and Atonement
The Holy Love of God in the Theology of P.T. Forsyth
Leslie McCurdy

Attributes and Atonement is an intriguing full-length study of P.T. Forsyth's doctrine of the cross as it relates particularly to God's holy love. It includes an unparalleled bibliography of both primary and secondary material relating to Forsyth.

1999 / 0-85364-833-6 / 323pp

Towards a Theology of the Concord of God
A Japanese Perspective on the Trinity
Nozomu Miyahira

This book introduces a new Japanese theology and a unique Trinitarian formula based on the Japanese intellectual climate: three betweennesses and one concord. It also presents a new interpretation of the Trinity, a co-subordinationism, which is in line with orthodox Trinitarianism; each single person of the Trinity is eternally and equally subordinate (or serviceable) to the other persons, so that they retain the mutual dynamic equality.

1999 / 0-85364-863-8

Your Father the Devil?
A New Approach to John and 'The Jews'
Stephen Motyer

Who are 'the Jews' in John's Gospel? Defending John against the charge of anti-Semitism, Motyer argues that, far from demonising the Jews, the Gospel seeks to present Jesus as 'Good News for Jews' in a late first century setting.

1997 / 0-85364-832-8 / 274pp

Origins and Early Development of Liberation Theology in Latin America
With Particular Reference to Gustavo Gutierrez
Eddy José Muskus

This work challenges the fundamental premise of Liberation Theology: 'opting for the poor', and its claim that Christ is found in them. It also argues that Liberation Theology emerged as a direct result of the failure of the Roman Catholic Church in Latin America.

2000 / 0-85364-974-X

'Hell': A Hard Look at a Hard Question
The Fate of the Unrighteous in New Testament Thought
David Powys

This comprehensive treatment seeks to unlock the original meaning of terms and phrases long thought to support the traditional doctrine of hell. It concludes that there is an alternative – one which is more biblical, and which can positively revive the rationale for Christian mission.

1999 / 0-85364-831-X / 500pp

Evangelical Experiences
A Study in the Spirituality of English Evangelicalism 1918–1939
Ian M Randall

This book makes a detailed historical examination of evangelical spirituality between the First and Second World Wars. It shows how patterns of devotion led to tensions and divisions. In a wide-ranging study, Anglican, Wesleyan, Reformed and Pentecostal-charismatic spiritualities are analysed.

1999 / 0-85364-919-7 / 320pp

Is World View Neutral Education Possible and Desirable?
A Christian Response to Liberal Arguments
(Published jointly with The Stapleford Centre)
Signe Sandsmark

This thesis discusses reasons for belief in world view neutrality, and argues that 'neutral' education will have a hidden, but strong world view influence. It discusses the place for Christian education in the common school.

1999 / 0-85364-973-1 / 205pp

The Extent of the Atonement
A Dilemma for Reformed Theology from Calvin to the Consensus
G. Michael Thomas

A study of the way Reformed theology addressed the question, 'Did Christ die for all, or for the elect only?', commencing with John Calvin, and including debates with Lutheranism, the Synod of Dort and the teaching of Moïse Amyraut.

1997 / 0-85364-828-X / 237pp

The Power of the Cross
Theology and the Death of Christ in Paul, Luther and Pascal
Graham Tomlin

This book explores the theology of the cross in St Paul, Luther and Pascal. It offers new perspectives on the theology of each, and some implications for the nature of power, apologetics, theology and church life in a postmodern context.

1999 / 0-85364-984-7 / 368pp

Constrained by Zeal
Female Spirituality amongst Nonconformists 1825–1875
Linda Wilson

Constrained by Zeal investigates the neglected area of Nonconformist female spirituality. Against the background of separate spheres, it analyses the experience of women from four denominations, and argues that the churches provided a 'third sphere' in which they could find opportunities for participation.

1999 / 0-85364-972-3

Disavowing Constantine
Mission, Church and the Social Order in the Theologies of John Howard Yoder and Jürgen Moltmann
Nigel G. Wright

This book is a timely restatement of a radical theology of church and state in the Anabaptist and Baptist tradition. Dr. Wright constructs his argument in dialogue and debate with Yoder and Moltmann, major contributors to a free church perspective.

1999 / 0-85364-978-2

The Voice of Jesus
Studies in the Interpretation of Six Gospel Parables
Stephen Wright

This literary study considers how the 'voice' of Jesus has been heard in different periods of parable interpretation, and how the categories of figure and trope may help us towards a sensitive reading of the parables today.

2000 / 0-85364-975-8

The Paternoster Press
P O Box 300
Carlisle Cumbria
CA3 0QS UK

Web: www.paternoster-publishing.com